Macmillan/McGraw-Hill TIMELINKS

People, Places, and Cultures

PROGRAM AUTHORS
James A. Banks
Kevin P. Colleary
Linda Greenow
Walter C. Parker
Emily M. Schell
Dinah Zike

CONTRIBUTORS
Raymond C. Jones
Irma M. Olmedo

Macmillan/McGraw-Hill

Europe and the Americas

PROGRAM AUTHORS

James A. Banks, Ph.D.
Kerry and Linda Killinger Professor of Diversity Studies and Director, Center for Multicultural Education
University of Washington
Seattle, Washington

Kevin P. Colleary, Ed.D.
Curriculum and Teaching Department
Graduate School of Education
Fordham University
New York, New York

Linda Greenow, Ph.D.
Associate Professor and Chair
Department of Geography
State University of New York at New Paltz
New Paltz, New York

Walter C. Parker, Ph.D.
Professor of Social Studies Education,
University of Washington
Seattle, Washington

Emily M. Schell, Ed.D.
Visiting Professor, Teacher Education
San Diego State University
San Diego, California

Dinah Zike
Educational Consultant
Dinah-Mite Activities, Inc.
San Antonio, Texas

CONTRIBUTORS

Raymond C. Jones, Ph.D.
Director of Secondary Social Studies Education
Wake Forest University
Winston-Salem, North Carolina

Irma M. Olmedo
Associate Professor
University of Illinois-Chicago
College of Education
Chicago, Illinois

HISTORIANS/SCHOLARS

Manuel Chavez, Ph.D.
Associate Director, Center for Latin American & Caribbean Studies,
Assistant Professor, School of Journalism
Michigan State University
East Lansing, Michigan

Lawrence Dale, Ph.D.
Director, Center for Economic Education
Arkansas State University
Jonesboro, Arkansas

Brooks Green, Ph.D.
Professor of Geography
University of Central Arkansas
Conway, Arkansas

Jason R. Young, Ph.D.
Assistant Professor of History
SUNY, Buffalo
Buffalo, New York

GRADE LEVEL REVIEWERS

Mary Beth Bridges
Sixth Grade Teacher
Erwin Middle School
Loveland, Colorado

June Montepeluso
Sixth Grade Teacher
Paul P. Gates Elementary School
Acton, Massachusetts

Ruth A. Nieboer
Humanities Teacher
LaSalle Intermediate Academy
South Bend, Indiana

Susan Sheskey
Sixth Grade Teacher
Pleasant View Elementary School
Franklin, Wisconsin

Cathy Sorger
Sixth Grade Teacher
Amity Elementary School
Boise, Idaho

Students with print disabilities may be eligible to obtain an accessible, audio version of the pupil edition of this textbook. Please call Recording for the Blind & Dyslexic at 1-800-221-4792 for complete information.

The McGraw-Hill Companies

Send all inquires to:

Macmillan/McGraw-Hill
8787 Orion Place
Columbus, OH 43240-4027

MHID 0-02-151343-0

ISBN 978-0-02-151343-7

Printed in the United States of America.

1 2 3 4 5 6 7 8 9 10 071/043 14 13 12 11 10 09 08

People, Places, and Cultures: Europe and the Americas

CONTENTS

Unit 3 The Geography and History of Latin America 81

EXPLORE The Big Idea How does geography affect civilizations?

Unit 4 Latin America Today 129

EXPLORE The Big Idea What causes a society to change?

Unit 5 The Geography and History of Europe 169

Explore The Big Idea: Why do civilizations change?

Unit 6 Europe Today 225

Explore The Big Idea: How do cultures influence each other?

Reference Section

Skills and Features

Maps

The Geography and History of the United States and Canada

Essential Question
How do people adapt to where they live?

Cause and Effect

Make and label a Two-Tab Book Foldable before you read Unit 1. Write: **Ways people change their environment** on the top tab. On the bottom tab write: **Ways people are affected by their environment**. Use the Foldable to organize information as you read.

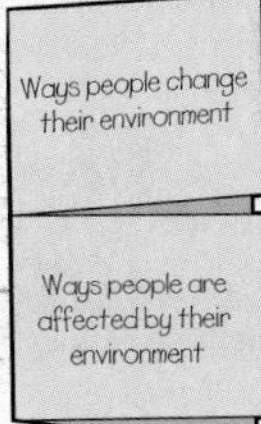

LOG ON For more about Unit 1, go to **www.macmillanmh.com**

Niagara Falls, Ontario, Canada

PEOPLE, PLACES, AND EVENTS

General James Wolfe

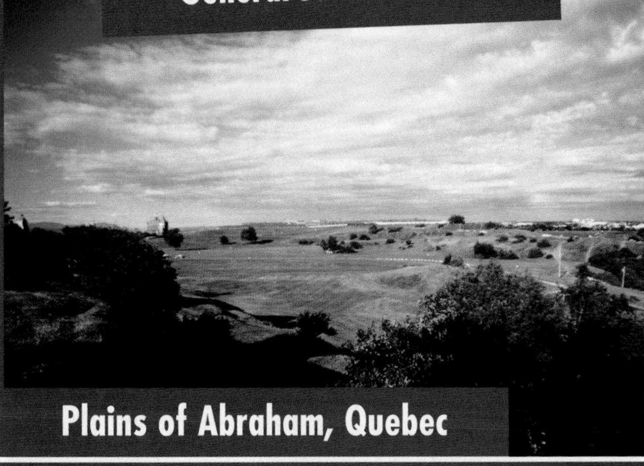

Plains of Abraham, Quebec

1759 | The British defeat the French in Canada during the Seven Years' War.

Martha Washington

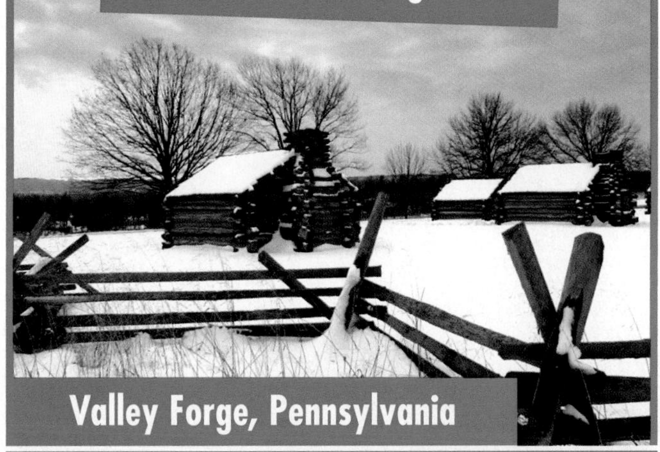

Valley Forge, Pennsylvania

1778 | Martha Washington helps troops during the winter at Valley Forge.

1750 1760 1770 1850

General James Wolfe and his troops scrambled to the **Plains of Abraham** to defeat the French and take **Quebec**.

Today you can see the park where the battle took place and even enjoy an outdoor concert.

Martha Washington nursed General George Washington's troops during the harsh winter at **Valley Forge, Pennsylvania**.

Today Valley Forge Historical Park re-creates how soldiers survived harsh conditions.

LOG ON For more about People, Places, and Events, visit www.macmillanmh.com

Abraham Lincoln

Fort Sumter, South Carolinia

1861 The Civil War begins with the first battle at Fort Sumter.

Martin Luther King, Jr.

Washington, D.C.

1963 Citizens march on Washington demanding civil rights.

1860 1870 1960 1970

After **Abraham Lincoln** was elected President, the South went to war. The first battle took place at **Fort Sumter, South Carolina**.

Today you can take a 30-minute boat ride from Charleston to visit Fort Sumter National Park.

Civil rights leader **Martin Luther King, Jr.**, gave a speech about equal rights at the march.

Today you can visit the Lincoln Memorial in **Washington, D.C.**, where Dr. King delivered his famous speech.

Lesson 1

VOCABULARY

- **prairie** p. 6
- **plateau** p. 7
- **tributary** p. 8
- **natural resource** p. 10
- **mineral** p. 10
- **scarcity** p. 11

READING SKILL

Cause and Effect

Copy the chart below. Use it to show how different forms of geography in North America affect the people that live there.

Cause	→	Effect
	→	
	→	
	→	

STANDARDS FOCUS

SOCIAL STUDIES People, Places, and Environments

GEOGRAPHY Places and Regions

PHYSICAL GEOGRAPHY OF THE UNITED STATES AND CANADA

Waterton National Park, Alberta, Canada

Visual Preview

How does the geography of an area affect living things?

A Grasses and mosses grow on treeless plains near the Arctic Ocean.

B Life is different in the highland, lowland, and mountain areas.

C Three waterways connect major cities and regions.

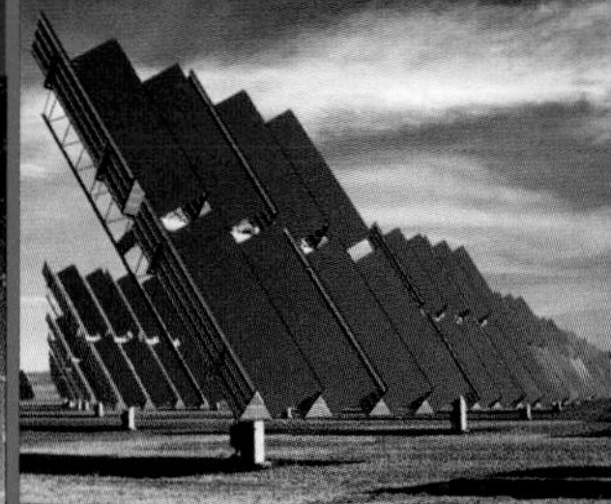

D People use natural resources in different ways in daily life.

Ⓐ THE UNITED STATES AND CANADA

The geography of North America played a big role in how the United States and Canada grew. Geography is the study of the interactions of Earth and its people.

The United States and Canada share most of North America. The west coast faces the Pacific Ocean. The west has high elevations, due to the rugged Rocky Mountains. The east coast faces the Atlantic Ocean. The north borders the cold Arctic Ocean. The tundra, or a treeless plain, covers Arctic lands in this region where only grasses and mosses can grow. The southern border of North America faces the Gulf of Mexico.

Canada occupies most of the northern part of North America. It is divided into 10 provinces and 3 territories. Canada is the second-largest country in the world. The United States is the fourth-largest country in the world. Forty-eight of the country's states are contiguous, or connected inside of a common boundary. Alaska borders Canada to the northwest. Hawaii is a group of islands southwest of California in the Pacific Ocean.

QUICK CHECK

Cause and Effect **Why can only grasses and mosses grow in the tundra?**

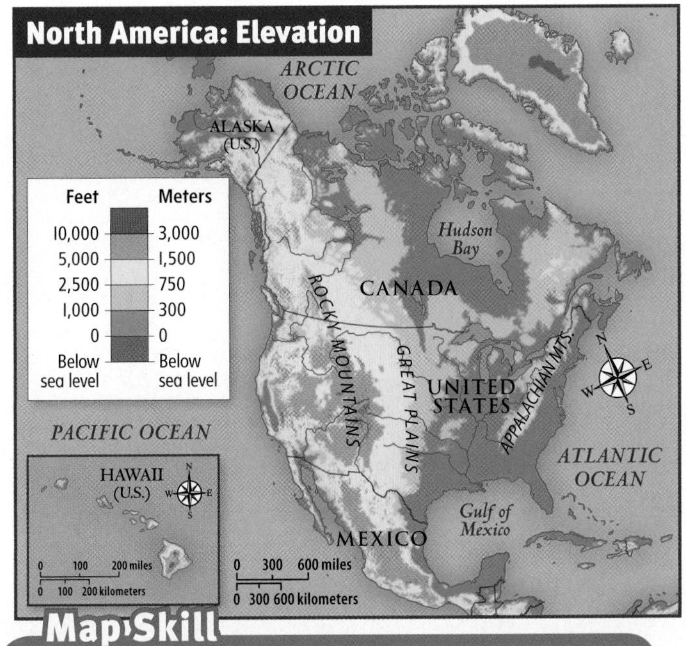

Map Skill

PLACE **About how high are the Rocky Mountains?**

▼ Low temperatures and a short growing season allow only tundra grasses and mosses to grow.

B LANDFORMS

A variety of landforms shape the United States and Canada. Two large, broad lowlands run along the Atlantic and Gulf of Mexico coasts. The Atlantic Coastal Plain has many shipping ports along the natural harbors of the Atlantic coast. The Gulf Coastal Plain is wide and has rich soil that is excellent for farming. Cotton is a major crop of the Gulf Coastal Plain.

Highlands

West and north of the Atlantic and Gulf Coastal Plains are highland areas. These include the Appalachian Mountains, which run from eastern Canada to Alabama. The Appalachian Mountains are the oldest mountains in North America. Their rounded peaks show their age. Water, wind, and ice have worn away mountain rock and soil in a process called erosion. The highest peak is Mount Mitchell in North Carolina. Even with erosion, it reaches 6,684 feet.

Interior Lowlands

Enormous interior lowlands lie to the west of the eastern highlands. In the north, the horseshoe-shaped area called the Canadian Shield wraps around Hudson Bay. It has rocky hills, lakes, and evergreen forests. With poor soil and a cold climate, the Canadian Shield cannot be farmed. It does have many minerals, such as iron ore, copper, and nickel.

South of the Canadian Shield and west of the Appalachian Mountains lie the Central Lowlands, or Central Plains. There you will find rolling hills, grassy flatlands, thick forests, and fertile farmland. This area also contains important waterways, such as the Great Lakes and the Mississippi River.

The Great Plains stretch west of the Mississippi River. Much of this vast region is a **prairie**. Prairies are flat, wide lands covered in grass. The soil is very fertile, and the land is rich in coal, oil, and natural gas.

▼ A Great Plains wheat farm

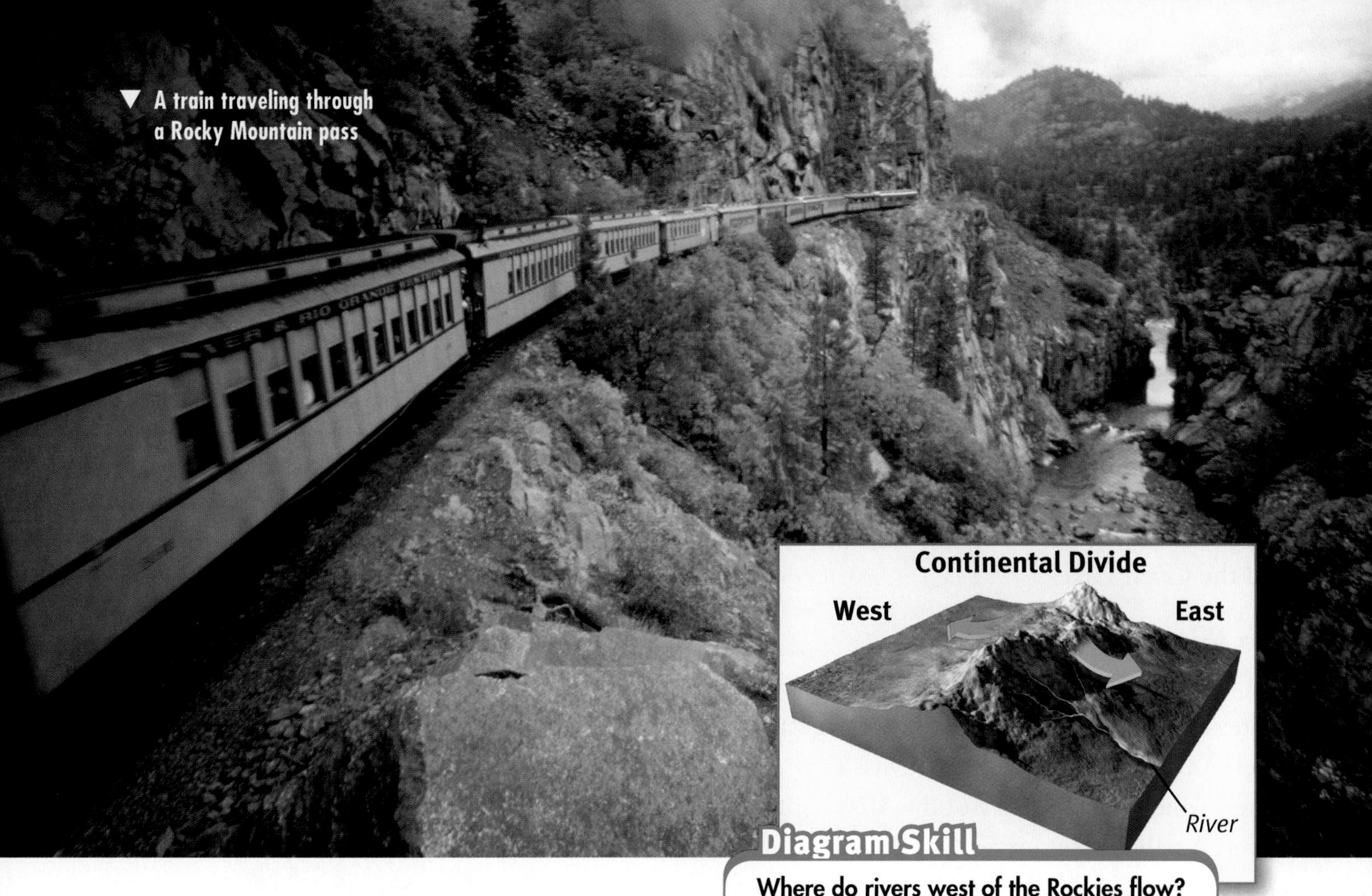

▼ A train traveling through a Rocky Mountain pass

Mountains in the West

Several mountain ranges exist west of the Great Plains. The Rocky Mountains are a long chain of mountains that run from Alaska south to New Mexico. The Rockies are a young and tall mountain range. People cross the Rockies through passes, or lower areas in the mountain.

The North American Continental Divide is an imaginary line that runs along the Rockies. A divide is a high point of a landmass that determines which direction rivers flow. Rivers to the east of the Continental Divide drain into the Arctic Ocean, the Atlantic Ocean, and the Gulf of Mexico. West of the Continental Divide, rivers flow into the Pacific Ocean and the Gulf of California. Each continent has its own continental divide.

Other mountain chains near the Pacific coast include the Sierra Nevada, the Cascade Range, the Coastal Ranges, and the Alaska Range. The Alaska Range has the highest point in North America, Mount McKinley (20,320 feet).

Canyons and Plateaus

Between these ranges and the Rockies are dry areas and high **plateaus**, or flat areas of raised land. To the south are canyons, or deep valleys with steep sides. Canyons are formed by rivers wearing through rock over time, such as the Grand Canyon of the Colorado River.

Quick Check

Cause and Effect **Why do people in the Canadian Shield focus more on mining than on farming?**

C MAJOR WATERWAYS

Waterways are found throughout the United States and Canada. Many of the region's rivers are navigable, or wide and deep enough to allow the passage of ships. Native Americans were the first to travel and trade on North American waterways. Over time, these same waterways connected major cities and regions of the continent. Two of the region's most important waterways are the Mississippi River and the Great Lakes.

The Mississippi River

The second-longest river in the United States is the Mississippi River. The longest river in the United States is the Missouri River, which is a **tributary** of the Mississippi River. A tributary is a river that flows into a larger river. The Mississippi begins as a narrow stream that flows from its source, Lake Itasca in Minnesota, to the Gulf of Mexico.

The Mississippi River Basin dominates the central part of the region. It drains over one million square miles of land. This means that as the river flows from its source to its mouth, the surrounding land is watered and made suitable for farming.

Because so much of the river is wide and deep, ships can navigate the Mississippi for a great distance. Products from port cities, such as St. Louis and Memphis, are shipped down the river to other ports.

Map Skill

REGION **What river regions make up the Mississippi River Basin?**

The mighty Mississippi River

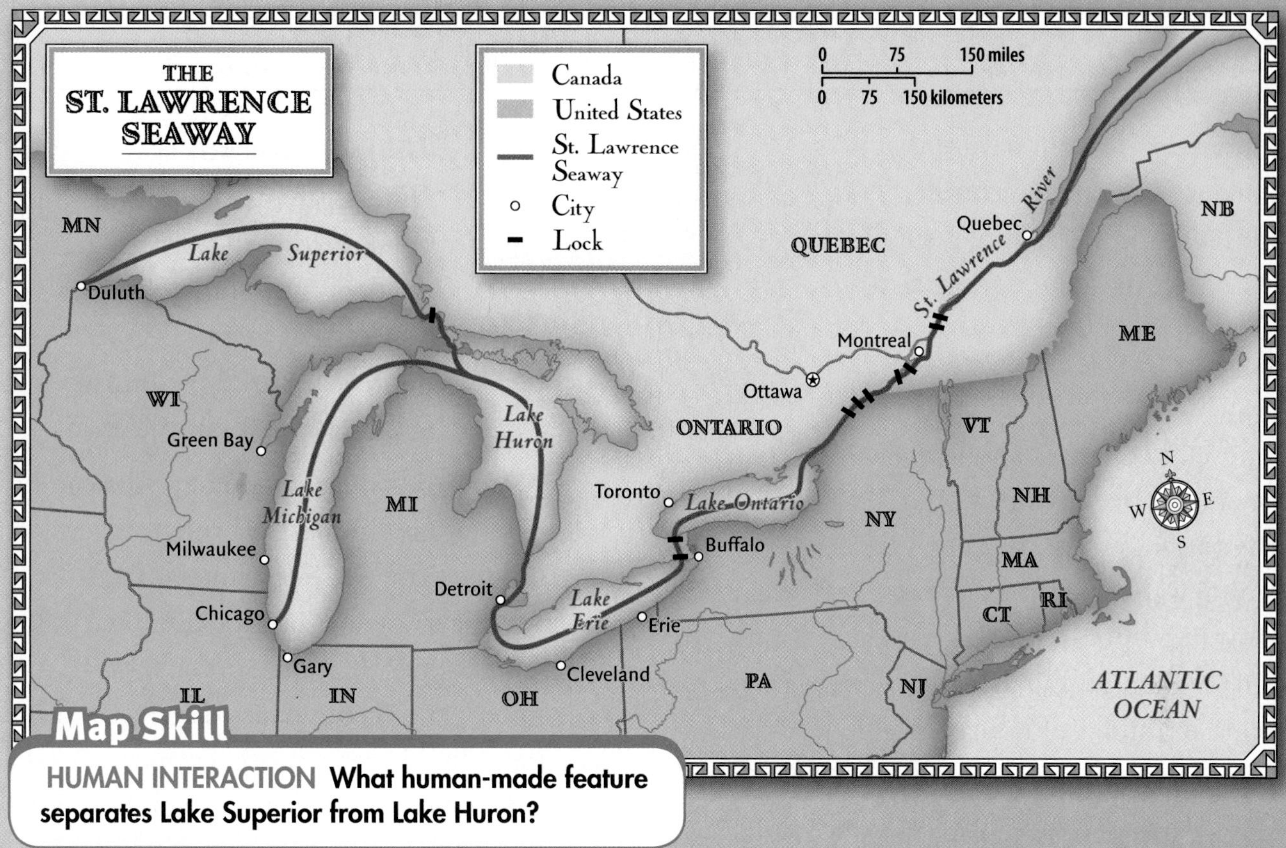

Map Skill

HUMAN INTERACTION **What human-made feature separates Lake Superior from Lake Huron?**

The Great Lakes

The Great Lakes—the world's largest group of freshwater lakes—lie in the central part of North America. Glaciers, or giant sheets of moving ice, carved Lake Huron, Lake Ontario, Lake Michigan, Lake Erie, and Lake Superior about 10,000 years ago. The largest and deepest of the Great Lakes is Lake Superior. Lake Erie is the most shallow and holds the least water of the Great Lakes.

St. Lawrence River

The waters of the Great Lakes flow into the St. Lawrence River. The St. Lawrence River flows for about 750 miles from Lake Ontario to the Atlantic Ocean. The Canadian cities of Montreal, Quebec, and Ottawa grew up along the St. Lawrence River and its branches. They depend on the St. Lawrence as an important transportation link.

For many years, rapids, waterfalls, and uneven water levels kept ships from navigating the entire route from the Great Lakes to the Atlantic Ocean. In 1959 the United States and Canada built a series of canals called the St. Lawrence Seaway. To cope with the problem of changing water levels, engineers built locks. A lock is a part of a canal where water is pumped in or out to raise or lower ships. Once a ship reaches the necessary sea level, the ship passes through the lock.

Today, ships on the St. Lawrence Seaway carry raw materials and manufactured goods from cities such as Chicago, Cleveland, and Toronto to the rest of the world.

Quick Check

Cause and Effect **Why did the United States and Canada build the St. Lawrence Seaway?**

D NATURAL RESOURCES

Materials found in nature that people use are called **natural resources**. These resources supply us with products and energy that we use every day.

A Canadian gold maple leaf coin

Energy Resources

The United States and Canada have energy resources that are both nonrenewable and renewable. Nonrenewable resources are resources that will eventually run out because there is only so much of them on Earth. Oil, natural gas, and coal are examples of nonrenewable resources.

Renewable resources are resources found in nature that can be replaced, such as sun, wind, and hydroelectric power. Solar energy harnesses the power of sunlight. Flat plates called solar panels collect sunlight energy and turn it into electricity. Wind can also be used to make energy. The force of the wind spins a turbine that produces electricity. Hydroelectric power is energy generated by falling water. Niagara Falls produces hydroelectric power.

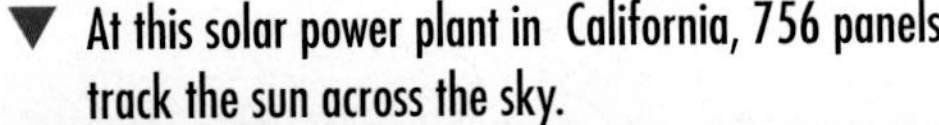

▼ At this solar power plant in California, 756 panels track the sun across the sky.

Mineral Resources

There are many **mineral** resources in the United States and Canada. A mineral is a natural resource that is found in Earth. Minerals are used by industries in the United States and Canada.

Large iron-ore deposits can be found in parts of the northern United States and eastern Canada. Iron-ore is used to make steel. The Rockies have gold, silver, and copper. Copper can be used to make wires, pipes, and frying pans. Deep within the Canadian Shield are iron ore, copper, nickel, and gold. In fact, the Canadian Shield supplies Canada with so many different minerals that it is often called "Canada's Storehouse."

Soil Resources

Rich soils in parts of the United States and Canada help farmers grow crops. The area along the St. Lawrence Seaway has fertile soil, and farmers grow grains, fruits, and vegetables.

The Midwest has flat land and fertile soil. Corn, grains, and livestock are all important to the economy of the Midwest. The warm, wet climate of the South favors crops that are not usually grown elsewhere, such as citrus fruits in Florida and Texas, and peanuts in Georgia and Alabama. People use irrigation, or bringing water to dry areas through ditches or pipes, to make the Central Valley of California a leading producer of fruits and vegetables.

A fishing boat in the Atlantic Ocean

Scarce Resources

Many resources are limited because they are nonrenewable. Renewable resources, however, can also become scarce. **Scarcity** happens when there is not enough of a resource to make all of the products people want.

Tree and fish resources have become scarce in North America. People have cleared land to farm or to make timber products, such as paper. This has led to a decrease in the number of forests in the United States and Canada.

The coastal waters of the Atlantic and Pacific Oceans and the Gulf of Mexico are important to both countries. These waters support fishing industries. Recently, some of these areas have been overfished, leading to a decrease in fish.

Quick Check

Cause and Effect **Why are scientists working to find renewable energy sources?**

Check Understanding

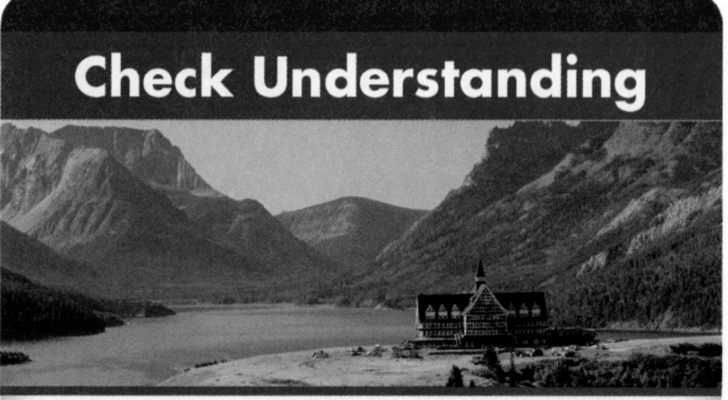

1. **VOCABULARY** Write a paragraph describing different land regions in North America.

   prairie **plateau**

2. **READING SKILL** Cause and Effect Use your chart from page 4 to write about how people have affected the amount of resources in North America.

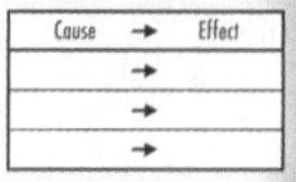

3. **Write About It** How might living near the Mississippi River affect job opportunities?

Lesson 2

VOCABULARY

temperate climate p. 13
current p. 14
precipitation p. 14
drought p. 15
arid p. 16

READING SKILL

Cause and Effect

Copy the chart below. Use it to show the factors that influence climate in North America.

Cause	→	Effect
	→	
	→	
	→	

STANDARDS FOCUS

SOCIAL STUDIES — People, Places, and Environments

GEOGRAPHY — The World in Spatial Terms

CLIMATE REGIONS OF THE UNITED STATES AND CANADA

Some plantlife, such as palm trees, can only exist in tropical climates.

Visual Preview

How does climate affect how people live?

A Long, cold winters and brief, cool summers make life harsh in the Far North.

B People in warm climates get different amounts of rainfall.

C In the Midwest and the East, people have plenty of snow, rain, and sun.

THE FAR NORTH

Climate is the usual pattern of weather in an area over a long period of time. It affects plant life and where people choose to live.

Climate is mainly determined by latitude, but it is also determined by landforms such as mountains and large bodies of water. The region of the United States and Canada has a great variety of climates. The Far North is a cold, arctic wasteland. Areas near the Tropic of Cancer are warm all year. Most people in the United States and Canada live in a **temperate climate**. Temperate climates have changing seasons and mild weather that is neither too hot nor too cold.

Cold Climates

In the northern arctic parts of Alaska and Canada, winters are long and cold, while summers are brief and cool. As a result, few people live in this harsh environment. The Arctic Ocean's coastline is a treeless tundra. This very cold climate prevents the growth of trees and most plants.

In the subarctic region farther south, dense forests of evergreen trees have adapted to the cold climate. For example, the waxy coating of evergreen needles keeps moisture inside during the bitterly cold winters.

Quick Check

Cause and Effect **Why do few people live in the Far North?**

Citizenship

Cooperation and Compromise

People living in harsh environments like the Far North need to practice cooperation and compromise. People use cooperation when they work together to make rules or laws or to solve a problem. People compromise when they give up a part of something they want. By getting along and working together, everyone contributes to a situation that everybody can live with.

Write About It Write a paragraph about a time you gave up something you wanted to solve a problem or settle a disagreement.

A village near the Arctic Ocean in Nunavut, Canada

B WESTERN AND TROPICAL AREAS

In addition to latitude, the movement of air and water helps create Earth's climates. Moving air and water help carry the sun's heat around the globe. In the ocean, the moving streams of water are called **currents**.

The Effects of Water

Near the Equator, air and water are heated the most. Warm wind and water currents move from the tropics toward the North and South Poles. A large, warm-water ocean current known as the Gulf Stream flows north from the Gulf of Mexico through the cool Atlantic Ocean along the east coast of North America.

Water temperatures do not change as much or as fast as land temperatures do. Thus, air over large bodies of water is warmer in winter and cooler in summer than it is on land. This keeps coastal air temperatures moderate.

The Great Lakes affect nearby land much as the ocean does in other parts of the country. This is called the lake effect. In summer, lake water and the air above it are cooler than the nearby land. Wind crossing a lake creates a cool breeze. In winter, the opposite is true. Sometimes, though, winds pick up moisture and form clouds that cause lake effect snow.

The Pacific Coast

The area from southern Alaska to northern California is called the Pacific Northwest. The Pacific Ocean's warm North Pacific Current keeps this area's climate mild and wet. Evergreen forests, ferns, and mosses are common. By contrast, southern California has a climate of warm, dry summers and mild, wet winters with less rainfall.

Deserts

Many parts of the southwestern United States are desert. A desert gets less than 10 inches of **precipitation**, or rainfall, each year. The Southwest is also closer to the Equator than other parts of the United States. The temperatures are high all year.

Venice Beach in southern California (left) and a home in Acoma Pueblo, New Mexico (below)

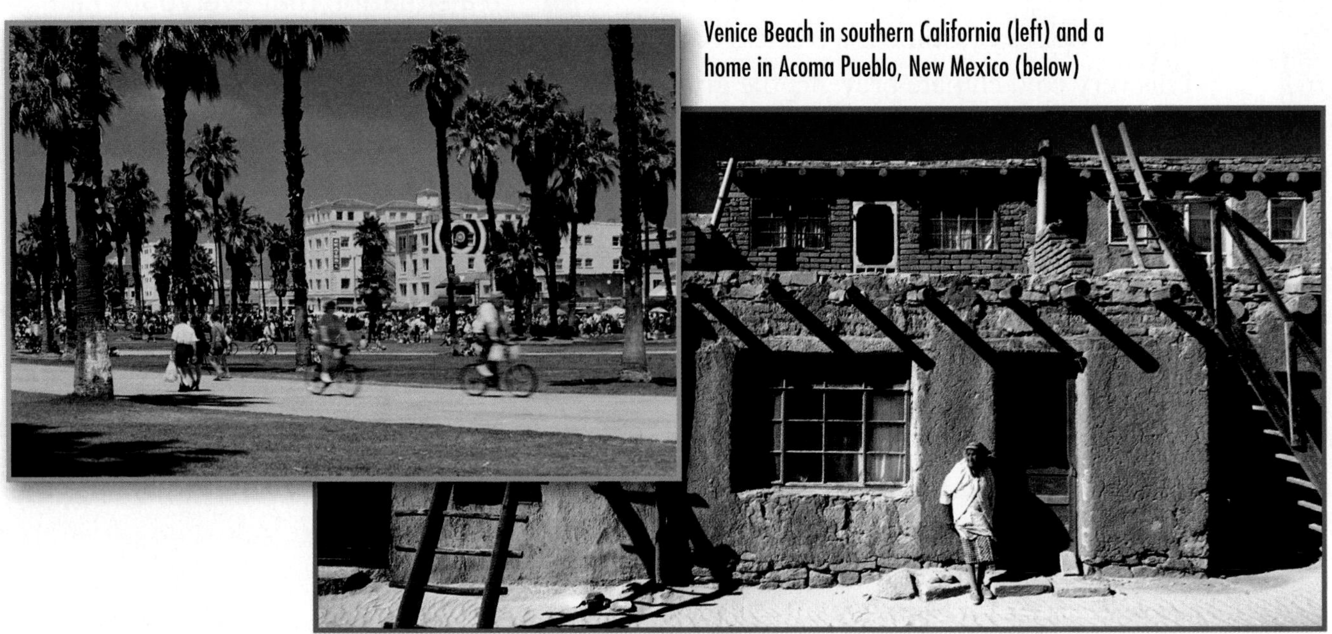

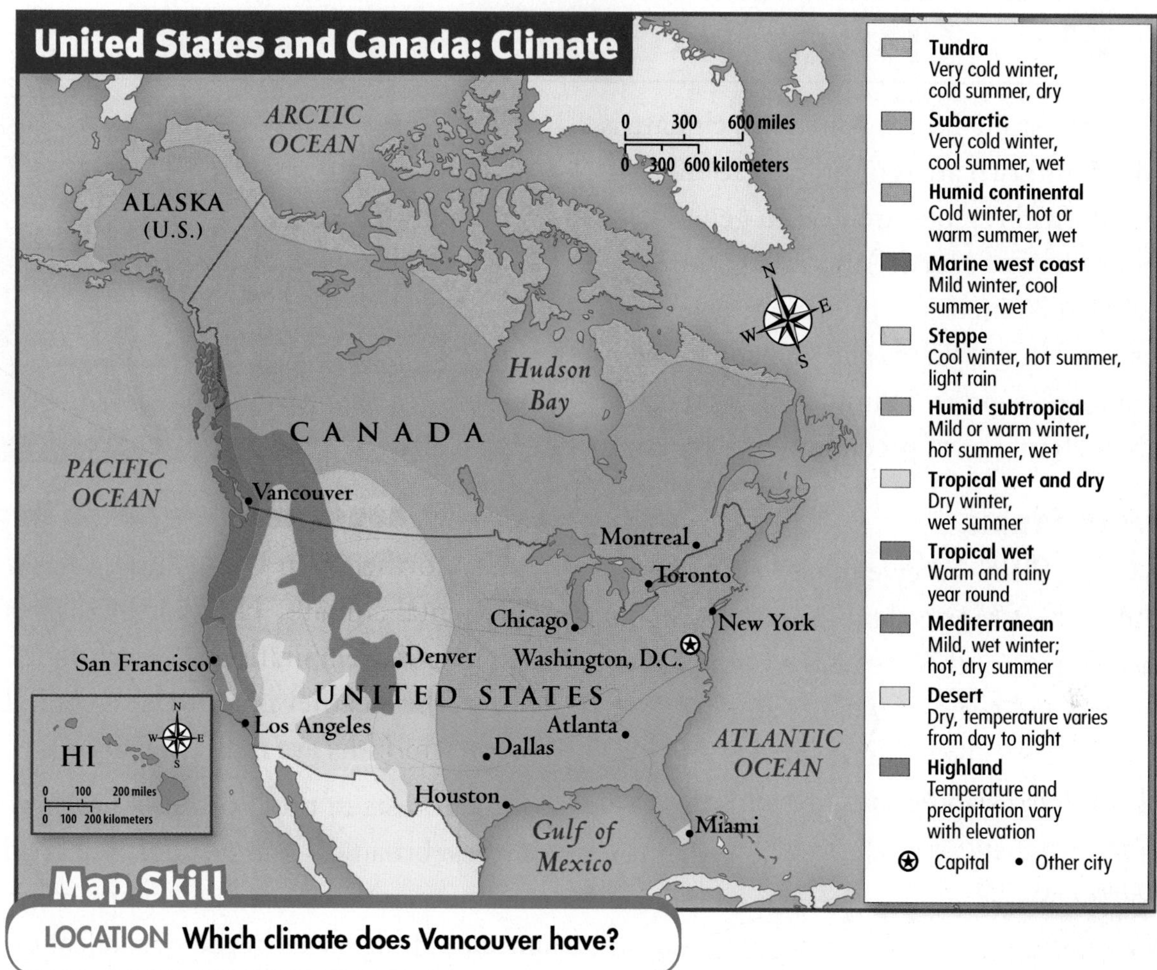

Map Skill

LOCATION **Which climate does Vancouver have?**

The Sonoran and Chihuahuan Deserts cover over 295,000 square miles along the United States–Mexico border. Plants and animals have adapted to this harsh climate over thousands of years. Many plants store rainwater so they can survive the long, dry season.

The Inland West

The Inland West stretches from the Sierra Nevada to the eastern Rocky Mountains. The Great Basin has a steppe climate of hot summers and mild winters. The Sierra Nevada blocks humid winds from the Pacific Ocean, causing little rainfall.

Areas on the eastern side of the Rockies have a partly dry climate. **Drought**, or a long period without rainfall, is a serious challenge. Droughts can kill crops and animals.

Tropical Areas

The tropics lie between the Tropic of Cancer and the Tropic of Capricorn. Temperatures here change little from season to season.

Two areas of the United States have tropical climates. South Florida has a tropical wet and dry climate, where summers are hot and wet and winters are warm and dry.

Hawaii has a tropical wet climate, which is wet in most months, with up to 100 inches of rain a year. Hawaii has average year-round temperatures between 70°F and 80°F. Monthly rainfall supports tropical rain forests.

Quick Check

Cause and Effect **How does water affect climate?**

C THE MIDWEST AND THE EAST

One way to study North America's climate is to divide it into two areas of precipitation, **arid** and humid. Arid regions are dry. In general, the western half of North America is arid. It gets less than 20 inches of precipitation a year. The eastern United States and Canada have humid climate regions. Humid regions receive more than 20 inches of precipitation a year.

EVENT

On April 14, 1935, twenty of the worst Dust Bowl storms turned the day into night. On **Black Sunday** some people could not see five feet in front of them.

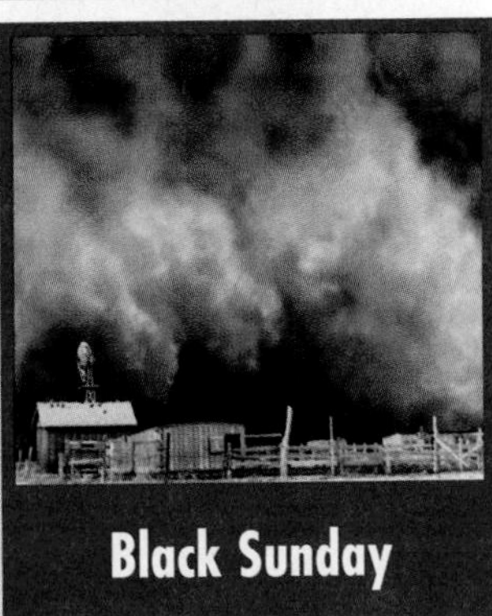

Black Sunday

The Great Plains

The Great Plains receive their moisture from the Gulf of Mexico and from the Arctic. The eastern part of this area has a humid climate, with cold, snowy winters and hot, humid summers. The western part has light rain. Short grasses and grains grow in this area.

Drought severely affected the Great Plains in the 1930s. Years of poor farming methods and drought caused the Dust Bowl, a series of windstorms that picked up loose topsoil and turned the central United States and Canada into a wasteland. Economic hardships forced many farmers to leave the Great Plains.

The Northeast and Northern Canada

The northeastern United States has a humid continental climate. The Northeast gets large amounts of precipitation all year round. In the winter, the weather is snowy and cold. The summer months are either warm or hot.

The forests in the Northeast have two types of trees: broadleaf and needleleaf. Broadleaf trees have wide leaves that change color in autumn. The leaves of the needleleaf evergreen trees are long and thin, like needles. The needleleaves stay green all year.

Northern Canada has a subarctic climate. This area lies just below the Arctic Circle.

Boston park in the summer

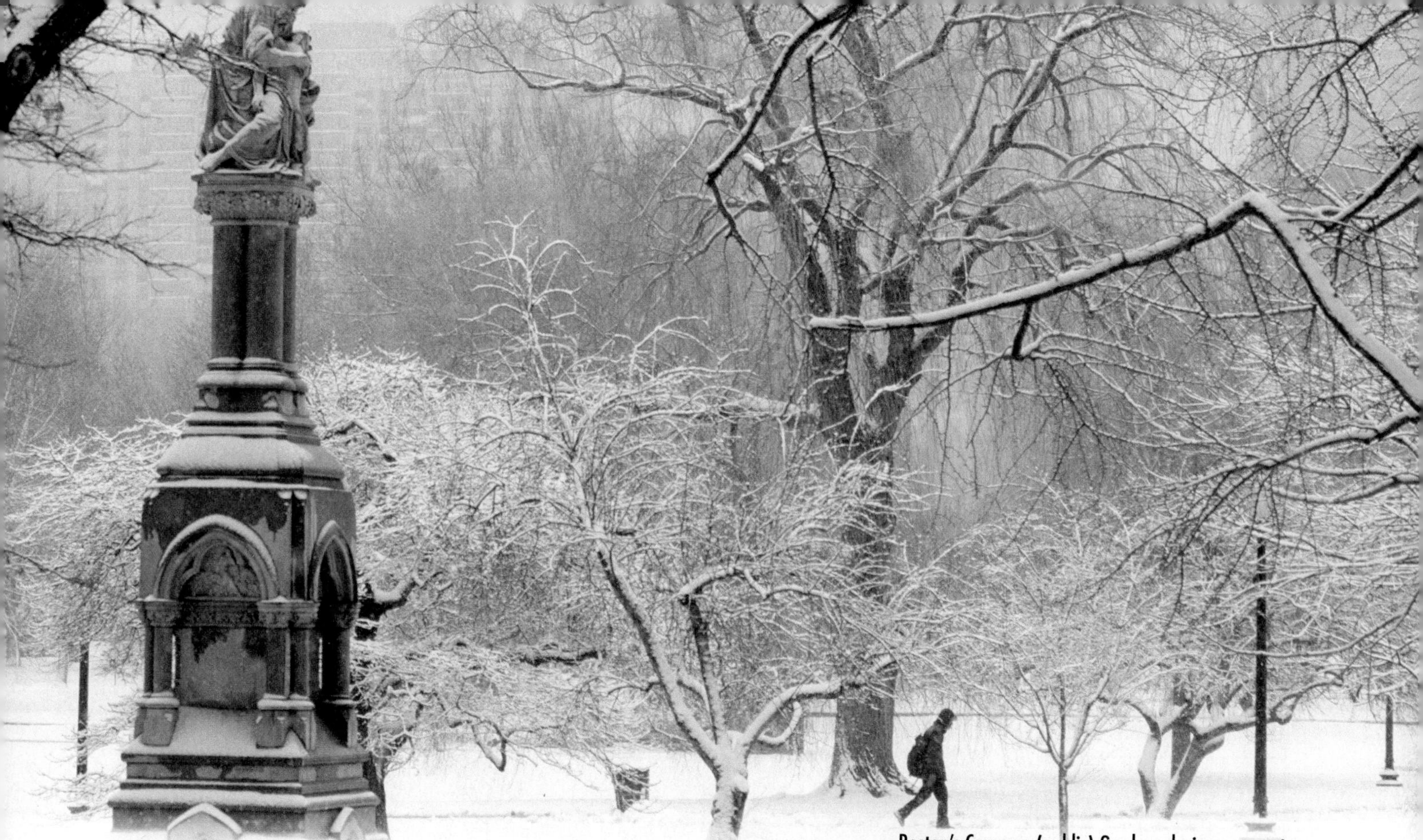

Boston's Common (public) Gardens during a snowstorm

The few people living here face severely cold and bitter winters, but temperatures do rise above freezing during summer months. Huge evergreen forests grow in this climate.

The Southeast

The Southeast has a humid subtropical climate. Rain falls throughout the year but is less heavy during the hot summer months. Humid subtropical winters are generally short and mild.

The warm Southeast region is the only place where certain crops, such as cotton, can be grown. This is because the Southeast has a longer growing season than some other regions of the United States.

Quick Check

Cause and Effect **Why can certain crops only be grown in the Southeast?**

Check Understanding

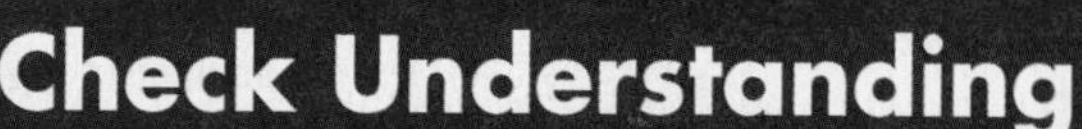

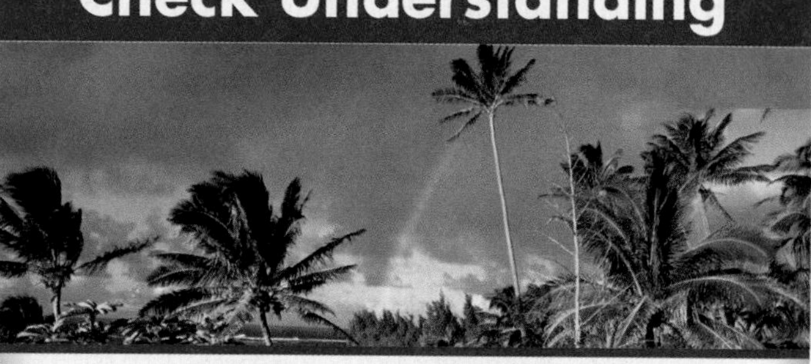

1. **VOCABULARY** Write about the Great Basin using the following words.

   precipitation **drought** **arid**

2. **READING SKILL** Cause and Effect Use your chart from page 12 to write about the climates in North America.

EXPLORE The Big Idea

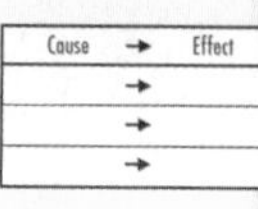

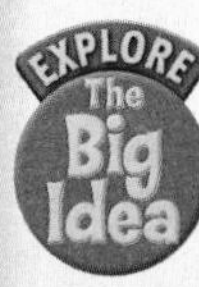

3. **Write About It** Write about how weather affects life in the region where you live.

Lesson 3

VOCABULARY

indigenous p. 19

Northwest Passage p. 20

voyageur p. 21

READING SKILL

Cause and Effect

Copy the chart below. Use it to show how native peoples and settlers helped shape North America.

Cause	→	Effect
	→	
	→	
	→	

STANDARDS FOCUS

SOCIAL STUDIES Time, Continuity, and Change

GEOGRAPHY Human Systems

EARLY CIVILIZATIONS AND COLONIALISM

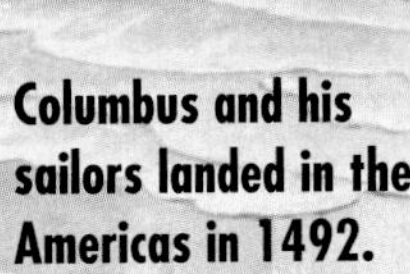

Columbus and his sailors landed in the Americas in 1492.

Visual Preview

How do people contribute to North America's history?

A Native peoples established ways of life in early North American history.

B Europeans came to North America and set up colonies.

C North America experienced internal and external conflicts.

Ⓐ EARLY NORTH AMERICANS

Much of what we have learned about early North Americans comes from studying things that they have left behind, such as buildings, tools, and pottery. This field of study is called archaeology.

The first people to settle in North America were hunters from Asia who probably followed herds of animals across a land bridge to Alaska. Many also may have come by boat. Their descendants are called **indigenous** people. In the United States, indigenous people are called Native Americans. In Canada, they are known as First peoples. First peoples include First Nations (known as Native Americans in the United States), Métis, and the Inuit.

Ways of Life

Over many centuries, Native Americans developed different ways of life based on the resources that were available to them. Some grew corn in the desert. Others hunted deer in the forests and cut down trees to build homes and canoes. In the Plains, buffalo provided food, clothing, and shelter. Other Native Americans caught fish in the Pacific Ocean. The Métis people came much later. The Métis have a mixture of First Nations, French Canadian, English, and Scottish ancestors. Métis culture includes fiddle playing and a dance called jigging.

The Inuit settled in the far north of Canada, where they still live today. They adapted to their environment by learning to hunt seals and walruses and by learning to catch fish from the icy waters. On land they traveled by dog sled. On the water they paddled single-person boats called kayaks. The First Nations and Inuit invented objects such as canoes, snowshoes, and a game called lacrosse.

QUICK CHECK

Cause and Effect **Why did the Inuit learn to hunt seals and walruses?**

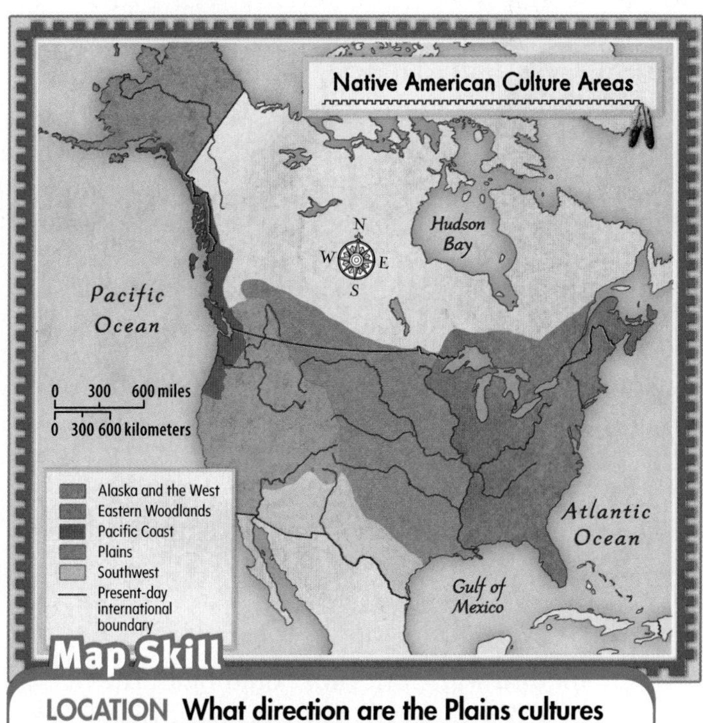

Map Skill

LOCATION **What direction are the Plains cultures in relation to the Eastern Woodlands cultures?**

B EUROPEAN COLONIZATION

▼ The Pilgrims arrived in Massachusetts in 1620.

Native American ways of life changed with the arrival of Europeans. In 1492 explorer Christopher Columbus, sailing west from Europe, reached islands in the Caribbean Sea.

European Settlements

Many Europeans believed there was a water route across North America to Asia. They called this shortcut the **Northwest Passage**. The search for the Northwest Passage brought explorers to North America.

England, France, and Spain claimed areas in North America called colonies. Colonies are settlements far away from the country that rules them.

Native Americans fought for their land. Some died in wars, but most died from the diseases that Europeans brought with them to the Americas.

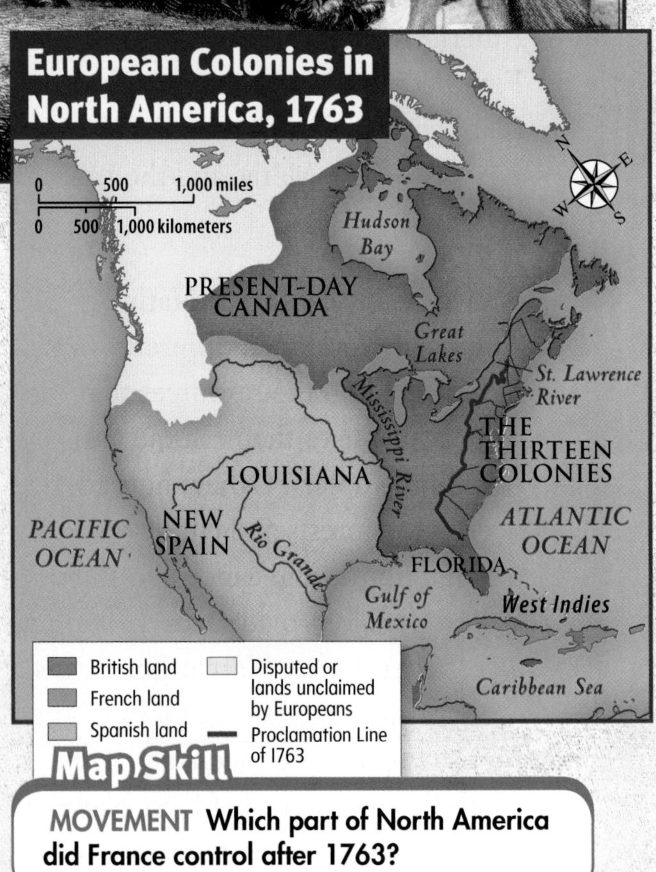

Map Skill

MOVEMENT Which part of North America did France control after 1763?

England settled in Virginia in 1607. Some people, such as the Pilgrims, came to North America seeking religious freedom.

Eventually England had 13 colonies along the Atlantic coast. England also controlled some areas in what is now Canada, including the Hudson Bay. France claimed land around the St. Lawrence River and called it New France.

The Fur Trade

French explorers, settlers, and missionaries founded several cities. The city of Quebec was founded in 1608 by French explorer Samuel de Champlain. Quebec quickly became an important trading post for France. The French traded with First Nations for beaver furs, which they sold in Europe for a lot of money.

The French fur traders were called **voyageurs**, which means "travelers" in French. The voyageurs paddled their canoes for 16 hours a day in rivers around the Great Lakes, sometimes singing as they went. They carried guns, kettles, fabrics, and other goods to trade for beaver furs. They worked for fur companies, which sold the furs in Europe to be made into hats.

▲ Beaver hats such as this one were popular in Europe.

◀ Voyageurs have become folk heroes in Canada.

New French Settlements

In 1682 Robert de La Salle led an expedition down the Mississippi River. La Salle continued down to the Gulf of Mexico, where he claimed the Mississippi River and its tributaries for France. He named the territory Louisiana after the French king, Louis XIV.

By 1690 France had claimed much of what is now the central United States and Canada. However, only a few thousand settlers lived in New France. Louis XIV tried to strengthen French control of the region. In 1706 the French created a new settlement in what is now New Orleans, Louisiana. New Orleans was the largest French settlement in Louisiana.

By 1760 France had 85,000 settlers and claimed land from Canada down to the Gulf of Mexico. The English had over 2 million settlers, but French control of the area prevented the English from moving west.

PLACES

Quebec City is the capital of the province of Quebec. It is one of the oldest cities in North America. The walls that once protected it still exist today.

Quebec City

Quick Check

Cause and Effect **Why was the fur trade profitable?**

C CONFLICTS AND INDEPENDENCE

During the 1600s and 1700s, the English and French fought each other for territory around the globe. In 1707 England and Scotland united to form Great Britain. This laid the foundation for the British Empire.

France Battles England

Both France and Great Britain wanted to control trade in Canada. Disagreements also arose when English colonists settled land claimed by France in the Ohio River Valley. The French feared that the settlers would cut down forests, which would hurt their fur trade.

These disputes over land and trade led to the Seven Years' War in 1754. In America this conflict is known as the French and Indian War. While warfare and diseases had killed most First Nations by this time, most of those who were left fought on the side of the French.

France Loses Canada

British General James Wolfe led a surprise attack at the Plains of Abraham in Quebec.

This battle ended the war. France and Britain signed the Treaty of Paris in 1763. This treaty ended the war as well as French control of Canada. Britain controlled Canada and all French land east of the Mississippi.

The American Revolution

The British victory in the Seven Years' War united the colonists. Many had joined together with the British to fight a powerful enemy. The colonists developed a new, independent spirit. The victory in the Seven Years' War set the stage for the American Revolution.

The Seven Years' War was costly for the British government. To help pay for the war debts, the British leaders decided to raise taxes on the colonists. The people in Great Britain's 13 colonies soon grew angry over British taxes and unfair trade policies.

In 1776 Thomas Jefferson wrote the Declaration of Independence, which stated that the colonies were now an independent nation. The final statement of the document made the most important point:

> "The good people of these colonies, solemnly publish and declare, that these United Colonies are … free and independent states."

Great Britain would not give up its colonies without a fight. This conflict is known as the Revolutionary War. The war lasted for eight years.

◀ The British and French fought battles across North America during the Seven Years' War.

▲ The British surrendered to the Americans at Yorktown, Virginia.

General George Washington was commander of the Continental army. One of the darkest times of the war was at the winter camp of Valley Forge, Pennsylvania. There, supplies were low, and 2,500 men died of disease. The Patriots did not give up. They fought on and won several battles.

The war finally ended in 1783. Britain officially recognized American independence. A new nation called the United States of America was born.

Quick Check

Cause and Effect What effect did British taxes and trade policies have on the colonists?

Check Understanding

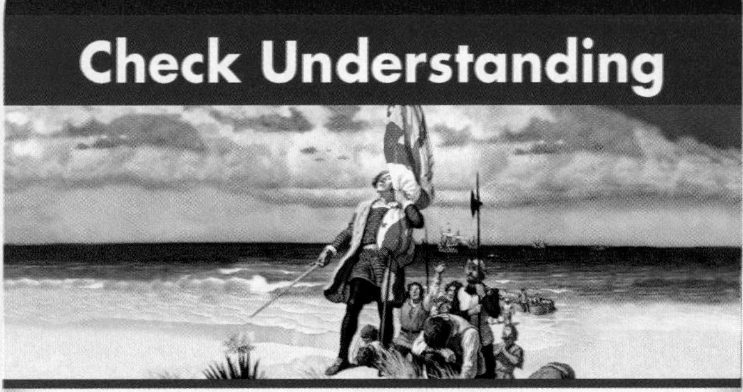

1. **VOCABULARY** Write a paragraph describing the fur trade in Canada.

   voyageur

2. **READING SKILL Cause and Effect** Use your chart from page 18 to write about the effects of European colonization in North America.

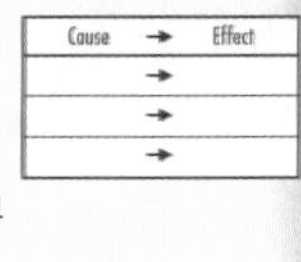

3. **Write About It** What impacts did Native Americans have on North American history?

Lesson 4

VOCABULARY

technology p. 25
annex p. 26
slavery p. 26
province p. 28
territory p. 28

READING SKILL

Cause and Effect
Copy the chart below. Use it to describe how the United States and Canada developed as nations.

Cause	→	Effect
	→	
	→	
	→	

STANDARDS FOCUS

SOCIAL STUDIES Production, Distribution, and Consumption
GEOGRAPHY Human Systems

NATION BUILDING in NORTH AMERICA

On July 1, Canada Day, there are special celebrations with fireworks, picnics, and the Royal Canadian Mounted Police.

Visual Preview

How did the United States and Canada develop as nations?

A The Industrial Revolution helped America grow into an economic power.

B The United States encountered conflict as it expanded westward.

C Canada united into one nation from several different colonies.

Ⓐ INDUSTRIALIZATION

As the United States and Canada became independent, both nations experienced growth and new challenges along the way.

A different kind of revolution took place in the mid-1700s. Before then most people used hand tools and worked at home or in workshops. In the mid 1700s, British inventors made machinery that could do some of the work that humans did. Many of these machines used waterpower, so mills were built along rivers. These inventions saved time and money and led to a boom in industry. This period is known as the Industrial Revolution.

Industrial Revolution in America

The Industrial Revolution came to America in the 1800s. The Industrial Revolution first appeared in the New England area. This area had many rivers where new factories and mills could be built. Because New England was so close to the coast, it had many ports to ship goods to other parts of the country and to the rest of the world.

New Inventions and Processes

The Industrial Revolution was propelled by new machines and **technologies**, or scientific discoveries that simplify work. In 1793 Eli Whitney invented the cotton gin, a machine which removed seeds from cotton fiber and made it quicker and easier to process cotton. Whitney also started the use of interchangeable parts, or a series of identical parts that make a finished product. These parts could be made more cheaply and quickly, which increased production and reduced the price of goods.

Francis Cabot Lowell of Massachusetts owned a cloth-making factory. He started the factory system, which increased production by putting all of the steps of the manufacturing process under one roof.

Quick Check

Cause and Effect **Why did the Industrial Revolution first come to New England?**

▲ A young woman working at a textile factory in the 1800s

B EXPANSION AND DIVISION

By 1783 the United States had gained land west of the Appalachian Mountains. During the 1800s, the United States expanded all the way to the Pacific Ocean.

A Growing Country

Some of this growth came through treaties, or written agreements, with other nations. Some came when the United States **annexed**, or took over, an area. This expansion, however, brought suffering to Native Americans who had lived on their land for centuries. They lost their land, their culture, and often their lives.

Throughout the 1800s, the United States grew in population as well. High birth rates, better public health, and the arrival of millions of Europeans increased the population.

The American economy also grew. Roads, canals, steamboats, and railroads were able to move goods more quickly to markets. The Industrial Revolution helped farmers as well as American manufacturers. New machines made it faster and easier for farmers to plant and harvest crops.

A Divided Country

By the 1850s, social and economic differences divided the country into two regions—North and South. Industry and trade were important in the Northern states. The Southern states built their economy on agriculture and **slavery**. Slavery is the practice of owning people and forcing them to work.

During this time, people in the North increasingly criticized slavery. Some worked on the Underground Railroad, a system of secret land routes, to help enslaved people reach the North. Harriet Tubman, a woman who escaped slavery, rescued hundreds on the railroad. Southerners worried that Northerners would move to end slavery.

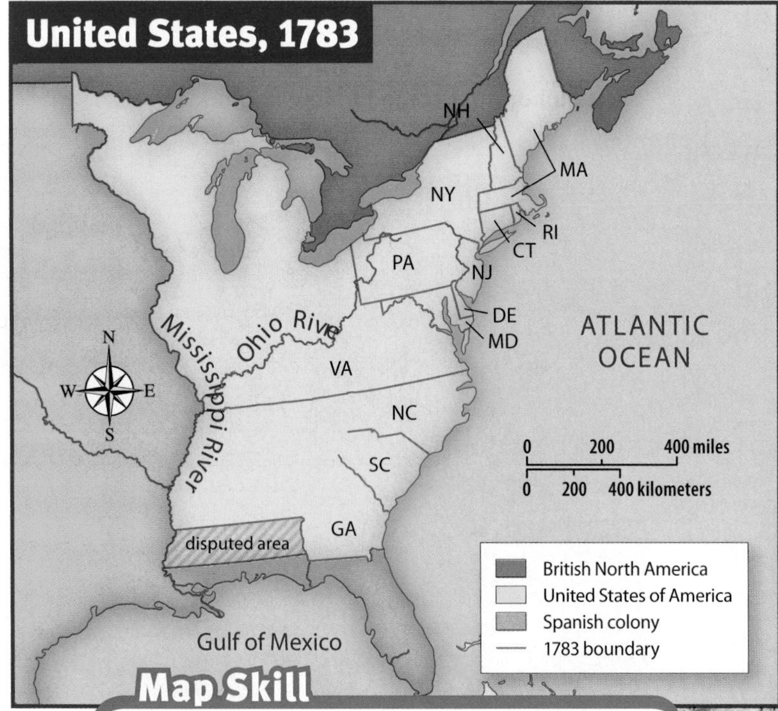

Map Skill

MOVEMENT **Why might settlers from the United States stop at the Mississippi River?**

▼ Sacagawea guided Lewis and Clark as they explored the Louisiana Territory.

▲ Harriet Beecher Stowe's novel *Uncle Tom's Cabin* described to many Northerners the evils of slavery.

Enslaved people working on a sugar plantation in the South

The Civil War

Abraham Lincoln did not want slavery to spread to other states. When he was elected President in 1860, the South set up its own country. The divided nation went to war.

For many, the Civil War was about keeping the Union together. That changed in January 1863, when President Lincoln issued the Emancipation Proclamation. It freed all enslaved people in the rebellious states. The Civil War was now a war to end slavery.

At the end of 1863, Lincoln delivered his Gettysburg Address, reminding Americans that the United States was based on the belief that "all men are created equal."

The fighting ended in 1865. The North had won. Slavery was ended. But the newly freed African Americans still faced poverty and discrimination in the years ahead.

Primary Sources

"I had reasoned this out in my mind, there was one of two things I had a right to, liberty or death; if I could not have one, I would have the other."

Harriet Tubman, as told to Sarah Bradford, *Harriet, the Moses of Her People*, 1869.

Write About It Suppose you worked to help people escape slavery. Write a journal entry describing what you would do in a day of work.

Quick Check

Cause and Effect **What effect did United States expansion have on Native Americans?**

C BRITISH CANADA

After the American Revolution, the British population increased in Canada. About 50,000 Loyalists, American colonists who had remained loyal to Britain, fled to Canada. They set up farms along the coast in what is now Ontario. French-speaking Canadians lived mostly in what is now Quebec.

Forming and Growing a Nation

Just as the United States gained its independence from Great Britain and grew from 13 states to 50, Canada also changed. It united, expanded, and gained its independence—only not quite in the same way. Canada's changes were more gradual and more peaceful.

From 1791 to 1867, British North America was a collection of six separate colonies in Canada. These colonies quarreled with each other over colonial government policies. Fears of being taken over by the United States, however, helped them to stay together.

On July 1, 1867, the British North America Act united Quebec, Ontario, New Brunswick, and Nova Scotia into one nation. July 1 is now celebrated as Canada Day.

Today, Canada is made up of 10 **provinces** and 3 additional **territories**—Yukon, the Northwest Territories, and Nunavut. A province is a division of a country, like a state. A territory is a part of a country that lacks the full rights of a province.

▼ American Loyalists draw lots for their land after arriving in Canada after the end of the American Revolution.

Quick Check

Cause and Effect **How did the American Revolution cause an increase in Canada's British population?**

Check Understanding

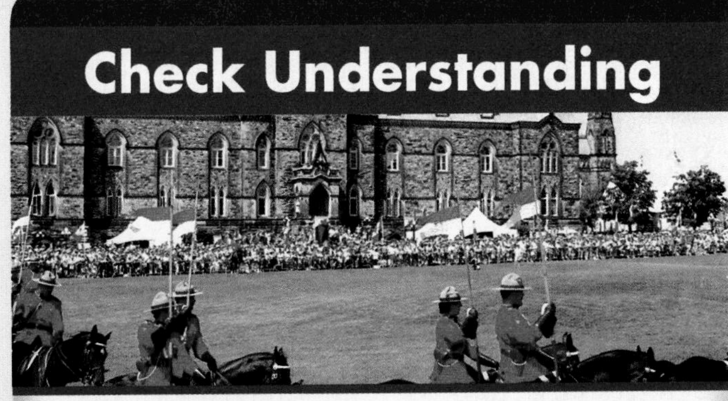

1. **VOCABULARY** Write a paragraph about how Canada has united and expanded.

   province **territory**

2. **READING SKILL Cause and Effect** Use your chart from page 24 to write about how the United States and Canada developed as nations.

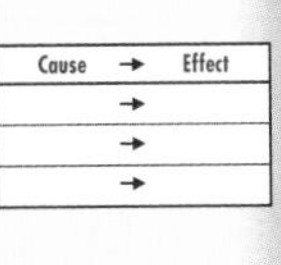

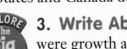

3. **Write About It** In what ways were growth and expansion different in Canada and in the United States?

Chart and Graph Skills

Read Parallel Time Lines

VOCABULARY

time line
decade
century
parallel time line

A **time line** is a diagram of events arranged in the order in which they took place. Time lines are often divided into single years, **decades** (ten-year periods), or **centuries** (hundred-year periods). Time lines can have a break in time that is shown with a symbol, meaning that a period of years is not shown.

The time line below is a **parallel time line**, which shows two sets of dates and events on the same time line. The time line below has events in United States history at the top and amendments, or additions, to the Constitution on the bottom.

Learn It

- Identify the years labeled on the time line. The time line below is labeled for every five years.
- Identify the events on a parallel time line.
- Compare the events on the top of the time line with the events on the bottom of the time line. Use the parallel time line to see what events happened at around the same time.

Try It

- Which amendment followed the election of Thomas Jefferson?
- Which two events happened at the same time on the parallel time line?

Apply It

- Which event led to the Fourteenth Amendment?
- Why do you think the Fifteenth Amendment was added?

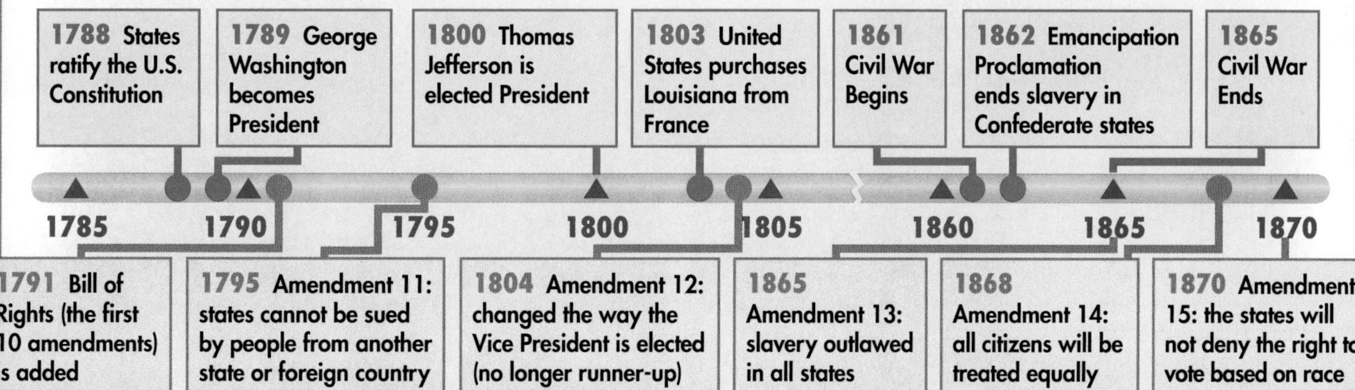

United States Events
1788 States ratify the U.S. Constitution
1789 George Washington becomes President
1800 Thomas Jefferson is elected President
1803 United States purchases Louisiana from France
1861 Civil War Begins
1862 Emancipation Proclamation ends slavery in Confederate states
1865 Civil War Ends
1785
1790
1795
1800
1805
1860
1865
1870
1791 Bill of Rights (the first 10 amendments) is added
1795 Amendment 11: states cannot be sued by people from another state or foreign country
1804 Amendment 12: changed the way the Vice President is elected (no longer runner-up)
1865 Amendment 13: slavery outlawed in all states
1868 Amendment 14: all citizens will be treated equally
1870 Amendment 15: the states will not deny the right to vote based on race
Amendments to the U.S. Constitution

Lesson 5

VOCABULARY

- **satellite** p. 35
- **arms race** p. 35
- **terrorism** p. 36

READING SKILL

Cause and Effect

Copy the chart below. Use it to show how the United States and Canada have changed in the modern era.

Cause	→	Effect
	→	
	→	
	→	

STANDARDS FOCUS

SOCIAL STUDIES Time, Continuity, and Change

GEOGRAPHY The Uses of Geography

THE MODERN ERA

World leaders gather in Alberta, Canada, to discuss global issues.

Visual Preview

How have the United States and Canada changed?

Canada 1861–1921

(in millions)

Years

A Canada's land and population have grown through westward expansion.

B The United States grew into an economic, political, and military world power.

C The Cold War caused changes at home and abroad for the United States.

D The United States and Canada face new challenges from terrorism.

Ⓐ CANADIAN EXPANSION

In the years after gaining independence, Canada and the United States became more involved with the international community.

During the late 1800s, Canada expanded quickly. Pioneers traveled west across the plains and prairies. Four new territories in the west joined Canada between 1870 and 1905. In 1885 the Canadian Pacific Railway linked the east and west together. Hundreds of thousands of European immigrants came to Canada to start farms in lands west of Quebec. Almost two million more immigrants settled in Canadian cities such as Toronto and Montreal.

Quick Check

Cause and Effect **What effect did the opening of the Canadian Pacific Railway have on western Canada?**

DataGraphic

Canada 1861 to 1921

Study the graph and the time line. Then answer the questions that follow.

Population of Canada 1861–1921

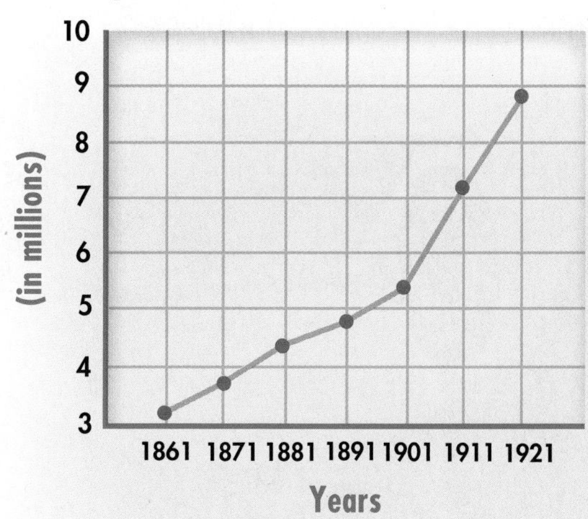

Events in Canada

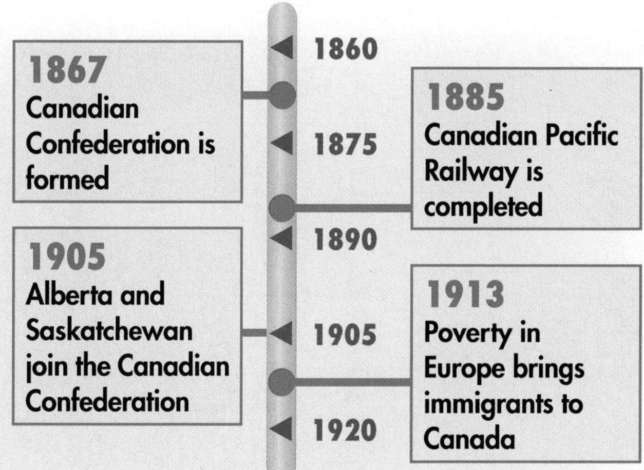

Think About History

1. In which decade did population grow the most?
2. Why did Canada's population grow from 1911 to 1921?

B BECOMING A WORLD LEADER

The map of the United States changed after the Civil War. Through wars, treaties, and purchases, the United States expanded its borders to the Pacific Ocean. People began to move west in search of a better life. Some came to California to look for gold.

PEOPLE

Bessie Coleman became the first African American woman to earn a pilot's license. She was also the first African American woman to become a stunt pilot, performing her first show in 1922.

Bessie Coleman

New Inventions, New Industries

Many new inventions in the late 1800s and early 1900s changed life in America. In 1876 Alexander Graham Bell invented the telephone, which was the first device to transmit speech. Thomas Edison invented the lightbulb in 1879. The first airplane took flight in 1903. By 1906 Henry Ford created the Model T, an automobile that was durable and affordable for the common consumer.

Many of these inventions led to new industries. As these industries grew, new cities grew around them. Cities became the centers of a new industrial age, as people flocked to them in search of work.

The railroad system helped industry spread to the West. Railroads made it easier for people to move to different parts of the country and to move into new cities. All of these changes helped industry grow in the United States. By the early 1900s, the United States industrial production was the greatest in the world.

Henry Ford created the assembly line, where each worker repeatedly performed one task. This made manufactured products, such as the Model T (inset) much cheaper and faster to produce.

World War I

In 1914 World War I began in Europe. After attacks by German submarines against American ships, the United States joined the war in 1917. World War I introduced new technologies to modern warfare, such as poison gas, machine guns, airplanes, and tanks. The American forces helped end the war. The involvement in the war made the United States a major political and military world power.

New technologies, such as airplanes, made World War I different from other wars.

The Great Depression

After the war, Americans enjoyed a boom in industry. By late 1929, however, the economy faced serious problems. Mass production led to more goods than people needed. When people stopped buying, companies could not make profits. This led to an economic crash. This period is called the Great Depression, a time of severe economic hardships in the 1930s.

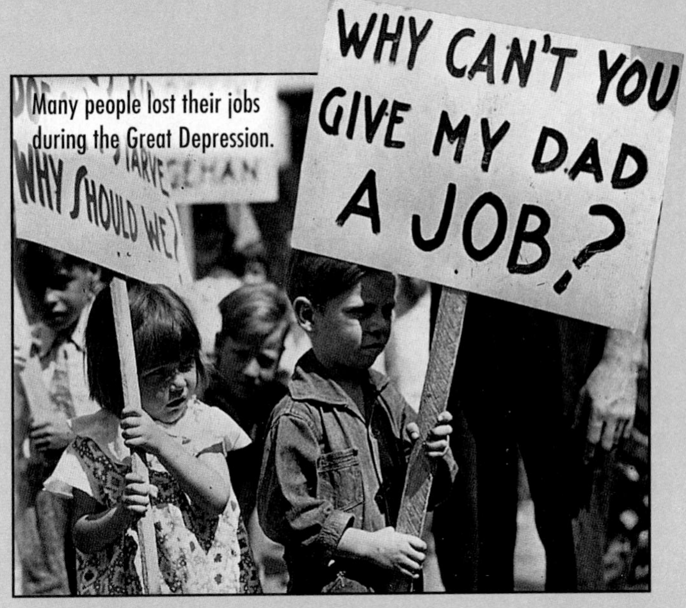

WHY CAN'T YOU GIVE MY DAD A JOB?
WHY SHOULD WE

Many people lost their jobs during the Great Depression.

World War II

In 1939 a new war began in Europe. Germany and its allies were fighting against Great Britain, France, and their allies. The United States entered the war after Japan, an ally of Germany, launched a surprise attack on Pearl Harbor, a naval base in Hawaii.

After years of difficult fighting, Germany surrendered on May 7, 1945. Japan surrendered on August 15, 1945, after the United States used a new weapon called the atomic bomb. The war left much of Europe in disarray. The United States stepped to the forefront to help the rebuilding effort.

The United States declared war on Japan after the attack on Pearl Harbor on December 7, 1941.

Quick Check

Cause and Effect Why did people move to cities in the late 1800s and early 1900s?

C THE COLD WAR ERA

After World War II, the United States and the Soviet Union—an American ally in World War II—became the world's two major powers. The Soviet Union sent troops into Eastern Europe and put these countries under Soviet rule. The Soviets did not allow the countries to hold free elections. These actions led to the Cold War, a war fought with ideas, words, money, and sometimes force.

In 1945 many nations formed the United Nations, or UN. The goals of this organization were to prevent future wars and to improve the lives of all people. In 1949 the United States and its allies formed the North Atlantic Treaty Organization, or NATO. This group pledged to fight the spread of Soviet influence. In response, the Soviet Union formed its own alliance called the Warsaw Pact.

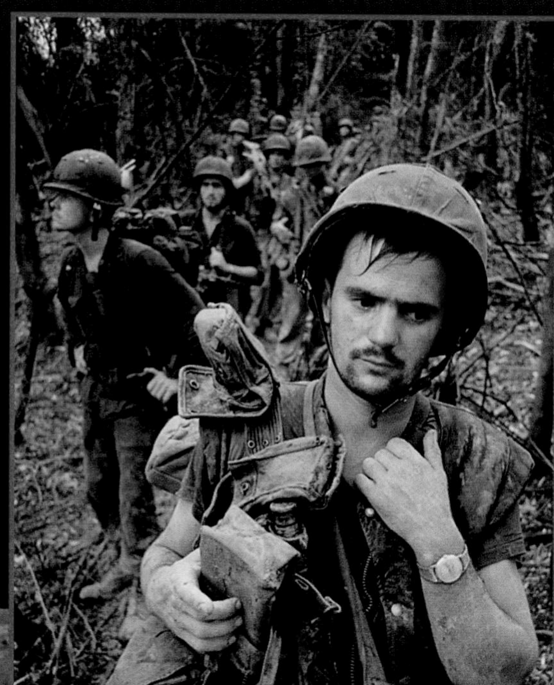

AMERICAN SOLDIERS IN VIETNAM
While the United States and Soviet Union never directly attacked each other, the United States did fight wars to support countries against the Soviet Union. Two such wars occurred in Korea in the 1950s and Vietnam in the 1960s.

A MISSILE FIELD IN THE UNITED STATES
The Soviet Union successfully tested its first atomic bomb in 1949. During the arms race that followed, U.S. missiles were built to carry nuclear weapons called warheads.

The United States and the Soviet Union were involved in a space race. The Soviets were the first to launch a **satellite**, or an object that circles another object, into space. The United States responded by sending a man to the moon in 1969.

The United States and the Soviet Union were also involved in an **arms race**, or a buildup of more powerful atomic weapons called nuclear weapons. People in each country were afraid that the other country would attack. These fears were most real during the Cuban Missile Crisis in 1962, when the Soviets placed missiles in Cuba. No attack ever took place, however. Later, the Soviets removed the weapons. In 1989 anti-Soviet protests began the break up of the Soviet Union. Two years later, the Cold War ended.

Quick Check

Cause and Effect **Why did the United States and its allies form the UN?**

Rosa Parks

THE CIVIL RIGHTS MOVEMENT
The Cold War era was also a time of great social changes in the United States. Rosa Parks (inset) sparked the civil rights movement in 1955 when she refused to move from the whites-only section of a Montgomery, Alabama bus. Leaders of the movement for equal rights included Martin Luther King, Jr., and César Chávez (above, right), who fought for rights for migrant farm workers. Other groups, such as women, Native Americans, and people with disabilities, also fought for equal rights.

On July 20, 1969, Neil Armstrong became the first human being to walk on the moon.

D THE WAR ON TERROR

American life has changed dramatically because of **terrorism**, or the use of violence or threats to reach a political goal. On September 11, 2001, terrorists crashed passenger planes into U.S. buildings. About 3,000 people died in the attacks. To help prevent further attacks, the United States and Canada have worked to increase security along their borders.

In 2001 the United States, Canada, and their allies invaded the country of Afghanistan and removed the Afghan government that was sheltering terrorists. In 2003 U.S. troops overthrew Iraq's government. Many people believed Iraq had weapons of mass destruction. In the years that followed, the United States worked with Afghanistan and Iraq to set up new governments.

QUICK CHECK

Cause and Effect **Why did the United States invade Afghanistan?**

Check Understanding

1. **VOCABULARY** Write a sentence for each of the following words.

   satellite **arms race** **terrorism**

2. **READING SKILL Cause and Effect** Use your chart from page 30 to write about how Canada and the United States have changed in recent years.

Cause	→	Effect
	→	
	→	
	→	

3. **Write About It** Describe some of the challenges the United States has faced as a world leader.

▼ Afghan children receiving school supplies from Canadian soldiers

Map and Globe Skills

Use Latitude and Longitude Maps

VOCABULARY

global grid
latitude
longitude
absolute location
relative location
parallel
meridian
prime meridian

Some maps divide the Earth into a **global grid**, or set of crisscrossing lines. Lines going from east to west are called **latitude**. Lines going from north to south are called **longitude**. Latitude and longitude are measured in units called degrees. The symbol for degrees is °. The point at which latitude and longitude lines cross is a place's **absolute location**.

Another way to determine the location of a place is by using **relative location**. Relative location tells you where a place or region is located in relation to another place. For example, the relative location of the United States is north of Mexico.

Learn It

- Lines of latitude are called **parallels**. They measure distance north and south of the Equator. The Equator is labeled 0° latitude. Lines of latitude north of the Equator are labeled **N.** Those south of the Equator are labeled **S.**
- Lines of longitude are called **meridians**. They measure distance east and west of the **prime meridian** (labeled 0° longitude). Meridians east of the prime meridian are labeled **E.** Meridians west of the prime meridian are labeled **W.**

Latitude and Longitude of the Western Hemisphere

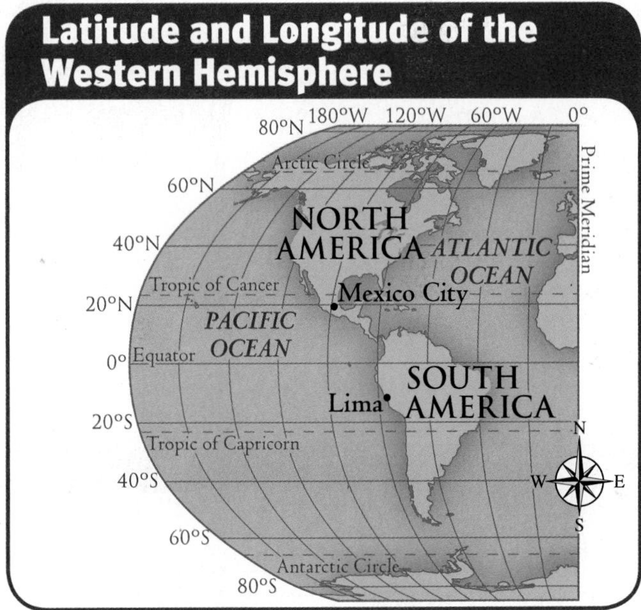

Try It

- Locate Mexico City. Which line of latitude is closest to this city?
- Locate Lima in South America. Which line of longitude is closest to this city?

Apply It

- Find the longitude and latitude lines that are closest to your community.
- Which city is closer to your community in longitude, Mexico City or Lima?

Unit 1 Review and Assess

Vocabulary

Number a paper from 1 to 4. Beside each number write the word from the list below that matches the description.

prairie **drought**
technology **province**

1. a long period without rain
2. a political division of a country
3. a flat or rolling land covered with grass
4. scientific discoveries that simplify work

Comprehension and Critical Thinking

5. Why is the Canadian Shield valuable despite its cold climate and rugged landscape?
6. Why did the colonists fight for independence from Great Britain?
7. **Reading Skill** What were the causes of the Seven Years War?
8. **Critical Thinking** Why did Loyalists flee to Canada after the American Revolution?

Skill

Use Latitude and Longitude Maps

Write a complete sentence to answer each question.

9. Toronto is about how many degrees north of Washington, D.C.?
10. What is the absolute location of Vancouver?
11. What is the location of Alaska relative to New Orleans?

Latitude and Longitude

160°W 140°W 120°W 100°W 80°W 60°W 40°W
60°N
40°N
ALASKA (U.S.)
CANADA
Hudson Bay
PACIFIC OCEAN
ATLANTIC OCEAN
UNITED STATES
Vancouver
Montreal
Toronto
New York
Chicago
Washington, D.C.
Denver
San Francisco
Los Angeles
Atlanta
Dallas
Houston
New Orleans
Miami
N S E W
0 300 600 miles
0 300 600 kilometers

Test Preparation

Study the map below. Then answer the questions.

United States and Canada: Physical

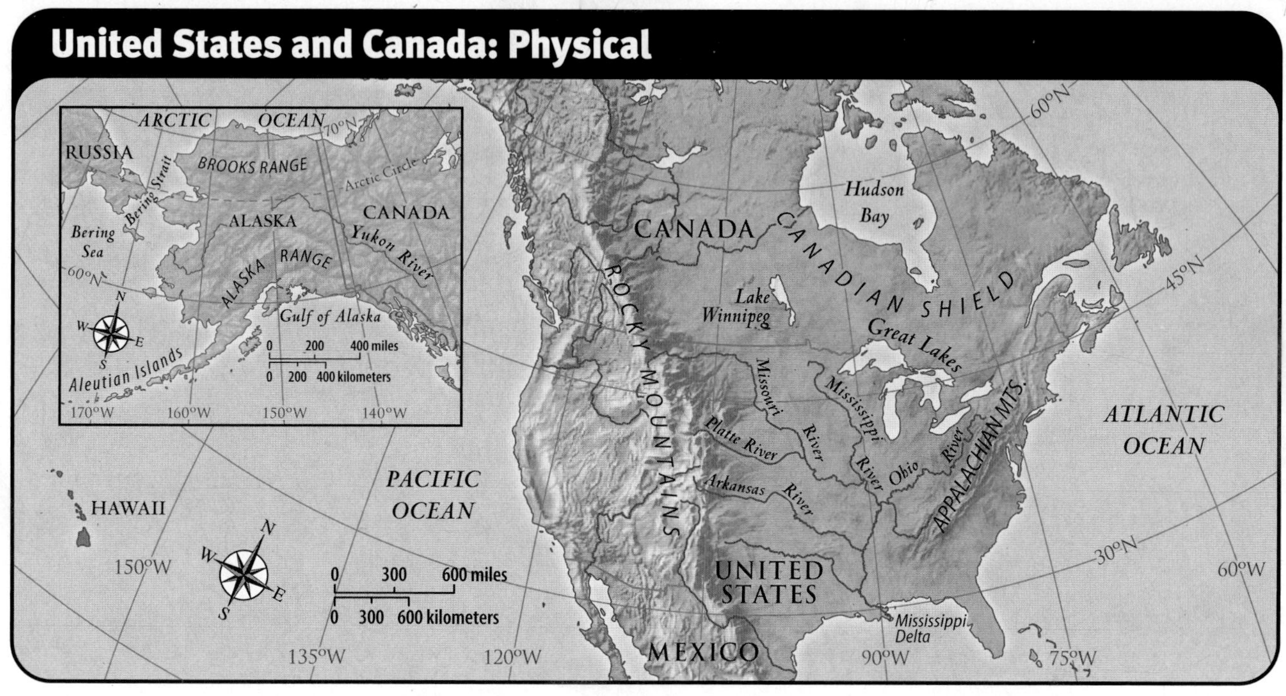

1. The information on the map is mostly about _________.
   A. elevation
   B. population
   C. landforms and latitude
   D. products and resources

2. In which direction would a person travel if he or she took a train directly from the Appalachian Mountains to Lake Winnipeg?
   A. northeast
   B. northwest
   C. southeast
   D. southwest

3. Which latitude is closest to the Mississippi delta?
   A. 30° S
   B. 30° N
   C. 90° W
   D. 90° E

4. Which stretches farther north: the Rocky Mountains or the Great Lakes?

5. What is the relative location of the Canadian Shield?

The Big Idea Activities

How do people adapt to where they live?

Write About the Big Idea

FOLDABLES™
Study Organizer

Expository Essay

Use the Unit 1 Foldable to help you write an expository essay that answers the Big Idea question, *How do people adapt to where they live?* Be sure to begin your essay with an introduction. Use the notes you wrote under the tabs in the Foldable for details to support each main idea. Be sure to include ways that people change their environment and ways that people are affected by it.

Ways people change their environment

Ways people are affected by their environment

Create a Time Line

Work with a partner to make a parallel time line. Place Canadian events on the top of your time line and U.S. events on the bottom.

1. Decide what period in history your time line will include.
2. Research events during that time at the library or on the Internet.
3. Illustrate your time line with drawings or photos of the events.

When you have finished your parallel time line, take turns explaining each event on your time line to the class.

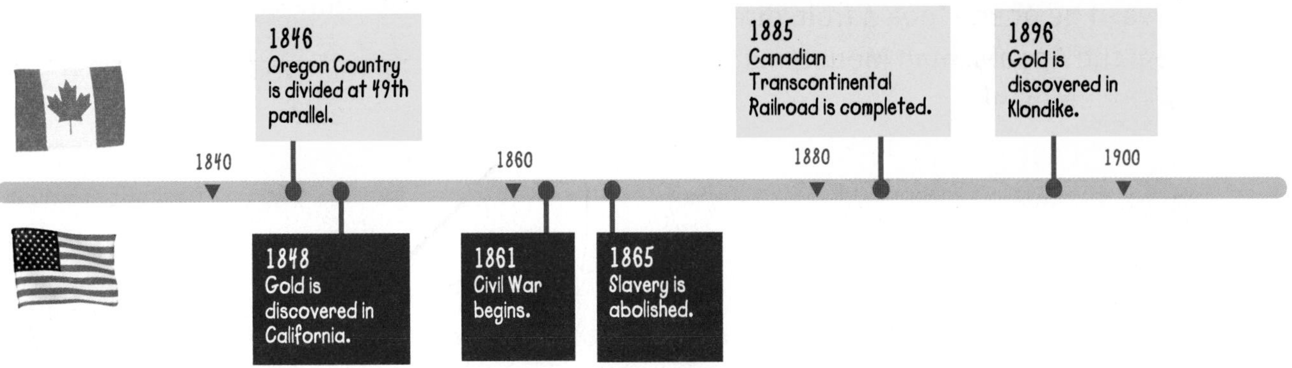
1846
Oregon Country is divided at 49th parallel.
1885
Canadian Transcontinental Railroad is completed.
1896
Gold is discovered in Klondike.
1840
1860
1880
1900
1848
Gold is discovered in California.
1861
Civil War begins.
1865
Slavery is abolished.

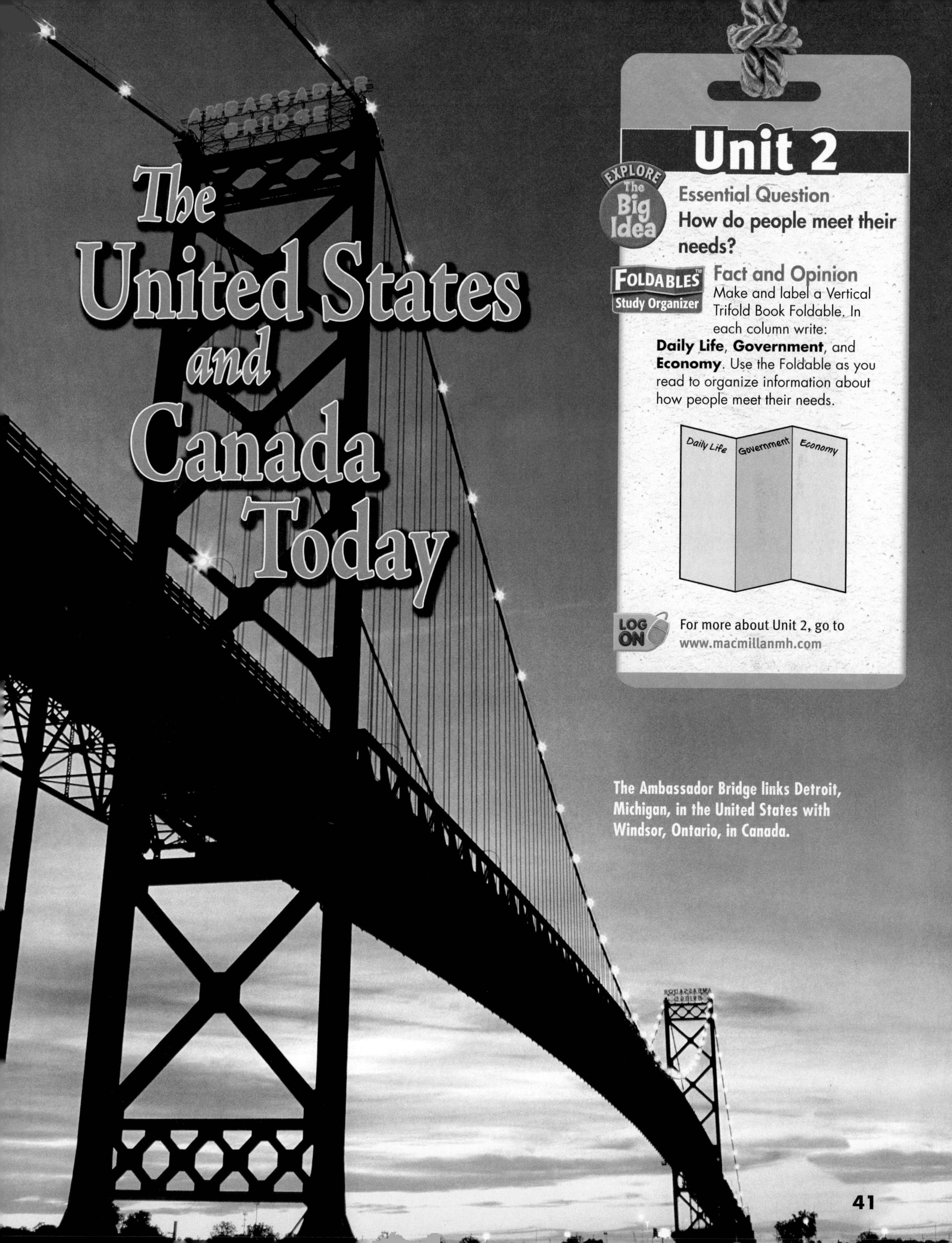

The United States and Canada Today

Unit 2

EXPLORE The Big Idea

Essential Question
How do people meet their needs?

FOLDABLES™ Study Organizer

Fact and Opinion
Make and label a Vertical Trifold Book Foldable. In each column write: **Daily Life**, **Government**, and **Economy**. Use the Foldable as you read to organize information about how people meet their needs.

Daily Life | Government | Economy

LOG ON For more about Unit 2, go to www.macmillanmh.com

The Ambassador Bridge links Detroit, Michigan, in the United States with Windsor, Ontario, in Canada.

PEOPLE, PLACES, AND EVENTS

Marjory Stoneman Douglas

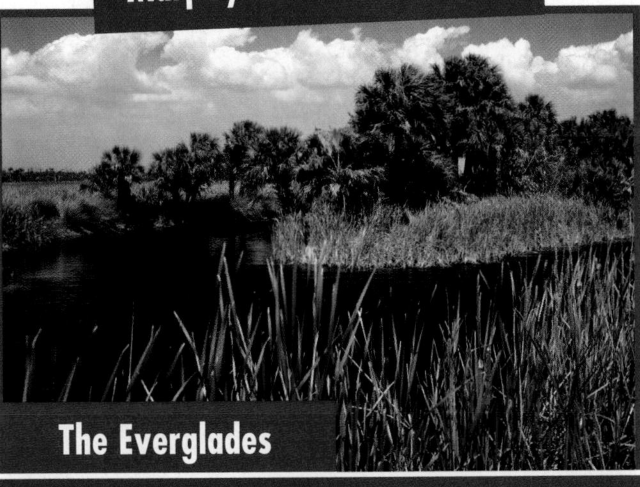

The Everglades

1947 Douglas writes a book to help save the Everglades.

Rachel Carson

Springdale, Pennsylvania

1962 Carson's book, *Silent Spring*, is published.

1905 1925 1945

Douglas fought to save **the Everglades** from being drained. Her book *The Everglades: River of Grass*, brought attention to her fight.

Today you can tour the Everglades on Florida's southern tip and see alligators in nature.

Rachel Carson wrote to warn of the dangers of using certain chemicals to kill pests.

Today you can find organic gardens and nature trails at Carson's birthplace in **Springdale, Pennsylvania**.

For more about People, Places, and Events, visit www.macmillanmh.com

Bill Gates

Hurricane Katrina Volunteers

Microsoft Redmond Campus

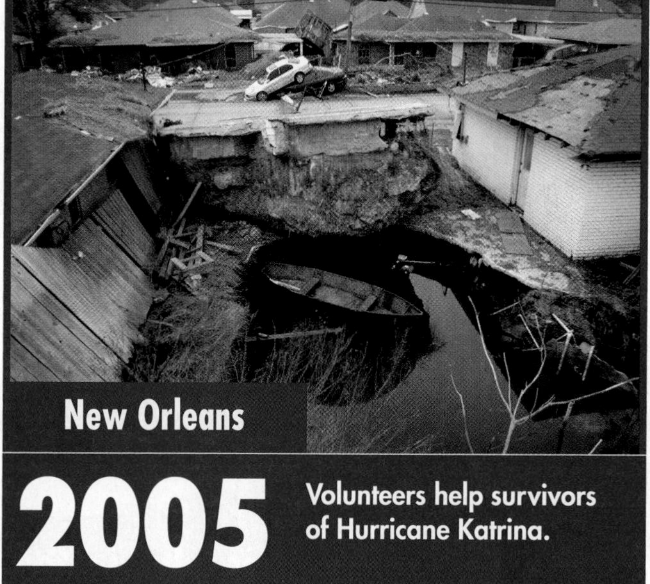
New Orleans

1975 Bill Gates founds Microsoft.

2005 Volunteers help survivors of Hurricane Katrina.

1965 1985 2005

Bill Gates was still in college when he and a friend developed the first computer language program for a personal computer.

Today you can tour **Microsoft's Redmond Campus** near Seattle, Washington.

Volunteers helped residents as soon as the storm made landfall, and they continued to provide assistance long after the storm.

Today New Orleans is still a favorite city among many tourists.

Cultures and Lifestyles

Lesson 1

VOCABULARY

immigrant p. 46
bilingual p. 47
urbanization p. 47

READING SKILL

Fact and Opinion

Copy the chart below. As you read, fill in the chart with facts and opinions about American and Canadian cultures.

Fact	Opinion

STANDARDS FOCUS

SOCIAL STUDIES Culture

GEOGRAPHY Places and Regions

Independence Day is an American national holiday that celebrates the signing of the Declaration of Independence on July 4, 1776.

Visual Preview

How does culture affect how people live and meet their needs?

A People from all over the world bring their culture with them to new lands.

B Immigration has shaped life in the United States and Canada.

C Distinct arts and entertainment have developed over time.

Ⓐ DIVERSE HERITAGE

Both the United States and Canada feature a rich mix of cultural traditions. Many of the foods, words, ideas, and traditions in the United States and Canada began in other countries. Yet, many of these traditions have been combined to make up unique parts of American and Canadian life.

The United States is known as a "melting pot." This means that over the years many cultures have come to the United States and blended together. The United States population is over 300 million, making it one of the largest countries in the world. As the chart shows, the population of the United States today contains a mix of ancestries from around the world.

United States Population, 2006

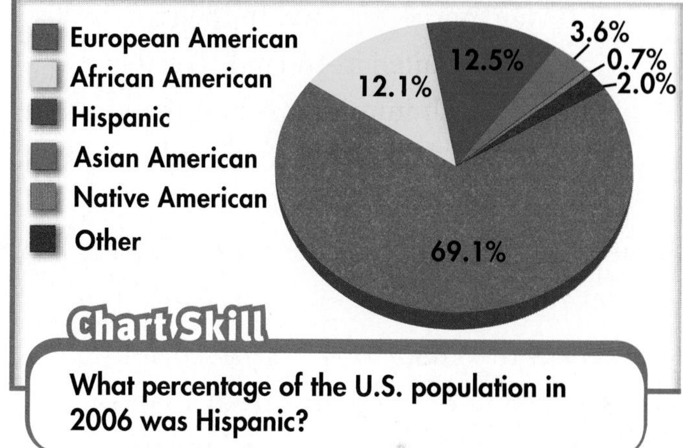

Chart Skill

What percentage of the U.S. population in 2006 was Hispanic?

The People of Canada

Canada has about 33 million people. About one-fourth have French ancestry and live mainly in Quebec. Another fourth have British ancestry.

Like the United States, Canada is a nation formed by immigrants with many different cultures. In addition to European ancestry, Canada is home to people of Asian, African, and Latin American backgrounds. First Nations also make up more than one million people in Canada. Most First Nations live on reserves, or land set aside for indigenous people.

QUICK CHECK

Fact and Opinion **Why are America and Canada so culturally diverse?**

Chinese characters cover storefronts in Sunset Park, Brooklyn. ▶

B GROWING POPULATIONS

The United States has been called a nation of **immigrants**. Immigrants are people who leave one country to live in another. Most immigrants came the United States and Canada for a better life.

A Changing People

In the late 1700s and early 1800s, most immigrants to North America came from Great Britain and Germany. In the mid-1800s, the potato crop failed in Ireland, causing a large flow of Irish immigrants into the United States and Canada. During the next forty years, 12 million immigrants came to the United States, mostly from Southern, Central, and Eastern Europe.

In 1924 the U.S. Congress passed a law keeping out immigrants from almost everywhere except northern and western Europe. A new law, passed in 1961, based entry into the United States on immigrants' work skills and links to relatives. In the 1960s and 1970s, Canada also loosened its immigration policies, basing entry into Canada on factors such as skills and family links.

Diverse Religions and Languages

The majority of Americans and Canadians are Christians, but religious life is diverse. Judaism and Islam each have about 5 million followers in America. Canada is about 1 percent Jewish and 2 percent Muslim. About 2 to 3 million Americans practice Buddhism, and another million are followers of Hinduism.

In the United States, Spanish is the most widely spoken language after English. More than one million people speak Chinese, French, Vietnamese, Tagalog, German, or Italian. In fact, one person out of six in the United States does not speak English as his or her first language.

▲ In the late 1900s, half of U.S. immigrants came from the Americas, one-third came from Asia, and less than 15 percent came from Europe.

▲ In the 1840s the potato famine in Ireland caused over one million people to come to the United States and Canada.

Map Skill

PLACE In which province is French spoken?

▲ People in British Columbia and Vancouver often eat fish and Asian food.

As you read in Unit 1, the French settled Canada in the 1600s, and the British won control of Canada in 1763. Today, Canada is a **bilingual** country. Bilingual means "two languages." Canada has two official languages—English and French.

Life in the United States

Before the Industrial Revolution, the United States was entirely made up of rural, or country, areas. During the Industrial Revolution, cities became ideal places to locate factories and workers. This led people to move to urban areas, or cities. This move from rural areas to cities is called **urbanization**.

Americans live in different types of houses, from one-story ranch houses to high-rise apartments. About two-thirds of American families own their homes. Many Americans enjoy watching movies, television, and sports. They exercise and play sports such as golf, tennis, and baseball.

Life in Canada

Canada has welcomed many immigrant families to its shores over the years. These families have kept many of the customs of their homelands. These customs appear in the form of foods from around the world that are found in different parts of Canada. You may find Italian and Eastern European food in Toronto and French cuisine in Quebec.

Canadians are also big sports fans. Hockey is the national sport in Canada. Lacrosse is also popular. Many Canadians enjoy outdoor activities, such as skiing, hunting, and fishing.

Quick Check

Fact and Opinion **What foreign influences are apparent in American and Canadian lives?**

THE ARTS

The earliest American and Canadian artists used materials from their environments to create works of art. For centuries Native Americans have carved wooden masks and made beautiful designs on pottery from clay found in their areas. The first Canadian artists were First Peoples who carved figures from bone, stone, and wood. They also made pottery and wove baskets.

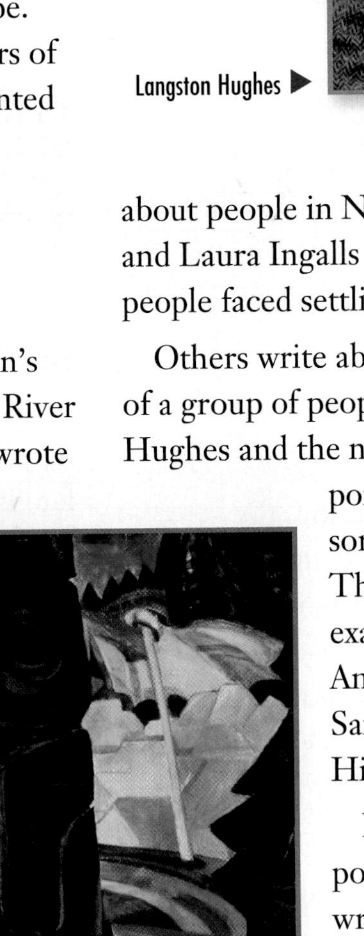

Langston Hughes ▶

Today, American artists have their own, uniquely American styles, while Canadian art reflects both European and Native influences. Painters are often inspired by the landscape. Winslow Homer painted the stormy waters of the North Atlantic. Georgia O'Keeffe painted the colorful deserts of the Southwest

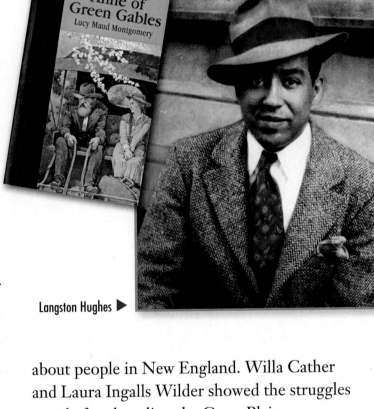

Literature

In their works many writers discuss the human condition, or experience, of the country. In the United States, Mark Twain's books tell about life along the Mississippi River in the mid-1800s. Nathaniel Hawthorne wrote about people in New England. Willa Cather and Laura Ingalls Wilder showed the struggles people faced settling the Great Plains.

Others write about the unique experience of a group of people. The poetry of Langston Hughes and the novels of Toni Morrison portray the triumphs and sorrows of African Americans. The novels of Amy Tan examine the lives of Chinese Americans. Oscar Hijuelos and Sandra Cisneros write about Hispanic Americans.

Nature and history have been popular subjects for Canadian writers. *Anne of Green Gables* by Lucy Maud Montgomery, the story of an orphan on Prince Edward Island, has been popular for one hundred years.

▲ *Skidegate, Graham Island, British Columbia,* 1928, by Emily Carr

▲ *Lion King* director Julie Taymor

Montreal-based Cirque du Soleil is a circus with no animals, no understandable language, and no average clowns.

Music, Theater, and Film

Americans have created unique musical styles. Country music grew out of folk music from the rural South in the 1920s. In the early 1900s, African Americans like Louis Armstrong, Ella Fitzgerald, and Dizzy Gillespie developed blues and jazz. Blues later inspired rock and roll in the 1950s. Recently, hip-hop and rap have gained popularity.

Plays and musicals are popular in both the United States and Canada. Ontario's Stratford Film Festival is known for its productions of William Shakespeare's plays. New Yorkers and visitors enjoy theater on Broadway. Musicals like *Beauty and the Beast* and *The Lion King* are especially popular with young people.

Starting in the early 1900s, movies attracted large audiences in America. Movies are also a big part of Canadian culture. Many American films are made in Toronto and Vancouver.

Quick Check

Fact and Opinion **Why do people enjoy American art?**

Check Understanding

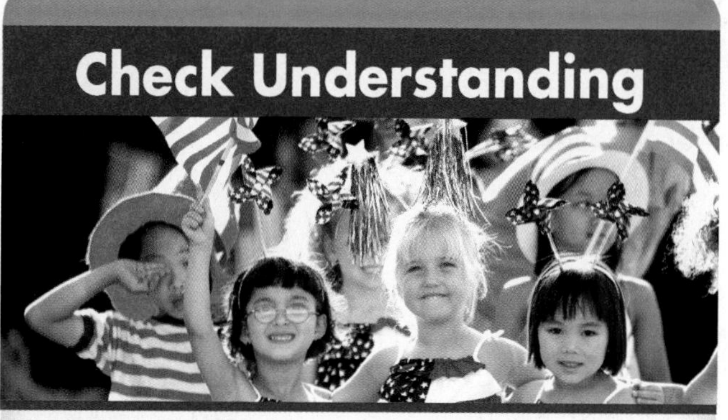

1. **VOCABULARY** Use the words below to write a paragraph about the mix of cultures in Canada.

   immigrant **bilingual**

2. **READING SKILL Fact and Opinion** Use your chart from page 44 to write facts and opinions about American art and literature.

Fact	Opinion

3. **Write About It** How might life in Canada be different if the British had never come to Canada?

Lesson 2

VOCABULARY

free enterprise p. 51

supply p. 51

demand p. 51

interdependence p. 56

gross domestic product p. 57

READING SKILL

Fact and Opinion

Copy the chart below. As you read, use the chart to write facts about the American and Canadian economies.

Fact	Opinion

Standards Focus

SOCIAL STUDIES Production, Distribution, & Consumption

GEOGRAPHY Human Systems

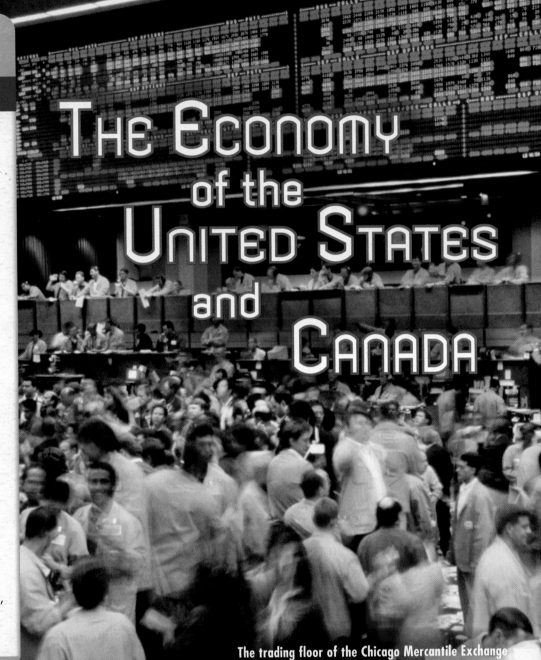

The Economy of the United States and Canada

The trading floor of the Chicago Mercantile Exchange

Visual Preview

How do people meet their economic needs?

A In the free enterprise system, people make money in different ways.

B Different regions of the United States specialize in different industries.

C Canadians use their vast resources to create jobs and make money.

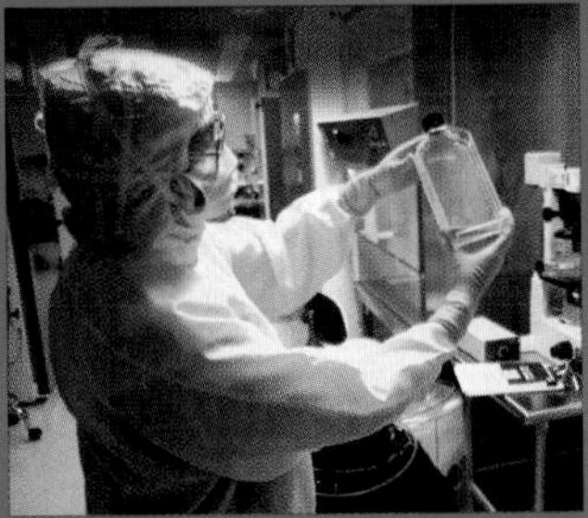

D The United States and Canada participate in global trade.

Ⓐ FREE ENTERPRISE

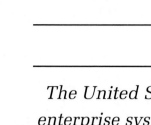

The United States and Canada have ***free enterprise*** *systems. In a free enterprise system, people can start any business they want. They decide what to produce, how to produce, and for whom to produce.*

Under free enterprise, also called capitalism, companies compete with each other to gain customers. As part of this competition, they may offer unique or better products, or they may lower prices.

Supply and Demand

Supply and **demand** determine the price of a product or service. Supply is the amount that producers are willing to sell at all prices. Demand is the amount people are wiling to buy at all prices.

All markets have a buying side and a selling side. Price determines how much of a good or service people will buy. Voluntary exchange occurs when buyers and sellers trade with anyone they chose.

Saving and Investing

People save and invest money in different ways. Many people have bank savings accounts or certificates of deposit (CDs). Over time, both accounts gain interest, or payment received when lending money. CDs have a set period of time before money can be withdrawn, but CDs also have higher interest rates.

People can also buy stock, or part ownership in a company. The value of the stock usually goes up when a company makes money. Stock can drop in value or become worthless if the company fails.

The amount of money left over after all the costs of production have been paid is called profit. Profit is how investors rate companies. The profit motive makes individuals and companies invest. It also drives the growth of capitalism. "Capitalism is this wonderful thing that motivates people, it causes wonderful inventions to be done," said Bill Gates, the founder of Microsoft.

Quick Check

Fact and Opinion **What is the best way to save?**

Shopping is part of the free enterprise system. ▶

B U.S. ECONOMIC REGIONS

Geographers group the United States into five economic regions—the Northeast, the Midwest, the South, the Interior West, and the Pacific. These regions have diverse resources and economic activities.

In recent years, the regions began to concentrate on technology industries, such as telecommunications. People can learn the job skills they need at trade schools and colleges throughout the country.

PLACES

The Chicago Mercantile Exchange (CME) began in 1898. Traders call out prices and quantities and use hand signals to talk to each other.

The Chicago Mercantile Exchange (CME)

The Northeast

The Northeast focuses on business, since it has poor soil and lacks mineral resources. New York has many media, or communications, companies. In its financial center, most of the stocks in the United States are traded on the New York Stock Exchange (NYSE), the American Stock Exchange, or an electronic stock market like the NASDAQ. Boston is an important center of biotechnology research, which is the study of cells to improve health.

The Midwest

People in the Midwest enjoy plenty of fertile, or rich, soil. Midwestern farmers grow corn, wheat, soybeans, and other crops. Farmers today use many new technologies, but many small farmers cannot afford to purchase the new machines. As a result, fewer people work in agriculture, usually on larger farms.

The Midwest also has mineral resources, such as iron ore, coal, and lead. The resources support manufacturing, including steel manufacturing in Cleveland the automobile industry in Detroit. Advances in technologies have led to a decline of older industries. Many people in the Midwest now work in telecommunications and similar industries.

The Interior West and Pacific

The mountains and plateaus of the Interior West support mining, ranching, and lumbering. The natural beauty and historical sites have lead to a thriving tourism industry. Information technology is important in the cities of Denver and Salt Lake City.

The western coastal states, Alaska, and Hawaii form the Pacific region. Los Angeles, California, is the world center of the movie industry.

◀ A new model electric hybrid car

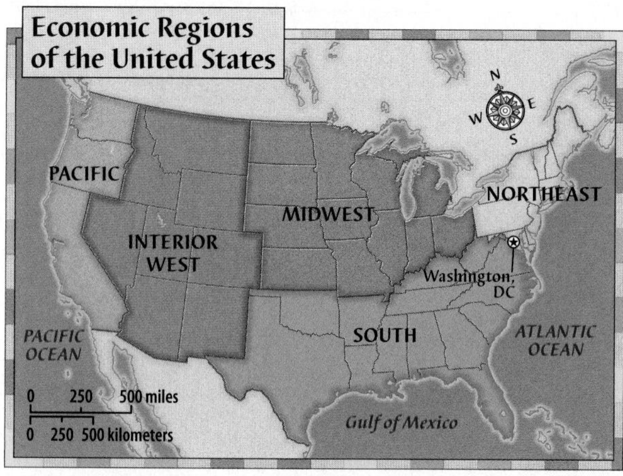

Major computer software companies have developed in California and Washington. This region also has valuable minerals, such as oil in Alaska and gold in California.

Agriculture is important to the region. Farmers raise fruits and vegetables in the fertile valleys of California, Oregon, and Washington. Sugarcane, pineapples, and coffee are grown in the rich soil of Hawaii.

The South

In the 1900s the manufacture of textiles, or cloth, became profitable in southern states due to favorable weather. Texas, Louisiana, and Alabama have long been producers of oil. Many people worked on small family farms.

In recent decades, the South has changed. The Southern economy is booming in areas such as information technology, software development, and biotechnology. As a result, cities and industries are growing in the region. For example, workers in cities such as Houston and Atlanta make textiles, electrical equipment, computers, and airplane parts.

Quick Check

Fact and Opinion **In your opinion, which region is the best for tourism? Why?**

DataGraphic

The United States Economy

The graph shows how different regions contribute to the U.S. economy. The map shows locations of select industries. Study the graph and map. Then answer the questions below.

U.S. Economy by Region, 2006

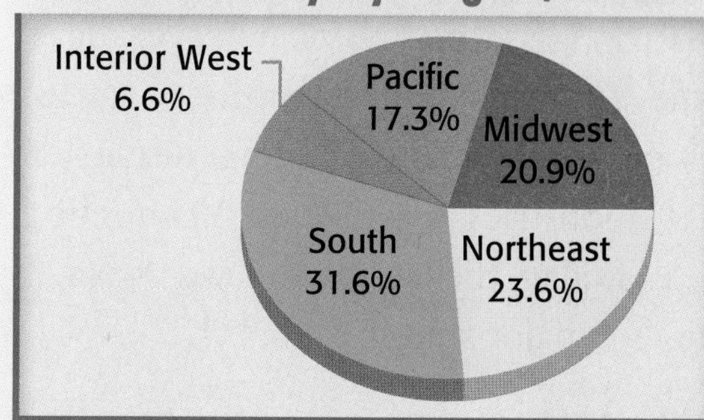

Source: U.S. Bureau of Economic Analysis

*SOURCE: CIA Factbook, 2006 *Percentages are rounded*

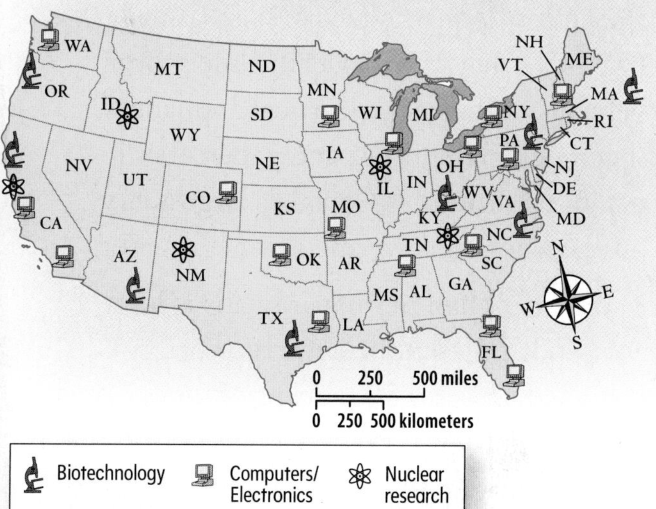

Think About the U.S. Economy

1. Which states have biotechnology?
2. How does the Interior West compare to the other regions of the country?

CANADA'S ECONOMIC REGIONS

In Canada's regions, people start and run businesses with limited government involvement. Like in most countries, the Canadian government also provides some services. This is called a mixed economy.

A hydroelectric plant in Quebec ▲

The Atlantic Provinces

Fishing was a major industry in the Atlantic provinces of Newfoundland and Labrador, Nova Scotia, Prince Edward Island, and New Brunswick. Offshore waters, however, have become overfished. The Atlantic provinces now focus on the manufacturing, mining, and tourism industries, which led to economic growth. Today, the city of Halifax, Nova Scotia, is a major shipping port.

The Central and Eastern Region

Ontario has the most people and the greatest wealth of Canada's provinces. It is the largest industrialized area in Canada. Ontario's major products include motor vehicles, iron, steel, electrical appliances, machinery, chemicals, and paper. Its capital, Toronto, is Canada's largest city and a major banking and business center.

Ontario's half of Niagara Falls is ideal for producing hydroelectric power. This accounts for 30 percent of the province's energy needs. Because of its manufacturing industries, in recent years the province has been forced to purchase power from other areas, such as Michigan and Quebec.

East of Ontario is the province of Quebec. In southern Quebec, the St. Lawrence River Valley is a fertile agricultural region, producing fruits, vegetables, and livestock. Northern Quebec is extremely rich in forest, lake, and river resources. Paper, lumber, and hydroelectric power are some of the province's most important industries.

Montreal, Quebec's largest city, has a knowledge economy. A knowledge economy makes a profit on the production and management of information. Industries in biotechnology, information and communication technologies, as well as aerospace are all important to Montreal.

◀ Canada's National Tower in Toronto is the tallest structure in the world.

The West

The west economic region of Canada includes the Prairie Provinces of central Canada and British Columbia on the Pacific Coast. In the Prairie Provinces of Manitoba, Saskatchewan, and Alberta, farming and ranching make up the main economy. This area produces large amounts of wheat and contains large reserves of oil and natural gas.

The province of British Columbia on the Pacific Coast has extensive forests. They help make Canada the world's largest producer of newsprint, the paper used for printing newspapers. Timber, mining, fishing, and tourism support British Columbia's economy. The capital of British Columbia, Vancouver, is Canada's main port city on the Pacific Coast.

The North

Canada's vast north covers about one-third of the country. This area includes the territories of Yukon, the North West Territories, and Nunavut. Many of the 25,000 people in this region are indigenous peoples. The main resources in the North are minerals, such as gold and diamonds. Diamond mines make the Northwest Territories one of the wealthiest regions in the world.

In the Yukon territory, manufacturing includes furniture, clothing, and handicrafts. Hydroelectricity is also produced. The traditional industries of trapping and fishing have declined in recent years. Today, the government is by far the biggest employer in the territory. It directly employs about 5,000 of the 12,500-person workforce.

Quick Check

Fact and Opinion **From which sources does Ontario get its power?**

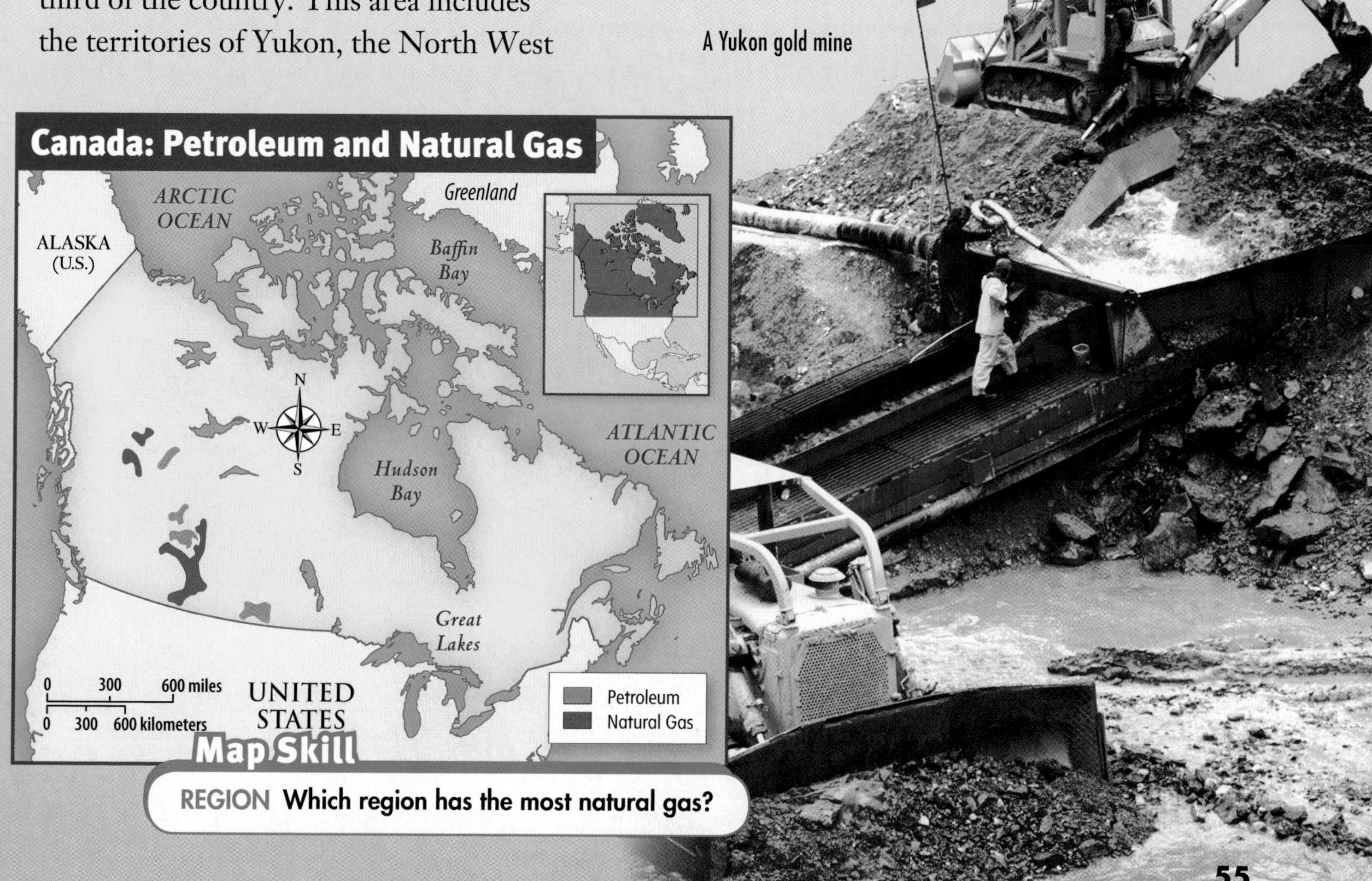

A Yukon gold mine

Map Skill

REGION **Which region has the most natural gas?**

D THE GLOBAL ECONOMY

You have learned that the regions in the United States and Canada specialize in certain products they can produce best. Countries also specialize in products. Trade allows them to export these goods and raw materials, and to import the goods and materials they need. This trade shows the global **interdependence**, or dependence on each other to meet needs and wants. Global trade fuels economic growth for both the United States and Canada.

Trade Agreements

Trade agreements help countries do business together. In 1994 the United States, Canada, and Mexico signed the North American Free Trade Agreement (NAFTA). The agreement promised to remove tariffs, or taxes, on goods brought into each country.

Since then, the value of goods shipped to each other has increased. Today the United States and Canada are each others' largest trading partners, and Mexico is the second-largest trading partner for the United States.

In a 2005 speech about free trade, former Canadian Prime Minister Paul Martin said:

"When we work together as countries to make North America safer and more competitive, . . . all of our citizens benefit."

Another agreement is the Central American Free Trade Agreement (CAFTA). CAFTA opens up trade among the United States, Nicaragua, Honduras, El Salvador, Guatemala, Costa Rica, and the Dominican Republic.

The Port of Vancouver ▼

GDP

One way to measure the economy of a country is the **gross domestic product**, or GDP. A country's GDP is the total value of all goods and services produced in a single year. Typically, countries with higher GDPs have stronger economies. At over $13 trillion, the United States has the largest GDP in the world. Canada's GDP is over $1.1 trillion.

Economic Differences

While the United States and Canada share economic connections, the two countries have many economic differences. Both countries rely on trade for economic growth, but the United States also depends on trade for energy resources. This is because Americans use three times the amount of oil our country produces. The United States must therefore import additional oil from countries such as Canada, Mexico, Venezuela, Saudi Arabia, and Nigeria.

The United States and Canada also differ in their balances of trade. Balance of trade is the difference between the value of a nation's exports and its imports. The United States spends far more on imports than it earns from exports. As a result, it has a trade deficit of hundreds of billions of dollars. A trade deficit means that the value of a country's imports is higher than its exports.

Canada, on the other hand, has seen its export earnings increase every year at a higher rate than those of the United States. It also enjoys a trade surplus. A surplus happens when a country exports more than it imports.

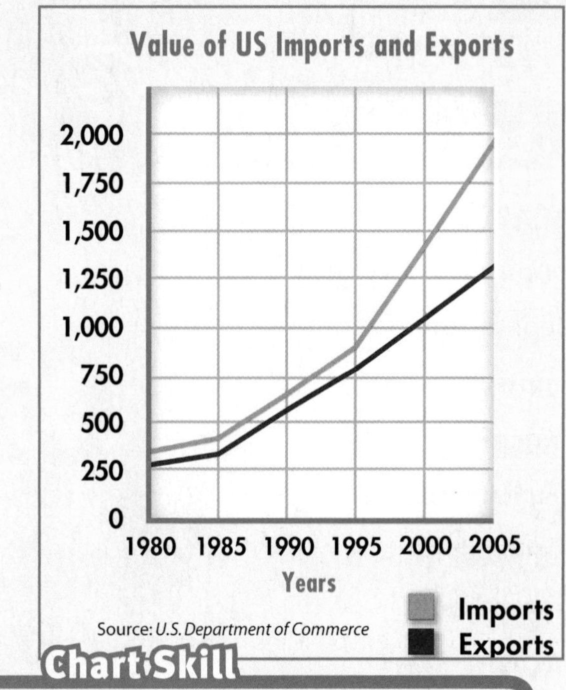

Chart Skill

In which year is the trade deficit the largest?

QUICK CHECK

Fact and Opinion How do countries around the world benefit from global interdependence?

Check Understanding

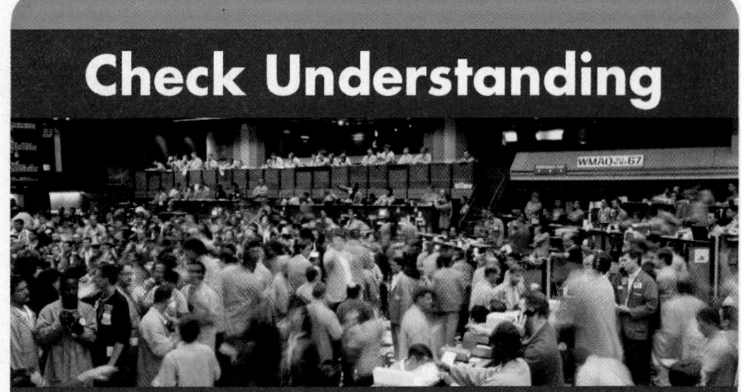

1. **VOCABULARY** Use the following words to write about global trade.

   interdependence **gross domestic product**

2. **READING SKILLS Fact and Opinion** Use your chart from page 50 to write about different economic regions in the United States and Canada.

Fact	Opinion

3. **Write About It** Write a paragraph describing how your life might be different in different economic regions of the United States.

Lesson 3

VOCABULARY

popular sovereignty p. 60
separation of powers p. 60
federalism p. 61
parliament p. 62
citizenship p. 64
amendment p. 64

READING SKILL

Fact and Opinion
Use the chart to write facts about the U.S. and Canadian governments.

Facts	Opinions

STANDARDS FOCUS

SOCIAL STUDIES Civic Ideals & Practices
GEOGRAPHY Human Systems

Government and Citizenship

The Peace Tower of the parliament building in Ottawa, Canada

Visual Preview

How do governments meet the needs of their people?

A Leaders of the United States created a framework for government in 1787.

B The U.S. government serves people on state and national levels.

C Canada has a parliament and prime minister to help meet its people's needs.

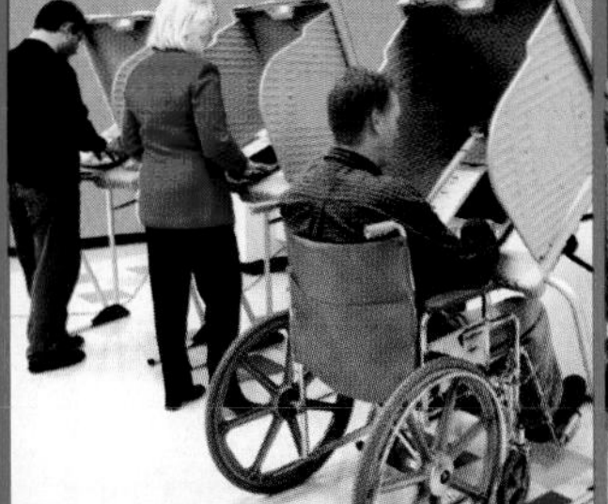

D People in the United States and Canada have both rights and duties.

Ⓐ THE U.S. CONSTITUTION

The governments of the United States and Canada have similar principles. However, the paths to creating those governments and the practices of those governments have many differences.

After declaring independence in 1776, the United States needed to create a plan of government. Many states had created their own constitution, or written plan of government. Each state could govern itself, but Americans realized that they needed a strong federal government to organize the Revolutionary War.

The Articles of Confederation

The first plan of government for the United States was called the Articles of Confederation. Under the Articles, each state was independent. Each state printed its own money and made its own laws.

There were many problems with the Articles. Congress could not pass laws without approval of nine of the states. Congress could not change the Articles without approval from all of the states. These restrictions made it difficult for Congress to do anything.

The Constitutional Convention

On May 25, 1787, a total of 55 delegates, or representatives from each state, were sent to a meeting in Philadelphia called the Constitutional Convention. The purpose of this convention was to fix the problems of the government. The delegates decided to abandon the Articles of Confederation altogether, and to create a new plan of government instead.

Creating this new plan of government was not easy. After nearly four months of debates, disagreements, and compromises, the delegates signed the United States Constitution on September 17, 1787.

QUICK CHECK

Fact and Opinion **Why did the Articles of Confederation not work?**

Copy of the original U.S. Constitution ▼

Weaknesses of the Articles of Confederation

Money	Central Power	Lawmaking
Congress had no power to: • collect taxes • control trade • enforce laws	• No central leader • No national court system	• Needed 9 states to approve laws • Needed all states to approve changes to Articles

CHECKS AND BALANCES IN THE UNITED STATES GOVERNMENT		
LEGISLATIVE BRANCH	EXECUTIVE BRANCH	JUDICIAL BRANCH
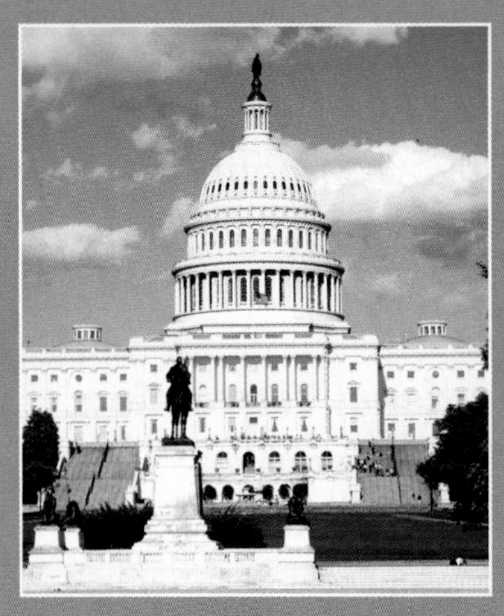		
• Congress • Passes laws • Approves taxes and spending • Can override vetoes	• President • Enforces laws • Commander-in-Chief of military • Signs or vetoes laws	• Supreme Court and federal courts • Appointed • Decides constitutional questions about laws

B PRINCIPLES OF THE CONSTITUTION

The Constitution is the plan that sets up how the United States government works. The United States is a representative democracy. This means voters choose leaders to govern on behalf of the people. The Constitution also specifies what the government may and may not do. This principle is called limited government.

Popular Sovereignty

The United States government operates under the idea of **popular sovereignty**. This is the idea that the power of the government belongs to all of the people in a nation. Because power belongs to all people, the idea of popular sovereignty emphasizes the belief that everyone is politically equal.

Dividing Power

The writers of the Constitution divided the government's power among three branches: legislative, executive, and judicial. The legislative branch makes laws. The executive branch enforces laws. The judicial branch interprets laws and decides if the laws follow the Constitution. This division of power in the government is known as **separation of powers**.

Each branch of the government has its own unique powers and can check, or limit, the powers of the other branches of government. This system is called checks and balances. It is a way to keep any one branch from becoming too powerful. The chart above describes these checks and balances in more detail.

Federalism

The principle of checks and balances also operates between the national government and the governments of the states. Our first leaders wanted to create a strong central government. They wanted state governments to have certain powers and responsibilities too.

The system they developed is called **federalism**. In federalism power is divided between the federal, or national, government and the state governments. Some powers are given to states, such as the power to establish schools. Other powers are given to the federal government, such as the power to declare war. Some powers are shared by both levels of government, such as collecting taxes and enforcing laws. The chart below shows some of the powers of each level of government.

Quick Check

Fact and Opinion **Why did our first leaders develop federalism?**

- makes treaties with other countries
- makes laws and regulations about trade between states
- declares war
- runs the post office
- mints money
- collects taxes

U.S. President George W. Bush

State Governments

- sets up local governments
- makes laws about education
- makes laws about health
- sets up public schools
- runs local elections
- collects taxes

Indiana Governor Mitch Daniels

C CANADA'S GOVERNMENT

Canada is a democracy like the United States. Yet, in some ways it is very different from the United States.

Structure of Government

Canada has a prime minister, who is the head of a democratic government, and a **parliament**. A parliament is an assembly of people who pass the laws governing a nation. Voters elect representatives to parliament. These representatives then choose a prime minister to head the government.

The British monarch, the king or queen, serves as Canada's head of state. The head of state has ceremonial duties but no real power. The British monarch visits Canada only once in a while. When the British monarch is not in Canada, a Canadian official called the governor general serves as head of state.

Canada's Constitution

Canada's form of government is based on its Constitution. Unlike the U.S. Constitution, Canada's is not just one document. The Constitution Act of 1867 is part of it. So is the Constitution Act of 1982. Long-standing customs and principles make up the third, unwritten, part of the Constitution.

Though the Constitution made Canada independent, many provinces in Canada remain divided. People in Quebec feel that their language and culture are different from the rest of Canada. Many there want to separate from Canada. Some people in Canada's western provinces have also considered separating. Plans for separation have all failed, but Canada's future as a united country is still uncertain.

Queen Elizabeth signs Canada's constitutional proclamation in Ottawa, Canada, on April 17, 1982. Prime Minister Pierre Trudeau, seated across from her, looks on.

Similarities and Differences

Like the United States, Canada has a federal system. The federal government is in charge of national matters that affect all of Canada. This includes making national laws, providing national defense, and setting foreign policies. Provincial and territorial governments are in charge of local matters. These governments take care of issues such as education, health care, and highways.

Unlike the United States, Canada does not have a complete separation of powers because the parliament chooses the prime minister. The prime minister depends on the support of parliament. If that support stops, a new national election must be called.

Quick Check

Fact and Opinion **Do you think voters should directly elect the head of their government?**

How the U.S. Government Works

- It is a representative democracy.
- The President is elected by voters through the Electoral College.
- The President is the head of government and head of state.
- The plan of the government is set out in the Constitution, a single document written in 1787.
- The three branches of government check each other's powers.
- It has a federal system with power divided between the central government and the states.
- It has a Bill of Rights to protect the basic liberties of United States citizens.
- Congress has two elected houses, the Senate and the House of Representatives.

How Canada's Government Works

- It is a parliamentary democracy.
- Members of parliament choose the prime minister.
- The prime minister is the head of government, and the British monarch is the head of state.
- The plan of government is set out in the Constitution, several written Acts, and unwritten customs.
- The prime minister depends on the support of parliament.
- It has a federal system with power divided between the central government and the provinces and territories.
- It has a Charter of Rights and Freedoms to protect the basic liberties of Canadian citizens.
- Parliament has two houses, the Senate and the House of Commons.

D RIGHTS AND RESPONSIBILITIES

Being a member of a country with all the rights, duties, and privileges that come with it is called **citizenship**. In the United States and Canada, people have the right to protection by the government and equal treatment under the law. Duties, or things citizens must do, include obeying the law, paying taxes, and attending school. Responsibilities, or things citizens should do, include being informed and voting, respecting the property and rights of others, and helping out in the community.

▼ Immigrant members of the U.S. Navy become United States citizens

The Bill of Rights

Protecting individual freedoms is an important value of the United States. In 1791 ten **amendments**, or additions, called the Bill of Rights, were added to the U.S. Constitution.

Citizenship

Rights and Responsibilites

As an American citizen, you have the responsibility to protect not only your own rights, but also the rights of others. Suppose you were asked to attend a meeting to suggest rules for the playground. You have a right to speak and give your suggestions. You also have a responsibility to be careful about what you say and to respect the ideas of others.

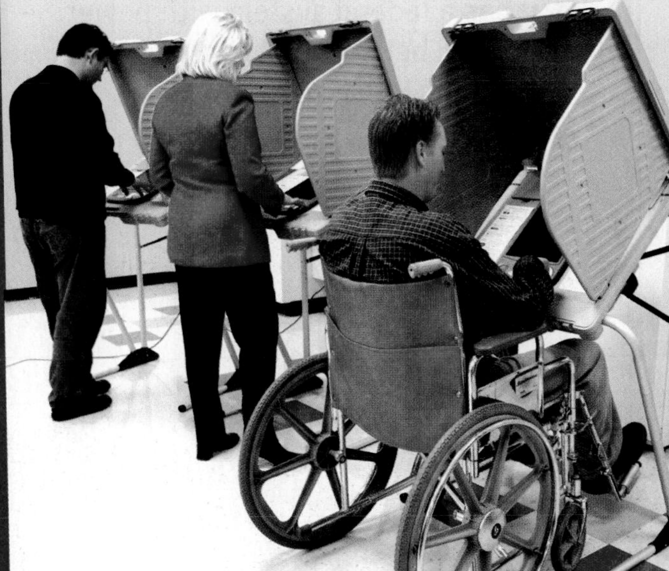

Write About It Explain the responsibilities citizens have when voting, and what might happen if people were not allowed to vote.

Their purpose was to prevent the government from taking away people's freedoms. The first amendment is the most famous and most important. It guarantees the freedoms of speech, the press, and religion.

Over the years other amendments have been added. The 14th Amendment, added after the Civil War, guarantees all citizens the same legal rights. The 15th Amendment granted African American males the right to vote. Women gained the right to vote in 1920 with the 19th Amendment.

Rights of Canadians

Canada's Charter of Rights and Freedoms lists its people's rights. These include the freedom of expression, conscience, religion, thought, and belief. It also includes equal rights without regard to "race, national or ethnic origin, color, religion, sex, age or mental or physical disability."

Unlike the government of the United States, Canada's government pays for the healthcare of its citizens. Together, local and national governments pay for about 70 percent of Canadian's health costs, including almost 100 percent of hospital and doctor care.

Quick Check

Fact and Opinion **Why is it important to be an informed voter?**

Check Understanding

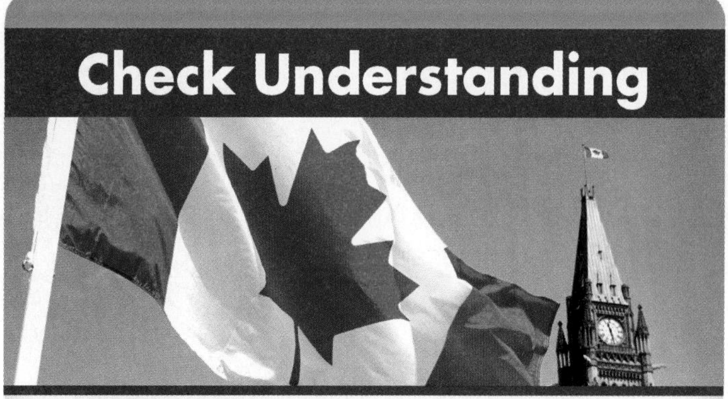

1. **VOCABULARY** Write about the U.S. Constitution using these words.
   separation of powers **federalism**

2. **READING SKILL Fact and Opinion** Use your chart from page 58 to write your opinion about whether you prefer the U.S. or Canadian form of government.

Fact	Opinion

3. **Write About It** How did the Constitution better meet the needs of Americans than the Articles of Confederation?

Members of the U.S. Senate met at the Democratic National Convention in 2004. Ninety women were serving in the U.S. Congress in 2007. ▼

Lesson 4

VOCABULARY

amnesty p. 67

Internet p. 68

READING SKILL

Fact and Opinion

Copy the chart below. As you read, use the chart to fill in facts and opinions about issues and technologies in the United States and Canada.

Fact	Opinion

STANDARDS FOCUS

SOCIAL STUDIES Science, Technology, & Society

GEOGRAPHY The Uses of Geography

ISSUES TODAY

The flags of Canada and the United States frame this across-the-border picnic in the village of Coutts, Alberta, Canada.

Visual Preview

How do current issues affect how people meet their needs?

A Changes in immigration pose new problems.

B New technologies have brought the world closer together.

C The United States and Canada work with the world on global affairs.

Ⓐ IMMIGRATION AND REFORM

New people and new technologies in the United States and Canada have led to advances and issues, not only in each country, but also around the world.

The population of the United States is changing. As you read in Lesson 1, most immigrants throughout U.S. history came from Europe. Today, most immigrants to the United States come from Latin America, Canada, and Asia.

In order to become a legal citizen of the United States, all immigrants must go through the naturalization process. The naturalization process involves filing the proper paperwork with the U.S. government and then pledging an oath of allegiance to the United States. This means that the person swears to be loyal to the United States.

Illegal Immigration

Many people come to the United States legally. However, nearly 12 million people have come to the United States illegally. Many of these immigrants risk their lives by crossing the U.S. borders illegally. Because they are in the country illegally, these immigrants often live in hiding and have to take jobs for extremely low pay.

There are different opinions on how to deal with illegal immigrants. Some want to send illegal immigrants out of the country. Others want to grant **amnesty**, or a pardon, to those who have already been in the country illegally. This would be done to help the illegal immigrants become citizens.

Many in the United States and Canada want increased patrols on the borders between the United States and Mexico and between the United States and Canada. Others have suggested building a wall to separate the two countries.

QUICK CHECK

Fact and Opinion **Should illegal immigrants be allowed to become U.S. citizens?**

A border patrol station along the Texas-Mexico border ▶

B THE IMPACT OF TECHNOLOGY

In the past few decades, the United States, Canada, and the world have been in the middle of a technology revolution. Many of the products we use every day, such as computers and cell phones, have only recently been in widespread use. As technology continues to advance, the world seems to be shrinking, with other nations and other cultures just a mouse-click away.

The Computer and the Internet

Early computers were developed in the 1930s and 1940s. Most of these machines were programmed to do a single function, often various math problems.

In the 1960s scientists developed the first computer circuits. More powerful circuits followed in the 1970s. These were called microprocessors. This led to the creation of personal computers. Since that time, computers have continually become smaller, faster, and more efficient.

Another major new technology is the **Internet**. The Internet is a worldwide system of connected computer networks. Web sites, or pages on the Internet, appear on the World Wide Web, which allows people to browse Internet sites. By 1996 over one billion people were using the Internet.

Few people had access to early computers (left). Today, many schools have computer labs where students can access the Internet (below).

Each day, billions of people from across the globe gather information and communicate with others online. Businesses can buy and sell goods using the Internet. People also use the Internet to purchase and sell goods.

New Ways to Communicate

In the 1980s the cellular phone, or cell phone, came into use in the United States. These early phones were bulky and expensive, and they had short battery lives. Today, people use their cell phones for more than just talking. People use their cell phones to play games, send messages, take pictures, and browse the Internet.

New communications technologies are found in automobiles as well. In the late 1990s, the U.S. government began allowing civilians to use government satellite systems. This technology was then placed in cars in the form of a navigation system. Some modern cars are equipped with communication links for roadside assistance or emergency situations.

Quick Check

Fact and Opinion How does technology bring the world closer together?

Cell phones have become smaller and more powerful over the years.

◀ Many people now have laptops, or portable computers.

GLOBAL COOPERATION

The United States and Canada have been close military allies since 1940. They share an active military exchange program. For example, Canadian navy ships train together with the U.S. Navy battle groups.

The Canadian military has fought alongside the United States in most major wars since World War II. Recently, the Canadian forces have helped the United States in the Persian Gulf War in 1991 and during the conflict in Afghanistan in 2002.

The United Nations

The United States and Canada also have strong roles in the United Nations. They provide much of the money that funds the organization. They take part in UN agencies that provide aid to people in areas affected by war or natural disasters. The United States and Canada have also sent soldiers to serve in UN forces that act as peacekeepers in troubled areas of the world.

▶ The United Nations headquarters in New York City

QUICK CHECK

Fact and Opinion **How do Canada and the United States cooperate on global issues?**

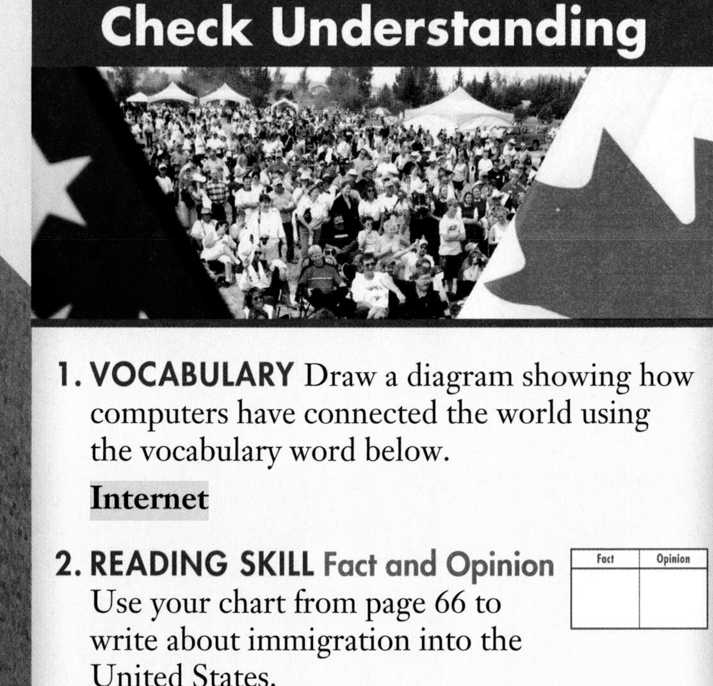

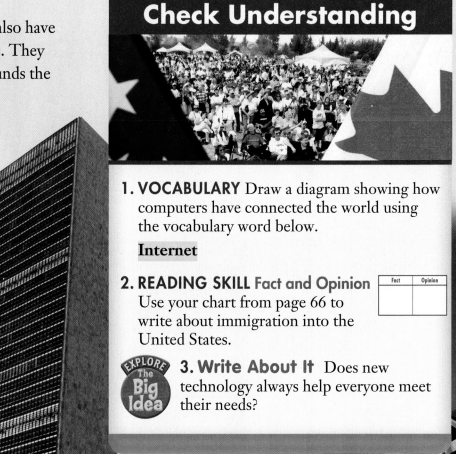

Check Understanding

1. **VOCABULARY** Draw a diagram showing how computers have connected the world using the vocabulary word below.

   Internet

2. **READING SKILL Fact and Opinion** Use your chart from page 66 to write about immigration into the United States.

Fact	Opinion

3. **Write About It** Does new technology always help everyone meet their needs?

Map and Globe Skills

Use GPS

VOCABULARY

geographer
Global Positioning System

New technologies are helping **geographers**, or people who study geography, make better maps. One system they use to make maps is the **Global Positioning System** (GPS). GPS uses radio signals from satellites to determine the exact location of places on Earth.

GPS was originally used by the U.S. military for navigation, map-making, and guiding missiles. Many people use GPS devices instead of using a traditional map when hiking. Others have a GPS device installed in their car to help them find their way while they are traveling.

Learn It

- Look at the image. You will notice that it shows different streets and where they intersect.
- Some GPS devices provide street names. Some even give audio directions as you approach your destination.

Try It

- How would this GPS device help you to decide where to cross the river on the map?
- How can you tell the difference between a street and a major highway?

Apply It

- Imagine that you are going on a vacation across the country. How might a GPS device be useful when going on vacation?

Lesson 5

VOCABULARY

global warming p. 73

acid rain p. 77

conservation p. 77

READING SKILL

Fact and Opinion

Copy the chart below. As you read, fill in the chart with facts about environmental issues and your opinions of those issues.

Fact	Opinion

STANDARDS FOCUS

SOCIAL STUDIES — People, Places, & Environments

GEOGRAPHY — Environment and Society

The Environment

Under these protective caps are cedar saplings that are part of the reforestation of British Columbia.

Visual Preview

How does the environment affect our lives?

A Scientists believe that global warming can have harmful affects.

B People in different areas must adjust to extreme weather in different ways.

C Pollution can cause problems that need to be addressed.

Ⓐ GLOBAL WARMING

People adapt to their environment to survive. In certain areas of North America, natural disasters bring vast destruction. Most natural disasters cannot be prevented. In some cases, however, people do play a role.

Human activity can affect Earth's environment. Most factories, automobiles, and power plants burn fossil fuels, such as coal, oil, or natural gas. Many scientists argue that this pollution has created a serious problem: **global warming**. Global warming is an overall rise in the temperature of Earth's atmosphere.

PEOPLE

Through books and television, **David Suzuki** has educated people about the threat of global warming. In 2004 television viewers voted Suzuki the greatest living Canadian.

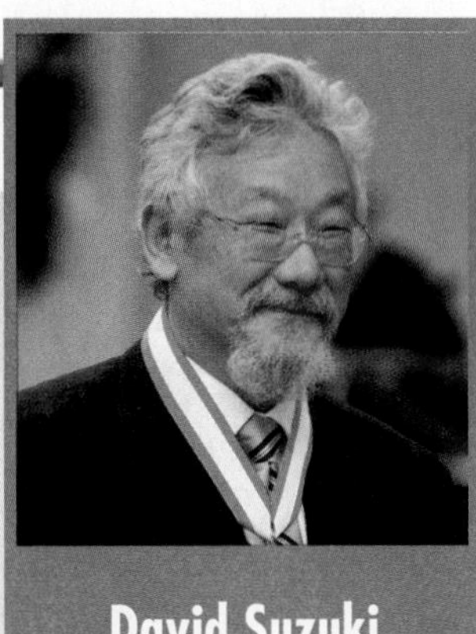

David Suzuki

Causes of Global Warming

Global warming is affected by what scientists call the greenhouse effect. The greenhouse effect is heat that is trapped in Earth's atmosphere and warms the planet. Many scientists claim that a rise in greenhouse gases leads to global warming. Greenhouse gases include water vapor, carbon dioxide, methane, nitrous oxide, and ozone. As we add greenhouse gases to the air, temperatures rise. Ice caps at the poles begin to melt, and ocean waters rise.

Some scientists believe that the rise in temperatures from global warming can also cause extreme weather conditions, rising sea levels, and changes in the amount and pattern of precipitation. These changes may cause floods, droughts, and heat waves.

The Future

Some scientists say that, to solve the problem of global warming, we need to change the way we produce energy. One way would be to use more clean and renewable sources of energy. These include sun, wind, and fuels such as ethanol, which is made from corn.

The United States and Canada have funded research to find cleaner sources of energy. Countries such as Denmark produce large amounts of energy with huge windmills. Someday, we may even place huge panels in space to collect solar energy and send it back to Earth.

QUICK CHECK

Fact and Opinion **How could one help solve the problem of global warming?**

A blizzard in New York City in 1888 (left), and a more recent blizzard (right)

B ENVIRONMENTAL EXTREMES

Some areas of the United States and Canada are more likely to experience severe weather than others. Severe weather includes wind, rain, and lightning. It can destroy buildings and result in massive flooding.

Blizzards

Blizzards are severe winter storms that last several hours and combine high winds with heavy snow that limits how far people can see. "White-out" conditions make driving dangerous. Also, the wind and snow can knock down electric power lines and trees. In the United States, blizzards are most common in the Northeast.

Blizzards can bring human activity in a busy city to a halt as cities work to clear the streets. The Great Blizzard of 1888 shut down New York City. It killed 400 people and sank 200 ships. The blizzard left snow drifts towering 15 to 50 feet high.

Tornadoes

A tornado is a powerful windstorm that has a funnel-shaped cloud which moves quickly over land. The high winds of a tornado can level houses, knock down trees, and toss cars around. Tornadoes are more likely to occur in a large part of the Midwest.

The central United States sees more tornadoes each year than any other place in the world. In fact, tornados are so common from Texas north to Nebraska that this area has been nicknamed "Tornado Alley."

Hurricanes

Similar to tornadoes, hurricanes are funnel-shaped wind systems, but hurricanes are much larger. They develop over large bodies of warm water and lose strength over land. Coastal regions can receive damage from a hurricane, but inland areas are relatively safe.

Hurricanes combine with normal tides to create a storm tide. Wind pushes the storm tide to shore, creating the storm surge. These high waters can flood low-lying coastal areas. Hurricanes generally develop from June to September. They often strike the southeastern Atlantic Coast and the Gulf of Mexico.

Earthquakes and Volcanoes

Scientists have developed a theory about Earth's structure called plate tectonics. This theory states that the surface of Earth is made up of moving plates, or huge slabs of rock. These plates fit together like a jigsaw puzzle. They move atop soft rock. Oceans and continents ride on top of the gigantic plates.

The plates can push against each other or pull apart from each other. These movements take place along faults, or cracks, that separate the plates. Shifts along a fault can cause earthquakes, or violent jolts, in the area around it. In coastal areas, earthquakes can cause huge waves called tsunamis. In 2004 a tsunami in the Indian Ocean killed about 230,000 people along coastal areas.

The area where two plates meet can also be the site of volcanoes. A volcano forms when magma, or molten rock, breaks through Earth's crust as lava. Volcanoes may explode in a fiery burst of ashes and rock. Then a cone-shaped mountain such as Washington's Mount Saint Helens results.

Volcanoes are found in the Pacific Coast mountains, southern Alaska, and Hawaii. Most volcanoes in North America are dormant, or not ready to erupt soon. A few volcanoes in Hawaii are still active.

EVENT

One of the most damaging hurricanes in history, **Hurricane Katrina**, struck the Gulf Coast in 2005. It damaged a wide area from Alabama through Louisiana.

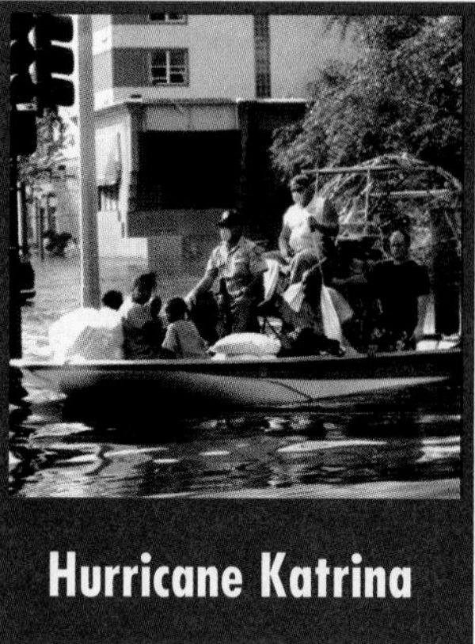

Hurricane Katrina

QUICK CHECK

Fact and Opinion **How do hurricanes form?**

▼ A damaged car after the 1980 eruption of Mount Saint Helens

C PROTECTING THE ENVIRONMENT

Environmentalist Rachel Carson once talked about how humans have the power to both help and harm the environment, or the world around us. In order to save the environment, countries around the world must work to end pollution.

Primary Sources

"There are no other Everglades in the world. They are, they have always been, one of the unique regions of the earth; remote, never wholly known. Nothing anywhere else is like them. . . ."

A section from *The Everglades: River of Grass* by Marjory Stoneman Douglas, 1947

Write About It Think about something that should be preserved. Write about ways people can work in your community to promote your cause.

The Everglades

One example of protecting the environment is the Everglades in southern Florida. The Everglades are home to many rare animals and plants. During the late 1800s and early 1900s, people built roads through the Everglades. Marjory Stoneman Douglas worked tirelessly to help preserve the Everglades. Her book, *The Everglades: River of Grass*, inspired people to protest the destruction of the Everglades. To protect and save the natural homes of the plants and animals, Everglades National Park was created in 1947.

Pollution

People in the United States and Canada burn fossil fuels—coal, oil, and natural gas—to power their factories and run their cars. Burning these fuels pollutes the air, which endangers those who breathe it.

Pollution from factories can also dissolve in rainwater. This causes **acid rain**, or rain containing high amounts of harmful chemicals. Acid rain has harmed forests and killed fish.

Our land and water are also polluted. Chemical spills can kill plants and animals. Fertilizers used on farms can run off into rivers. Oil spills from ships pollute water and beaches. An important way to reduce different kinds of pollution is through **conservation**. Conservation is the protection and careful use of our natural resources.

Forests and Carbon Dioxide

Another problem is deforestation, or the removal of trees. Some trees are removed for farmland, logging, or to make room for cities. Trees, however, help protect the environment by absorbing a greenhouse gas called carbon dioxide.

Carbon dioxide occurs naturally, but it has increased steadily with the burning of more and more fossil fuels. At high levels carbon dioxide contributes to global warming.

The United States and Canada have passed many laws to protect the environment. Some laws lower the amount of fossil fuels that are allowed to be burned.

Quick Check

Fact and Opinion How does the environment benefit from conservation?

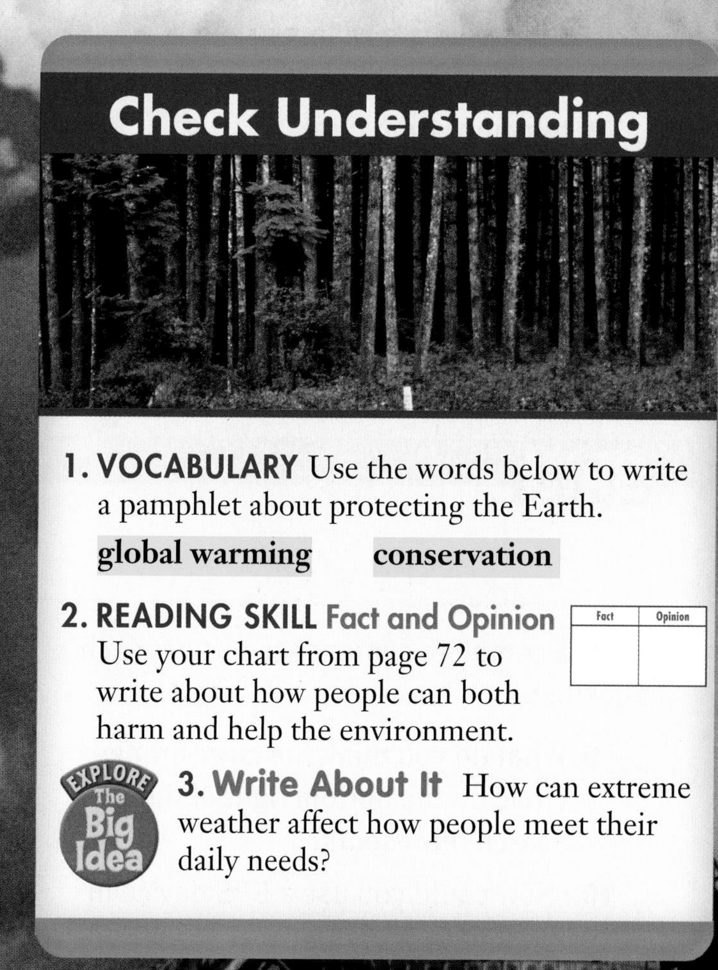

Check Understanding

1. **VOCABULARY** Use the words below to write a pamphlet about protecting the Earth.

   global warming **conservation**

2. **READING SKILL Fact and Opinion** Use your chart from page 72 to write about how people can both harm and help the environment.

Fact	Opinion

3. **Write About It** How can extreme weather affect how people meet their daily needs?

Review and Assess

Vocabulary

Write the word from the list that matches the description.

urbanization	**supply**
amendment	**conservation**

1. an addition to the U.S. Constitution
2. the amount of a product or service producers are willing to sell at a given price
3. the move from rural areas to cities
4. the protection and careful use of natural resources

Comprehension and Critical Thinking

5. What are the differences between the American and Canadian governments?
6. How has the Internet affected daily life in the United States and Canada?
7. **Reading Skill** How do you think immigration impacts the economy?
8. **Critical Thinking** What are ways the United States and Canada can celebrate the diversity of their populations?

Use GPS

Write a complete sentence to answer each question.

9. What do you think the large orange circle on the bottom right of the screen represents?
10. How could you use a GPS device in your daily life?

Test Preparation

In 1999 Nunavut became an official territory in Canada. Nunavut is the homeland for the Inuit people. Read the passage below. Then answer the questions.

> For thousands of years the people of Nunavut have thrived on top of the world. . . .
>
> Nunavut is also a land of opportunity. Our economy has excellent prospects [chances] for growth and we expect significant development in the mining, fisheries, arts, culture, film, and tourism industries over the next decade. We look forward to gaining control of our natural resources . . . so we can take full advantage of the economic opportunities that arise from our human and natural resources. . . .
>
> We have a wealth of resources, a growing economy, breathtaking landscapes and a unique culture to share with Canada and the rest of the world.
>
> —Paul Okalik, Premier of Nunavut

1. Why does Premier Okalik want to gain control of Nunavut's resources?

A. to pay for Nunavut's arts

B. to take advantage of economic opportunities

C. to share the Inuit culture

D. to improve Nunavut's landscape

2. The word "thrived" most likely means ___.

A. ended

B. failed

C. succeeded

D. started

3. What is the main idea of this passage?

A. Nunavut has an economy that is diverse and growing.

B. Nunavut does not have a film industry.

C. Nunavut only shares its unique culture with other Canadians.

D. Nunavut's economy will not grow in the next 10 years.

4. Why does Premier Okalik call Nunavut a "land of opportunity"?

5. Why might the premier of Nunavut speak in such positive terms about the economy of his territory?

The Big Idea Activities

How do people meet their needs?

Write About the Big Idea

Use the Unit 2 Foldable to help you write a persuasive essay that answers the Big Idea question, *How do people meet their needs?* Form an opinion about a fact you wrote under the Daily Life, Government, or Economy heads. In the body of the essay, be sure to use persuasive language to support your opinion. End with a conclusion about what you feel is important in order for people to meet their needs.

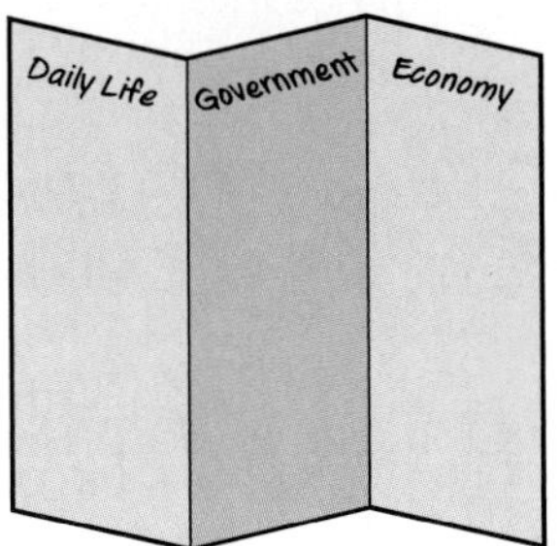

Create a Newspaper Article

Work in small groups to create a front page news story about an event that you have read about in Unit 1. There are several parts to an article.

1. One person should write the article.
2. One person should find and cut out or copy photographs and illustrations for the page.
3. Another person should find and make a copy of a map or chart that helps to explain the story.

Decide as a group how you want your page to look. Then decide as a group what the headline will be.

GLOBAL WARMING
Polar Bears' Habitat Melting

Global warming is a threat to the survival of polar bears. The World Conservation Union has estimated that the polar bear population will drop by 30 percent over the next 45 years. In Canada numbers fell by 22 percent between 1997 and 2004.

The Geography and History of Latin America

Unit 3

EXPLORE The Big Idea

Essential Question
Why do civilizations change?

FOLDABLES™ Study Organizer

Draw Conclusions
Make and label a Three-Tab Book Foldable before you read Unit 3. Write: **How does geography affect civilizations** across the top. On the tabs write: **Climate, Settlement,** and **Economics**. Use the Foldable to organize information as you read.

LOG ON For more about Unit 3, go to www.macmillanmh.com

This mural shows the people who helped Mexico win its fight for independence from Spain.

PEOPLE, PLACES, AND EVENTS

Moctezuma II

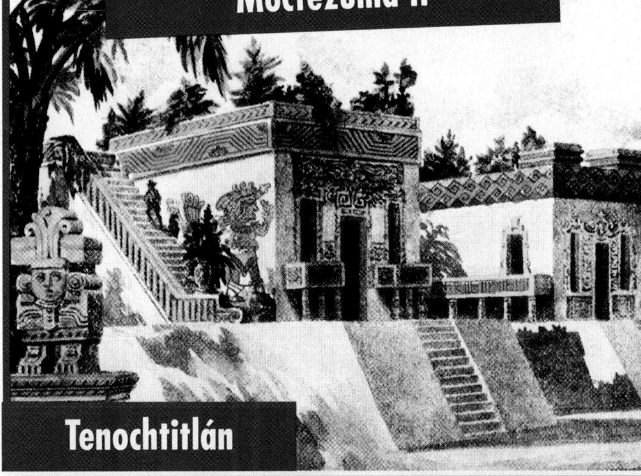
Tenochtitlán

1519 Moctezuma welcomes Cortés to Tenochtitlán.

Sor Juana Inéz de la Cruz

Convent of San Jerónimo

1690 Sor Juana Inéz de la Cruz defends women's right to receive an education.

1500 1600 1700

Moctezuma welcomed Cortés with gifts of gold. Eager for more, Cortés took Moctezuma prisoner. Moctezuma was later killed in a riot.

Today Tenochtitlán is part of Mexico City, one of the most populated cities in the world.

Sor Juana joined the **Convent of San Jerónimo** to continue her education. Through poetry, she fought for women's rights.

Today the Convent of San Jerónimo is a museum named in honor of Sor Juana.

LOG ON For more about People, Places, and Events, visit www.macmillanmh.com

Simón Bolívar

Colombia

1819 Bolívar defeats the Spanish in South America.

Marina Silva

Brazilian rain forest

2005 Silva cut deforestation of the rain forest by half.

1800 1900 2000

Bolívar led the fight for independence in what are now the countries of Venezuela, **Colombia**, Ecuador, Peru, Panama, and Bolivia.

Today every city and town in Colombia has a main square named Plaza Bolívar.

Brazil's environment minister **Marina Silva** works with many groups to stop the deforestation of the rain forest.

Today you can visit the magnificent **Brazilian rain forest**.

Physical Geography of Latin America

Lesson 1

VOCABULARY

- **subregion** p. 85
- **archipelago** p. 85
- **Llanos** p. 87
- **Pampas** p. 87

READING SKILL

Draw Conclusions

Copy the chart below. As you read, use it to draw conclusions about the geography of Latin America.

Text Clues	Conclusion

STANDARDS FOCUS

SOCIAL STUDIES — People, Places, and Environments

GEOGRAPHY — Places and Regions

Farmers in Peru build terraces on the sides of the Andes to grow crops.

Visual Preview

How are people affected by Latin America's landforms?

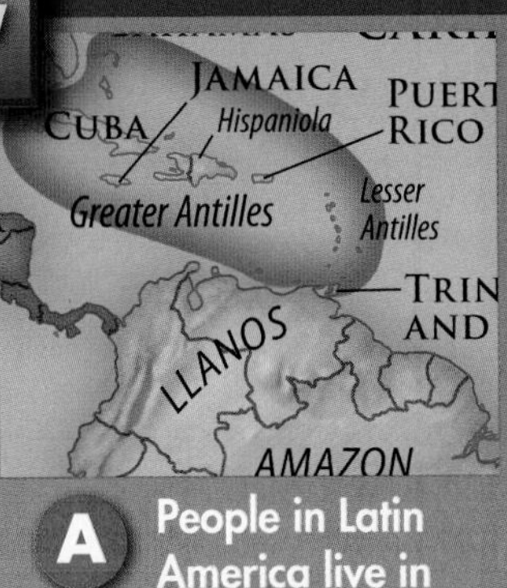

A People in Latin America live in three subregions.

B Latin America has diverse landforms.

C Waterways in Latin America are used for many different purposes.

Ⓐ LATIN AMERICA'S SUBREGIONS

Soaring, snowcapped mountains, tropical islands with sandy beaches, lonely stretches of wide-open Pampas, and many volcanoes make Latin America's scenery some of the most dramatic in the world.

Latin America is in the Western Hemisphere, south of the United States. The region has an area of nearly 8 million square miles. Geographers divide Latin America into three **subregions**, or smaller areas. They are Middle America, the Caribbean, and South America.

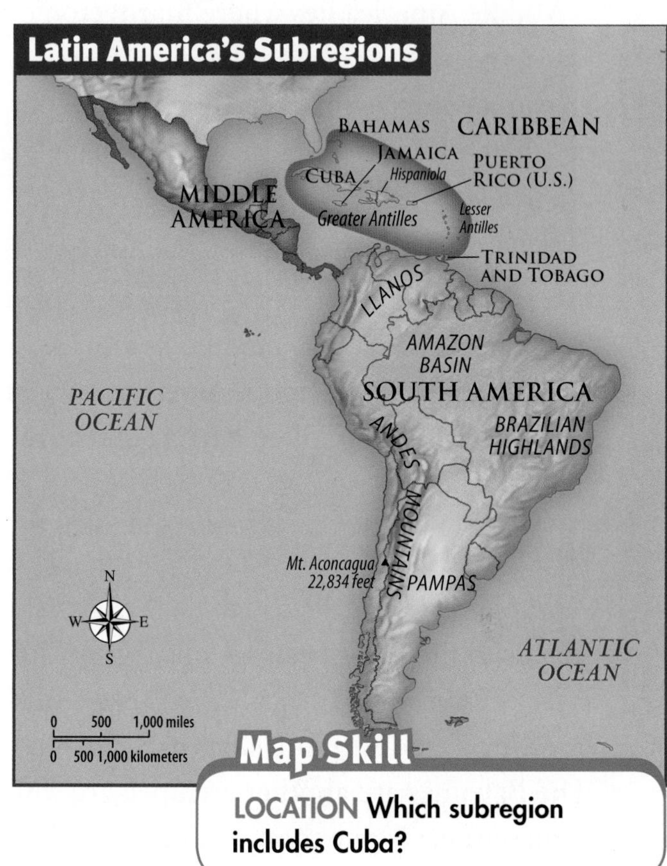

Map Skill

LOCATION **Which subregion includes Cuba?**

Middle America

Mexico and Central America make up Middle America. Mexico is a large country that borders the United States. Central America is an isthmus, or a narrow strip of land that links two larger areas of land. It links North and South America.

The Caribbean

The islands of the Caribbean Sea, also known as the West Indies, can be divided into the Greater Antilles, the Lesser Antilles, and the Bahamas. The Lesser Antilles and the Bahamas each form an **archipelago**, or a group of islands.

South America

South America is one of the seven continents on Earth. It is the largest landmass of Latin America. The Andes, a long chain of mountain ranges, and the vast Amazon Basin are South America's major landforms. The high Andes have many peaks over 20,000 feet. To the east of the Andes, the Amazon rain forest covers much of the continent. It is home to more than one third of all Earth's plant and animal species.

Quick Check

Draw Conclusions **Why do a large number of species live in the Amazon rain forest?**

B HIGHLANDS AND LOWLANDS

The three main subregions of Latin America are unique because of their physical features. These features influence where people settle and how they live.

Middle America

Middle America lies where four tectonic plates meet. As a result, it has many active volcanoes and frequent earthquakes. Deposits of ash and lava left over many years have made the soil very fertile.

Mexico has mountain ranges along its eastern and western coasts, with a high plateau between. In the south, mountains rise like a backbone through Central America. Lowlands along the coasts are often narrow and have frequent floods.

The Caribbean

The Greater Antilles include the largest islands in the Caribbean—Cuba, Hispaniola, Puerto Rico, and Jamaica. The Lesser Antilles curve from the Virgin Islands to Trinidad. The Bahamas are another archipelago, which contains nearly one thousand tiny islands.

PLACES

Lava flowing from the nearby volcano Parícutin buried **San Juan Parangaricutiro**. All that remains is this church.

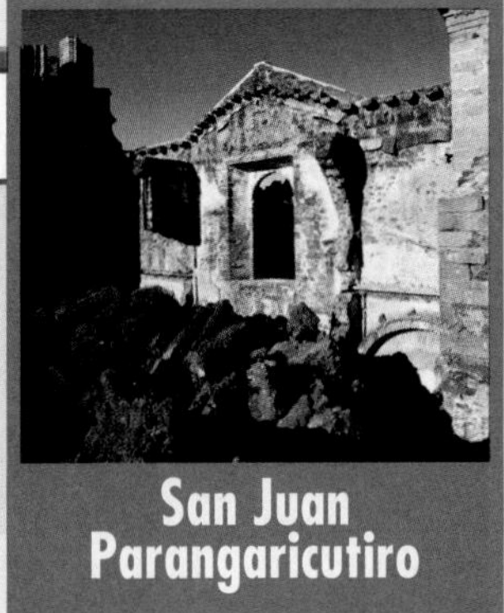

San Juan Parangaricutiro

Most of the Caribbean islands are small. The two large islands of Cuba and Hispaniola are the exceptions. Together they contain over half the subregions's land area. The remaining land area of the Caribbean subregion comes from nearly 7,000 smaller islands.

The Caribbean islands are lush and fertile. Many different species of plants and animals can be found in the Caribbean. Volcanic eruptions have deposited fertile soil. Good soil and frequent rainfall make agriculture an important activity. Farmers grow a wide variety of crops, including bananas, eggplants, flowers, citrus fruits, and cacao.

South America

Two giant landforms dominate the continent of South America. They are the Andes mountain ranges along the western edge and the vast Amazon Basin in the center. Two lowland plains of tropical grasslands also stretch across the continent, to the north and south of the Amazon Basin.

Fishers on the island of Tortola in the Virgin Islands

The Andes

The Andes are the world's longest mountain system. They stretch along the Pacific coast of South America for almost 5,500 miles. Between the mountain chains lie deep valleys and tall plateaus where most people live and farm the land.

The Amazon Basin

East of the Andes, the Amazon River crosses the huge Amazon Basin. This low-lying area covers 2.7 million square miles. Highlands border the basin to the north and south. The Brazilian Highlands, in the south, end with a sharp drop to the Atlantic Coastal Plain.

Lowland Plains

Other lowland plains are found north and south of the Amazon Basin. Tropical grasslands known as the **Llanos** stretch through eastern Colombia and Venezuela. These are similar to the prairies in the western United States. The **Pampas** covers much of Argentina and Uruguay. Like North America's Great Plains, the Pampas provide grazing land for beef cattle and fertile soil for growing grains.

Quick Check

Draw Conclusions Which parts of Latin America are most suitable for farming?

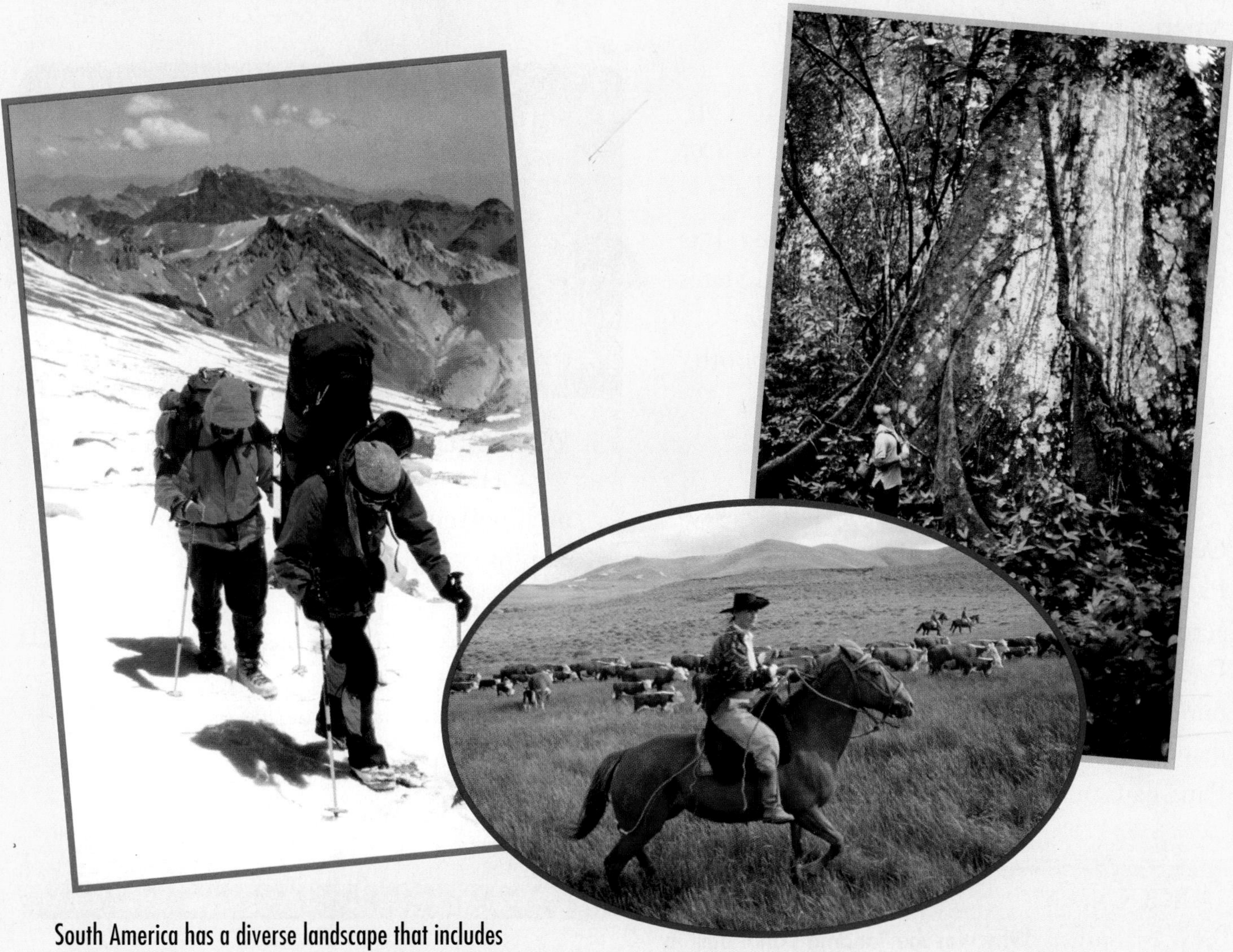

South America has a diverse landscape that includes snowy mountain ranges, vast plains, and dense rain forests.

C WATERWAYS

Throughout the world, towns and cities are founded along rivers. Like the rest of the world, Latin Americans make use of their rivers to survive and thrive.

Rivers

The Amazon River in South America is one of the longest rivers in the world. It begins as a trickle of snow in the Andes. Along its route, it is joined by over 1,000 tributaries. The entire Amazon River is 3,900 miles long and is so wide that no bridges have been built across it.

The second-largest river system in South America is made up of three rivers—the Paraná, Paraguay, and Uruguay rivers. Together they drain the rainy eastern half of South America. Parts of the Paraná River drop from the highlands to form the Iguazú Falls.

Mexico's Río Bravo is 1,885 miles long. It is known as the Rio Grande in the United States. The Río Bravo forms most of the border between Mexico and the United States. Both countries use it for irrigation.

The Panama Canal

Many nations attempted to dig a canal across Central America to connect the Atlantic and Pacific Oceans. A canal is a waterway dug across land for ships to travel through. The French began work on the canal in the 1800s but did not finish. In 1904 the United States made a deal with Panama. Ten years later the Panama Canal construction was completed.

QUICK CHECK

Draw Conclusions **Why was the Panama Canal built in Central America?**

Check Understanding

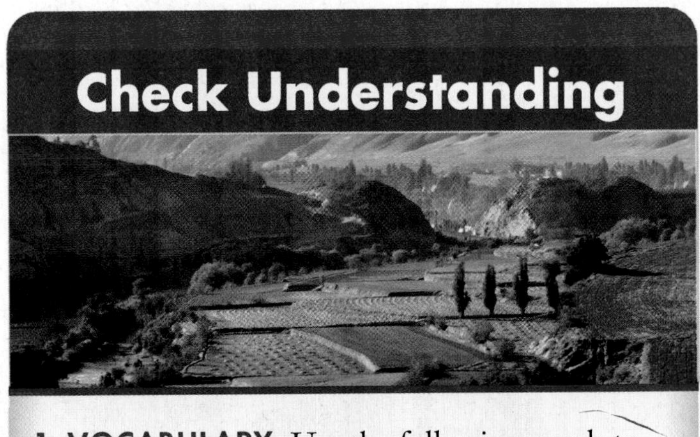

1. **VOCABULARY** Use the following words to write a paragraph about Latin America:

   archipelago **subregion** **Llanos**

2. **READING SKILL Draw Conclusions** Use your chart from page 84 to write about the three subregions of Latin America.

Text Clues	Conclusion

3. **Write About It** Write about how people use waterways.

Chart and Graph Skills

Use a Climograph

VOCABULARY

climograph

In the next lesson, you will learn about the climate in Latin America. One way to learn about climate is to study a **climograph**. A climograph is a graph that shows the temperature, precipitation, and other climate information of a place over time. The climograph below shows the climate of Rio de Janeiro, Brazil.

Learn It

- Study the labels on the climograph. Notice that it is really two graphs in one—a bar graph and a line graph.
- Study the key in the climograph. It tells you what the bars and lines mean.
- Study the scales of measurement on the sides of the climograph. The precipitation scale, shown on the left, is measured in inches. The temperature scale is shown on the right. It is measured in degrees Fahrenheit.

Try It

- What is Rio de Janeiro's average high temperature in January?
- Which month has the greatest amount of precipitation? Which has the least?

Apply It

- Research the climate of a place you would like to visit.
- Why would a climograph be useful to you?

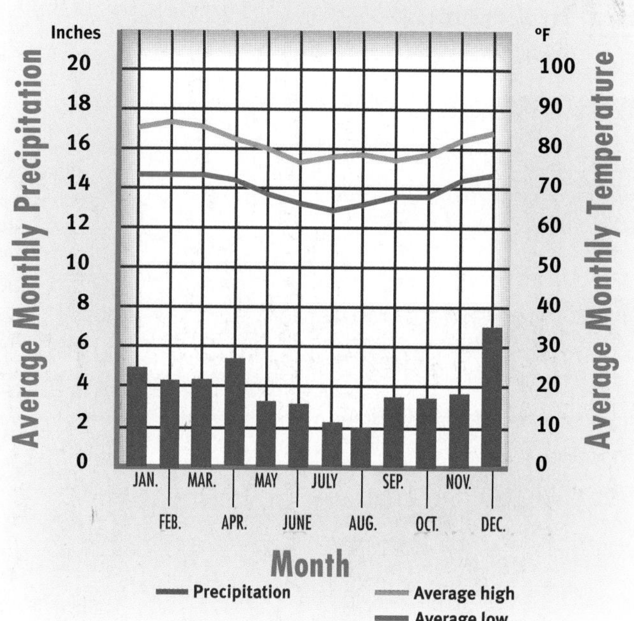

Climate Regions of Latin America

Lesson 2

VOCABULARY

altitude p. 94

El Niño p. 95

La Niña p. 95

READING SKILL

Draw Conclusions

Copy the chart below. Use it to draw conclusions about the climate of Latin America.

Text Clues	Conclusion

STANDARDS FOCUS

SOCIAL STUDIES — People, Places, and Environments

GEOGRAPHY — Environment and Society

A fisherman on a river in the Brazilian rain forest

Visual Preview

How does climate affect life in Latin America?

A Most of Latin America lies within the tropical climate zones.

B Latin America has both tropical and temperate climates.

C Mountains and winds affect climate and the crops people grow.

Ⓐ CLIMATE ZONES

Most of Latin America's rain falls in the tropics, near the Equator. On Colombia's Pacific coast, rainfall can reach 280 inches a year. In contrast, parts of coastal Peru and Chile get little rain.

Look at the map of Latin America's climate zones. Most of Latin America lies within the tropics—the area between the latitudes of the Tropic of Cancer and the Tropic of Capricorn. Farther south the climate generally becomes drier and cooler. The tip of South America is very cool in the summer.

Climate is not determined by latitude alone, however. Mountain ranges and wind patterns create a variety of climate zones that affect the way people live.

QUICK CHECK

Summarize What affects Latin America's climate?

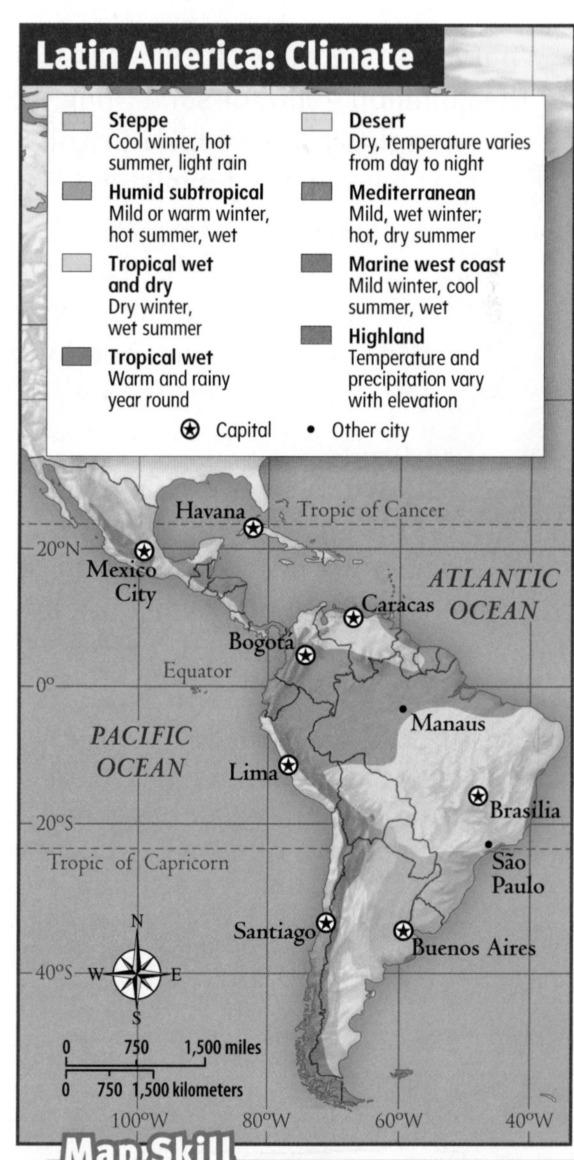

Map Skill

REGION Which climate does Santiago have?

◀ Palm trees grow in tropical climates.

B TROPICAL AND TEMPERATE ZONES

Citizenship

Working for the Common Good

What are some ways citizens can work for the common good, or something that benefits most people? Brazil's environment minister Marina Silva is working for a rain forest economy that provides jobs and helps farmers, but does not destroy the rain forest at the same time. Like Silva, you can work for the common good by becoming involved in solving a community problem or by volunteering for an organization that helps others.

Write About It Write a list of five projects you and your classmates can do to make your school a better place for everyone.

The tropics generally have warm to hot temperatures, because this area often receives the direct rays of the sun. There are two main kinds of tropical climates.

Tropical Dry Climate

A tropical dry climate zone extends over parts of Middle America, most Caribbean islands, and north-central South America. This area has hot temperatures and abundant rainfall, but also experiences a long dry season.

Tropical Wet Climate

Some Caribbean islands have a tropical wet climate, as does much of Central and South America. A tropical wet climate has year-round hot temperatures and heavy rainfall. Vast areas of rain forest cover much of this climate zone. Warm temperatures and heavy rains cause rain forests to grow.

South America's Amazon Basin holds the world's largest rain forest. The Amazon rain forest is home to more species of plants and animals than any other area on planet Earth.

A canopy of trees in the Brazilian rain forest

In the rain forest, trees grow so close together that their tops form a dense canopy, an umbrella-like covering of leaves. The canopy may soar to 130 feet above the ground.

Temperate Climates

Temperate climates are common in the parts of South America that lie south of the Tropic of Capricorn. A humid subtropical climate dominates much of southeastern South America from southern Brazil to the Pampas of Argentina and Uruguay. In this area, winters are short and mild, and summers are long, hot, and humid. Summers occasionally bring short dry periods.

Temperate climates are also found in parts of southwestern South America. Central Chile has a Mediterranean climate of dry summers and rainy winters. Farmers there grow fruits in summer and export them to North America during that area's winter season. Farther south is a marine west coast climate, where rain is heavier and falls throughout the year.

Quick Check

Summarize **Why do the tropics tend to have warm temperatures?**

DataGraphic

Summer and Winter Temperatures

Buenos Aires, Argentina, is about as far south of the Equator as Atlanta, Georgia, is north of it. Study the graphs, then answer the questions.

Average July Temperatures

City	High	Low	Absolute Location
Atlanta	89°F	71°F	33.45°N 84.23°W
Buenos Aires	60°F	46°F	34.35°S 58.23°W

Average January Temperatures

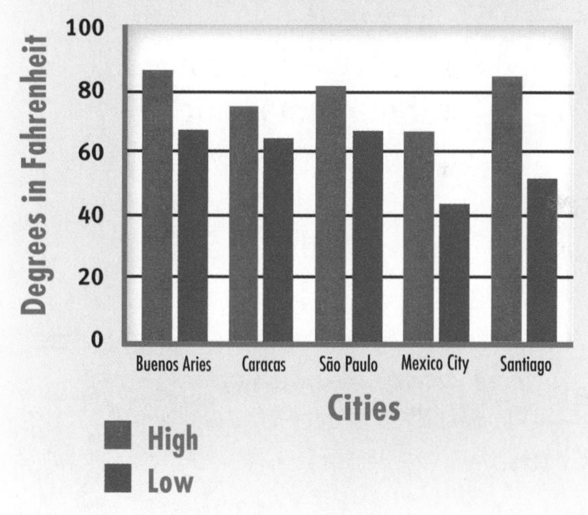

Think About Temperatures

1. Why is Atlanta warmer in July than Buenos Aires?
2. Why are January temperatures warm in Latin America?

ELEVATION AND CLIMATE

As you have read, mountains and highlands cover much of Latin America. **Altitude**, or height about sea level, affects climate in these rugged areas. The higher the altitude, the cooler the temperatures are—even within the warm tropics. The Andes, for example, have five altitude zones of climate. Terms in the Spanish language are used to label the different zones. temperatures become cooler the higher up you go.

The Five Climate Zones

Tierra caliente, or "hot land," refers to the hot and humid elevations near sea level. There is little change in temperature here from one month to another. Farmers in the tierra caliente grow tropical crops such as bananas, sugarcane, cacao, and rice.

From 3,000 feet to 6,000 feet above sea level the air becomes cooler. There large amounts of rainfall encourage forest growth. This moist, pleasant climate zone is called tierra templada, or "temperate land". Mild temperatures make tierra templada the most densely populated of the climate zones.

The next zone is the tierra fría, or "cold land." It begins at 6,000 feet and stretches up to 12,000 feet. The tierra fría has forested and grassy areas. Farming can take place in this zone during the warmer summers. The crops grown are those that thrive in more difficult conditions such as potatoes and grains.

Above the tree line at 12,000 feet lies the puna. The puna is so cold that only hardy livestock can live there. Next is the tierra helada, or "frozen land," which lies above 15,000 feet. This land is covered in snow and ice that does not melt.

El Niño and La Niña

Winds, rain, and mountains all affect the climate throughout Latin America. In some years, changes in the Pacific Ocean's surface temperature cause **El Niño**. In an El Niño year, heavy rains fall on western South America, causing floods. El Niño can also bring a long dry season to northeastern Brazil, causing crop failures.

In some years the opposite happens, producing conditions called **La Niña**. La Niña causes unusually cool water and low rainfall in the eastern Pacific. In the western Pacific, rains are heavy and hurricanes can destroy buildings. La Niña can bring a greater chance of powerful and destructive hurricanes to Mexico and Central America.

Tall Mountains

The Atacama Desert in northern Chile is one of the driest places on Earth. It lies along the Pacific coast in the rain shadow of the Andes. Winds bring rain from the Atlantic Ocean across South America, but the tall mountains keep them from falling in the Atacama Desert.

Northern Mexico, northeastern Brazil, and southeastern Argentina also have dry climates. Northern Mexico gets less than one inch of rain per month.

EVENT

Hurricane Wilma hit Cancún, Mexico, on October 21, 2005. It was the most intense storm ever to form in the Americas.

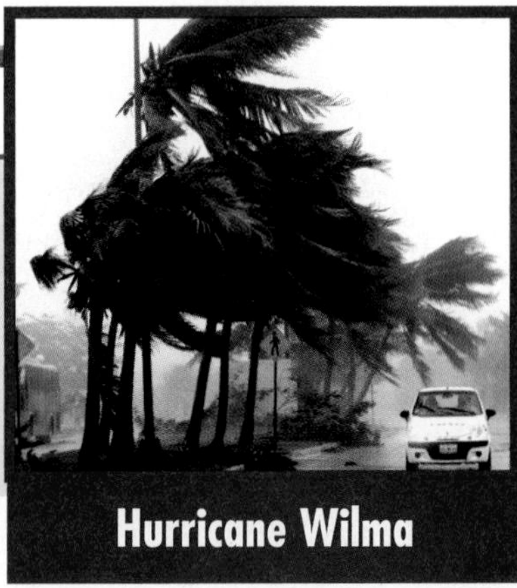

Hurricane Wilma

Check Understanding

1. **VOCABULARY** Write a paragraph about weather using these words.
   altitude **El Niño** **La Niña**
2. **READING SKILL** Draw Conclusions Use your chart from page 90 to write about the climate of South America.

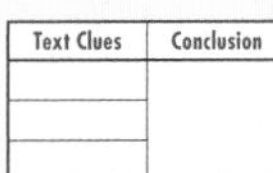

3. **Write About It** Write about how altitude affects the way people live.

QUICK CHECK

Draw Conclusions **Why is the Atacama Desert so dry?**

Lesson 3

Early Civilizations

VOCABULARY

glyph p. 98

empire p. 102

READING SKILLS

Draw Conclusions

Copy the chart below. As you read, use it to draw conclusions about early Latin American civilizations.

Text Clues	Conclusion

STANDARDS FOCUS

SOCIAL STUDIES Time, Continuity, and Change

GEOGRAPHY The Uses of Geography

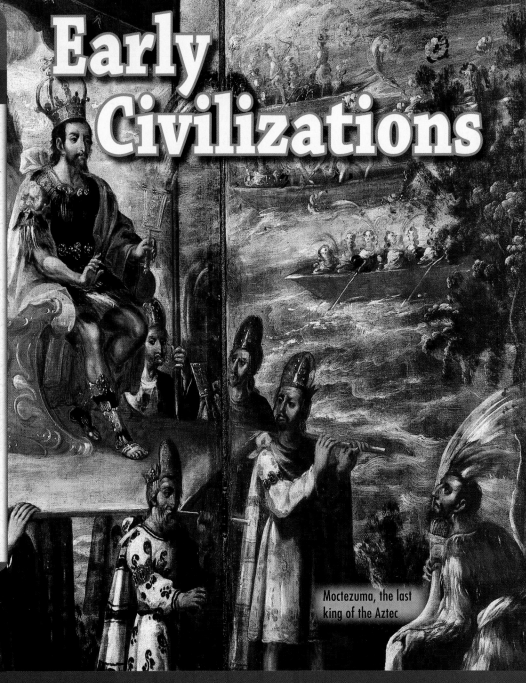

Moctezuma, the last king of the Aztec

Visual Preview

How did geography affect early civilizations?

A Trade helped the Olmec become Latin America's first civilization.

B The Maya developed a great civilization, studied the stars, and built cities.

C The Aztec captured the Toltec and built an empire.

D The Inca Empire grew through farming, strong leaders, and trade routes.

Ⓐ THE FIRST PEOPLES

No one knows how farming first started. We do know that in the Americas it started in Mexico. By about 7000 B.C., people in Mexico and Central America were raising three crops—corn, beans, and squash.

Early Latin Americans are often discussed in the field of anthropology, or the study of human beings. The first people to live in Latin America were the ancestors of today's Native Americans. These groups created advanced cultures.

The Olmec

The Olmec of southern Mexico built Latin America's first civilization. It lasted from about 1500 B.C. to 300 B.C. Each Olmec city focused on a certain activity, and they all depended on one another. Some cities were at the heart of farming areas that grew maize (corn), squash, and beans. Others controlled valued mineral resources, such as jade, a shiny green stone, and obsidian, a hard, black volcanic glass. Some cities were religious centers, with pyramid-shaped stone temples. The Olmec traded with people hundreds of miles away. As a result, Olmec culture spread along these trade routes to other parts of Mexico and Central America.

QUICK CHECK

Draw Conclusions **Why do you think the Olmec traded with people hundreds of miles away?**

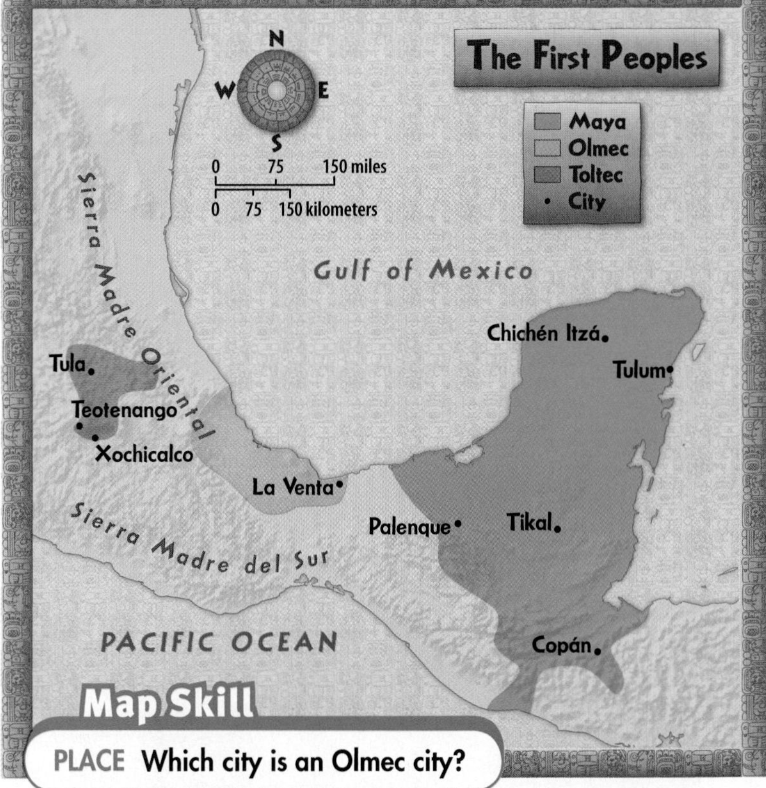

Map Skill

PLACE **Which city is an Olmec city?**

An Olmec stone statue ▼

B THE MAYA

Another civilization that grew from trade was the Maya. The Maya lived in Mexico's Yucatán Peninsula and surrounding areas from about A.D. 300 to A.D. 900. The Maya civilization began to decline in about A.D. 900. No one knows exactly why.

Maya Wealth

Why were the Maya able to develop a great civilization? The Maya grew enough food to feed their people and trade with other groups. This allowed them the wealth and time for building projects, writing, and other studies.

The Maya built huge stone temples in the shape of pyramids with steps. Skilled at astronomy, the Maya used their knowledge of the stars, moon, and planets to develop a calendar. They also had a number system based on 20. Using **glyphs**, a form of writing that uses signs and symbols, the Maya recorded the history of their kings.

Maya Cities

Ancient Maya cities had palaces, observatories, temple-pyramids, and ball courts built around a central plaza. The Maya knew much about the sun. They built their cities with compass directions so the sun's rays would shine through small openings on special days of the year. At Chichén Itzá, the Pyramid of the Feathered Serpent is placed to show the first days of spring and fall. Sunlight pours through the temple's openings, lighting up the stairs and making it look like a huge snake.

The largest city was Tikal, with 60,000 people. Another center of Maya culture was Copán, in what is today Honduras.

A pyramid in the Maya city of Chichén Itzá has 365 steps, one step for each day of the year. ▶

Art and Religion

The Maya were talented sculptors and painters. They used symbols as backgrounds for images, such as the sun, moon, and stars. Maya artists were among the few to sign their work at the time.

Many Maya artists used images of the maize god in their artwork. The cycle of the maize crop lies at the heart of Maya beliefs. The maize god was an important religious figure.

Because religion was so important, religious leaders were at the top of the Maya social pyramid. Religious leaders decided where and when cities should be built.

Quick Check

Draw Conclusions Why do you think the Maya built their cities with compass directions?

Statue of a Maya religious leader

C THE TOLTEC AND AZTEC

As the Mayan civilization declined, the Toltec took over what is now northern Mexico. They built the city of Tula northwest of present-day Mexico City. From Tula, they conquered lands to the Yucatán Peninsula.

Toltec rulers controlled trade. For example, they held a monopoly, or sole right, in the trade of obsidian. Obsidian was used to make weapons. This monopoly gave the Toltec power over other groups.

The Aztec

Around A.D. 1200, the Aztec people from the north moved into central Mexico and captured Tula. They adopted Toltec culture and took control of the region's trade. Tenochtitlán, the Aztec capital, was a city built on an island in a lake. It held about 250,000 people—a huge population at that time.

Tenochtitlán had huge temples, including one over 100 feet tall. Roads and bridges joined the city to the mainland, allowing the Aztec to bring food and other goods to their busy markets. Aztec farmers grew their crops on "floating gardens," or rafts filled with mud. After a time, the rafts sank to the lake bottom and piled up, forming fertile islands where farmers could grow crops.

Then and Now

The Aztec built Tenochtitlán in A.D. 1325 on an island in Lake Texcoco. Today Tenochtitlán is part of Mexico City, the tenth largest city in the world, with a population of over 8.6 million.

Building an Empire

Like the Maya, the Aztec had a steady food supply that gave them more time to do other things. Aztec culture soon spread. To expand their empire, the Aztec often waged war with other groups.

War was important to the Aztec because they demanded tribute from those they conquered. Tribute was a tax that was paid in goods or services. Tribute often included food, clothing, precious stones, or feathers. People were also taken as tribute. Many were forced into slavery and used as laborers on large building projects.

By the mid-1400s, Tenochtitlán was one of the largest cities in the world. On market day, the Aztec and other people met and exchanged news. They danced, played music, and performed juggling tricks. They also sold many beautiful items at the market.

Some historians believe the Aztec market was one of the largest in the world. This growth was achieved with the help of workers from groups the Aztec had conquered and enslaved. The Aztec were feared and hated by the survivors of the people they had conquered. In 1521 these groups joined with European invaders to conquer the Aztec.

Quick Check

Draw Conclusions **Why do you think Tenochtitlán was built on an island in a lake?**

Then and Now

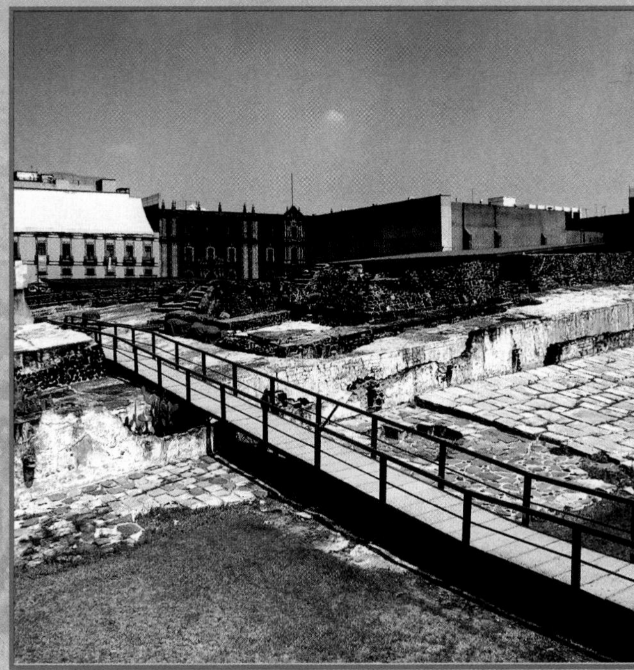

The Great Pyramid, or Templo Mayor, was the main temple of the Aztec capital of Tenochtitlán. Today Templo Mayor is a museum with eight halls exhibiting thousands of objects.

D THE INCA

During the 1400s, the Inca had a powerful civilization centered in what is now Peru in South America. Their **empire**, or many different lands under one ruler, stretched more than 2,500 miles along the Andes. The Inca lived in environments that varied from the desert coastal lowlands to the rugged Andes mountain ranges.

The Inca rulers founded military posts and put in place a highly developed system of record keeping. Work crews built irrigation systems, roads, and suspension bridges that linked regions of the empire to Cuzco, the capital. You can still see the remains of magnificent fortresses and buildings erected centuries ago by the skilled Inca builders.

The Inca Capital

Cuzco served as the center of government, religion, and trade. The temples and government buildings at the center of Cuzco were built of stone blocks. These blocks fit together so well that it is impossible to put a knife between them. They also can withstand earthquakes.

Inca leaders ruled their empire from Cuzco. Each Inca leader was an emperor, or an absolute ruler. According to Inca legend, the emperor was descended from the sun. His ancestor was Inti, the sun god. The Inca worshiped many gods, but the sun god was the most important. In fact, all Inca called themselves "Children of the Sun."

The Inca built Machu Picchu about 500 years ago. It is thought that it was used as a royal retreat.

The Inca built their buildings from blocks formed into different shapes and sizes to create a perfectly fitting puzzle.

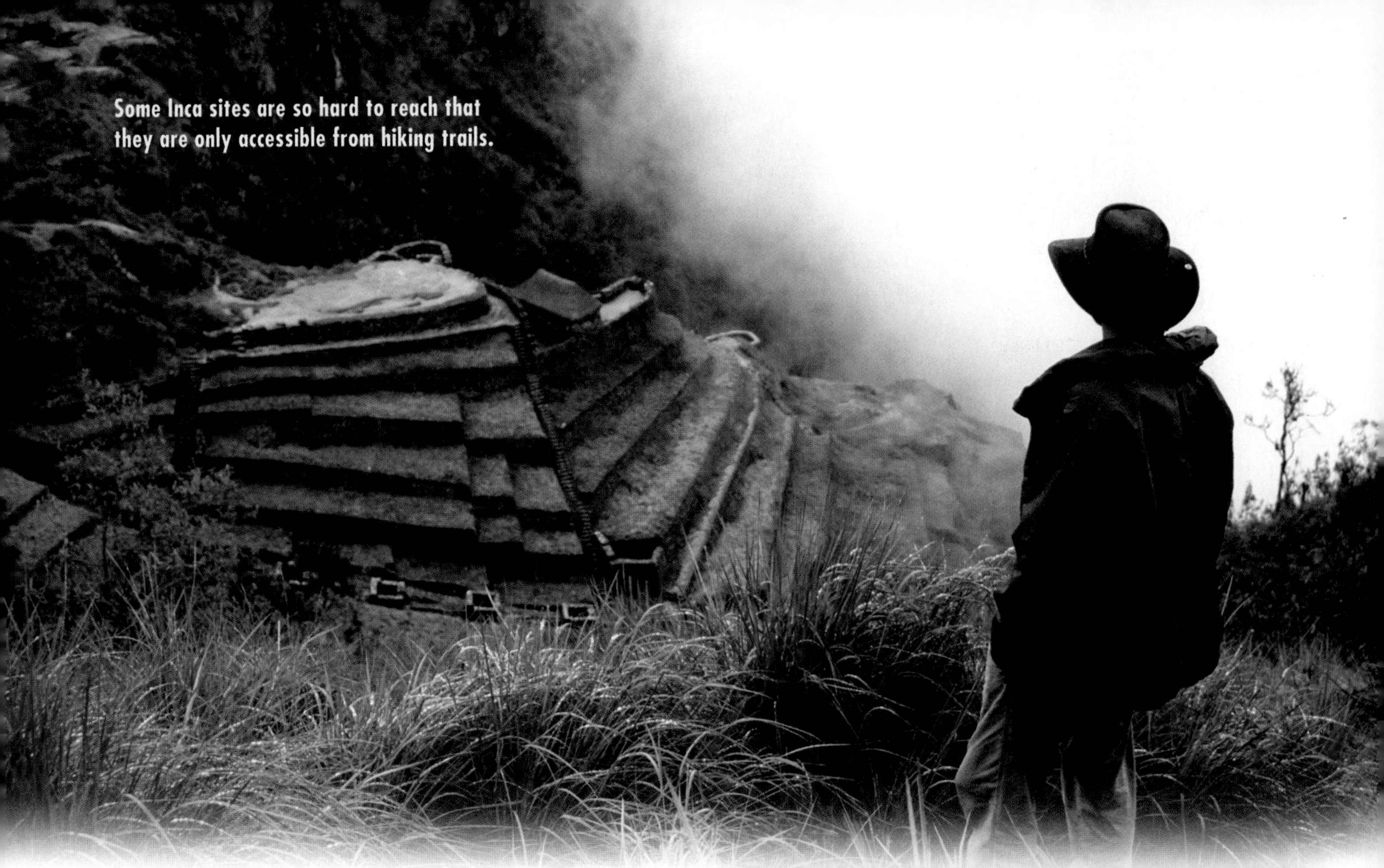

Some Inca sites are so hard to reach that they are only accessible from hiking trails.

The Amazing Inca Farmers

Did you know that the Inca grew more than half the foods people all over the world grow today? Among the many crops they grew were beans, potatoes, corn, squash, tomatoes, and peppers. The Inca also raised llamas for their meat and wool. Llamas were especially helpful in carrying goods up the steep Andes.

Llamas probably helped workers build the city of Machu Picchu high in the Andes. This town was forgotten until an explorer named Hiram Bingham came across it in 1911. No one knows why Machu Picchu was built high in the Andes or why it was abandoned.

Quick Check

Draw Conclusions **Why do you think Machu Picchu was built high in the Andes?**

Check Understanding

1. **VOCABULARY** Write a paragraph about early Native Americans using these words.

   glyph **empire**

2. **READING SKILL** Draw Conclusions Use your chart from page 96 to write about early Latin American civilizations.

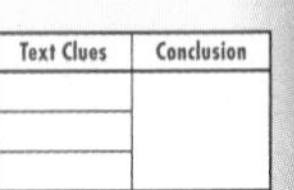

3. **Write About It** Write about how Native Americans adapted to their environment.

Lesson 4

VOCABULARY

Line of Demarcation p. 105

Columbian Exchange p. 108

encomienda p. 111

cash crop p. 111

plantation p. 111

READING SKILL

Draw Conclusions

As you read, use the chart to draw a conclusion about Europeans in Latin America.

Text Clues	Conclusion

STANDARDS FOCUS

SOCIAL STUDIES Global Connections

GEOGRAPHY Human Systems

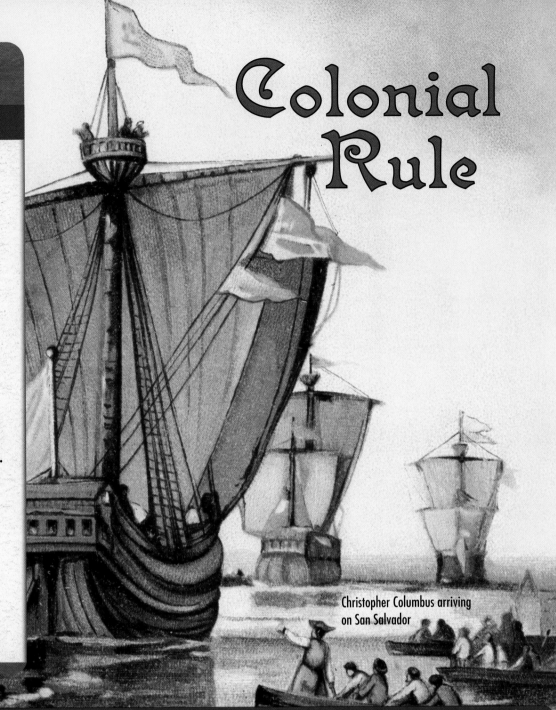

Colonial Rule

Christopher Columbus arriving on San Salvador

Visual Preview

How did Europeans change Latin America?

A Columbus's discovery led Spain and Portugal to claim the Americas.

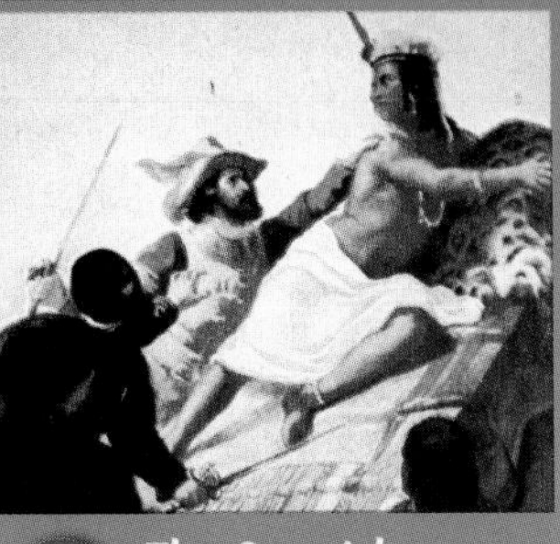

B The Spanish defeated the Aztec and Inca and took control of their empires.

C A global exchange of food and ideas changed the world.

D Spain and several other European countries colonized Latin America.

Ⓐ EUROPEAN CONQUESTS

In the late 1400s and early 1500s, Spanish explorers arrived in Middle America and South America. They were impressed by the magnificent cities and the great riches of Native Americans.

An Italian sailor, Christopher Columbus, asked Spain's rulers to finance his plan to reach Asia by sailing west. In 1492 Columbus first saw land in the Western Hemisphere. It was an island in the Bahamas he called San Salvador. He thought it was Asia. Columbus claimed the lands he saw for Spain. He also traded with people he called "Indians" because he thought he was near India.

Dividing the Americas

Columbus's discovery started a race in Europe to claim land and find riches in the Americas. In 1494 Portugal and Spain signed the Treaty of Tordesillas. The treaty created the **Line of Demarcation**, an imaginary line dividing the Americas. All territory west of the line was Spanish. Territory to the east was Portuguese.

In 1500 Portugal discovered the land that is now Brazil because of a sailing accident. Pedro Cabral was sailing off the coast of Africa when a storm forced his ship off course. His ship reached the eastern coast of South America. Cabral was the first of many Portuguese explorers to reach the Americas in the 1500s.

Columbus's dream of finding a western water route to Asia became a reality with the Portuguese explorer Ferdinand Magellan. In 1519 Magellan led a fleet of five ships for Spain. He thought he could sail around the southern tip of South America and cross the Pacific Ocean to reach Asia. In 1521, after a year and a half at sea, Magellan finished his journey and landed in the Philippines.

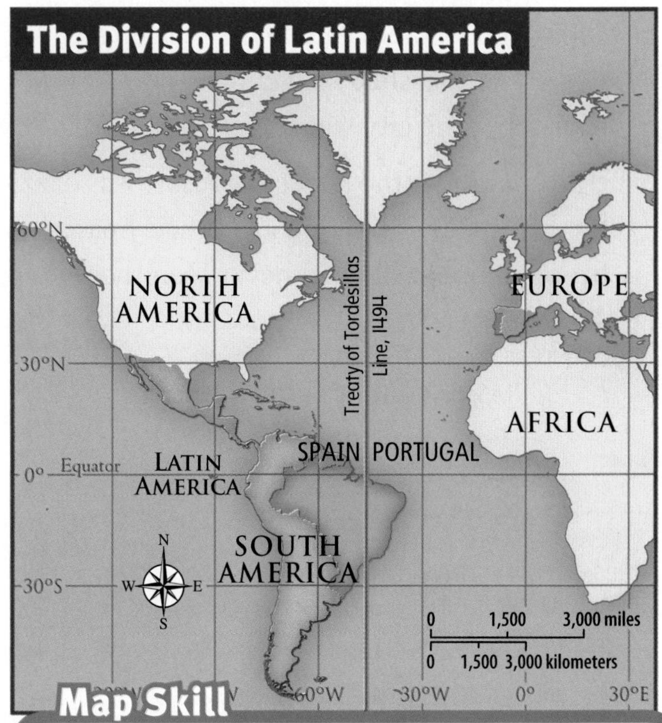

REGION **What part of Latin America was controlled by Portugal?**

Quick Check

Draw Conclusions **Why did Columbus think he could reach Asia by sailing west?**

B CORTÉS AND PIZARRO

While some explorers continued to search for sea routes, others wanted to learn more about the new lands. Hernán Cortés and Francisco Pizarro were two such men.

Cortés and the Aztec

In 1519 Hernán Cortés and an army of about 600 soldiers landed on Mexico's Gulf Coast and marched to Tenochtitlán. They heard that the city was filled with gold.

Moctezuma, the Aztec emperor, was dazzled by the horses, guns, and armor the Spanish had brought along. He had never seen these before. Moctezuma welcomed them into the city, but the Spanish kidnapped him. The emperor was later killed in a riot in Tenochtitlán.

Native Americans who opposed the harsh rule of the Aztec joined the Spanish. Within two years, Cortés's army and allies defeated the Aztec, who had only simple weapons.

However, European diseases eventually killed more Aztec than weapons. One fourth of the Aztec died from smallpox. This weakened the Aztec army and their government and made their empire easy to conquer.

The Spanish defeating the Aztec at Tenochtitlán

The Battle of Cajamarca, where Pizarro defeated the Inca

Pizarro and the Inca

Another Spanish explorer, Francisco Pizarro, wanted the gold and silver of the Inca. In 1532 Pizarro took a small group of Spanish soldiers to South America. The Inca emperor, Atahualpa, had heard about Pizarro's arrival and had planned to meet him. Before this could happen, the Spanish attacked the Inca.

Pizarro captured Atahualpa and held him prisoner for months. Atahualpa offered to fill Pizarro's room with gold in exchange for his freedom. On the same day Atahualpa finished filling the room, Pizarro ordered the Inca emperor killed.

Like the Aztec, the Inca were affected by diseases the Europeans brought. Many of these diseases were new to the Inca people and thus very dangerous. People from all parts of Inca society were affected. Like the Aztec, more Inca were killed by these diseases than by Spanish weapons. Nearly 75 percent of the Inca died from smallpox alone. Weakened by disease, and having lost their leaders, the Inca were conquered within a few years.

Quick Check

Draw Conclusions **What led the Spanish to conquer the Aztec and Inca Empires?**

C THE COLUMBIAN EXCHANGE

As Europe traded with the Americas and other parts of the world, a global exchange of food, animals, people, goods, technology, and even diseases began. Today we call this process the **Columbian Exchange**.

Changes in the Americas

Among all the items included in the Columbian Exchange, horses and diseases changed life in the Americas most. Some of the horses the Spanish brought got away and lived in the wild. They changed the lives of hunter-gatherers, or people who hunt animals and gather plants to eat. Native American groups such as the Plains Indians learned to tame them. Horses made hunting bison easier.

Disease was another European import. Native Americans had never been exposed to smallpox, malaria, yellow fever, and other deadly diseases. Millions of indigenous people caught these diseases from Europeans and died.

Europe and Beyond

Some foods exchanged in this period had an important effect in the countries where they were introduced. Corn, potatoes, sweet potatoes, cassava, peanuts, and beans all have important vitamins, which improved the European diet. These foods were planted in areas where traditional Eastern Hemisphere crops could not be grown as easily or at all.

Once American foods gained acceptance in other regions of the world, they quickly spread. The Columbian Exchange led to increased food production in many countries in Africa, Asia, and Europe. As a result, populations across the Eastern Hemisphere grew.

Ireland offers a dramatic example. Its population more than doubled between the mid-1700s and the mid-1800s, in large part because the Irish people came to rely on the potato as their chief food.

Quick Check

Draw Conclusions **How did the Columbian Exchange affect countries in the Western Hemisphere?**

The Columbian Exchange

From the Americas

- Pumpkins
- Chocolate
- Peanuts
- Turkeys
- Potatoes
- Beans
- Corn
- Pineapples

To the Americas

- Wheat
- Rice
- Bananas
- Sugar
- Coffee
- Oranges
- Horses
- Cattle
- Sheep

D COLONIAL LATIN AMERICA

As a result of the Aztec and Inca conquests, Spain was able to build an empire that included much of South America, the Caribbean, Central America, and parts of what is now the United States. Other European countries seized other parts of the Americas. Portugal became the colonial ruler of what is today Brazil. France, Britain, and the Netherlands took control of some Caribbean islands and parts of North America.

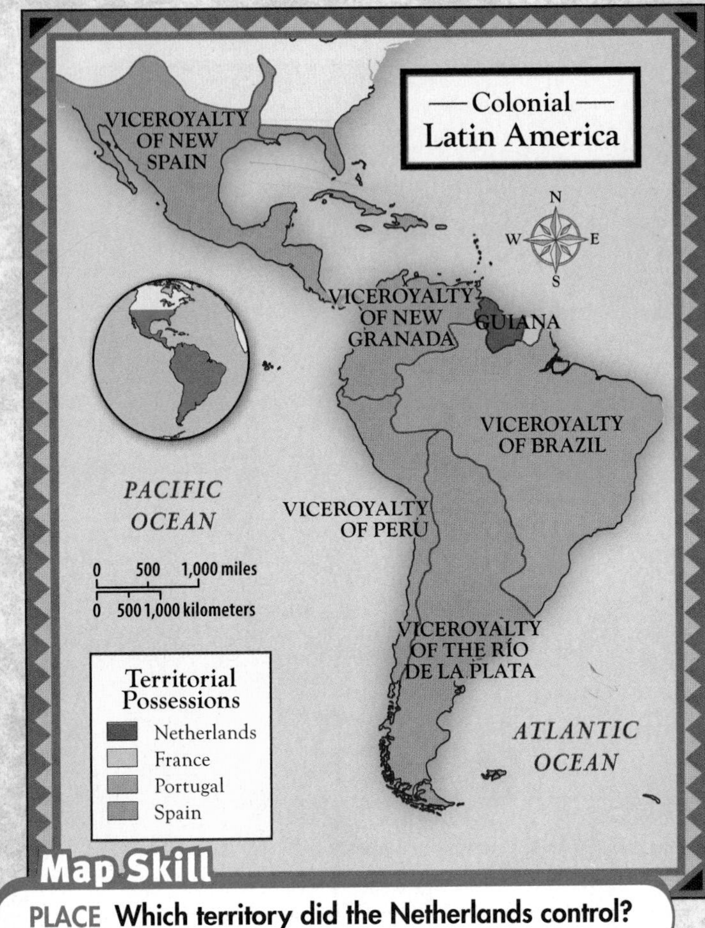

Map Skill

PLACE Which territory did the Netherlands control?

Viceroyalties

To help him govern the Latin American colonies, the Spanish king divided them into divisions called viceroyalties. During the early 1500s, there were two viceroyalties, the Viceroyalty of New Spain and the Viceroyalty of Peru. In the 1700s, the viceroyalties of New Granada and Río de la Plata were carved out of the Viceroyalty of Peru.

Wealthy Mexican hacienda owners with their overseers

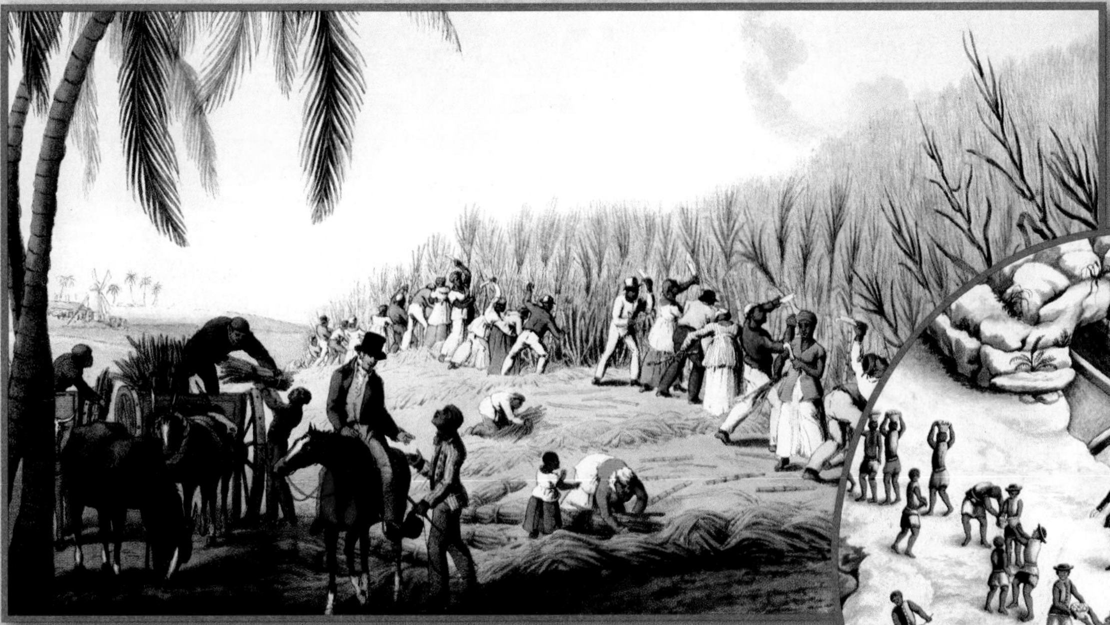

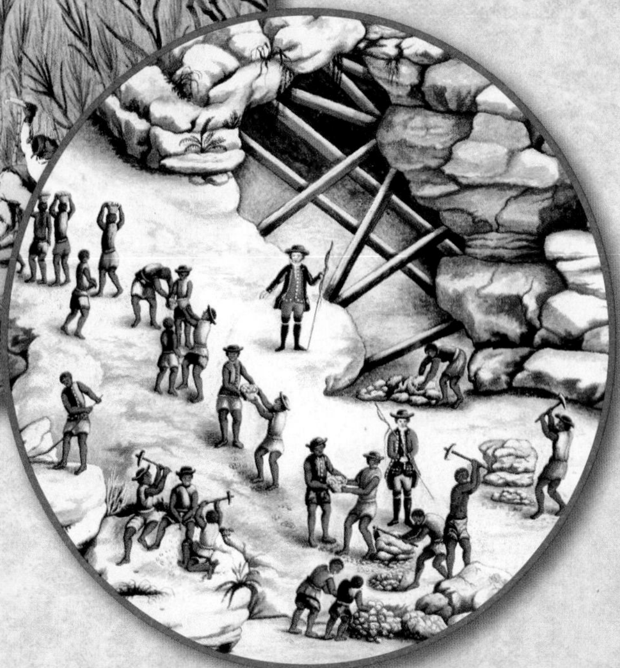

Enslaved Africans cutting sugarcane in Antigua, 1823 (above), and a diamond mine in Brazil (right)

A New Way of Life

Colonists greatly changed the way Native Americans lived. Spanish rulers gave **encomiendas**, or large areas of land, to Spanish colonists. Encomiendas included all of the Native Americans living on the land. Europeans spread Christianity among Native Americans. They also used Native Americans as enslaved workers to grow **cash crops**, or farm products grown for export.

When diseases greatly reduced the numbers of Native Americans, European landowners brought enslaved Africans to work on large farms called **plantations**. A busy trade eventually resulted. Ships carried enslaved people from Africa and manufactured goods from Europe to the Americas. Products such as sugar, cotton, tobacco, gold, and silver, went from the Americas to Europe.

Quick Check

Draw Conclusions **What effects did Europeans have on Native Americans?**

Check Understanding

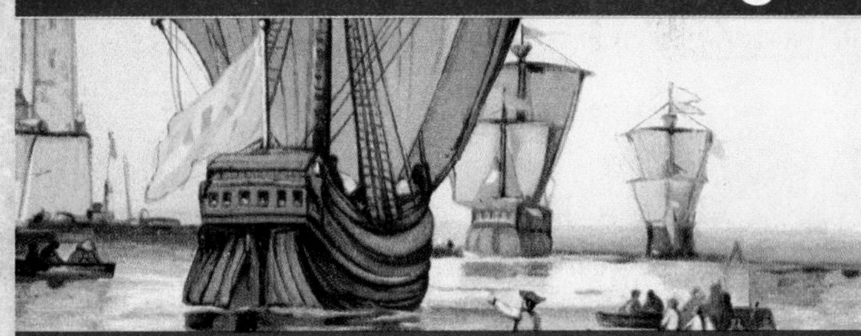

1. **VOCABULARY** Write about colonial Latin America using the following words.

   cash crop **plantation**

2. **READING SKILLS** Draw Conclusions Use your chart from page 104 to write about European conquests in Latin America.

Text Clues	Conclusion

EXPLORE The Big Idea

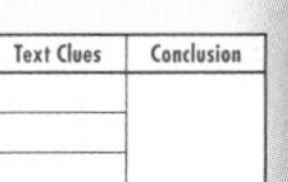

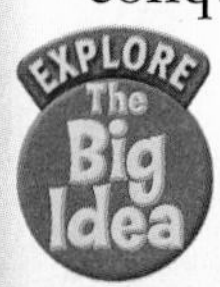

3. **Write About It** Write about how civilizations changed in Latin America after Europeans arrived.

Lesson 5

VOCABULARY

mestizo p. 114

decree p. 117

READING SKILLS

Draw Conclusions

Copy the chart below. As you read, use it to draw a conclusion about Mexico's struggle for independence from Spain.

Text Clues	Conclusion

STANDARDS FOCUS

SOCIAL STUDIES — Power, Authority, and Governance

GEOGRAPHY — Human Systems

Forming New Nations

A bronze statue of Simón Bolívar

Visual Preview

How did the idea of independence spread across Latin America?

A L'Ouverture led Latin America's first successful fight for independence.

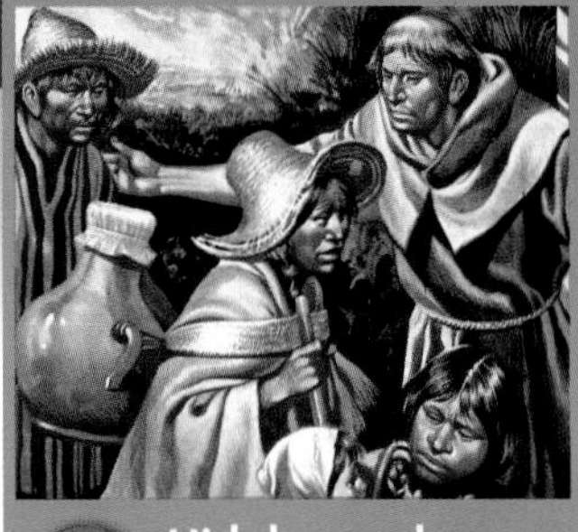

B Hidalgo and Morelos inspired the fight for Mexico's freedom.

C Many of South America's colonies defeated Spain to gain their independence.

D Bolívar and San Martín fought for independence in Peru.

Ⓐ REVOLUTION IN HAITI

Enslaved Africans and Native Americans had been kidnapped, separated from their families, forced to work, and punished harshly. In Haiti, enslaved people decided to fight for their freedom.

In the late 1700s, revolutions in the United States and France inspired the people of Latin America to fight for their independence. While European colonists called for self-rule, Native Americans and Africans wanted to be free from slavery.

The End of Slavery

The first successful revolt of enslaved persons broke out in the French colony of Haiti. In August 1791, enslaved Africans attacked their owners, shouting, "Better to die than be slaves." Two months later, 1,000 people were dead and 180 plantations had become mounds of ashes.

Toussaint L'Ouverture, a Haitian soldier, shaped 100,000 rebels into a strong army. This army conquered all of Hispaniola. The army also named L'Ouverture its ruler. His first act was to emancipate, or free, all enslaved islanders. When the ruler of France, Napoleon Bonaparte, heard the news, he was furious.

In 1802 Napoleon sent a large force of French troops to Hispaniola. However, the Haitians fought back. In 1804 Napoleon's forces were defeated. Haiti became the first colony in Latin America to gain independence.

After Haiti, a movement to end slavery began to spread across Europe. Between 1833 and 1863, Great Britain, France, and the Netherlands all ended slavery.

QUICK CHECK

Draw Conclusions **Why did the Haitians defeat Napoleon?**

Toussaint L'Ouverture

B FREEDOM FOR MEXICO

Under Spanish rule, it was illegal to grow olives and grapes in Mexico. Spain wanted Mexicans to buy only olives and grapes grown in Spain. Many felt Spanish laws kept Native American and **mestizo** farmers in a life of poverty. A mestizo is a person of mixed Spanish and Native American heritage.

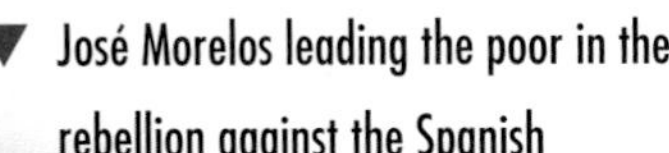

▼ José Morelos leading the poor in the rebellion against the Spanish

Miguel Hidalgo

In 1803 a Catholic priest called Miguel Hidalgo was assigned to a church in Dolores. Dolores was a very poor village in central Mexico. Hidalgo tried to help the farmers by teaching them to grow olives and grapes. Officials chopped down the new olive trees and grapevines. Hidalgo was shocked. He felt that the only way to help his people was to end Spanish control of Mexico. He decided to organize a march, but first he gave a speech:

> Come march with us for country and religion. . . .
>
> —MIGUEL HIDALGO

The Cry of Dolores

On September 16, 1810, church bells rang in the village of Dolores. Hidalgo told the crowd his people had been in bondage for 300 years.

His speech, known as the "Cry of Dolores," was the beginning of the Mexican War for Independence. Eight hundred men, women, and children followed Hidalgo out of the village on the way to Mexico City.

When they reached Mexico City, their rebel army had grown to 80,000. But the rebels were poorly armed and lacked training. A force of 7,000 Spanish soldiers attacked and scattered Hidalgo's army. In 1811 Hidalgo was captured and later killed.

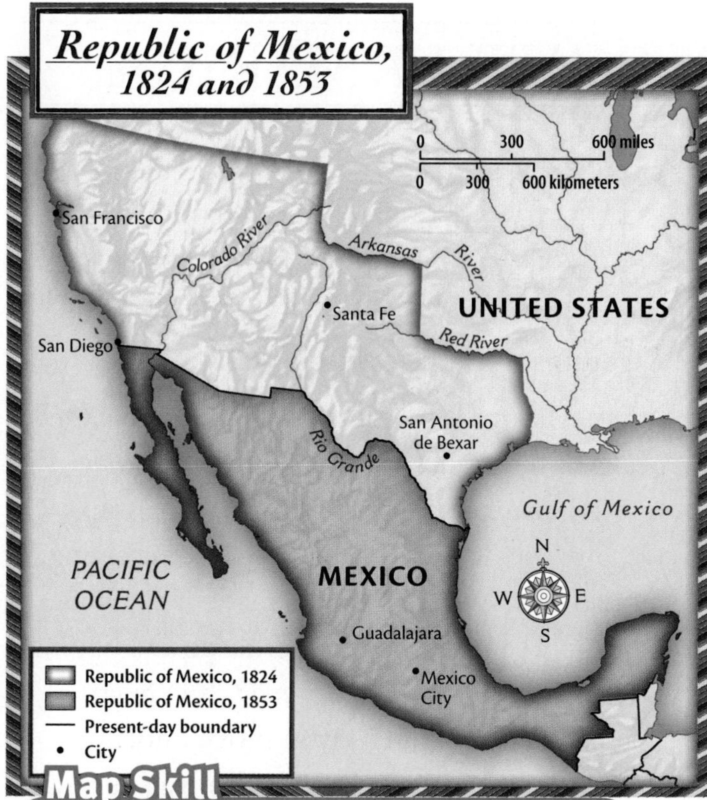

Map Skill

HUMAN INTERACTION **About how much land did Mexico lose between 1824 and 1853?**

▲ José Morelos

Morelos and Iturbide

After Hidalgo's death, José Morelos, a mestizo priest, continued to lead the struggle for independence. Morelos became a skillful leader. Still, the well-armed Spanish troops finally exhausted the rebels. Morelos was captured and killed.

Small bands of rebels continued to make scattered raids on the Spanish troops. A creole officer, Agustín de Iturbide, was assigned to defeat the rebellion. Creoles were descendants of the Spanish and Portuguese settlers and often owned huge farms. Iturbide decided to support the rebels as a way to gain power. In August 1821, Iturbide's troops surrounded the Spanish viceroy and forced him to sign a plan for independence.

Iturbide also wanted control of Central America. On September 15, 1821, Central America declared independence from Spain and became part of Mexico. However, Iturbide ruled poorly and was driven from power. Mexico became a republic in 1823. Central America became the United Provinces of Central America. By 1840 this union had fallen apart, creating Guatemala, Honduras, Nicaragua, El Salvador, and Costa Rica.

Quick Check

Draw Conclusions **Why did Spain assign Iturbide to defeat the rebellion?**

EVENT

Cinco de Mayo celebrates Mexico's victory over the French on May 5, 1862. In the Battle of Puebla, Mexico's force of 4,500 men faced 6,000 men of Napoleon III's well-trained French army.

Cinco de Mayo

C INDEPENDENCE IN SOUTH AMERICA

By 1808 people in the northern part of South America began a revolt against Spain.

Simon Bolívar

Simón Bolívar led the fight for independence in Venezuela. An earthquake in 1812 forced him out of the country, but Bolívar was determined to continue the fight against Spanish rule. By 1813 he had freed most of Venezuela, and a year later, he had freed Bogotá, the capital of Colombia. By 1819 nearly all of northern South America had been set free. The nations of Colombia, Venezuela, and Ecuador joined together in 1821 as Gran Colombia, and Bolívar was named president.

José de San Martín

In the meantime, José de San Martín, a former Spanish officer, led the fight in the south. In 1816 he defeated Spanish forces in Argentina. Next he turned to Chile.

San Martín knew crossing the snow-covered peaks of the Andes would be difficult, so he trained his troops to survive great hardship. Despite the dangers of the mountain crossing, most of San Martín's troops made it to Chile. They joined rebels led by Bernardo O'Higgins. By 1818 these forces had freed Chile from Spanish control. San Martín moved north to Peru, where he hoped to meet Bolívar's army.

Bolívar defeats the Spanish in the Battle of Araure, 1813

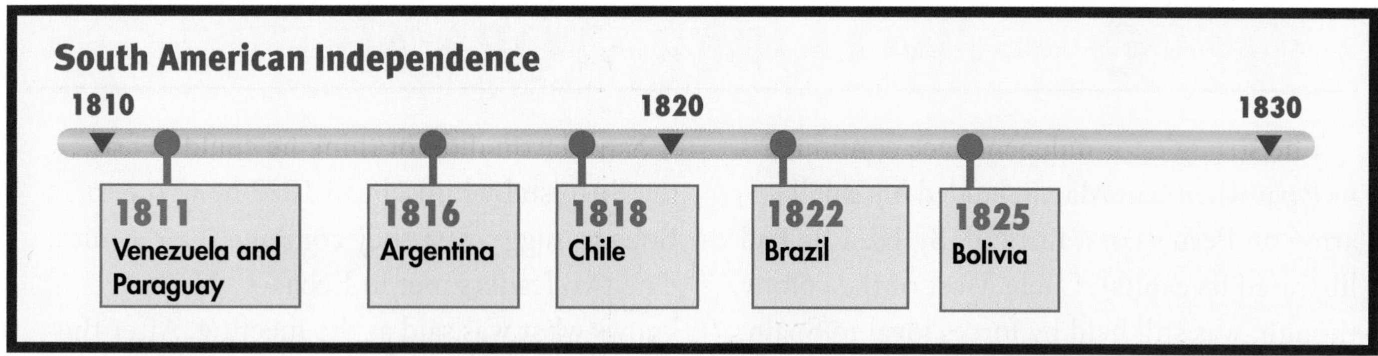

Independence for Brazil

When Napoleon invaded Portugal in 1807, the Portuguese king, John VI, set sail for Brazil. King John was popular in Brazil. He opened Brazilian ports to all countries and built libraries and schools. Then he issued a **decree**, or royal command, making Brazil part of Portugal rather than a colony.

After Napoleon was defeated, King John returned to Portugal. He left his son, Pedro, in charge of Brazil. Trouble soon broke out between Portugal and Brazil. Portuguese leaders wanted Brazil to be a colony again, not a part of Portugal. Brazilian leaders passsed laws to end many of the improvements King John had made.

People in Brazil wanted Pedro to declare independence from Portugal. In 1822 Pedro called an assembly and declared independence. He called himself Emperor Pedro I of Brazil.

The Last Emperor

The people of Brazil soon found Emperor Pedro I to be a harsh ruler. He made many enemies. In 1831 the emperor was forced to give up his throne and leave Brazil. His 5-year-old son became Emperor Pedro II.

Emperor Pedro II was a much wiser ruler than his father. He ruled Brazil for 50 years and helped it grow into a strong nation.

Brazil was a rich agricultural country, with sugar and coffee as its two leading exports. Both crops were grown on large plantations using enslaved Africans. Pedro II wanted to end slavery, but the plantation owners were the most powerful group in Brazil.

The emperor first approved laws that freed enslaved children and people over the age of 60. Then, in 1888, the General Assembly passed a bill freeing all enslaved people.

The plantation owners were angry because they were not paid for the people who were freed from slavery. They blamed Pedro II for the end of slavery. With the landowners' support, the army rebelled against the emperor and declared Brazil a republic.

Quick Check

Draw Conclusions **Why did Brazil have many enslaved people?**

PEOPLE

Emperor **Pedro II** was widely respected by Brazilians of all social levels. He was known to be bright, level-headed, and moderate. Pedro II spent his final year in Portugal, but his remains were returned to Brazil in 1939 for burial.

Pedro II

Ⓓ TWO LIBERATORS MEET

The struggle for independence continued in Peru when San Martín landed his small army on Peru's coast in 1820. By 1821 he had liberated its capital, Lima. Most of the colony, though, was still held by forces loyal to Spain.

Primary Sources

On August 10, 1819, Simón Bolívar issued a proclamation to the people of Colombia:

"Venezuela marches with me to free you, as in past years you marched with me to free Venezuela....The sun will not have completed the course of its present round through the heavens without beholding in all your territory the proud altars of liberty!"

Write About It The year is 1819 and you have just read Bolívar's proclamation. Write a letter to a friend explaining how you feel about independence from Spain.

San Martín did not think he could defeat the Spanish by himself. In 1822 he wrote to Bolívar, suggesting they combine their armies. The two leaders met in Ecuador. No one knows what was said at the meeting. After the meeting, San Martin gave command to Bolívar. On December 9, 1824, this new army met Spanish troops near Ayachucho, Peru. Even though the Spanish army was larger, Bolívar's army achieved a quick victory. Spanish troops left Peru within weeks.

Quick Check

Draw Conclusions **Why do you think San Martín gave up command of his troops?**

Check Understanding

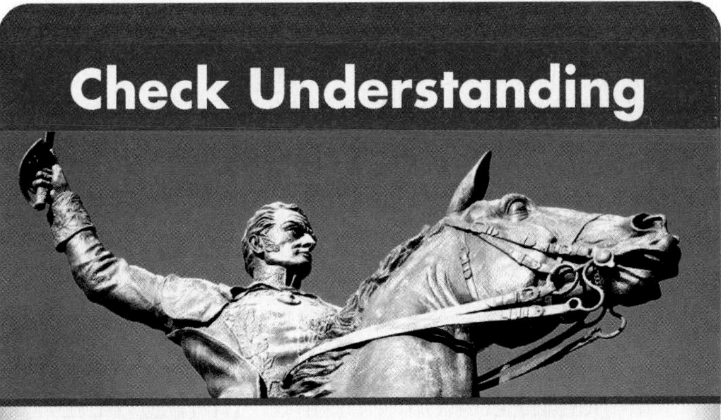

1. **VOCABULARY** Write a sentence for each of the following words.

   mestizo **decree**

2. **READING SKILLS** Draw Conclusions Use your chart from page 112 to describe Mexico's fight for independence.

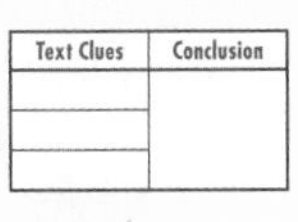

3. **Write About It** Write about why the colonies of Latin America wanted independence from Spain.

Map and Globe Skills

Use a Battle Map

VOCABULARY

battle map

One way to learn about historical battles is to explore a **battle map**. A battle map shows important places, events, and troop movements during a battle. The map on this page explains the Battle of Chacabuco. By looking at a battle map, you can better understand details from your reading. The map on this page has several features that tell you that it is a battle map.

Learn It

- Look at the map key, or legend. It tells the meaning of the symbols on the map. On this map, the red line shows San Martín's route to Chacabuco. The blue soldier represents Martín's troops. The red soldier represents Spanish troops.
- Look for a scale to find out how far troops traveled. Look at the compass rose to tell you in which direction they moved.

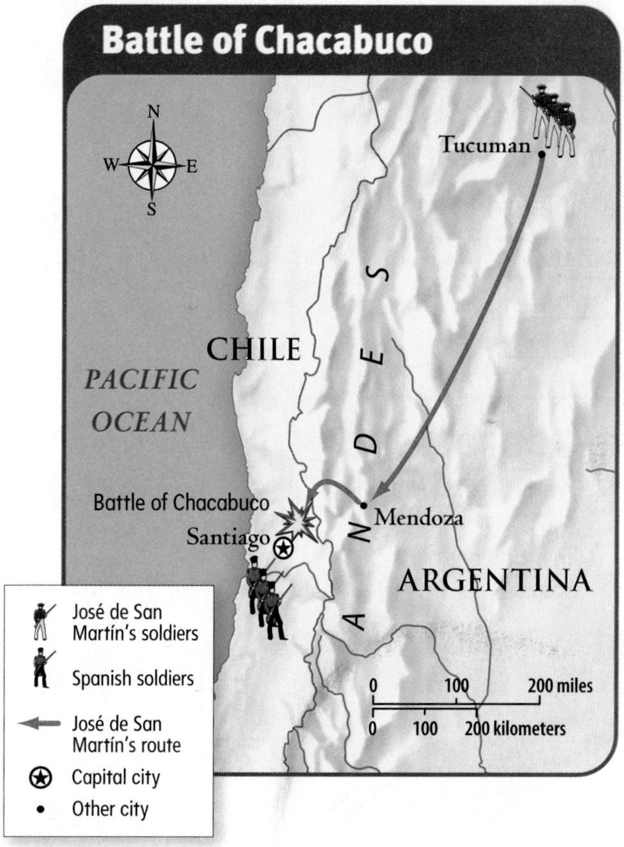

Battle of Chacabuco

Try It

- What direction is Chacabuco from Santiago?
- How far did the troops have to travel?

Apply It

- What information can you get from a battle map that is not in the text?
- What have you learned about the Battle of Chacabuco from the map?

Lesson 6

Political and Economic Challenges

VOCABULARY

dictator p. 121
caudillo p. 121
communism p. 124
command economy p. 124
socialism p. 125

READING SKILL

Draw Conclusions

Copy the the chart below and use it to draw conclusions about recent Latin American history.

Text Clues	Conclusion

STANDARDS FOCUS

SOCIAL STUDIES Production, Distribution, and Consumption

GEOGRAPHY Environment and Society

A Jamaican banana plantation

Visual Preview

How did Latin America change after colonial rule ended?

A Economic growth benefited some, but others stayed poor.

B Exports are growing, but economic expansion brings challenges.

C Castro led a revolution, and other countries became more democratic.

A INDEPENDENCE AND CONFLICT

Although Spanish South America was now independent, life there continued with only few changes. A small group of creoles controlled the land and the wealth in the new countries.

Each of the nations of Latin America has its own history. However, they all have faced many similar problems since gaining their independence. Latin American nations hoped their countries would become democracies. Instead, many were ruled by **dictators**, or leaders with complete power over a country.

The Rise of Dictators

One major problem was frequent political conflicts. Individual countries fought over boundary lines. Tensions also developed between the rich and the poor.

Meanwhile, strong leaders known as **caudillos** made it difficult for democracy to develop. Caudillos were usually rich men, supported by the upper class. They often ruled as dictators. Some built roads, schools, and new cities. Many, however, favored the wealthy over the poor.

In order for a dictator to maintain control, he usually had to control the army. Dictators used the army to put down opposition. If a dictator lost control of the army, he could sometimes be removed from power.

The Economy Grows

In the late 1800s, events throughout the world brought other changes to Latin America. The growth of industry in Europe and the United States created new demands for South America's natural resources. These demands expanded economies throughout Latin America.

Over time, old colonial seaports, such as Rio de Janeiro in Brazil, and Buenos Aires in Argentina, grew into booming centers of trade. These bustling cities were home to a new and growing middle class.

Quick Check

Draw Conclusions Why were many leaders in Latin America rich dictators?

The busy port of Valparaiso, Chile

B LATIN AMERICA AND THE WORLD

The United States and other industrial countries began to demand more Latin American products. Businesspeople from these countries set up companies in Latin America to export products such as bananas, sugar, coffee, copper, and oil.

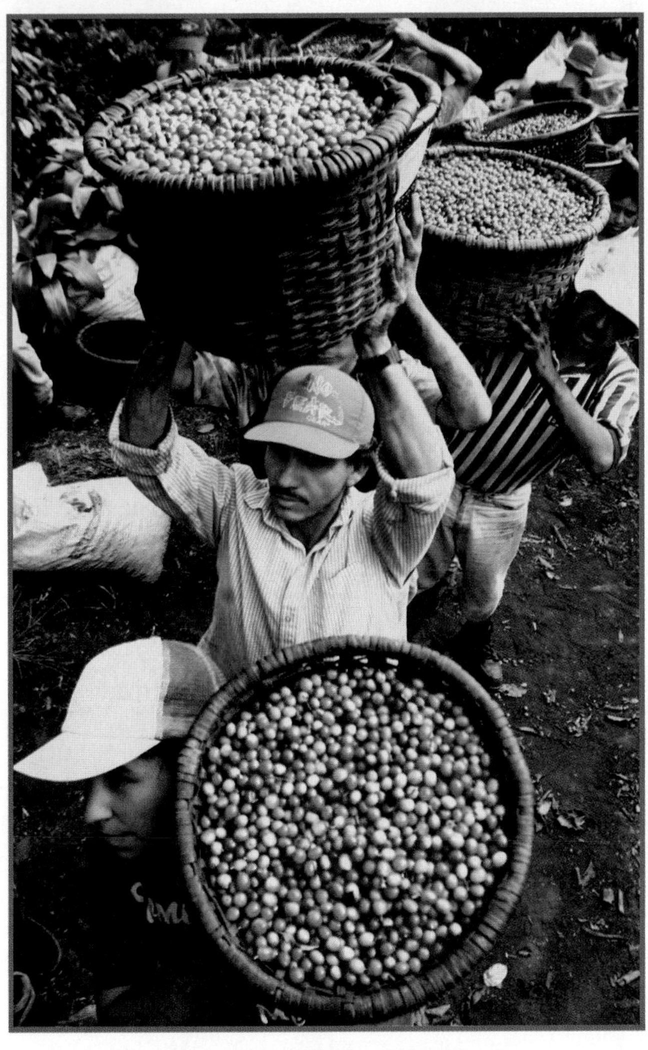

▲ Costa Rican workers wait in line to measure baskets of freshly harvested coffee.

Rising Exports

As the number of Latin American exports grew, many countries began to grow only one or two products. These exports created income for Latin America, but they could also cause problems. If the price or demand for a product dropped by a large amount, that change could seriously hurt a country that grew a lot of that product. Large price drops were often followed by losses in jobs and incomes. Usually, the people most hurt by economic problems were the poor.

Latin American exports did bring some benefits. Foreign investors built ports, roads, and railroads. Cities increased in size and population, and a middle class of lawyers, teachers, and businesspeople grew.

SHARE OF MAJOR LATIN AMERICAN EXPORTS, 2005

MEXICO 40.9%	Petroleum and petroleum products, vehicles, engines, cotton, machinery, coffee, fish, fertilizers, and minerals
BRAZIL 22.6%	Iron ore, coffee, fruits, timber, sugar, vehicles, and beef
VENEZUELA 10.6%	Coffee, oil, iron ore, textiles, fruits, and aluminum
ARGENTINA 7.7%	Wheat, corn, rice, meat, hides, and wool
CHILE 7.6%	Copper, iron, fruits, and wood pulp
COLOMBIA 4.1%	Coffee, emeralds, petroleum, coal, flowers, and meat
PERU 3.1%	Copper, lead, fish products, iron, zinc, oil, coffee, llama and alpaca wool, cotton, and sugar

The Spanish-American War

By the 1890s, Spain had only two colonies in the Western Hemisphere—the Caribbean islands of Puerto Rico and Cuba. In 1895 the people of Cuba began a revolt against their colonial government. Thousands of Cubans were jailed or killed by Spanish troops.

"Remember the Maine"

In January 1898, U.S. President William McKinley sent the battleship USS *Maine* to Havana, Cuba, to protect Americans there. On February 15, an explosion sank the *Maine* and killed 260 United States sailors. There was no proof that Spain was involved, but many Americans blamed Spain for the sinking. "Remember the Maine" became the country's battle cry. A few weeks later, on April 25, 1898, the U.S. Congress declared war against Spain.

The U.S. Navy defeated Spain's ships near Cuba. On July 1, 1898, Theodore Roosevelt led a charge against the Spanish in Puerto Rico called the Battle of San Juan Hill. Roosevelt's troops were victorious. U.S. battleships also sailed to the Spanish colony of the Philippines and destroyed a Spanish fleet there.

In August 1898, the Spanish-American War was over. The treaty that ended the war gave Cuba its independence from Spain. The United States gained control of Puerto Rico and the Spanish colonies of Guam and the Philippines in the Pacific Ocean. In 1946 the Philippines gained independence from the United States. Guam and Puerto Rico are part of the United States today.

Quick Check

Draw Conclusions **Why did the United States go to war with Spain?**

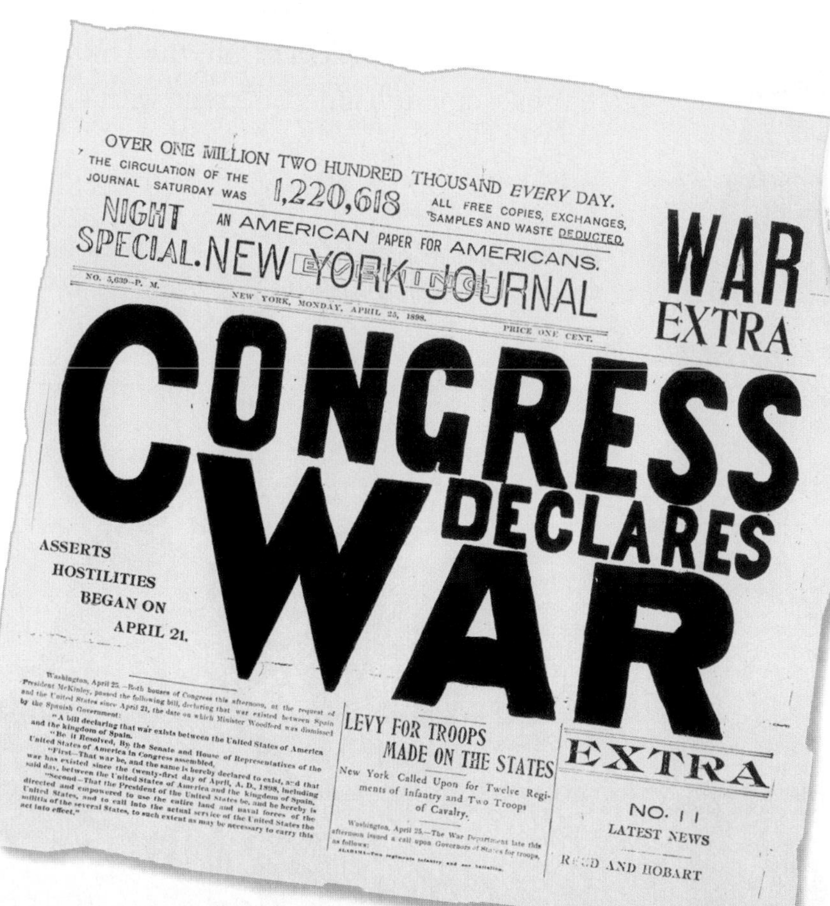

OVER ONE MILLION TWO HUNDRED THOUSAND EVERY DAY.

THE CIRCULATION OF THE JOURNAL SATURDAY WAS 1,220,618 ALL FREE COPIES, EXCHANGES, SAMPLES AND WASTE DEDUCTED.

NIGHT SPECIAL. AN AMERICAN PAPER FOR AMERICANS.

NEW YORK JOURNAL

WAR EXTRA

NEW YORK, MONDAY, APRIL 25, 1898. PRICE ONE CENT.

CONGRESS DECLARES WAR

ASSERTS HOSTILITIES BEGAN ON APRIL 21.

Washington, April 25.—Both houses of Congress this afternoon, at the request of President McKinley, passed the following bill, declaring that war existed between Spain and the United States since April 21, the date on which Minister Woodford was dismissed by the Spanish Government:

"A bill declaring that war exists between the United States of America and the kingdom of Spain.

"Be it Resolved, By the Senate and House of Representatives of the United States of America in Congress assembled,

"First—That war be, and the same is hereby declared to exist, and that war has existed since the twenty-first day of April, A. D., 1898, including said day, between the United States of America and the kingdom of Spain.

"Second—That the President of the United States be, and he hereby is directed and empowered to use the entire land and naval forces of the United States, and to call into the actual service of the United States the militia of the several States, to such extent as may be necessary to carry this act into effect."

LEVY FOR TROOPS MADE ON THE STATES

New York Called Upon for Twelve Regiments of Infantry and Two Troops of Cavalry.

Washington, April 25.—The War Department late this afternoon issued a call upon Governors of States for troops, as follows:

EXTRA

NO. 11

LATEST NEWS

REED AND HOBART

Newspaper announcing the Spanish-American War (left), and a button asking citizens to remember the USS *Maine* (above)

C MODERN TIMES

After the Spanish-American War, large businesses quickly became important to the economies of Cuba and Puerto Rico. They bought up the best land to plant sugarcane. By the 1950s, companies had gained control of more than 75 percent of Cuba's farmland.

Struggling Economies

Similar to Cuba, the economies of many other parts of Latin America were controlled by a small number of people. Owners of big businesses made profits, but they often did not share the wealth with farmers and factory workers. Poverty was widespread throughout most of Latin America. To aid their countries, Latin American leaders often borrowed large amounts of money from the United States and other countries. These debts seriously weakened Latin American economies. Prices rose, wages fell, and people lost jobs.

Fidel Castro

Many leaders in Latin America were ruthless. In some countries, people rebelled against these leaders. In 1959 a young lawyer named Fidel Castro led a revolution in Cuba. He set up a system of government based on **communism**. People under communist rule have limited rights to own property. Under communism, the entire economy of a country is controlled by the central government. This is called a **command economy**.

In 1960 Castro ended free elections and began to nationalize United States companies in Cuba. To nationalize means to place formerly private property under the control or ownership of the government. Many people in the United States were angry that they were not paid for this property. They were also concerned about Castro's ties to other communist countries. As a result, the United States government banned all trade with Cuba.

Fidel Castro led a revolution in Cuba and set up a communist government.

▲ In 2006 Michelle Bachelet became the first woman elected president of Chile.

Allende and Pinochet

By 1970, changes were also taking place in Chile. Salvador Allende was elected president of Chile in 1970. Allende believed that **socialism** would help solve many of Chile's problems. Under socialism, major businesses, factories, and farms are owned and run by the government, rather than by individuals. Allende was the first socialist to be democratically elected to lead a country in the Western Hemisphere.

Allende nationalized some of Chile's industries and large farms. However, the people in Chile and the United States who lost land and businesses did not approve of those changes. In 1973 the United States helped one of the top generals in Chile's army named Augusto Pinochet take control of the country by force. After this short revolt, Pinochet became dictator of Chile.

A Return to Democracy

By the 1980s, the people of Latin America began to demand a return to democracy. In many countries, the dictators were forced to give up control to elected leaders. For example, elections in 1989 toppled the rule of Augusto Pinochet in Chile. In some countries, one political party had controlled the government for so long, that it was no longer effective. In the early 2000s, angry voters in Venezuela, Bolivia, Peru, Mexico, and Chile elected new leaders. These leaders promised sweeping changes that would treat the poor more fairly.

Quick Check

Draw Conclusions **Why did the people of Latin America demand a return to democracy?**

Check Understanding

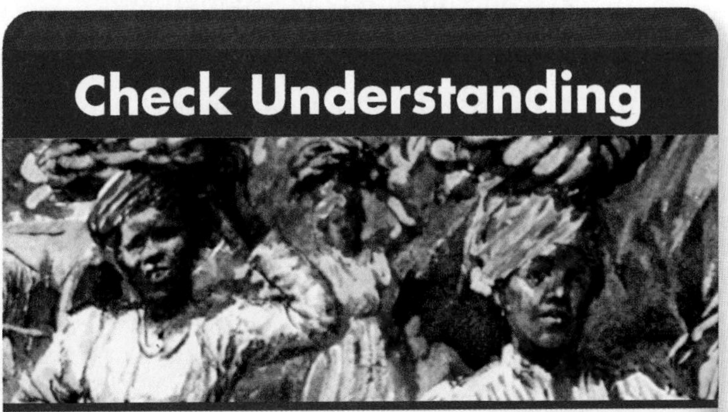

1. **VOCABULARY** Write about Cuba and Chile using the following words.

   communism **socialism**

2. **READING SKILLS** Draw Conclusions Use your chart from page 120 to write about recent Latin American history.

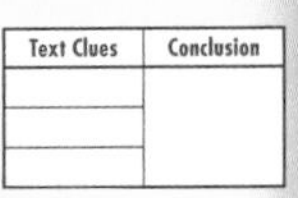

3. **Write About It** Write about why Latin America changed during the 20th century.

Unit 3 Review and Assess

Vocabulary

Number a paper from 1 to 4. Beside each number write the word from the list below that matches the description.

altitude **mestizo**
plantation **communism**

1. a system where the economy is controlled by a central government
2. a person of mixed Spanish and Native American heritage
3. the height above sea level
4. a large farm that grows cash crops

Comprehension and Critical Thinking

5. Why did the Olmec culture spread to other parts of Mexico and Central America?
6. Name two major landforms of Latin America.
7. **Reading Skill** What caused colonial governments to fall in South America?
8. **Critical Thinking** Why did the U.S. Congress declare war on Spain?

Skill

Use a Battle Map

Write a complete sentence to answer each question.

9. What mountains did San Martín cross?
10. In which country is Tucuman?

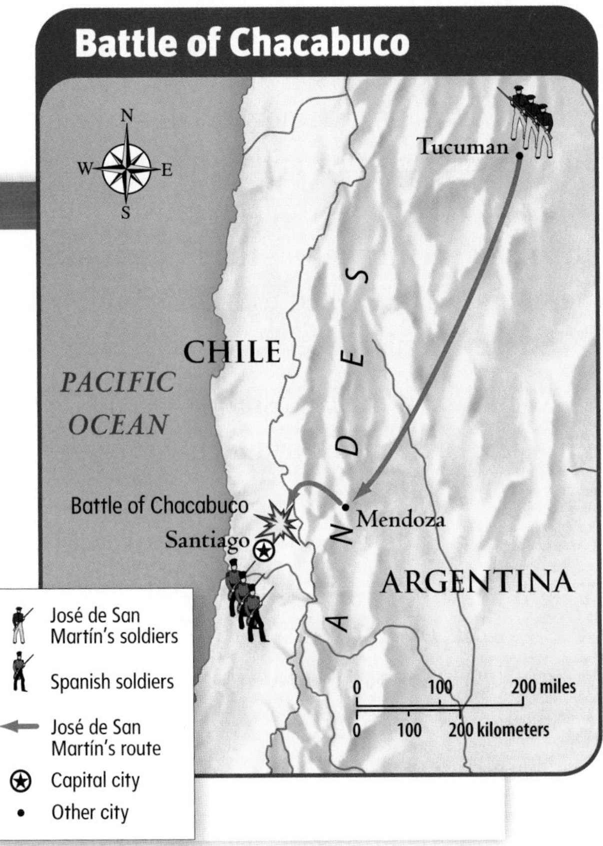

Test Preparation

Look at the time line. Then answer the questions.

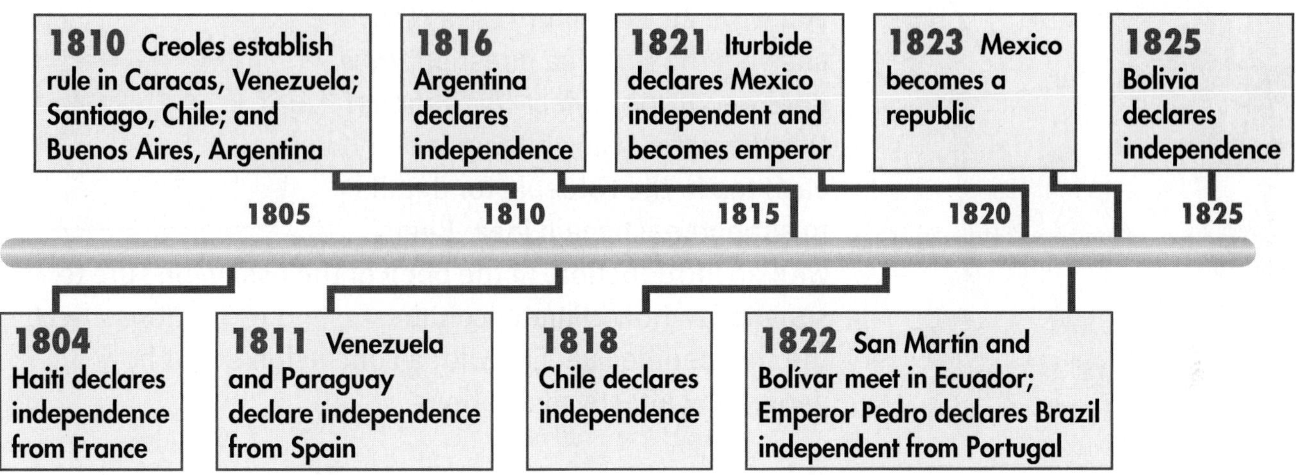
1810 Creoles establish rule in Caracas, Venezuela; Santiago, Chile; and Buenos Aires, Argentina
1816 Argentina declares independence
1821 Iturbide declares Mexico independent and becomes emperor
1823 Mexico becomes a republic
1825 Bolivia declares independence
1805
1810
1815
1820
1825
1804 Haiti declares independence from France
1811 Venezuela and Paraguay declare independence from Spain
1818 Chile declares independence
1822 San Martín and Bolívar meet in Ecuador; Emperor Pedro declares Brazil independent from Portugal

1 In which year did Chile declare independence?

A 1804
B 1810
C 1811
D 1818

2 Based on the information provided by this time line, which statement is true?

A Argentina declared its independence after Paraguay.
B Haiti declared its independence after Chile.
C Brazil declared its independence before Mexico.
D Bolivia declared its independence before Venezuela.

3 The first Latin American nation to declare independence was ruled by which country?

A Spain
B France
C England
D Portugal

4 Which nation was the first to declare independence?

5 What happened in Mexico after Iturbide became emperor?

The Big Idea Activities

Write About the Big Idea

An Expository Essay

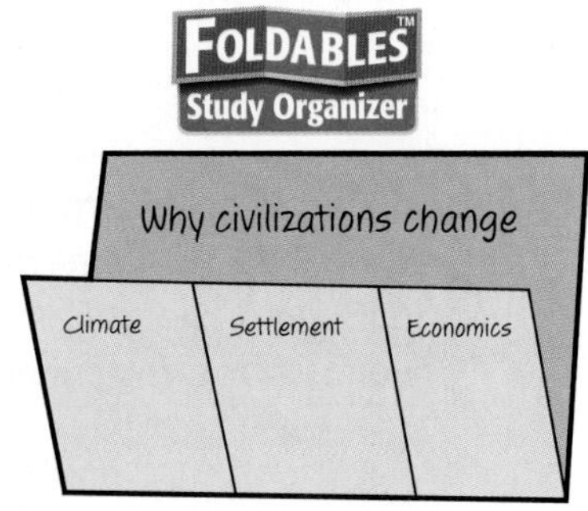

Use the Unit 3 Foldable to help you write an expository essay that answers the Big Idea question, *How does geography affect civilizations?* Use the notes you wrote under each tab in the Foldable for details to support each main idea. Begin with an introduction. In the body of the essay, be sure to summarize how climate, conquests, and revolutions affect the way people live. End with a conclusion about how geography affects civilizations.

Make a Photo Collage

Work individually to make a photo collage of the Columbian Exchange. Here's how to make your collage:

1. Study the examples on pages 108–109 of food and animals that made up the Columbian Exchange.
2. Choose one example, and use magazines, newspapers, or the Internet to find photos of that food or animal.
3. Make a photo collage of the ways that food or animal is used today.

When you finish your collage, present it to your class. Discuss what you have learned about the food or animal you chose.

LATIN AMERICA TODAY

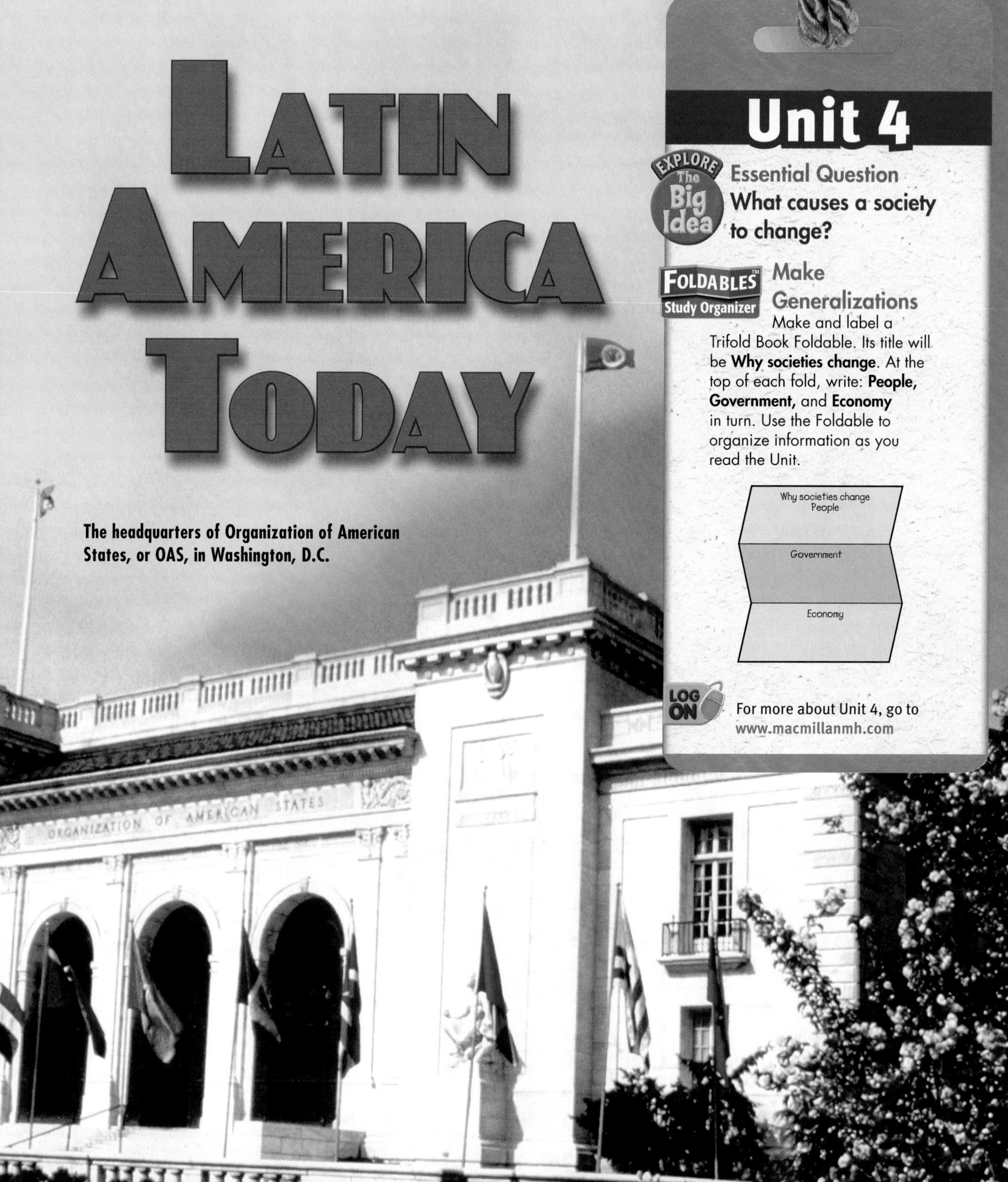

The headquarters of Organization of American States, or OAS, in Washington, D.C.

Unit 4

EXPLORE The Big Idea

Essential Question
What causes a society to change?

FOLDABLES™ Study Organizer

Make Generalizations

Make and label a Trifold Book Foldable. Its title will be **Why societies change**. At the top of each fold, write: **People, Government,** and **Economy** in turn. Use the Foldable to organize information as you read the Unit.

Why societies change
People

Government

Economy

LOG ON For more about Unit 4, go to **www.macmillanmh.com**

PEOPLE, PLACES, AND EVENTS

Luis Muñoz Marín

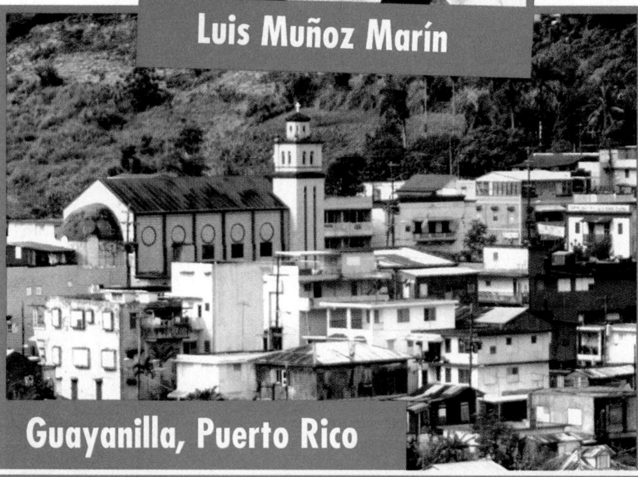

Guayanilla, Puerto Rico

Eva Perón

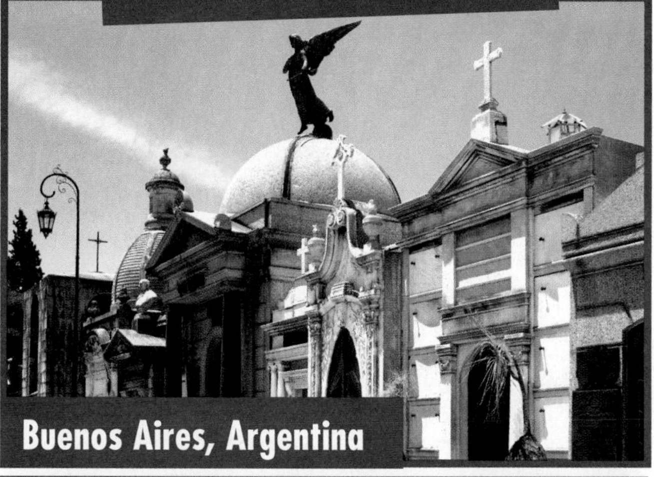

Buenos Aires, Argentina

1950 | Luis Muñoz Marín launches "Operation Bootstrap" in Puerto Rico.

1952 | Eva Perón, first lady of Argentina, dies at age 33.

1950 — 1960 — 1970

Under the leadership of Governor **Luis Muñoz Marín,** Puerto Rico industrialized rapidly.

Today visitors at **Guayanilla**, **Puerto Rico**, can see a monument dedicated to him in the Plaza de Recreo Luis Muñoz Marín.

Argentina's first lady **Eva Perón** was loved for her work helping the poor. July 26, 1952, the day she died, was a day of national mourning.

Today Perón's tomb is in the La Recoleta Cemetery in **Buenos Aires**, **Argentina**.

LOG ON For more about People, Places, and Events, visit www.macmillanmh.com

Rigoberta Menchu

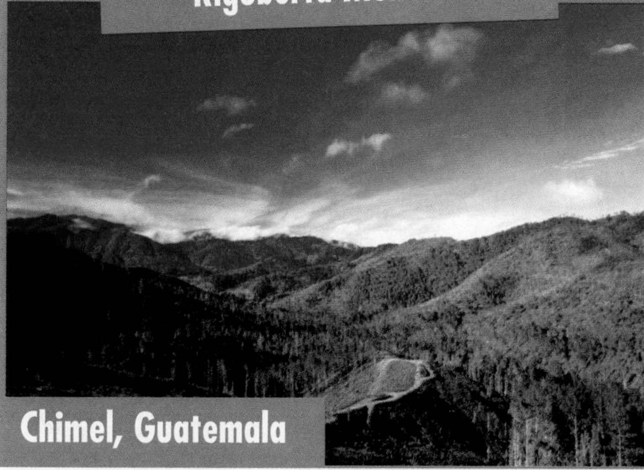

Chimel, Guatemala

1980 Rigoberta Menchu leads striking farmworkers in Guatemala.

Oscar Arias Sánchez

San José, Costa Rica

1987 Oscar Arias Sánchez develops a peace plan for Central America.

1980 — 1990 — 2000

Rigoberta Menchu won the Nobel Peace Prize for her fight to help the Maya of Guatemala gain their rights.

Today you can read about her early life in the book *The Girl From* ***Chimel***.

Oscar Arias Sánchez won the Nobel Peace Prize in 1988. He used the money to found the Arias Foundation for Peace and Human Progress.

Today you can see the foundation's Peace Museum in **San José**, **Costa Rica**.

Lesson 1

VOCABULARY

pidgin language p. 135
carnival p. 136
mural p. 138

READING SKILL

Make Generalizations
Copy the chart below. As you read, use it to make generalizations about the cultures of Latin America.

Text Clues	What You Know	Generalization

STANDARDS FOCUS

SOCIAL STUDIES Culture

GEOGRAPHY Places and Regions

Cultures and Lifestyles

Carnival in Rio de Janeiro, Brazil, is a celebration known for its color, costumes, and excitement.

Visual Preview

How has Latin America's past affected its culture?

Latin America Population Estimate

Population (in thousands): 650,000; 600,000; 550,000; 500,000; 450,000; 400,000

Years: 1985; 2000; 2015

A The population in Latin American countries is increasing rapidly.

B Latin America is a melting pot of many different ethnic groups.

C Religion, music, sports, and dance reflect different aspects of daily life.

D The arts address problems and influence people all over the world.

Ⓐ POPULATION PATTERNS

Population growth changes the landscape of a region. Once-small villages in Latin America are now growing cities. These cities attract many people of different cultures.

Latin America is growing fast. Rapid population growth is putting new pressures on less developed areas, such as the Amazon Basin, where urban areas have grown in recent years.

High Birth Rates

Some of the region's highest birth rates are in Central America. Guatemala and Honduras, for example, are expected to double in population by 2050. Most of these people will be living and working in cities such as Guatemala City and San Pedro Sula, Honduras's most industrial city.

Geography also affects where people live. Most people live along the coasts of South America, or in the valleys of Mexico and Central America. These areas provide favorable climates, fertile land, and easy access, or reach, to transportation.

QUICK CHECK

Make Generalizations **Why do people live in valleys?**

DataGraphic

Population of Latin America

The population of Latin America is growing quickly. Study the graphs. Then answer the questions below.

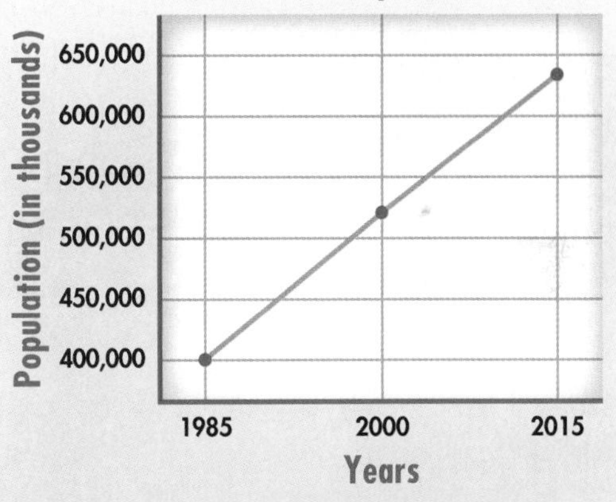

Source: Economic Commission for Latin America and the Caribbean

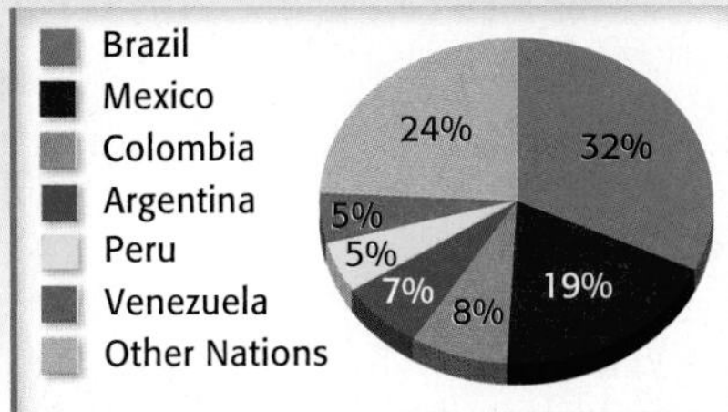

Source: Economic Commission for Latin America and the Caribbean

Think About Population Growth

1. Which country has the largest percentage of Latin America's population?
2. By how much did Latin America's population grow from 1985 to 2000?

B ETHNIC GROUPS AND LANGUAGES

Latin America is a melting pot of European, African, Native American, and Asian cultures. Many people are of mixed ancestry. Mestizos are people of mixed Native American and European ancestry. Others combine African with European or Native American ancestry.

Most Native Americans live in Mexico, Central America, and the Andes countries of Ecuador, Peru, and Bolivia. Native Americans in these areas have worked to keep their languages and traditions.

Settling Latin America

Since the 1400s millions of Europeans have settled in Latin America. At first, most were Spanish or Portuguese. Later, Italians, British, French, and Germans came. In the 1800s many Spanish and Italian immigrants settled in Argentina, Uruguay, and Chile. As a result, these three nations are populated mainly by people of European descent today.

Latin Americans of African ancestry form a higher percentage of the populations in the Caribbean islands and northeastern Brazil. They are the descendants of enslaved Africans. Over the years, Africans have added their rich cultural influences to the food, music, and arts of Latin America.

Many Asians live in the Caribbean islands and in some countries of South America. Most came during the 1800s to work as temporary laborers and remained to form communities. In Guyana about one-half the population is of South Asian or Southeast Asian ancestry.

Many people of Chinese descent make their homes in Peru, Mexico, and Cuba. About one million people of Japanese descent live in Brazil, the largest number of Japanese people outside Japan.

Over the centuries, there has been a blending of these different cultures throughout Latin America. In countries such as Mexico, Honduras, and El Salvador, mestizos make up the largest part of the population. In Cuba, the Dominican Republic, and Brazil, people of mixed African and European descent form a large percentage of the population.

Languages

Spanish is the most widely spoken language in Latin America. In Brazil most people speak Portuguese. Native American languages are still spoken in many countries. For example, Quechua, spoken centuries ago by the Inca, is an official language of Peru and Bolivia.

In the Caribbean English and French are widely spoken. In some countries people have developed a **pidgin language** by combining parts of different languages. An example is Haitian Creole, which is spoken in Haiti. Most Haitian Creole words are from French, but the grammar is from African languages. Other Creole languages in the Caribbean are based on English, Spanish, and Dutch.

Quick Check

Make Generalizations **Why do people migrate to Latin America?**

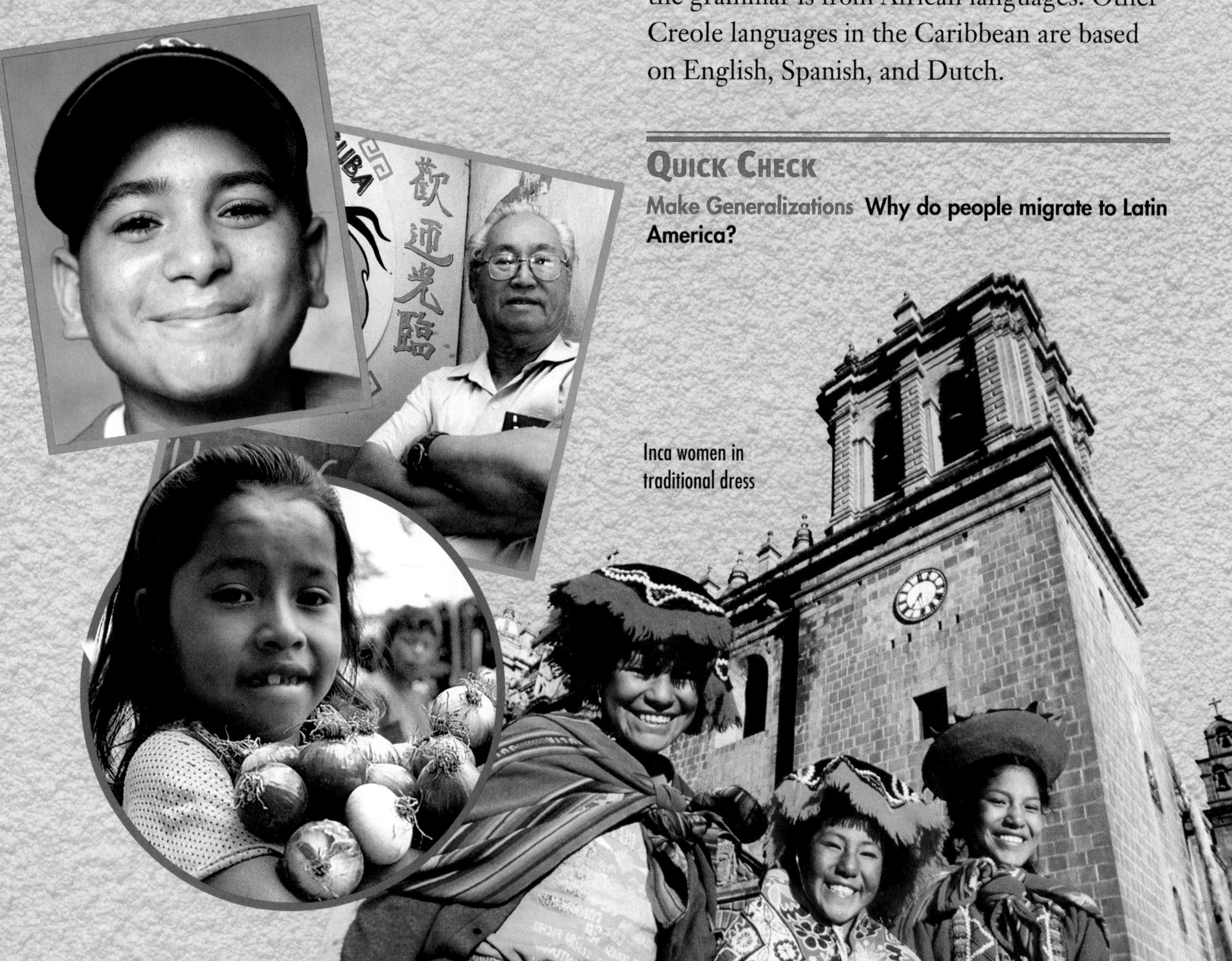

Inca women in traditional dress

C DAILY LIFE

For most people in Latin America, family is one of the most important parts of their lives. Often, several generations live together in one home, and adults are expected to care for their parents. Adult brothers and sisters often live near each other, and their children—who are cousins—can be very close.

Religion

Religion has long played an important role in Latin America. During colonial times most Latin Americans became Christians, and Christianity still has the most followers.

Other faiths include traditional Native American and African religions. These often mix with Christianity and other faiths. Islam, Hinduism, and Buddhism came to Latin America with Asian immigrants. Judaism has followers in the largest Latin American cities.

Holidays

Some holidays are celebrated throughout the Americas, such as Christopher Columbus Day. In Latin American countries, the day is called Día de la Raza, the Day of the Race.

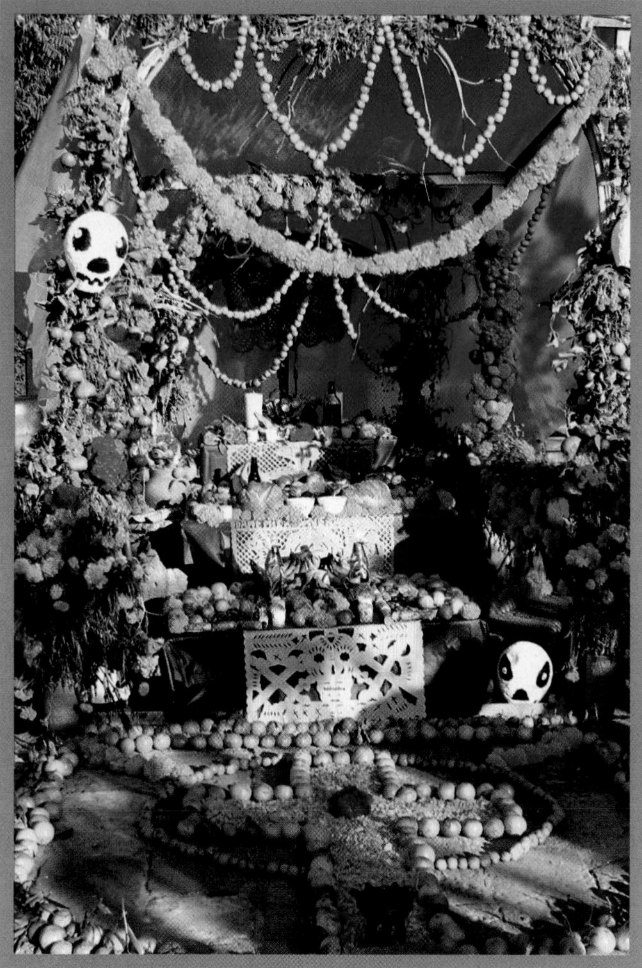

▲ On the Day of the Dead, families in Mexico build altars to give offerings to dead relatives.

Many countries have a large festival called **carnival**. It takes place on the last day before the Christian holy period of Lent and is marked by huge parades. The carnival held in Rio de Janeiro, Brazil, is the largest and is famous for its color and excitement.

Another holiday is the Day of the Dead. It is a day to honor family members who have died. Latin Americans believe that death is the beginning of a new stage of life.

◀ Latin American families try to balance tradition and modern life.

▼ Dominican Republic native, José Reyes, plays for the New York Mets.

Sports

Many Latin Americans are avid sports fans. Latin Americas enjoy a variety of ball games. Soccer is popular throughout the region, and Brazil and Argentina have produced outstanding players and many world championship teams.

Baseball is popular throughout the Caribbean, Central America, and northern South America. Cuba was the second country in the world—after the United States—to play baseball. Several countries have their own baseball leagues, and many players have left Latin America to play for teams in the United States.

In areas of the Caribbean once ruled by the British, cricket is a favorite sport. Cricket is a ball-and-bat sport similar to baseball. Since 1975 many Caribbean nations have participated in an international cricket league with other English-speaking countries such as India, Australia, and the United Kingdom.

Music and Dance

Latin Americans have a love of music and dance. Latin American music is a blend of European and African rhythms. Caribbean music styles, such as salsa and meringue, are based on African rhythms. In Argentina the tango has its roots in European rhythm and dance. In Brazil samba, jazz, and classical music combine to form bossa nova music.

Quick Check

Make Generalizations **Why is baseball popular in northern Latin America?**

▶ A Mexican dancer performs a traditional dance at a festival.

D THE ARTS

It is easy to see how Latin American art has been affected by rich history and a mix of many ethnic groups. During the 1930s Mexican artist Diego Rivera painted **murals**, or large paintings that are painted on walls. Rivera's murals recalled the artistic traditions of the ancient Maya and Aztec.

Many works of Rivera and other Latin American artists focused on the region's history and political issues. In Latin America many writers, such as Pablo Neruda, have used their work to address, or talk about, social divisions and political conflicts in their countries and in the world.

Chilean writer Isabel Allende

Mexican painter Frida Kahlo

Mexican director Alfonso Cuarón, director of a *Harry Potter* movie

Cuban Buena Vista Social Club singer Ibrahim Ferrer

International Influences

Latin American artists have inspired artists in other parts of the world. The music of Cuba and Brazil has strongly influenced American jazz. Writers around the world have used a Latin American style of writing called magic realism that combines fantastic events with the ordinary.

Quick Check

Make Generalizations **How has history influenced art in Latin American and beyond?**

Colombian singer and dancer Shakira

Jamaican reggae singer Bob Marley

Primary Sources

"My ambition as a writer, if there is an ambition, is to write about all the things that I see, that I touch, that I know, that I love, or that I hate."

An interview with Pablo Neruda by Radio Canada, 1971

Write About It Write an essay about the things you would write about if you were a writer.

Check Understanding

1. **VOCABULARY** Write a sentence for each of the following words.

   carnival **mural**

2. **READING SKILL**
   Make Generalizations Use your chart from page 132 to write about Latin American music, dance, and art.

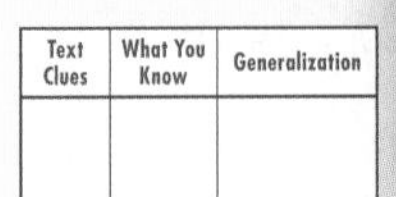

Text Clues	What You Know	Generalization

3. **Write About It** How can people change a language? Why would they want to do that?

Lesson 2

VOCABULARY

maquiladora p. 142

national debt p. 143

campesino p. 144

cash crop p. 145

READING SKILL

Make Generalizations

Copy the chart below. As you read, use it to make a generalization about the economy of Latin America.

Text Clues	What You Know	Generalization

STANDARDS FOCUS

SOCIAL STUDIES Production, Distribution, and Consumption

GEOGRAPHY Human Systems

The Economy of Latin America

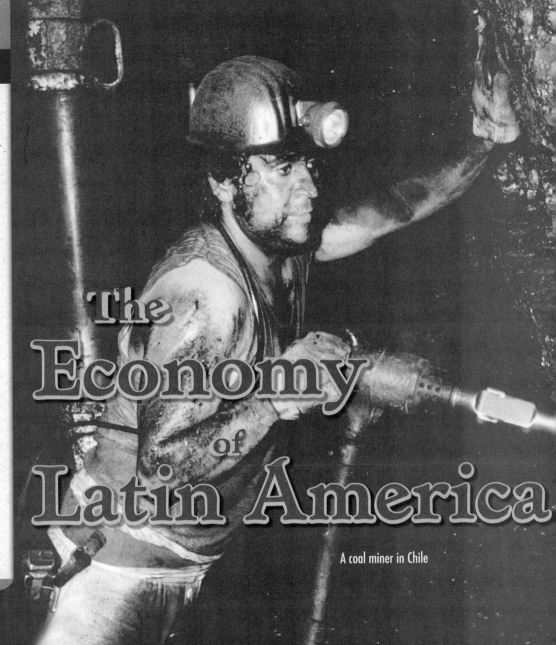

A coal miner in Chile

Visual Preview

What changes brought growth to Latin America's economy?

A Latin America is rich in resources, but many are hard to get.

B Growth of industry has brought trade and challenges to Latin America.

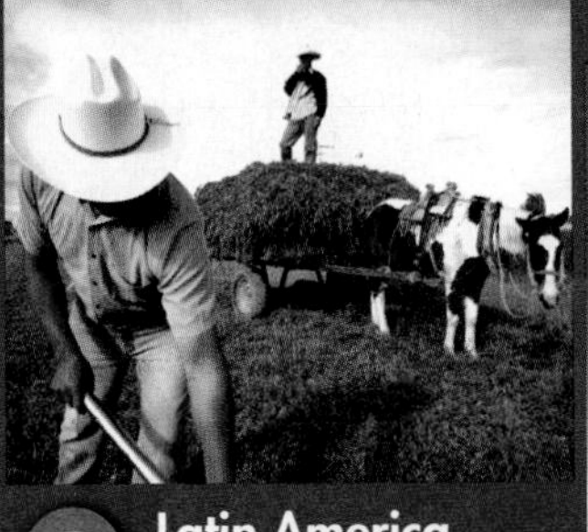

C Latin America grows produce for local use and export.

D Trade and tourism are central to Latin American economies.

Ⓐ RESOURCES IN THE REGION

Take a look around your local supermarket. You will see bananas, pineapples, coffee, sugar, and many other farm products imported to the United States from Latin America. The region's economy grows every day.

Minerals, forests, land, and water make up Latin America's main natural resources. All countries share equally in this wealth. Remote locations and a lack of money have kept many natural resources from being fully developed.

Natural Resources

Mineral resources found in Latin America include silver from Mexico, copper from Chile, and bauxite from Jamaica. Venezuela has, by far, the region's largest oil and natural gas reserves. Mexico has large amounts of oil and natural gas along the coast of the Gulf of Mexico. Both countries use these supplies for their own energy needs, as well as for export.

Uneven Supply

Brazil has large amounts of ore. Its rain forests provide rubber, palm oil, and nuts. Due to its size, Brazil has the region's greatest wealth of natural resources.

Other Latin American nations are not so lucky. Some lack resources or are not able to develop those they have. Sometimes, resources are too difficult to reach, or political problems prevent development. Latin Americans are trying to solve these problems and make use of their resources.

QUICK CHECK

Make Generalizations **Why is oil a valuable economic resource?**

Oil Reserves In Latin America

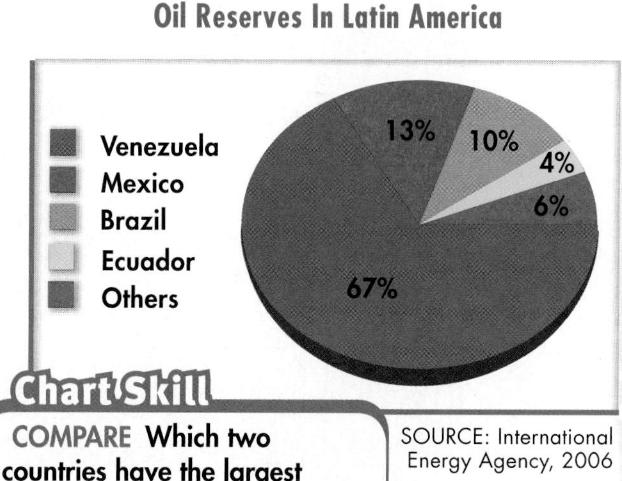

SOURCE: International Energy Agency, 2006

Chart Skill

COMPARE **Which two countries have the largest oil reserves?**

▼ A worker on an oil rig off the coast of Mexico

B INDUSTRY

Most Latin American countries are developing nations because they have limited industry, agriculture remains important, and incomes generally are low. Physical geography, limited development, and weak governments all can limit growth.

Industrial Growth

Some countries have found ways to overcome these problems. Between 2004 and 2007, the gross domestic product (GDP) of all Latin American countries grew by 5 percent. GDP is the total value of all the goods produced in one year.

Many Latin American countries have free market economies. In most, agriculture and tourism are more important than industry. Other nations have found ways to use their natural resources, and money from other countries, to develop their industries.

Venezuelans once depended on crops such as coffee and cacao to earn a living. Since the 1920s, however, Venezuela has become one of the world's leading producers of oil and natural gas. Venezuela also benefits from mining bauxite, gold, diamonds, and emeralds. The country's factories manufacture steel, chemicals, and various food products.

In Mexico many companies from the United States and elsewhere have built **maquiladoras**, or factories, in which workers assemble parts made in other countries. The finished products are then exported to the United States and other countries. Thousands of Mexicans now work in maquiladoras, making cars, textiles, computers, and other goods. These industries add greatly to Mexico's economy and standard of living.

These oil-drilling rigs are near Cabimas, Venezuela, 300 miles west of the capital, Caracas. Oil is very important to the economy of Venezuela and is its number one export.

This worker in a maquiladora in Mexico inserts electronic components into circuit boards at an assembly line for video tuners at the Samsung Electromechanics plant in Tijuana.

Brazil

Brazil has the tenth-largest economy in the world. Some people believe that Brazil could become an economic superpower like the United States and China. Brazil's diverse economy includes manufacturing, mining, and many different service industries.

Most of Brazil's manufacturing takes place in São Paulo and other southeastern cities. There, factory workers produce heavy industrial goods such as machinery, airplanes, and cars. They also make food products, medicines, paper, chemicals, and clothing.

Brazil's growing population and industries use lots of oil and natural gas. However, Brazil's supply of these resources is limited. To reduce its need for oil imports, Brazil uses sugarcane and gasoline to produce a fuel for cars called gasohol. Gasohol is praised as a helpful, environmentally friendly fuel source.

Argentina's Recovery

To help its economy grow, Argentina borrowed money from foreign banks during the late 1900s. This led to **national debt**, or money owed by the government. In 2001 Argentina had to default on its debt. To default is to miss a debt payment. Other countries stopped investing in Argentina's businesses. This brought a severe economic slowdown.

By 2005 Argentina was paying off its debts and the economy had begun to recover. Today, Argentina is one of the most industrialized countries in South America. Most factories are near Buenos Aires, the nation's capital. The leading manufactured goods are automobiles, chemicals, and textiles.

Quick Check

Make Generalizations **What happened after Argentina defaulted on its debt?**

Sugarcane grown in the Brazilian countryside is processed into fuel at a nearby gasohol factory. As a result of gasohol, Brazil uses less gasoline than other countries.

A Volkswagen employee is busy grinding car-body panels in the German carmaker's factory in Buenos Aires. Foreign investment in Latin America is becoming common.

Ⓒ AGRICULTURE

Much of Latin American still operates under a traditional economy. In a traditional economy, people produce most of what they need to survive. People fill roles and make decisions based on tradition, or what has been done for decades and even centuries.

Latifundia and Minifunda

Many in Latin America are **campesinos**, or poor farmers. Campesinos work small farms where they grow corn, beans, and rice to feed only their families. These farms are called minifundia.

Farms or plantations owned and operated by companies or wealthy families are called latifundia. These farms are often very large and use new technology to produce crops to be sold for profit.

Slow Change

This system is centuries old, but it is starting to break down. As latifundia use more technology and need fewer people, many farmworkers are leaving to find work in the cities. Campesinos are starting to work together. Many campesinos are combining their minifundia into jointly run farms. By bringing their resources together, they can compete with bigger farms.

Latin American farmers grow a wide variety of crops. On the left is an alfalfa farm, and on the right is a large coffee plantation.

Cash Crops

Latin America's geography makes it a good region for growing many different **cash crops**. Cash crops are valuable crops produced in large numbers for export. Because they are expensive to produce, cash crops usually benefit latifundia more than minifundia. Latin America's major cash crops are coffee, bananas, and sugarcane.

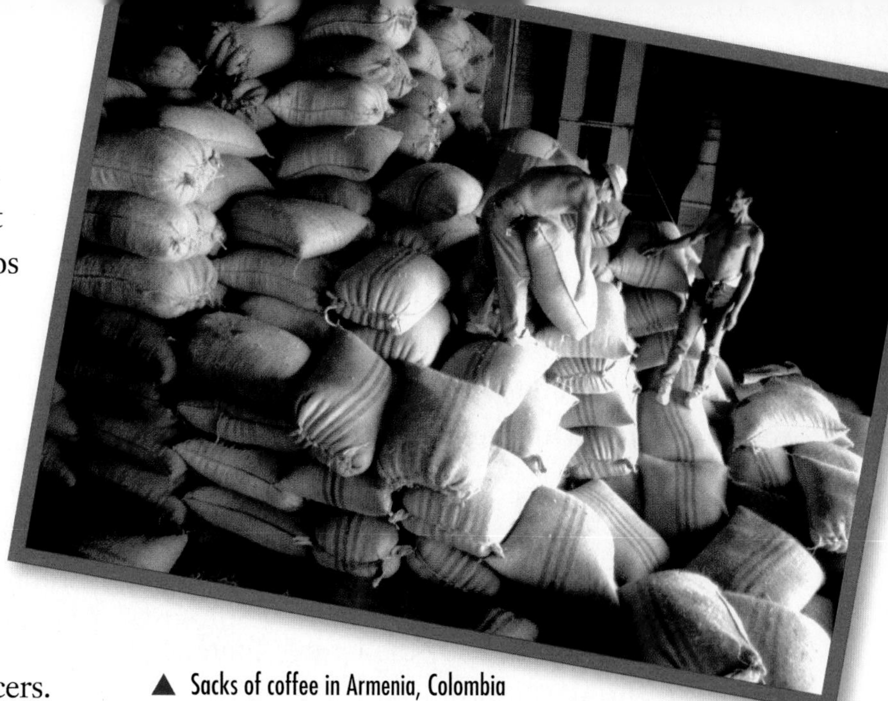

▲ Sacks of coffee in Armenia, Colombia

Fertile highlands turned Brazil, Mexico, Guatemala, and Colombia into some of the world's leading coffee producers. Lush, tropical coastal areas helped Central America become a major banana-growing region. Tropical climates and fertile soil allow Brazil, Mexico, and Cuba to grow much of the world's sugarcane.

Argentina's economy depends heavily on farming and ranching. Huge ranches cover the Pampas. Gauchos, or cowhands, take care of the livestock on these ranches. The livestock that the gauchos herd and tend are a vital part of the economy. Beef and beef products are Argentina's chief exports.

▼Gauchos driving cattle in Argentina

Risks

Depending on just one or two cash crops can be dangerous. Droughts, floods, or volcanoes can destroy a cash crop harvest. Diseases can wipe out herds of livestock. Such loss can cause serious harm to a country's economy. In 1998 Hurricane Mitch destroyed almost 90 percent of the Central American banana crop.

Quick Check

Make Generalization **Why can having only one or two cash crops create problems?**

Ⓓ TRADE AND TOURISM

Latin American countries depend on trade to buy goods they do not have, and to sell the products they produce. In recent years Latin America has begun to promote trade within the region and with the rest of the world.

NAFTA and CAFTA

In 1994 Mexico, the United States, and Canada signed the North American Free Trade Agreement. In 2005 the United States and five Central American countries signed the Central American Free Trade Agreement. The purpose of these agreements is to make trade among these nations easier and cheaper. After NAFTA went into effect, trade among the three countries grew by 10 to 15 percent.

▼ Each year more than eight million tourists are attracted to the Caribbean's beautiful scenery, mild weather, and sandy beaches.

Tourism

Tourism is also a major industry, especially along the coasts and in the Caribbean. Some countries, such as the nation of Dominica, specialize in ecotourism. Ecotourists enjoy the wilderness and local culture. Many ectourists travel to Dominica each year because of its natural beauty. Its nickname is "The Nature Island of the Caribbean."

QUICK CHECK

Make Generalizations **What makes tourism such an important industry to small Caribbean nations?**

Check Understanding

1. **VOCABULARY** Write a sentence for each of the following words.

   maquiladora **cash crop**
   national debt **campesino**

2. **READING SKILL** Make Generalizations Use your chart from page 140 to make a generalization about Latin America's economy.

Text Clues	What You Know	Generalization

3. **Write About It** Write about how industry is changing the economy of Latin America.

Map and Globe Skills

Use a Cartogram

VOCABULARY

cartogram

Population can be shown on a map in different ways. One way is with a special kind of map called a **cartogram**. A cartogram is a map that shows information that can be measured in numbers. For example, to compare population numbers for different places, a cartogram changes the size of these places. You can compare populations by looking at the size of places.

Learn It

- Identify what is being shown in a cartogram. This cartogram shows the population of the Caribbean in 2006 and the real sizes of the countries in the lower left-hand corner.
- Read the map key to learn what each box represents. Each box in this cartogram represents 100,000 people.

Try It

- Which country on the cartogram has the largest population? Which countries have the smallest population?
- About how many people live in Barbados?

Apply It

- Draw a cartogram to compare the population of the largest and smallest states in the United States. Don't forget to include a legend and a title for your cartogram.

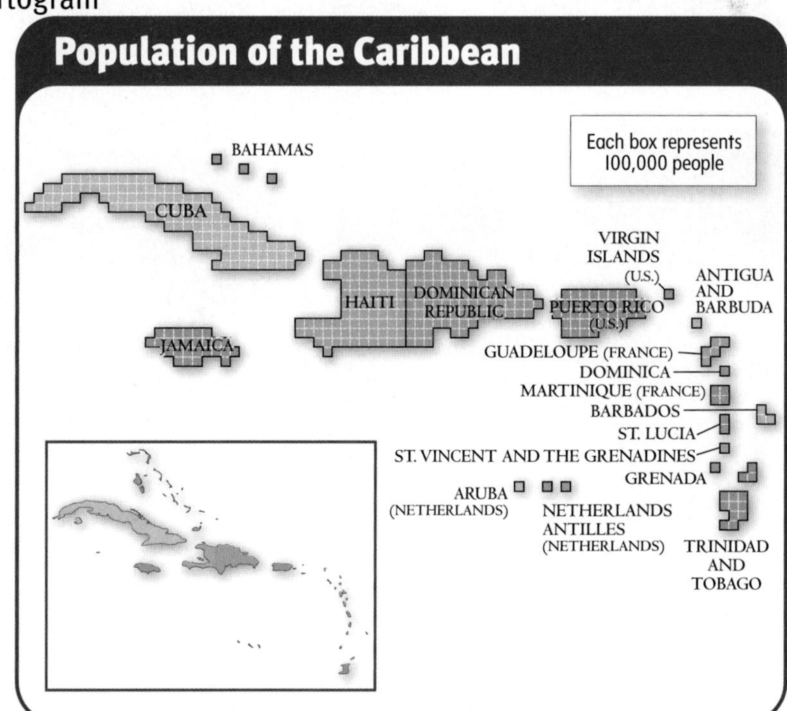

Lesson 3

VOCABULARY

coalition government p. 151

literacy rate p. 152

commonwealth p. 153

READING SKILL

Make Generalizations

Copy the chart below. As you read, use it to make generalizations about democracy in Latin America.

Text Clues	What You Know	Generalization

STANDARDS FOCUS

SOCIAL STUDIES — Power, Authority, and Governance

GEOGRAPHY — Human Systems

GOVERNMENT AND CITIZENSHIP

El Ángel, in Mexico City, was built in 1910 to celebrate the 100th anniversary of the beginning of Mexico's War of Independence.

Visual Preview

How has political change affected Latin America?

A Most Latin American governments have turned into democracies.

B Brazil, like most Latin American nations, is now a federal republic.

C Some Latin American countries struggle, while others find success.

(A) STRUGGLES AND SUCCESSES

Many Latin American governments are thriving democracies today. This has not always been the case. Most Latin American countries have struggled to establish democracies after gaining independence.

After independence, many Latin Americans hoped their countries would become strong democracies. Numerous problems, faced during their early years, made this difficult. One major problem was frequent political conflict. Countries fought with each other over land and resources. Another issue was the gap between the rich and the poor. In most Latin American countries, this gap was very wide.

Strong leaders took advantage of these issues to gain power and become dictators. Almost all Latin Americans were ruled by dictators at one time. Often, dictators supported the wealthy and kept the poor from participating in government. Their rule made it difficult for democracy to develop. Some countries remained under such leaders until recently.

PEOPLE

Anastasio Somoza
This general became dictator of Nicaragua in 1934. His family ruled this nation until 1979.

Anastasio Somoza

Today, few Latin American countries are ruled by dictators. Most Latin American governments are democracies or are slowly becoming democracies. The region is coming close to reaching its original goals.

QUICK CHECK

Make Generalizations **Why did Latin American countries have problems forming democracies?**

Years as an Electoral Democracy

Map Skill

PLACE: **Which three countries have been democracies for the longest amount of time?**

B BRAZIL'S GOVERNMENT

Today, most Latin American countries are representative democracies. Brazil, the largest Latin American nation in size and population, is a good example of how Latin American government works. Most Latin American democratic governments today are organized similar to that of Brazil.

Brazil declared independence from Portugal in 1822. During most of the 1800s, emperors ruled. From 1889 to 1985, Brazil alternated from republican governments to dictatorships. Today, Brazil is a democratic republic, and people elect a president and other leaders. Most citizens cannot choose whether or not to vote. People from ages 18 to 70 who can read are required by law to vote.

Three Branches of Government

Like the United States, Brazil's government has three branches. The president heads the executive branch, which carries out the laws. The National Congress is the legislative branch, which makes the laws. It is made up of the Federal Senate and the Chamber of Deputies. These are like the Senate and the House of Representatives the United States.

Chart Skill

COMPARE: **How can the National Congress check the powers of the executive branch?**

A Supreme Federal Tribunal, or court, heads the judicial branch, which interprets the laws. It works much like the Supreme Court of the United States.

Federal System

Brazil is divided into twenty-six states and one Federal District. The Federal District was created in 1960 for the new city of Brasília, which is Brazil's capital. The Federal District is similar to Washington, D.C., in the United States.

Each of Brazil's twenty-six states has its own government, much like the fifty states of the United States. City governments, too, are separate from the governments of the states and the nation. Brazil's federal government is much larger and stronger than the governments of its states and cities.

Political Parties

In the United States, candidates are usually from only two political parties, Republican or Democratic. Brazil has four major parties and sixteen minor parties. Usually, no single party gains a majority, so parties must work together.

To work together, different political parties will form a **coalition government**. In a coalition government, two or more political parties cooperate in leading the government. Coalition governments are also common in other Latin American countries. Most of these countries have many small political parties, rather than two or three large parties.

EVENT

In 1960 **Brazil moved its capital** from Rio de Janeiro to the newly built city of Brasília, 600 miles inland. Today, it is a thriving city with more than 2 million people.

Brazil moves its capital

Citizenship

Be a Leader

Simón Bolívar was one of the early Latin American leaders. He helped much of Latin America become independent, so that they could develop democracies.

Leaders are able to identify problems and find solutions. Consider being a leader in your community or school. Find others to help solve a problem, and make sure everyone has a chance to contribute.

Write About It Identify a problem in your community or at your school. Then write an essay about how you would work with others to find a solution to that problem.

Quick Check

Make Generalizations **How is a coalition government different from the government in the United States?**

Ⓒ OTHER NATIONS

Most nations in Latin America have governments similar to Brazil's. There are a few nations that differ.

Cuba

As you read in Unit 3, in 1959 revolutionary leader Fidel Castro took over Cuba and soon established a communist government. Since then, the country has been tightly controlled. The government sets most prices for goods and controls most workers.

Primary Sources

"Because our country is a country of teachers, we closed the army camps, and our children go with books under their arms, not with rifles under their arms. We reject violence...."

A section from a speech by Oscar Arias, 1987

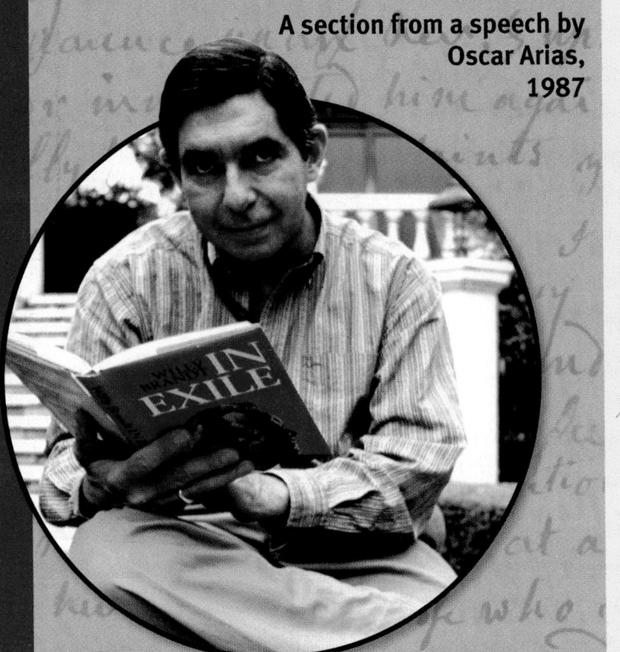

Write About It Write a journal entry about your reaction to President Arias's speech.

Cuba's government is one of the few remaining communist systems in the world today. The government controls society as tightly as it controls the economy. People who criticize the Cuban government are often arrested and jailed. This is the main reason the United States opposes Cuba's communist government and refuses to trade with it. Partly as a result, the Cuban economy has struggled for many years.

Fidel Castro retired as Cuba's head of state in early 2008. Cuba's National Assembly selected Raul Castro, Fidel's brother, as Cuba's new president. Castro's retirement means an uncertain future for communist Cuba.

Costa Rica

Costa Rica is one of the most developed countries in Central America. It has a strong economy and a **literacy rate**, or percentage of people who can read and write, close to that of the United States.

Costa Ricans overthrew their military government in the late 1940s. Since then, a stable democratic government has ruled, and the army has been disbanded. There have been no civil wars or conflicts between Costa Rica and other countries since the overthrow of the military government. Costa Rica keeps only a police force to maintain law and order.

In 1987 Oscar Arias Sánchez, the president of Costa Rica, worked to get the Central American Peace Accord signed. This was a plan to bring about democracy and peace in the region. President Arias won the Nobel Peace Prize in 1987 for this important work.

Panama

The Panama Canal is important to many trading nations across the globe. For 85 years the United States controlled the canal that it built across Panama in 1914. As a result, it had taken a special interest in the government of Panama during that time.

In 1989 it was found that Manuel Noriega, Panama's leader, was selling and shipping illegal drugs. He also rejected the results of an election in which his side lost. The United States helped remove Noriega from power and restore the country's democratic government.

On December 31, 1999, the United States took an important step to end its long political involvement in Central America. In a ceremony, it gave full control of the Panama Canal over to Panama.

This factory in Puerto Rico produces medicine for a U.S. company (top). The Panama Canal has not always been controlled by Panama (left).

Puerto Rico

Since 1952 Puerto Rico has been a **commonwealth**, or partly self-governing territory, of the United States. It handles its own local issues, but the Unites States handles defense, the postal system, money, and similar national concerns.

Puerto Ricans are American citizens. They have a high standard of living, and they can come and go as they wish between Puerto Rico and the United States.

QUICK CHECK

Make Generalizations Why has Costa Rica decided not to rebuild its army?

Check Understanding

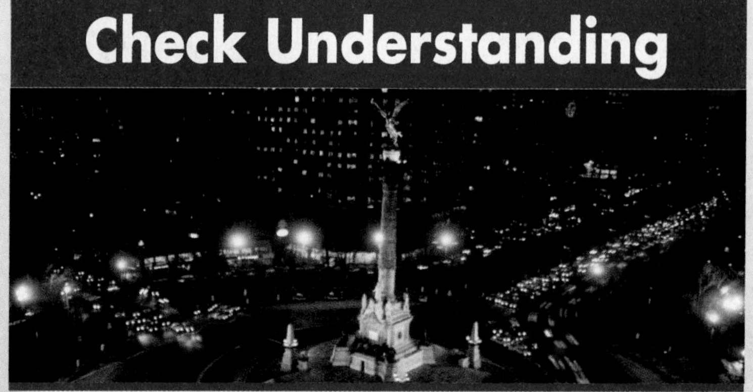

1. **VOCABULARY** Write about Puerto Rico using the following term.
   commonwealth
2. **READING SKILL**
   Make Generalizations Use your chart from page 148 to make a generalization about the governments of Latin America.

Text Clues	What You Know	Generalization

3. **Write About It** Write about why Panama has a special relationship with the United States.

Lesson 4

VOCABULARY

migrate p. 158

emigrate p. 158

READING SKILL

Make Generalizations
Copy the chart below. As you read, use it to make a generalization about Native American relations in Latin America.

Text Clues	What You Know	Generalization

STANDARDS FOCUS

SOCIAL STUDIES Civic Ideals and Practices

GEOGRAPHY Place and Regions

Issues Today

The border between Mexico, on the left, and the United States, on the right.

Visual Preview

How has change affected Latin Americans?

A Political changes in some countries have not always been easy.

B Native Americans are speaking out for their rights.

C People move into, out of, and within Latin America for different reasons.

Ⓐ CIVIL WARS

Not all countries were able to create stable governments. In some countries different groups of people fought over who would lead. Today, many of these countries are working hard for positive changes.

Many countries in Latin America have struggled to find stability since independence. Some have even had costly civil wars, or wars between groups within a country. During the last century, many Central and South American governments were ruled by brutal dictators. Civil war erupted when rebel groups formed to overthrow these dictators.

Nicaragua

In 1979 a group called Sandinistas took control of Nicaragua. They began to limit freedoms. A rebel group called the Contras opposed the Sandinista government and gained support from United States.

The Contras started a civil war to fight for control of the government. In 1990 Sandinista leader Daniel Ortega agreed to hold free elections in Nicaragua to end the war. Ortega lost the 1990 election, but he won in 2006.

Haiti

Haiti has had a troubled history. The government has been unstable because of conflicts among political groups. Each group has accused the other of cheating in elections or accepting support from outside sources, such as the United States. In 2004 president Jean-Bertrand Aristide was forced to leave office and the country after violent riots erupted across Haiti. A new president was elected in 2006.

QUICK CHECK

Make Generalizations **What generalizations can you make about civil wars in Latin America?**

▲ Sandinista leader Daniel Ortega

Ⓑ NATIVE AMERICAN ISSUES

Native Americans are a major part of the population of Latin America. Today, they play an active role in their nations' societies.

Guatemala's Native Americans

Guatemala was once home to the Maya civilization. About half its people are descendents of the Maya, while some are of mixed Native American descent. The Maya language is still spoken today alongside Spanish in many parts of Guatemala.

Guatemala experienced a terrible civil war in the 1970s and 1980s. Native Americans united with poor farmers and other rebels to fight the government. They demanded changes that would give them land and better lives. The fighting finally ended in 1996, after many people had been killed.

Fighting for Her People

During the civil war, many Maya Native Americans were killed. Among those killed were family and friends of Rigoberta Menchu.

This led Menchu to dedicate her life to helping Native Americans fight for their rights. During the civil war, she worked to bring world attention to human rights violations committed against local Native Americans by the Guatemalan army.

In 1992 Menchu won the Nobel Peace Prize for her efforts. When she accepted the prize, she said that bringing about peace is very hard work. Today, Menchu is still active in Guatemalan politics. She also promotes better cultural understanding in her country by bringing together people of different ethnic backgrounds.

Rigoberta Menchu (top), and members of a Maya family (left)

Mexico's Native Americans

About a quarter of Mexico's people are mostly or completely Native American. About two-thirds of Mexicans are mestizos, with mixed Spanish and Native American ancestry.

Mexico's Native American population has faced struggles. Most live in rural areas, and many are poor. In 1994 the Zapatistas, a group of Native Americans in the state of Chiapas, rose up against the Mexican government. They demanded changes to improve the quality of their lives.

Some of these conflicts turned violent. By the early 2000s, the struggle between the Zapatistas and the Mexican government still had not been settled. Today, protests continue; however, these protests are much less violent.

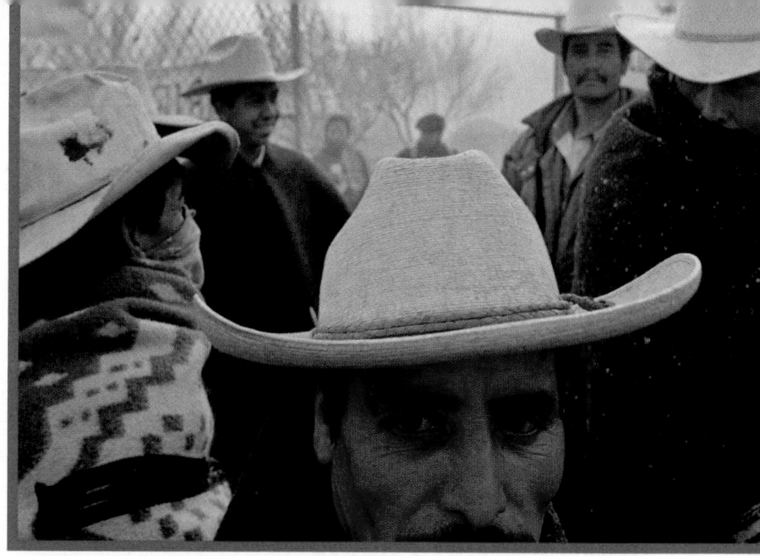

▲ Zapatistas at a gathering in southern Mexico

MATSES

In Peru an organization called MATSES, or Movement in the Amazon for Tribal Subsistence and Economic Sustainability, exists to help preserve the culture and way of life of the Matsés group. MATSES also works to provide the Matsés with medical care. However, the Matsés live in an isolated part of the Amazon and are difficult to reach. The Matsés live a traditional way of life, and did not make permanent contact with Peru until 1969.

Quick Check

Make Generalizations **What made Menchu a success?**

▼ Children of the Matsés group in a local school

C MIGRATIONS

In the past Europeans, Africans, and Asians came to Latin America in large numbers. Some came willingly, while others came by force. Immigrants, or people who come to a country from another country to live, have greatly shaped Latin American's population.

Movement of People

Many Latin Americans **migrate**, or move, within their country or region. As in many parts of the world, Latin America's urban areas have increased greatly in population. Fertile land is often in short supply in rural areas. Farming cannot always support a family, and many people leave to find jobs in cities. Most cities are areas of industrialization and offer more hope for getting a job.

Emigration

Latin America also has people who **emigrate**, or leave their own country to live in another. Many Latin American emigrants move to Canada, Europe, or to the United States, hoping to escape political unrest or to find a better way of life. Many keep in close contact with friends and family back home. Many also plan to return when economic conditions improve in their home countries.

A mall in São Paulo, Brazil (below), and a young woman with her family before moving to a different city (right)

Migrant Workers

Some people cannot find work or want to earn more money than they do in in their native country. These people might become migrant workers. Migrant workers are people who travel from place to place where workers are needed. They bring parts of their culture, such as language or traditions, along with them.

Many migrant workers in the United States come from Mexico. They often cross the border to work in the United States, where the pay is better and work is safer.

Some migrant workers find jobs in construction, where they work building roads and houses. Others without these job skills work in low-paying jobs, such as planting or harvesting crops on farms.

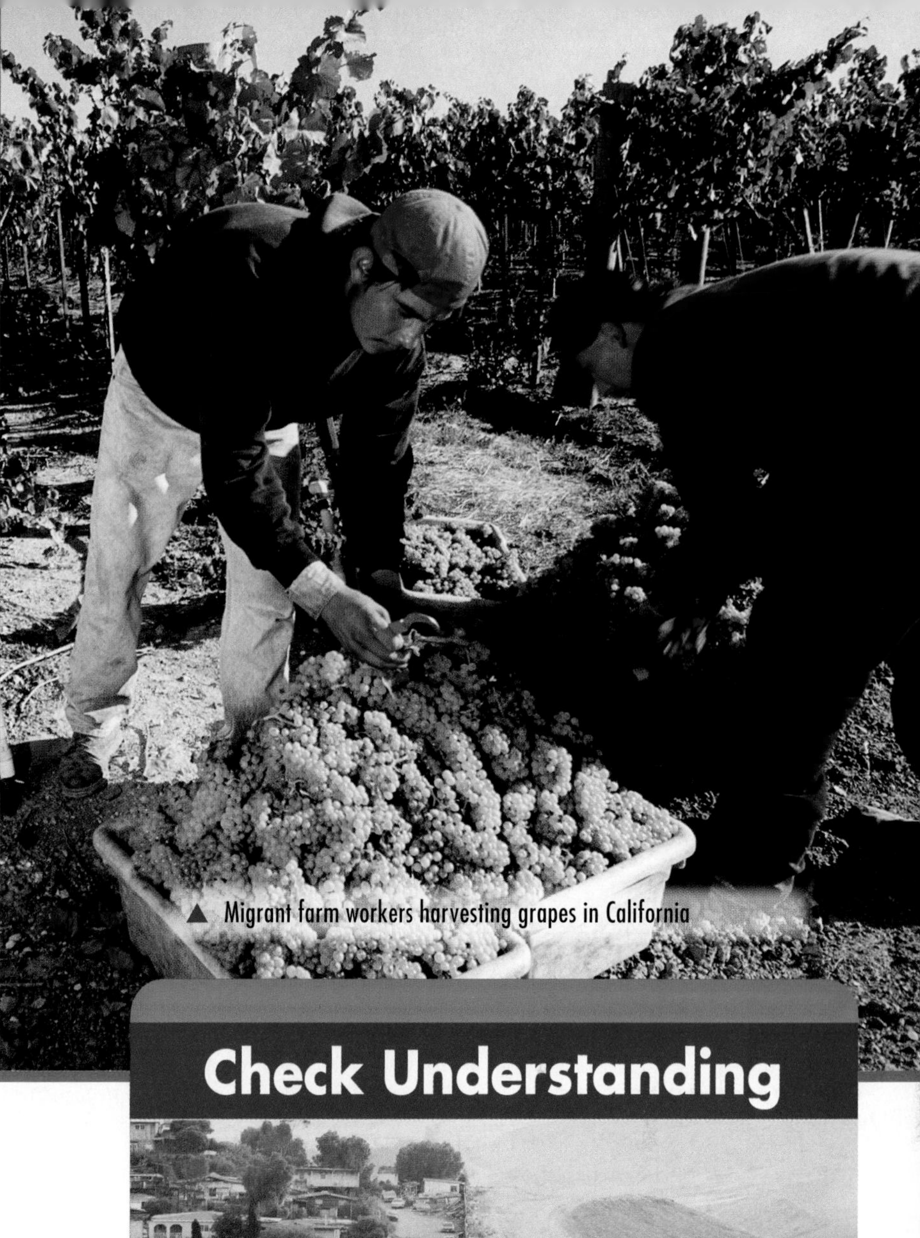

▲ Migrant farm workers harvesting grapes in California

Illegal Immigration

Many migrants enter the United States legally, but migrant workers do not always cross the U.S.–Mexico border legally. About one million job seekers cross the border illegally each year. There are many problems with this kind of immigration. Often, workers make the trip through dangerous desert areas. Also, many people in the United States do not want border laws to be broken. Many lawmakers in the United States are working to solve the problem of illegal immigration.

Quick Check

Make Generalizations **Why do some people become migrant workers?**

Check Understanding

1. **VOCABULARY** Write a paragraph about the movement of people. Use these words:
   migrate **emigrate**

2. **READING SKILL**
   Make Generalizations Use your chart from page 154 to write about the civil wars in Latin America.

Text Clues	What You Know	Generalization

3. **Write About It** What are some of the reasons people move from place to place?

Lesson 5

VOCABULARY

selva p. 162

ecosystem p. 162

smog p. 164

READING SKILL

Make Generalizations
Copy the chart below. As you read, use it to make generalizations about the environmental issues facing Latin America.

Text Clues	What You Know	Generalization

STANDARDS FOCUS

SOCIAL STUDIES Production, Distribution, and Consumption

GEOGRAPHY Environment and Society

The Environment

Patagonia in the southern Andes

Visual Preview

How can people change Latin America's environment?

A Latin America often faces deadly natural disasters.

B The rainforest is one of Latin America's most threatened areas.

C Latin Americans are finding a balance between growth and pollution.

Ⓐ NATURAL DISASTERS

Latin Americans are trying to protect the environment while taking care of growing human needs. The environment itself can be a large threat to people when natural disasters strike.

Latin America is a region of great natural beauty. This beauty can be deceiving, however, because Latin America faces some of the deadliest natural disasters in the world.

Volcanoes and Earthquakes

Mexico and Central America are crossed by the Trans-Mexican Volcanic Belt. This is a long mountain chain with several active volcanoes. The 1982 eruption of El Chichón, in Mexico, killed about 2,000 people who lived near the volcano.

Latin America also sees frequent earthquakes, especially in the Andes. In 2007 a strong earthquake hit Peru, destroying up to 58,000 homes and killing over 1,000 people.

Hurricanes

Mexico, Central America, and the Caribbean often deal with hurricanes. A hurricane is a large, dangerous tropical storm with powerful winds and heavy rains. Hurricanes often bring high waves and heavy floods to coastal areas.

In 1998 Hurricane Mitch swept over Middle America, killing thousands of people and leaving many more homeless. Hurricane Mitch destroyed homes, bridges, and roads and caused billions of dollars in damage.

The heavy rains and winds of a hurricane can be devastating.

Quick Check

Make Generalizations **Why is the Caribbean especially threatened by hurricanes?**

Assai palm forest
in the Serra do Mar of Rio de Janeiro, Brazil

B THE AMAZON RAIN FOREST

The Amazon rain forest is located in nine South American nations. It is the largest rain forest biome, or environmental community, in the world. Brazil has 60 percent of the rain forest within its borders. Brazilians call the Amazon rain forest the **selva**. The selva has the world's highest rate of deforestation. Each year, trees are cut down in an area the size of New Jersey in the Amazon rain forest.

Causes of Deforestation

In the 1950s Brazil's leaders set out to develop the Amazon. They saw it as a solution to the nation's problems of poverty and unemployment. Poor Brazilians could make new lives for themselves in the Amazon frontier. However, there were no highways in the rain forest until 1958.

In the 1970s government leaders began offering free land in the rain forest to anyone who was willing to settle there. Buses soon streamed along the Trans-Amazon Highway, filled with people hoping to carve out a life in the rain forest.

In the 1980s Brazil's government encouraged mining, logging, farming, and cattle ranching in the rain forest. Unfortunately, the soil in the rain forest is very fragile. Once the land has been cleared, it becomes almost useless. Farmers must move on, hoping to find better soil elsewhere. These activities lead to soil erosion. They also harm the rain forest's **ecosystem**. An ecosystem is all the living and nonliving things in a certain area, including plants, animals, soil, and water.

Deforestation

Saving the Rain Forest

Rain forests are home to a huge variety of plants and animals. Three-quarters of Earth's living things are found in rain forests.

In addition tropical forests give off huge amounts of oxygen and play a role in maintaining the earth's climate patterns. Although most of the Amazon rain forest belongs to Brazil, the effects of deforestation are felt worldwide.

Because deforestation is a global issue, other nations are working with Brazil to protect at least part of the rain forest from development. These efforts to preserve the rain forest have seen some success. From 2002 to 2006, deforestation of the Amazon rain forest was down 60 percent. At the same time, protected land almost tripled.

PLACES

In Guatemala the **Maya Biosphere Reserve** was created in 1990 to help preserve the largest rain forest in Central America. The Guatemalan government has encouraged tourists to visit the reserve. The interest of tourists might help protect these fragile areas from threats, such as cutting down trees and drilling for oil.

Maya Biosphere Reserve

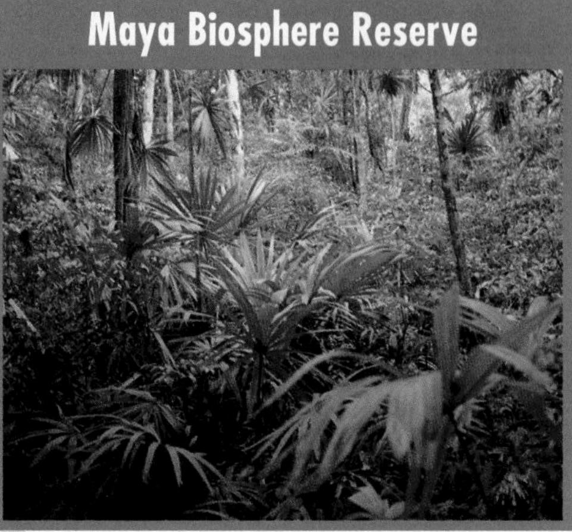

Quick Check

Make Generalizations **What are some of the benefits of protecting areas of the rain forest?**

C POLLUTION

Latin America's economy relies less on farming and more on manufacturing than it once did. This is good for the economy, but it can be harmful for the environment.

Growth of Industry

Thousands of Latin Americans now work in factories making cars, textiles, computers, and other consumer goods. Many service industries, such as banking and tourism, also add greatly to the economy.

Economic advances have raised the standard of living. Many Latin Americans can now afford automobiles and other luxuries. The speed of this growth has brought concerns about damage to the environment.

Challenges

Pollution has become a major national challenge in many Latin American countries. The Rio Grande, the river along much of the Mexico–United States border, is heavily polluted. Air and soil pollution, too, are a concern in many places.

Because many people have moved to cities to find jobs, the cities have grown. This combination of many millions of people in one location and an increase in industrial jobs has had an effect on the environment. For example, Mexico City is often covered by **smog**, or a thick layer of fog and chemicals created by factories and automobile exhaust.

Planning for the Future

The smog in Mexico City is becoming a major health and environmental risk. The government is planning to increase public transportation to reduce the number of cars on city streets. It hopes that this will reduce harmful exhaust of cars and will lower smog levels across the city.

Smog is a major problem in Mexico City.

Latin Americans in all countries are working today to protect their environment and reverse some of the damage done. Individuals are more aware of the impact they have on the environment. Companies are making safer and more responsible choices. Governments are finding ways to work together on the issue. By cooperating at the regional level, Latin Americans can find ways to protect their environment.

▲ The Rio Grande River has become polluted because of industry growth.

Quick Check

Make Generalizations **Why is slowing industrial growth a difficult choice to make?**

▲ Efforts to clean up pollution often start as small community projects, such as this park.

Check Understanding

1. **VOCABULARY** Write a sentence for each of the following terms.

   selva **ecosystem** **smog**

2. **READING SKILL** **Make Generalizations** Use your chart from page 160 to write about the environmental issues of Latin America.

Text Clues	What You Know	Generalization

3. **Write About It** Write about how you can improve the environment of your community.

Unit 4 Review and Assess

Vocabulary

Number a paper from 1 to 4. Beside each number write the word from the list below that matches the description.

maquiladora **smog**

command economy **mural**

1. a thick layer of smoke generated by cars and factories
2. a system where the government sets most of the prices for goods and employs most of the workers
3. a large painting drawn on a wall
4. a foreign-owned factory in Mexico where workers assemble parts made in other countries

Comprehension and Critical Thinking

5. What are the risks of growing cash crops?
6. Why did Rigoberta Menchu win the Nobel Peace Prize?
7. **Reading Skill** What are Latin Americans doing to balance rain-forest protection with economic growth?
8. **Critical Thinking** How is voting in Brazil different from voting in the United States?

Skill

Use a Cartogram

Write a complete sentence to answer each question.

9. About how many people live in Jamaica?
10. Why is Puerto Rico larger than Jamaica in the cartogram?

Population of the Caribbean

Each box represents 100,000 people

BAHAMAS
CUBA
JAMAICA
HAITI
DOMINICAN REPUBLIC
PUERTO RICO (U.S.)
VIRGIN ISLANDS (U.S.)
ANTIGUA AND BARBUDA
GUADELOUPE (FRANCE)
DOMINICA
MARTINIQUE (FRANCE)
BARBADOS
ST. LUCIA
ST. VINCENT AND THE GRENADINES
GRENADA
ARUBA (NETHERLANDS)
NETHERLANDS ANTILLES (NETHERLANDS)
TRINIDAD AND TOBAGO

Test Preparation

In 2002 Mexican President Vicente Fox gave a speech on "International Migrants' Day," where he declared the 21st century the "century of the migrant." Read the passage from the speech below. Then answer the questions that follow.

> Migration is a clear sign of our times. In ways never seen before, nations and cultures all over the planet today are getting to know each other, are getting closer to each other, [and] are mutually enriching each other.
>
> We ourselves, in Mexico, have benefited from the arrival of thousands of men and women from other nations, whom Mexico has always welcomed with open arms, and who also have contributed a lot, so very much, to our country.
>
> The challenge today is finding the right mechanisms [ways] to guarantee their rights in an orderly and secure framework [system]. All countries are responsible for this task. We must strengthen migrants' rights together.
>
> —President Vicente Fox

1. How does President Fox believe the migrant community has affected Mexico?

A. He believes Mexico has too many migrants.
B. He believes Mexico is held back by its migrants.
C. He believes Mexico has benefited from the contributions of migrants.
D. He believes Mexico has seen little change because of migrants.

2. President Fox believes that migrations are ___ the world.

A. enriching
B. developing
C. shrinking
D. damaging

3. What is the main idea of this passage?

A. Mexico has a large migrant community.
B. All countries are responsible for the rights of migrants.
C. Migrants have too many rights.
D. President Fox welcomes migrants.

4. Why does President Fox call the 21st century the "century of the migrant"?

5. Why might President Fox welcome migrants to Mexico?

The Big Idea Activities

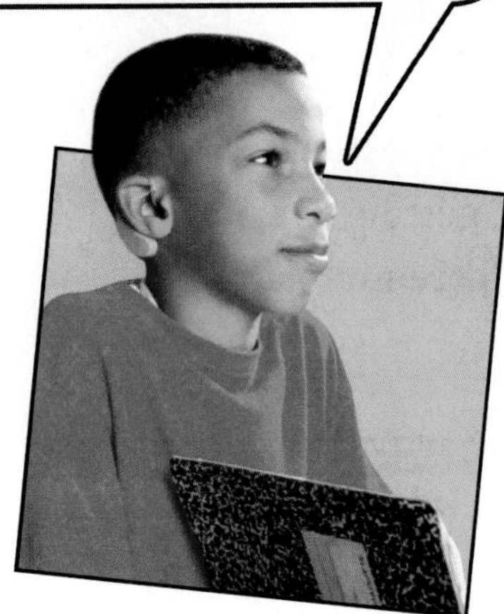

Write About the Big Idea

A Persuasive Essay

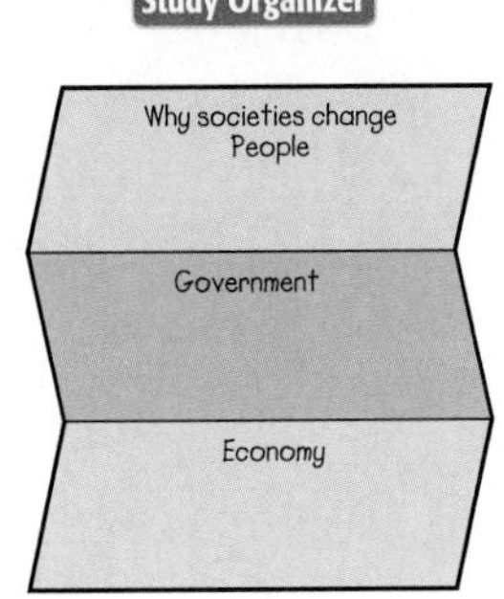

Use the Unit 4 Foldable to help you write a persuasive essay that answers the Big Idea question, *What causes a society to change?* Form an opinion about a fact you wrote about under people, government, or economy. Begin with an introduction. In the body of the essay, be sure to use persuasive language to support your opinion. End with a conclusion about what you feel is important for a society to grow.

A Newscast

Work with a partner to present a newscast. You and your partner will be co-anchors of a nightly news program. Follow these steps to produce your newscast.

1. Use the Internet or newspapers to find a news topic about a Latin American country.
2. Research your topic and compare the information you gather with your partner.
3. Divide your newscast into two parts. The first part will be facts about the topic. The second part will be an editorial expressing an opinion about the topic.

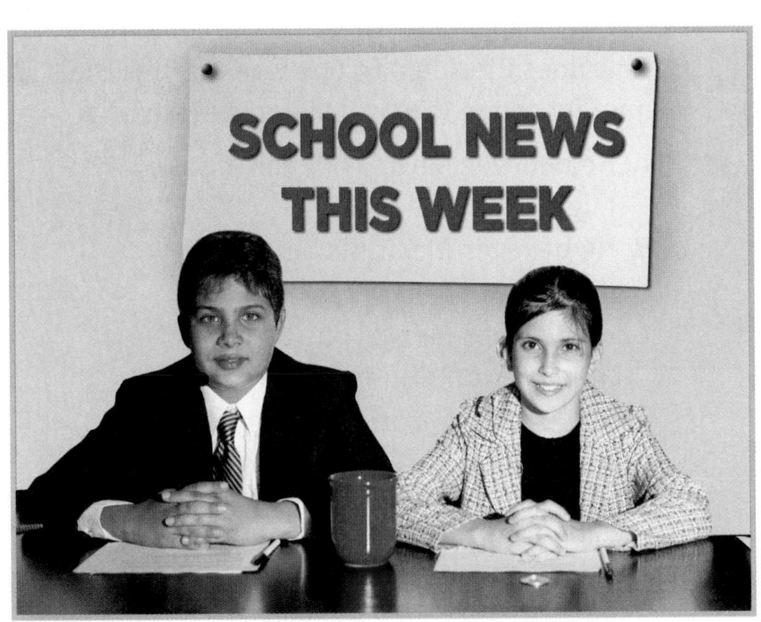

After you have rehearsed your newscast, present it to the class.

The Geography and History of Europe

Unit 5

Essential Question
Why do civilizations change?

Foldables Study Organizer

Make Inferences
Make an Accordion Foldable to take notes as you read Unit 5. Your Foldable's title will be **Changes in Civilizations**. Use one fold for each of the lessons in Unit 5. Use your Foldable to organize information as you read the unit.

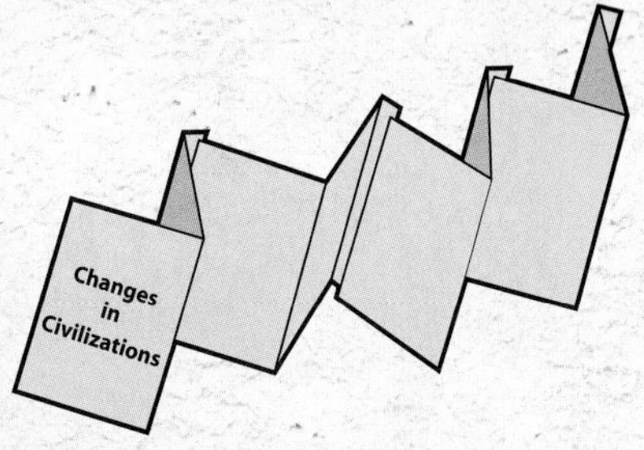

Log On For more about this unit go to **www.macmillanmh.com**

Mont St. Michel, Normandy, France

PEOPLE, PLACES, AND EVENTS

Homer

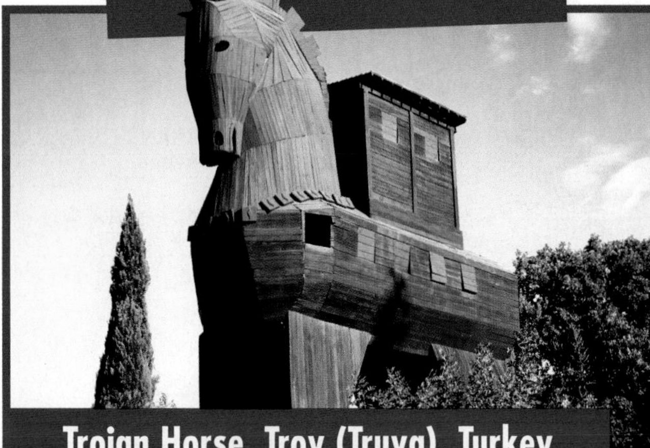

Trojan Horse, Troy (Truva), Turkey

700 B.C. Homer creates the *Iliad* and the *Odyssey.*

Charlemagne

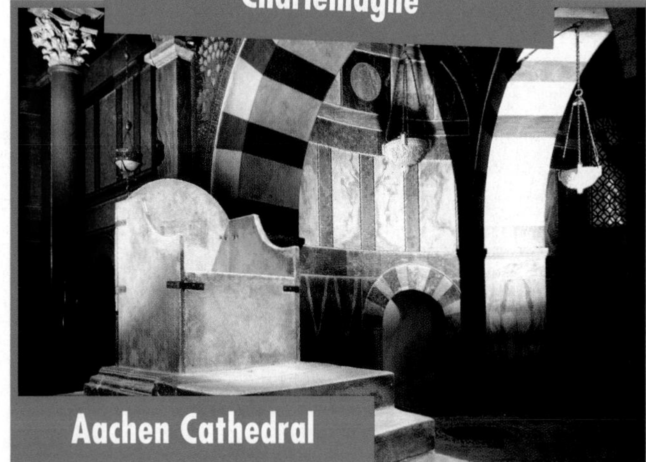

Aachen Cathedral

A.D. 800 Charlemagne becomes the Holy Roman Emperor.

1000 B.C — A.D. 1 — 1000

The Greek poet **Homer** was blind, but he created two poems about a long-ago war between Greece and the city-state of **Troy**.

Today you can visit the ruins of Troy and see a copy of the famous Trojan Horse.

After conquering much of western Europe, **Charlemagne** was crowned emperor by Pope Leo III on Christmas Day, 800.

Today you can still see Charlemagne's throne in **Aachen**, Germany.

LOG ON For more about People, Places, and Events, visit www.macmillanmh.com

Queen Victoria

Suez Canal, Egypt

1869 European royalty attends the opening of the Suez Canal.

Winston Churchill

London, England

1940 German bombers attack London during the Battle of Britain.

1600 | 1800 | 2000

Queen Victoria ruled England and India.

Today you can travel through the **Suez Canal**, which connected her two kingdoms. The opera *Aida* was written for the opening of this canal.

Winston Churchill, Great Britain's World War II leader, led by example and delivered stirring speeches.

Today you can see ruined **London** buildings preserved as monuments to the Battle of Britain.

Lesson 1

VOCABULARY

landlocked p. 173

navigable p. 173

peninsula p. 174

pass p. 175

READING SKILL

Make Inferences

Copy the chart below. Then fill in the chart with details about the physical geography of Europe.

Text Clues	What You Know	Inference

STANDARDS FOCUS

SOCIAL STUDIES People, Places, and Environments

GEOGRAPHY Places and Regions

Physical Geography of Europe

The Danube River flows from southern Germany to the Black Sea. It is a beautiful river and also an important transportation route.

Visual Preview

How do the landforms in Europe affect its people?

A Europeans use waterways for transportation, trade, and leisure.

B Plains, mountains, and highlands dominate Europe.

C Europeans depend on many "clean" energy sources that cause less pollution.

Ⓐ WATER SYSTEMS

The continent of Europe shares a landmass with Asia. Together they are called Eurasia, but each continent is considered a distinct region.

Geographers divide the continent of Europe into four subregions. They are Northern, Eastern, Western, and Southern Europe. Europe has a long, jagged coastline that is framed by many bodies of water. Most of Europe lies within 300 miles of a seacoast. Only a few countries are **landlocked**, meaning they do not border an ocean or a sea.

Being close to the sea has shaped the lives of Europe's people over time. Europeans have developed skills in sailing and fishing, which helped trade and made Europe's economy grow.

Waterways

Europeans depend on rivers, lakes, and canals for transportation, trade, and leisure. They have connected many rivers with canals to create important transportation links. Rivers and canals also provide rich soil and sources of electricity.

Many of the rivers flow from inland mountains into the oceans and seas. For example, the Volga River is the longest river in Europe. Canals off the Volga link to the Baltic Sea, providing a water reoute to Northern Europe. Most of the rivers are **navigable**, or wide and deep enough for ships to use.

Europe has a small number of lakes. They provide important places for Europeans to boat, fish, and swim.

QUICK CHECK

Make Inferences **Why do you think the people of Europe depend on their waterways?**

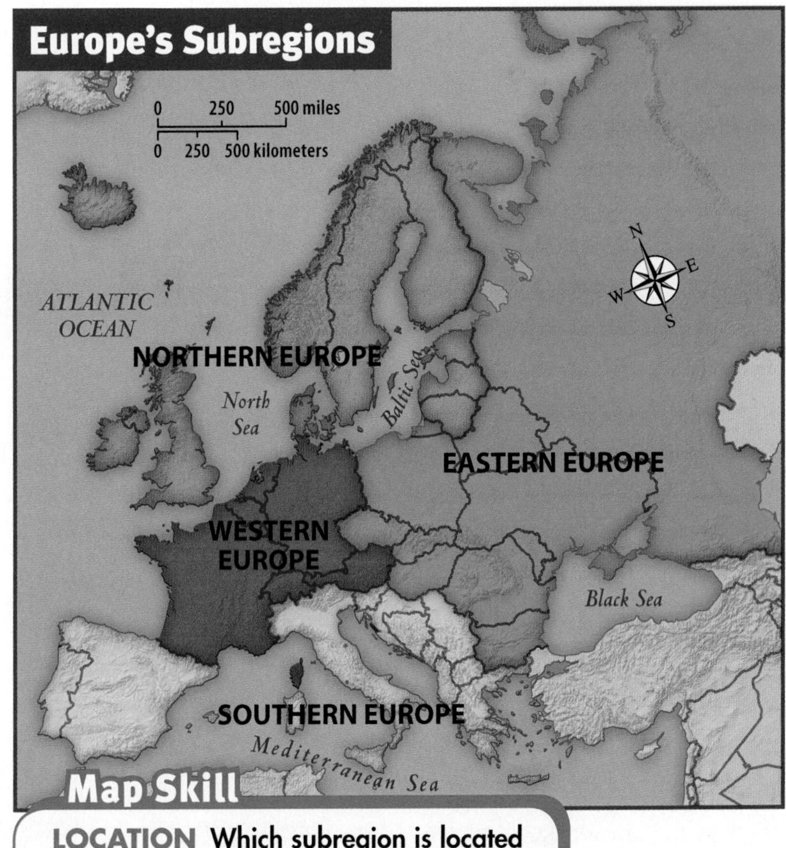

Map Skill

LOCATION **Which subregion is located closest to the Black Sea?**

Ⓑ LANDFORMS

Europe is a large **peninsula** with many smaller peninsulas branching out from it. A peninsula is a body of land almost entirely surrounded by water, projecting out from a large land mass. There are also many islands scattered around Europe. Great Britain and Ireland are two of the main islands found in the Atlantic Ocean. Sicily and Crete are large islands that are located in the Mediterranean Sea. There are a variety of landforms throughout Europe, including amazing mountains, shimmering seas, rolling farmland, and temperate islands.

Plains

The Northern European Plain is Europe's chief landform. The large lowland area extends across the northern half of mainland Europe. It reaches from southeastern England and western France eastward to Poland, Ukraine, and Russia.

The plain's rich soils drew farmers to the area. The farms grow grains, fruits, and vegetables. The Northern European Plain also has deposits of coal, iron ore, and other mineral resources, which led to Europe's industrial growth.

The plain is densely populated because it is rich agriculturally and industrially. Today, many of Europe's largest cities, such as Paris, Warsaw, and Berlin, are located on the plain. There are two additional lowland areas located in Eastern Europe—the Hungarian Plain and the Ukraine Steppe. These also have rich soil that supports farming.

A village in the French Alps

Mountains and Highlands

The North European Plain is interrupted by steep mountains that create its southern border. The Alpine Mountain System contains the region's most recognizable and tallest mountain ranges. They stretch from southern France to the Balkan Peninsula. The system includes the Alps in south-central Europe, the Pyrenees between France and Spain, and the Carpathians located in east-central Europe. Mont Blanc is the highest peak in Europe. It is found in the Alps on the border of France and Italy and rises 15,771 feet.

Mountains have helped to isolate certain countries and peoples in Europe. However, they did not completely stop movement. **Passes**, or low areas between mountains, allow people and goods to move through.

Three other highland areas are older and have been rounded by millions of years of erosion. The Uplands are located in northwest Europe and stretch from Sweden through Great Britain to Iceland. The land in this area is best for raising livestock, such as sheep. Another highland area, the Central Uplands, contains most of Europe's coal supply. It is located in Southern Poland and extends to France. The third highland area is the Meseta and is located in Spain. It is a plateau where people grow grains and livestock.

Quick Check

Make Inferences **Why do you think many of Europe's largest cities are located on the North European Plain?**

C NATURAL RESOURCES

Europe is a leader in the world economy because of its abundant supply of natural resources. A major resource found in Europe is its fertile soil. Europe has some of the best farmland in the world. Farmers grow many grains, including nearly all the world's rye, most of its oats, and nearly half of its wheat. Europe also produces more potatoes than any other region in the world.

The United Kingdom exports special clay used to make fine china dishes. Marble from Italy and granite from Norway and Sweden are used as fine building materials.

Energy Resources

Coal has been the main energy source in Europe for many years. Today, almost half the world's coal comes from Europe. Coal mining provides jobs for many people throughout the region. European mines also produce about one-third of the world's iron ore.

Europe produces more electricity with wind turbines than any other region in the world.

Petroleum and natural gas are other energy resources found in Europe. The region's most valuable oil fields lie beneath the North Sea.

Europe also relies on several "clean" energy sources that cause less pollution. In the highlands and mountains, fast moving rivers are used to create hydroelectric power. Germany, Spain, and Denmark are leaders in building wind farms, which use large turbines to create electricity from the wind.

Quick Check

Make Inferences **Why do you think "clean" energy sources are important?**

Check Understanding

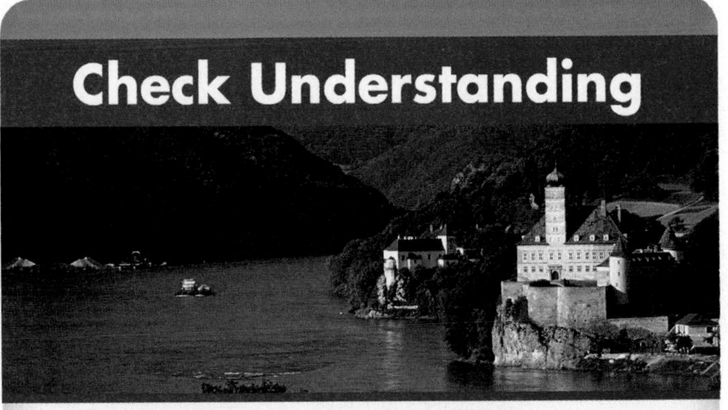

1. **VOCABULARY** Write a paragraph about the physical geography of Europe. Use the vocabulary words in your paragraph.

   landlocked **navigable** **passes**

2. **READING SKILL** Make Inferences Use your chart from page 172 to write about how people use landforms in Europe.

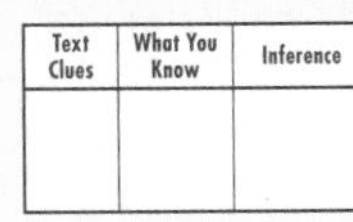

Text Clues	What You Know	Inference

3. **Write About It** Write about how the mountains and highlands affect the people of Europe.

Map and Globe Skills

Use a Time Zone Map

VOCABULARY

time zone
Greenwich Mean Time

The concept of **time zones** was developed to allow people living in the same region or country to share the same time frame. Europe spans four different time zones.

Since 1884 the world has been divided into 24 time zones, one for each hour of the day. Since there are so many different time zones, it was necessary to choose one time zone as a reference. The Prime Meridian, which passes through Greenwich, England, starts the day. This time is called **Greenwich Mean Time** or **GMT**.

Learn It

- The map shows the world divided into time zones.
- To find the time in any region, look at the clocks. They show the time when it is noon at the Prime Meridian.

Try It

- What time is it in your time zone? How many hours are you from GMT?

Apply It

- Look at your classroom clock. What is the GMT when you read this page?

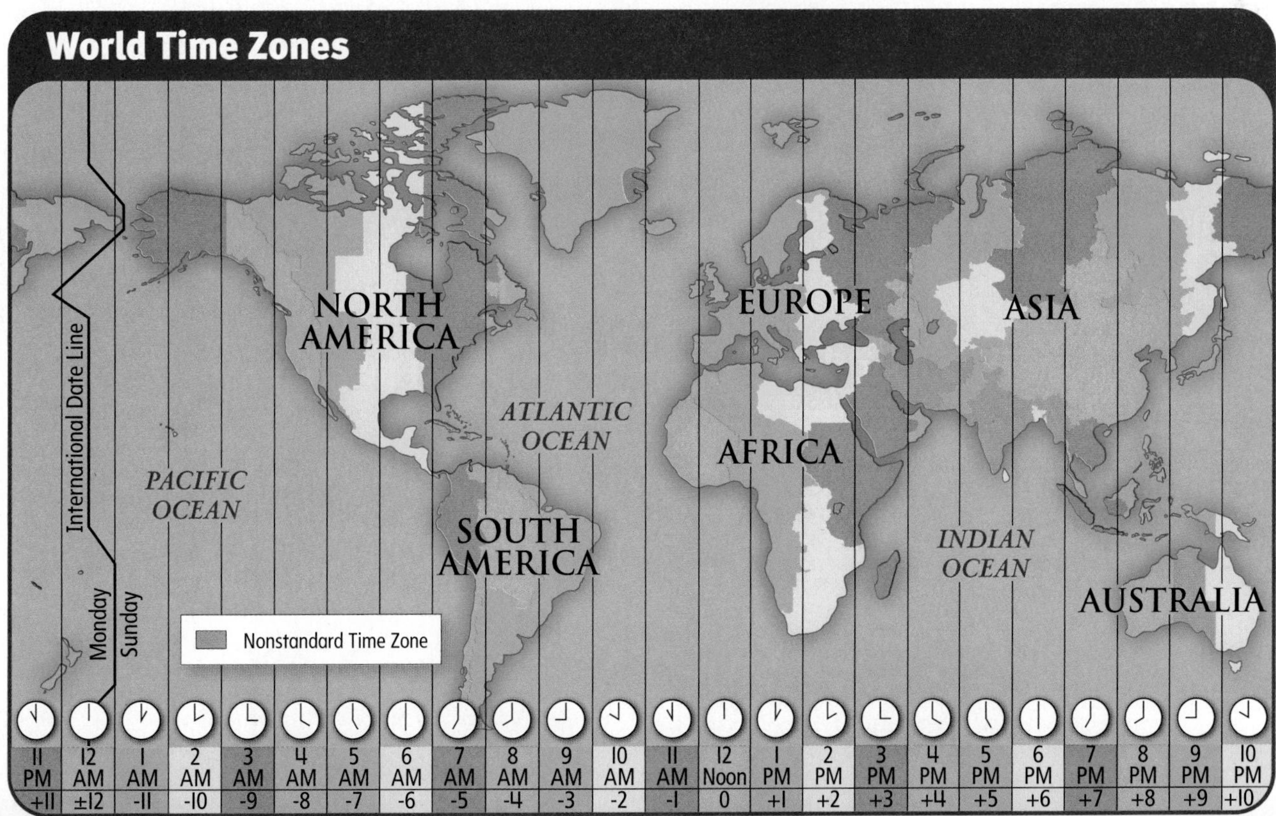

Lesson 2

VOCABULARY

westerlies p. 179

deciduous p. 180

coniferous p. 180

mistral p. 180

sirocco p. 181

READING SKILL

Make Inferences

Copy the chart below. Use it to write details about the climate of Europe.

Text Clues	What You Know	Inference

STANDARDS FOCUS

SOCIAL STUDIES People, Places, and Environments

GEOGRAPHY Physical Systems

Climate Regions of Europe

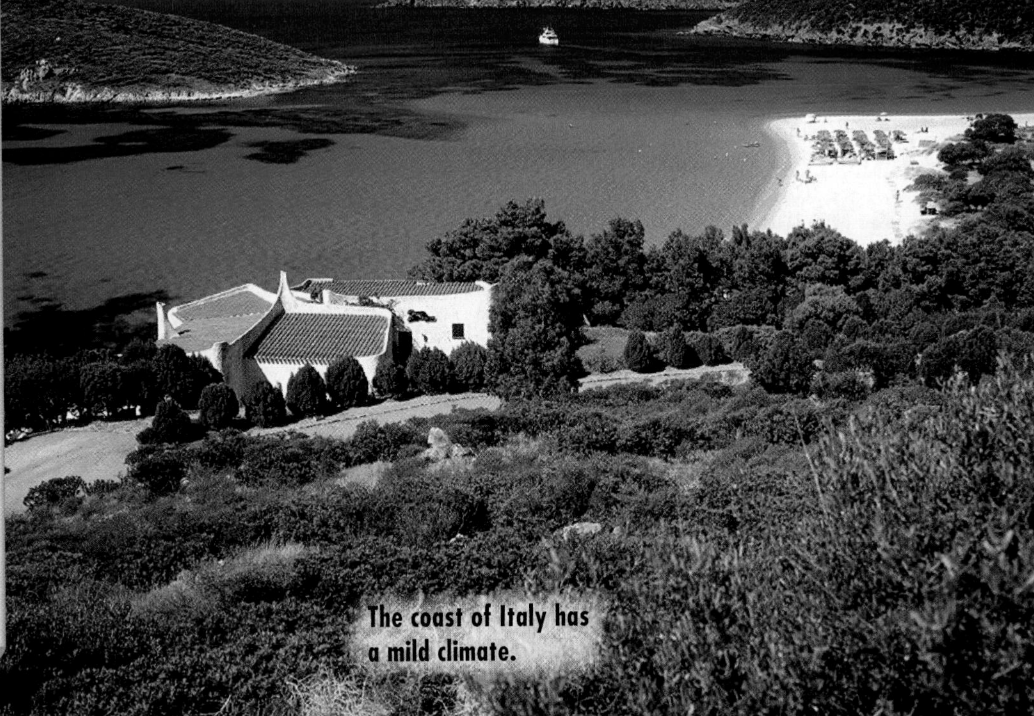

The coast of Italy has a mild climate.

Visual Preview

How does the climate in Europe impact people's lives?

A Westerlies play a major role in warming the climate of Europe.

B Europe has eight different climate regions, each with different vegetation.

Ⓐ INFLUENCES ON CLIMATE

Wind patterns and water currents shape Europe's climate. Together they create a mild climate throughout much of the continent.

Madrid, Spain, and Columbus, Ohio, are at about the same latitude, yet January temperatures in Spain are much milder than those in Ohio. This is because the North Atlantic Current carries warm waters from the Gulf of Mexico to Europe. Winds from the west pass over the water and carry more warmth to the coasts of Europe. These winds are known as **westerlies**, and they play a major role in warming the European climate.

Other wind patterns also have an effect on Europe's climate. Winds from Africa warm parts of southern Europe. Winter winds from Asia lower temperatures throughout most of Eastern Europe.

The water surrounding Europe also affects the continent's climate. Winds blowing off the water cool the land in the summer and warm the land in the winter.

As in other parts of the world, location influences what vegetation grows in Europe. Agricultural goods can be grown further north here than in North America. The vegetation in the region varies from forests to grasslands to tundra plants. The types of vegetation in Europe are closely linked to the climate regions.

Quick Check

Make Inferences **How might the climate of Europe affects its people?**

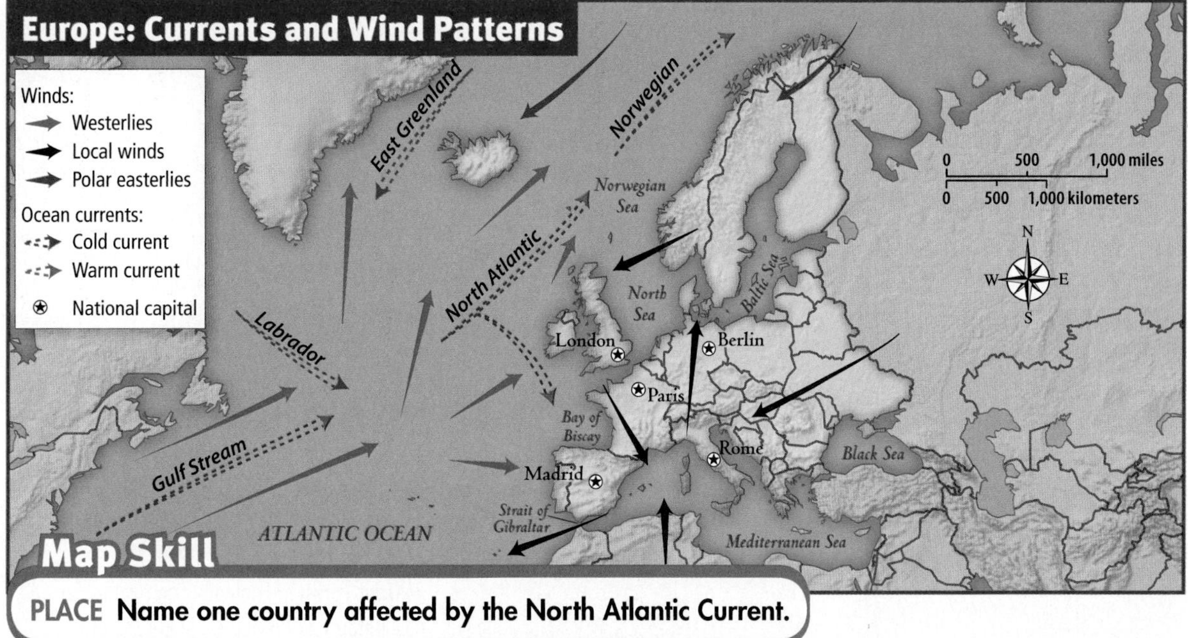

Map Skill

PLACE **Name one country affected by the North Atlantic Current.**

B CLIMATE REGIONS

Europe has eight climate regions, each with different vegetation. Wind, ocean currents, latitude, and landforms all help determine Europe's varied climates. Most of Europe falls into three main climate regions—marine west coast, humid continental, and Mediterranean.

Marine West Coast

Much of northwestern and central Europe has a marine west coast climate. This region has mild winters, cool summers, and large amounts of rainfall. The North Atlantic Current brings warm waters to this part of Europe. Because of the mild temperatures, the region has a long growing season. Forests thrive in this climate. Some forests consist of **deciduous** trees, which lose their leaves in the fall. **Coniferous** trees, also called evergreens, grow in the cooler areas of this climate.

Humid Continental

Most of Eastern Europe has a humid continental climate. Cool, dry winds from the Artic and Asia give this region cool summers and very cold winters. Because of drier winds, the humid continental region also gets less rain and snow. The region has mixed forests of deciduous and coniferous trees.

Mediterranean

The Mediterranean region includes most of Southern Europe. This region is known for its hot, dry summers and mild, rainy winters. The mountains of Southern Europe affect the Mediterranean climate. The Pyrenees and Alps block chilly northern winds from reaching Spain and Italy. In southern France, the lack of a mountain barrier allows a cold, dry wind to blow in from the north. This wind, the **mistral**, can occur in the winter and spring.

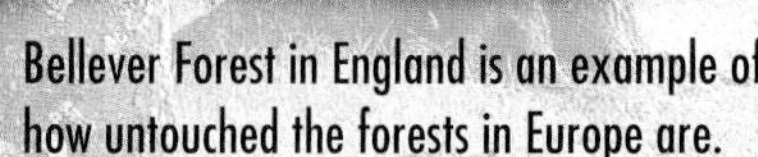

Bellever Forest in England is an example of how untouched the forests in Europe are.

The Mediterranean climate is also affected by hot, dry winds that sometime blows from Africa. These winds are called **siroccos** in Italy. They pick up moisture as they cross the Mediterranean Sea and make southern Europe hot and humid. Plants that grow in the region need to be drought resistant because of the overall lack of rain. This is why olive trees and grape vines are able to thrive in the region.

Other Climate Regions

Northern Europe has two regions of extreme cold. The subarctic zone covers parts of Norway, Sweden, and Finland. Evergreens grow in the low altitudes of this region. The tundra region is found in the very north of these countries and in Iceland. The tundra is an area of vast treeless plains near the North Pole. The higher altitudes of the Alps and Carpathians have a highland climate, which is generally cold.

Europe's last two climate regions cover a relative small part of land. The steppe region is located in southern Ukraine. Steppes are dry grasslands. A small piece of land north of the Adriatic Sea falls into the humid subtropical region. This climate has hot, wet summers and mild, wet winters.

Quick Check

Make Inferences **Explain why forests thrive in the marine west coast climate.**

Map Skill

LOCATION **Which climate does Oslo have?**

Check Understanding

1. **VOCABULARY** Write one sentence for each vocabulary word.

   westerlies **deciduous** **coniferous**
   mistral **sirocco**

2. **READING SKILL** Make Inferences Use your chart from page 178 to describe the climate regions of Europe.

Text Clues	What You Know	Inference

3. **Write About It** Write about why climate regions in Europe differ.

Lesson 3

VOCABULARY

city-state p. 184
philosopher p. 184
polytheism p. 184
consul p. 186
aqueduct p. 187

READING SKILL

Make Inferences

Copy the chart below. Fill in the chart with details about ancient Europe.

Text Clues	What You Know	Inference

STANDARDS FOCUS

SOCIAL STUDIES Time, Continuity, & Change
GEOGRAPHY World in Spatial Terms

ANCIENT EUROPE

A temple porch in Athens, Greece

Visual Preview

How did the Greek and Roman civilizations develop?

A Ancient Greeks depended on the sea for food and trade.

B The people of Athens developed the world's first democracy.

C Rome began as a monarchy, changed into a republic, and grew to an empire.

D When the Roman Empire split, the eastern part became the Byzantine Empire.

Ⓐ THE RISE OF GREECE

Ancient Greece and Rome laid the foundations for European civilizations. More than 2,500 years ago, the ancient Greeks and Romans settled near the Mediterranean Sea. Eventually, their cultures spread throughout Europe and beyond.

Greece is a mountainous land on the European coast of the Mediterranean Sea. Over 400 islands lie off the coast, while two peninsulas make up mainland Greece. The earliest Greek civilizations began in farming and fishing communities. The people felt deep ties to the land, which is both rugged and beautiful. At the same time, mountains, islands, and seas divide the areas from one another. As a result, early Greek communities grew up fiercely independent.

Farming

Much of Greece is covered with mountains and rocky soil, mostly unsuitable for farming. Greek farmers met the challenges of rocky soil by planting crops that grew well in the harsh environment. One major crop was olives, which were a staple of Greek life. They were served as food and made into oil, which was used for cooking and fuel.

Greek farmers also raised sheep and goats. Food was scarce, however, no matter how hard the farmers worked. Most Greeks had to rely on the sea to survive.

The Greek Economy

Most Greeks lived within 40 miles of the sea, which helped link them to the rest of the world. They became fishers, sailors, shipbuilders, and traders. Greek merchants, with their sturdy boats and sailing knowledge, brought grain from surrounding areas. These traders traveled as far as Egypt and Spain to do business.

Quick Check

Make Inferences **How do you think the geography of Greece affected its people?**

A Greek ship used oars and sails. ▼

B ANCIENT GREECE

The early trading civilizations helped create the ancient Greek culture. The Minoans lived on the island of Crete, the Mycenaeans controlled the Greek mainland, and the Phoenicians sailed from land that is today Lebanon. By 700 B.C. Greek culture had spread around the Aegean Sea.

Athens

After warfare led to the decline of these civilizations, independent territories called **city-states** developed throughout Greece. Though separated by geography, these city-states had the same language and culture.

One of the most prosperous and powerful city-states was Athens. The people of Athens introduced the world's first democracy.

A democracy is a political system in which all citizens share in running the government. Athenian democracy set an example for later nations, including the United States.

Culture and Religion

Learning and the arts thrived in Athens. Among the city-state's great thinkers were Socrates, Plato, and Aristotle. These Greek **philosophers** studied history and mathematics. A philosopher is a "lover of wisdom."

The Greeks enjoyed poems that described Greek history. One of the most famous ancient Greek poets was Homer. He created two epics, or long poems that tell the story of legendary figures. In the *Iliad*, Homer described a war between the Greeks and Trojans. In the *Odyssey* he described the adventures of the hero, Odysseus.

The Greeks practiced **polytheism**, or the belief in many gods and goddesses. According to Greek mythology, there were 12 main gods and goddesses who lived on Mount Olympus, Greece's highest mountain.

PEOPLE

Socrates was a sculptor whose true love was philosophy. Socrates left no writings, so we know about him only by the writings of his pupils, such as Plato. Socrates taught many pupils, but he accepted no pay. He believed that the goal of education was only to improve the individual.

Socrates

The ancient Greeks believed that their gods and goddesses played roles in daily life. They also believed that their gods controlled natural events, such as storms. Many festivals honored the Greek gods. For example, the Olympic Games honored Zeus.

Sparta Versus Athens

By about 500 B.C., the two most powerful city-states in Greece were Athens and Sparta. They had different values and cultures, and they often fought with each other and with other city-states.

Athens became rich and powerful. Other city-states grew jealous and afraid of Athens. In 431 B.C., Sparta and its allies attacked Athens, beginning the Peloponnesian War. Weakened by disease and a lack of a strong leader, Athens had to surrender in 404 B.C. The victory did Sparta little good. Greece was exhausted by war, and a new empire was rising in the north.

New Power

By 338 B.C. Phillip II, the king of Macedonia, a country north of Greece, had conquered all of the mainland Greek city-states. Phillip II was killed two years later, leaving Alexander, his 20-year-old son, ruler of the Greek world.

From the age of 16, Alexander was trained to be a general. In 334 B.C. he led his army on a war of conquest. By the age of 32, Alexander was ruler of the largest empire in the world.

Trade boomed, Greek culture mixed with Egyptian and Persian cultures, and scientific advances spread. When Alexander suddenly died in 323 B.C., his empire quickly broke into several smaller kingdoms. By about 130 B.C., the Romans had conquered most of the Greek kingdoms.

Quick Check

Make Inferences **How might you have ruled Greece?**

Most city-states were built around an acropolis, a walled hill where people could seek safety from attack.

C ROME

While Greece ruled the eastern Mediterranean, Rome became a dominant power on the Italian Peninsula.

A Republic

Rome was first ruled by kings, but it changed into a republic in 509 B.C. In a republic, government leaders are voted into office. A group called patricians, from Rome's wealthiest families, became rulers. Beneath them were plebeians, poor farmers and shopkeepers who could not hold office.

Rome had two elected leaders, called **consuls.** Both consuls had to agree on any public plan, and either consul could veto, or turn down, a plan of the other consul. The Senate, or the lawmaking body of Rome, had to approve the consuls' plans.

The Plebeians also wanted political power. They decided to go on strike until the patricians agreed to share power. The plebeians gained an assembly with elected representatives called tribunes.

The Roman government developed a code of laws. Written on bronze tablets known as the Twelve Tables, the laws stated that all free citizens had the right to be treated equally. Roman law led to principles we use today.

Julius Ceasar

By 146 B.C., the Romans defeated their enemy, Carthage, a Phoenician city-state in northern Africa. They now ruled the Mediterranean world. Several civil wars erupted between wealthy Romans and powerful generals. One of the generals, Julius Caesar, took power.

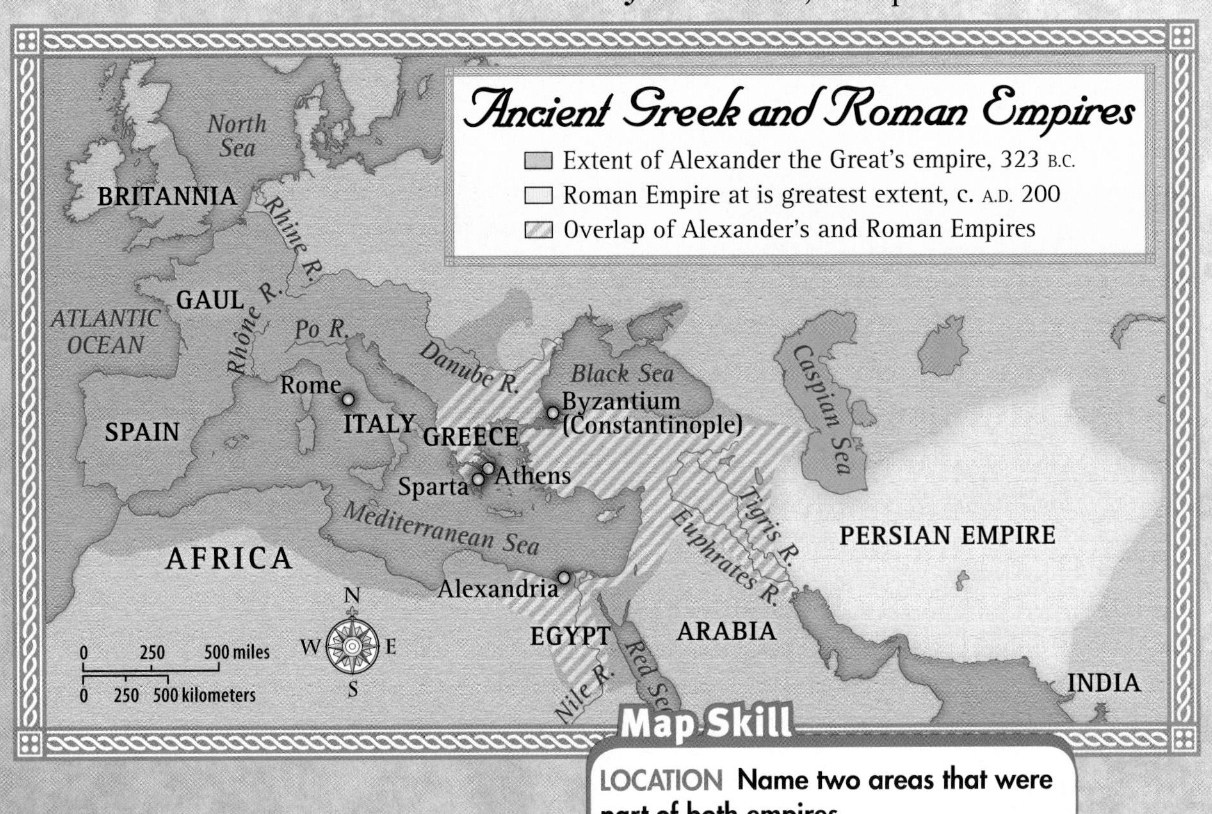

Map Skill

LOCATION **Name two areas that were part of both empires.**

Caesar became popular after conquering Gaul, present-day France, and made himself dictator for life. Although he was later killed, Caesar set the stage for the Roman Empire.

Augustus

The first emperor, or all powerful ruler, was Augustus. His rule brought order to Rome's vast lands. This period, called *Pax Romana*, was a time of peace, artistic growth, and expanding trade that lasted 200 years.

Augustus rebuilt Rome with stately palaces, fountains, and splendid public buildings. The arts flourished as never before. Augustus ordered a system of roads built to connect Rome to every part of the empire. Once built, the roads helped to make communication and trade throughout the empire possible.

Roman cities enjoyed police and fire protection. **Aqueducts**, long stone structures, were built to bring fresh water into the cities. Many Roman cities had huge public baths with picture galleries and libraries.

The Fall of Rome

By A.D. 200 the Empire began to decline. New civil wars, combined with Germanic and Persian invasions, weakened the economy. A common problem was inflation. Inflation is a rapid increase in prices. One effect of inflation was less income. With less income, fewer taxes were paid and the Empire could not afford to defend its borders.

To better govern the empire, the emperor Diocletian divided it into a western and eastern empire in A.D. 293. His successor, Constantine, moved the center of power to a city in the east called Byzantium. In honor of himself, he renamed the city Constantinople.

Citizenship

Citizenship Then and Now

Roman citizenship was a prized possession. To gain Roman citizenship, a person could serve in the army or work for the government. Some bought their citizenship but for a very high price. Today, immigrants to the United States must pass a test and promise to obey the laws before they can become American citizens.

Write About It Write a letter telling what you think a good citizen of any country should know.

The western empire shrank in importance and power. Finally, in A.D. 476, a Germanic tribe conquered the city of Rome. Even so, the influence of Rome would outlive its empire. Roman traditions continued in the eastern, or Byzantine, empire for almost one thousand years. In the west, small Germanic kingdoms adopted Roman laws, customs, and language.

Quick Check

Make Inferences **Do you believe the government of Rome was fair?**

D CHRISTIANITY

During the *Pax Romana*, Christianity was developing in Judea, the Jewish state that the Romans conquered and renamed Palestine.

Jesus's Teachings

In Palestine, a Jewish teacher, Jesus of Nazareth, preached a message of love and forgiveness. His teachings often used parables, or simple stories that contain a message. Some of these stories taught that people should seek eternal life, and not possessions. Others stressed the importance of loving all people. His teachings attracted followers, known as Christians, as well as enemies.

The Death of Jesus

The Roman governor became afraid that Jesus wanted to be king of Judea. He feared there would be a revolt. When Jesus came to Jerusalem to celebrate the Passover festival, Roman authorities arrested him. The governor had him executed by crucifixion, meaning "putting to death by hanging from a cross."

Within three days Christians reported that Jesus had risen from the dead. He rejoined his followers and told them of the coming kingdom of God. His followers took this as proof that Jesus was the son of God. Today, Christians celebrate his renewed life on Easter Sunday.

Christians wanted to spread their faith. Two early leaders, Peter and Paul, set up Rome's first Christain Church. At first, officials persecuted them, but the new religion spread quickly. When the emperor himself became a Christain in A.D. 392, Christainity became the official religion of the Roman Empire.

The Byzantine Empire

When the Roman Empire was split into eastern and western parts, the eastern part remained strong and prosperous. Known as the Byzantine Empire, it lasted about a thousand years after the fall of Rome.

The center of the Byzantine Empire was Constantinople. It grew rich from trade and manufacturing. Its walls were a marvel of engineering that stopped all attackers for nearly a thousand years. The city also had the largest church in the world, called Hagia Sophia, or "holy wisdom."

In A.D. 527, Justinian became emperor of the Byzantine Empire. He conquered new lands and even tried to win back the territory of the western Roman Empire.

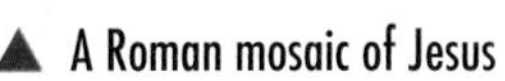

▲ A Roman mosaic of Jesus

Justinian reorganized the laws of the Roman Empire. His code of laws covered property, marriage, women, slaves, and criminals. The Justinian Code was the basis of Byzantine law and became very influential in shaping future legal systems.

Split of the Church

There were almost constant arguments between Rome and Constantinople about religion. In 1054 the Church split. Eastern Christians became known as Orthodox Christians. The Byzantines sent missionaries to spread the Orthodox Church's beliefs to Russia, Africa, and southwest Asia.

QUICK CHECK

Make Inferences **Explain why you believe the Justinian Code is still important.**

Check Understanding

1. **VOCABULARY** Write a paragraph about ancient Greece using these vocabulary words.

   city-state **philosopher**
   consul

2. **READING SKILL** Make Inferences
   Use your chart from page 182 to describe the importance of Rome's government.

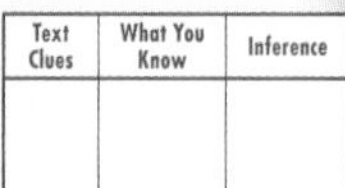

Text Clues	What You Know	Inference

3. **Write About It** Write about how the Roman Empire developed.

Hagia Sophia, Istanbul, Turkey

Lesson 4

VOCABULARY

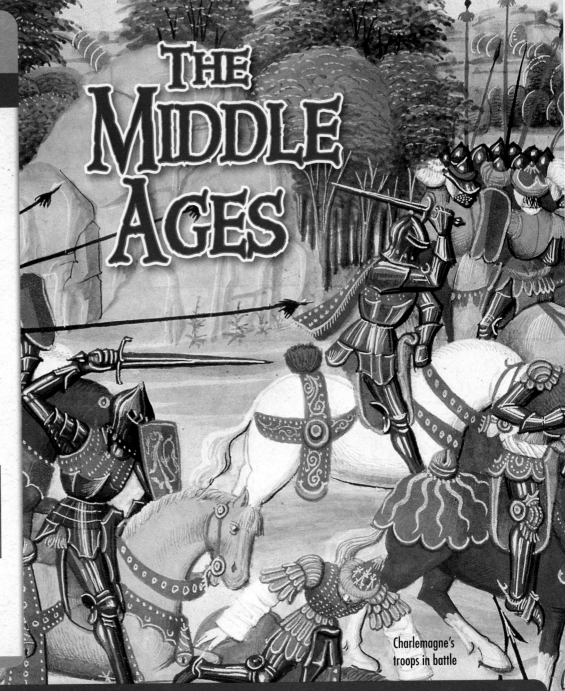

feudalism p. 192
manor p. 192
vassal p. 192
serf p. 192
guild p. 192
nation-state p. 195

READING SKILL

Make Inferences
Copy the chart below. Then use it to make inferences about the Middle Ages in Europe.

Text Clues	What You Know	Inference

STANDARDS FOCUS

SOCIAL STUDIES — Time, Continuity, & Change
GEOGRAPHY — Human Systems

THE MIDDLE AGES

Charlemagne's troops in battle

Visual Preview

How did life change for Europeans during the Middle Ages?

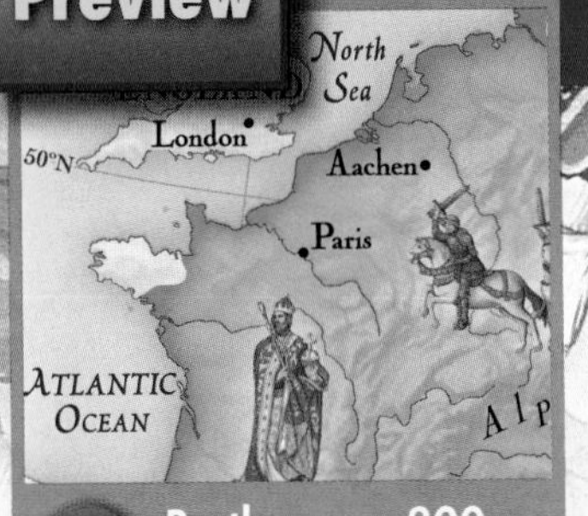

A By the year 800, Charlemagne had reunited much of western Europe.

B When feudalism became a way of life in Europe, everyone in society had a set role.

C Popes urged Christians to join in Crusades to capture Jerusalem.

D A plague called the Black Death helped to end feudalism.

Ⓐ EUROPE AFTER ROME

After Rome's fall, Europe entered the Middle Ages, a period that lasted until the 1400s. During this time European society, religion, and government underwent great changes.

Long after the Roman Empire fell, its culture still connected Europeans—through its roads, its aqueducts, and the Latin language. In most ways though, Europe had split apart. No one felt safe or secure. This time was the Middle Ages.

Charles the Great

Around 790 Charles the Great, also known as Charlemagne, became the ruler of a Germanic group called the Franks. Charlemagne's armies conquered territory in today's France, Italy, and Germany.

The early Middle Ages are often called "the Dark Ages" because few Europeans could read or write. Charlemagne built schools and hired judges to write down his laws. He also tried to spread Christianity wherever his troops went.

The Holy Roman Emperor

On Christmas 800, Charlemagne visited Pope Leo III in Rome. As Charlemagne bowed his head to pray, the pope surprised him by placing a gold crown on his head and declaring him emperor. Charlemagne claimed he never expected the crown. From then on he was the "Holy Roman Emperor." Charlemagne's empire did not last long, though. It split up soon after he died in 814.

QUICK CHECK

Make Inferences **Why might Charlemagne have pretended to be surprised when he was crowned emperor?**

LOCATION **Which major city was at the southeastern corner of Charlemagne's empire?**

B LIFE IN THE MIDDLE AGES

For many Europeans life during the Middle Ages was hard and short. Much of Europe suffered periods of war, disease, and hunger.

Feudal System

The system that helped keep order in Charlemagne's time was **feudalism**. In most places kings divided their land into **manors**, or large areas of farmland controlled by local leaders called lords. A lord divided control of his land among other nobles called **vassals**. The part of a manor controlled by a vassal was called a fief. One way a vassal served his lord was by defending the manor as a knight, or armored soldier on horseback.

At the bottom of feudal society were the farmers called **serfs**, or peasants. Serfs farmed a manor's land and, in return, were protected by the lord and his knights. Serfs had few rights. They could not leave their manor or marry without their lord's permission.

At around age seven, the sons of lords and vassals were sent to live with knights who taught them how to fight and follow the knights' code of conduct, known as chivalry. The daughters of nobles were taught how to take care of the manor. The children of serfs, on the other hand, did not get any formal education. They joined their parents in the fields.

The Rise of Towns

Europe's towns began to grow around the year 1000. Manors had surplus crops to sell in the towns. Craftworkers in the towns formed **guilds**, organized groups who set prices and rules for their businesses. Serfs moved to the towns as well because, under feudal rules, if they could avoid capture in a town for a year and a day, then they were free.

The towns were not pleasant places to live. People threw waste and garbage into the crowded streets. Pigs and rats spread disease.

Kings and queens

Lords and ladies

Knights

Peasants and serfs

Under Feudalism each level of society had duties to groups above and below it.

Invaders from the North

During the early Middle Ages, Norsemen, or "North men," came in ships from northern Europe—today's Denmark, Norway, and Sweden. In surprise attacks, they looted towns and then sailed off.

Some Norsemen started a settlement on the northwest coast of France. Today, this area is called Normandy after the "Normans," or Norsemen, who lived there. As happened in other cultures around the world, the Norse invaders began following some of the customs of the places they conquered. Soon, the Normans were French-speaking Christians.

▲ King John signing the Magna Carta

William the Conqueror

The greatest Norman leader was William the Conqueror. King Edward of England promised William that he could become King of England after Edward's death. When Edward died in 1066, William led a Norman army across the English Channel to claim the throne. As king William took land from English lords and instead gave it to his Norman knights.

William wanted to learn more about the large country he now controlled. He ordered a census, or official counting, of every person, animal, and manor in the land. Today, William's census gives us an accurate picture of life in England during the early Middle Ages.

The Magna Carta

One of William's descendants, King John, raised taxes and sent his enemies to prison without fair trials. By 1215 angry English nobles and their soldiers gave John a choice: sign their Magna Carta, or "Great Charter," or lose the throne. The Magna Carta was the first document that gave nobles and other people in England certain basic rights the king could not take away. For example, the king could not throw nobles in jail without a fair trial or raise taxes without a noble's permission.

Quick Check

Make Inferences **In what ways do you think the Magna Carta has influenced our government today?**

Ⓒ THE CRUSADES

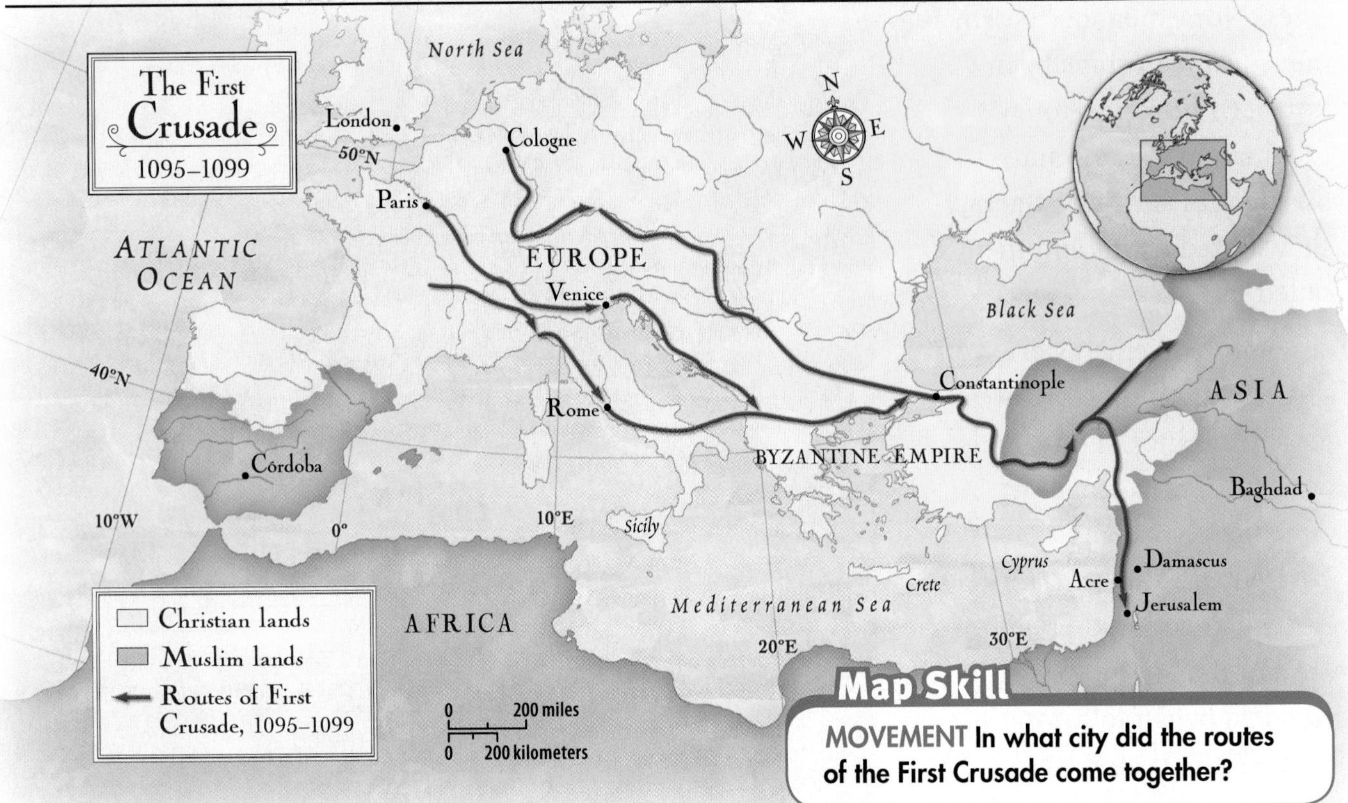

Map Skill

MOVEMENT In what city did the routes of the First Crusade come together?

By the year 1000, most people in Europe had become Christians. This time period became known as the Age of Faith. As European towns grew wealthy, they showed their faith by building churches and cathedrals.

The Crusades Begin

In 1071 the Seljuk Turks, Muslim soldiers from Central Asia, captured Jerusalem. The city was holy to Jews, Christians, and Muslims. Christians had been making pilgrimages, or religious journeys, to Jerusalem for years. Europeans worried that the Muslim Turks would stop Christian pilgrimages to the city.

The Christian leaders of the Byzantine Empire had split from the church in Rome years before. However, now they asked the pope for help in fighting the Turks. In 1095 Pope Urban II called on European Christians to march to Jerusalem to take the city.

As many as 100,000 Christians answered the pope's call. They believed God had called them to fight a holy war, later called a Crusade. The soldiers were called Crusaders.

Many Crusaders wore a red cross on their clothes as a sign of their obedience to the pope's call. Their journey was difficult and poorly planned. Almost half of the Crusaders died of hunger or sickness before they even reached Jerusalem.

The Crusaders who survived the journey reached Jerusalem in 1099. In a bloody one-month battle, they captured the city. After their victory most of the Crusaders went home to Europe and their families.

Christians lost control of Jerusalem less than 100 years after the First Crusade. Popes called for nine Crusades in all, but by 1291 all the lands won were back under Muslim control.

Crusades Change Europe

The Crusades had a major effect on Europeans. Goods began to flow more easily between European and Muslim lands. This trade benefited European kings, who taxed the goods that crossed their borders.

Kings also took over land from nobles who left to fight in the Crusades. As a result, feudalism slowly faded away, and Europe's kingdoms grew stronger and larger. Many of them later became modern Europe's **nation-states**, or countries made up of people who share a common culture or history.

EVENT

The **Council of Clermont** was a meeting of over three hundred clergy members. At the Council, Pope Urban II called for the first Crusade. He challenged Christians to join in a holy war. The pope promised: "All who die . . . shall have immediate remission [forgiveness] of sins."

Council of Clermont

Marco Polo

In 1271 near the end of the Crusades, a young explorer from Venice, named Marco Polo, traveled the entire length of the Silk Road—the trade route that linked China to the Mediterranean Sea. Then he stayed in China for 21 years. When Polo returned home, he shared amazing tales of his adventures. Polo inspired other Europeans to travel the Silk Road, which increased trade with China and paved the way for the Age of Exploration.

Quick Check

Make Inferences **Why would serfs decide to join the Crusades?**

Crusaders marching toward Jerusalem

D THE BLACK DEATH

DataGraphic

The Plague

The map below shows when the Black Death reached different regions of Europe. The chart shows how the population of Europe changed during the plague years.

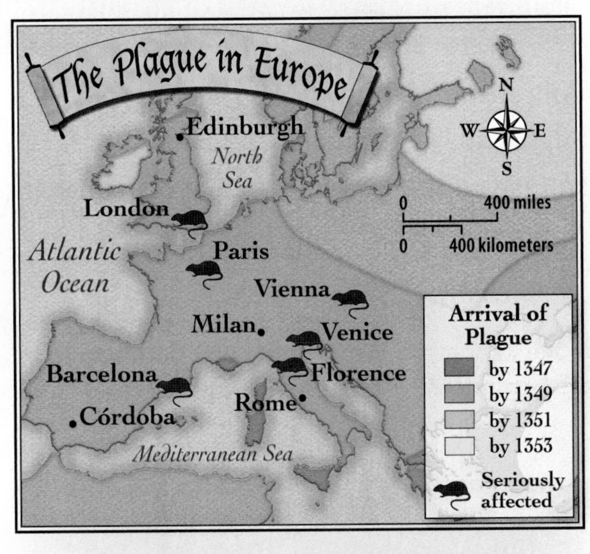

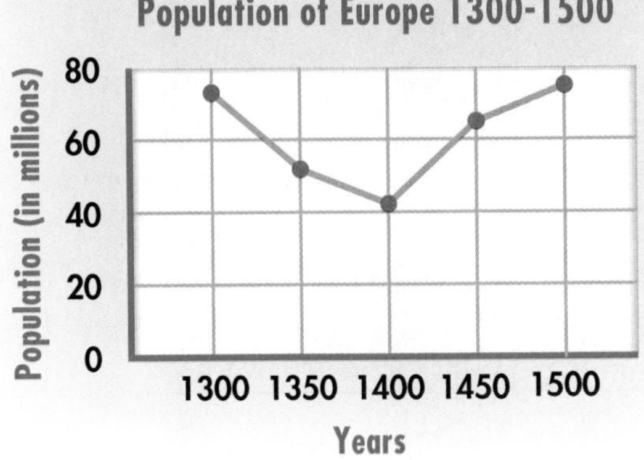

Think About the Plague

1. How long did it take for the plague to spread across Europe?
2. How was life in Europe in 1400 different from life there in 1300?

In the 1300s a plague struck Europe. A plague is a terrible disease that spreads quickly. The plague, called the Black Death, killed about 38 million people. Today, scientists believe the disease was the bubonic plague, which is carried from rats to humans by fleas. European cities of the time were filled with rats and fleas, and many people were exposed to the illness.

The plague probably began in the Gobi, a desert in Asia, and spread west along the Silk Road. It struck Asia in the 1330s, killing millions of people in China and the Middle East. By 1347 the Black Death had reached Europe. At least one in three Europeans died from the plague. The plague affected Europeans for about 130 years.

One writer, Robert Avesbury, described life in England during the plague years:

> “Those marked for death were scarce permitted to live longer than three or four days. It showed favor to no one, except a very few of the wealthy. On the same day, 20, 40, or 60 bodies, and on many occasions many more, might be committed for burial together in the same pit.”

Serfs No More

The death of so many millions of people changed Europe's economy. As demand for food dropped, prices for farm goods fell.

Trade also declined because many merchants died while they traveled. So many serfs died that lords had to begin to pay workers to plant their crops. Serfs then began to ask for higher pay and freedom from their lords. Some of these workers used their wages to rent their own land and earn more money. These changes sped up the decline of feudalism in Europe.

QUICK CHECK

Make Inferences **How did the Black Death change life for lords?**

Check Understanding

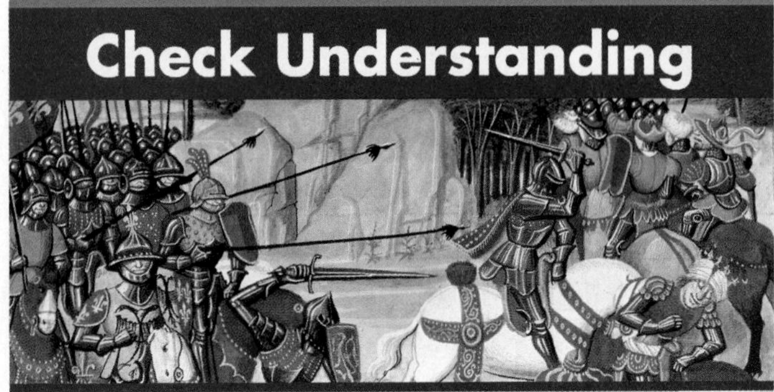

1. **VOCABULARY** Use these words in a paragraph about feudalism during the Middle Ages.

   manor **vassal** **serf** **guild**

2. **READING SKILL Make Inferences** Use your chart from page 190 to describe the importance of the Crusades.

3. **Write About It** Write about what life would have been like for you during the Middle Ages.

EXPLORE The Big Idea

◀ A doctor tries to help a plague patient by treating the sores that were a symptom of the disease.

Renaissance and Reformation

Lesson 5

VOCABULARY

Renaissance p. 199
humanism p. 199
Inquisition p. 202
Reformation p. 202
caravel p. 204
circumnavigate p. 205

READING SKILL

Make Inferences
Copy the chart below. Use it to write details about the Renaissance and the Reformation.

Text Clues	What You Know	Inference

STANDARDS FOCUS

SOCIAL STUDIES Time, Continuity, & Change
GEOGRAPHY Human Systems

In this painting, *The Procession of the Magi*, by Benozzo Gozzoli, the young man on the horse is Lorenzo the Magnificent.

Visual Preview

How did new ideas and conflicts change Europe?

A Artists and thinkers were supported by rulers such as the Medicis of Italy.

B During the Renaissance the arts and sciences thrived.

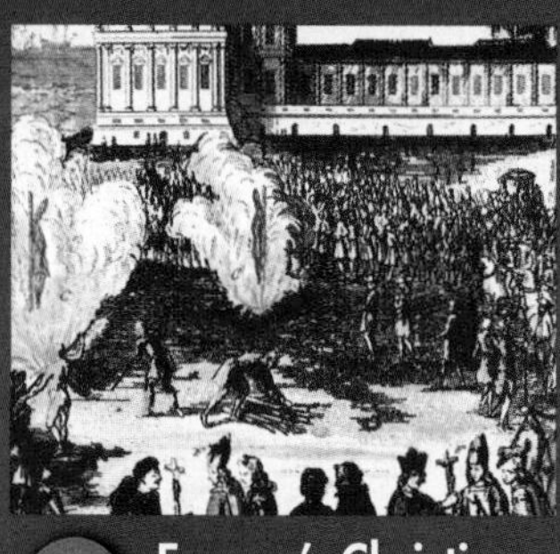

C Europe's Christians split into two religious groups.

D Europeans began to look for a water route to Asia.

A TIME FOR NEW IDEAS

The plague caused terrible suffering in Europe. For 130 years, people had lived with death and despair every day. Now that the plague had ended, the people were ready for something new.

A period called the **Renaissance** began in Italy around 1350. *Renaissance* is a French word meaning "rebirth." The Renaissance in part was a result of the rise of trade between cities around the world. During the Renaissance many people began to study and value art, literature, and science.

Trade and Cities

The Renaissance began in the Italian city-state of Florence. By 1400 Florence had become one of the wealthiest city-states in Italy. The city was a major trading center for goods from all over. Meanwhile, towns in Flanders—which today is part of Belgium—became the center of trade for Northern Europe.

Flanders and Italy exchanged goods regurlary. During this time people bartered, or traded goods for other goods. As trade increased, demand for gold and silver coins rose. Slowly, people began using money again to pay for goods. A money economy emerged. Merchants set up banks and trading companies to manage the sale of goods and the use of money.

Renaissance Ideas and Writings

Scholars in Florence and elsewhere began to study humans and the world they lived in. This way of thinking was called **humanism**. Humanist ideas were inspired by ancient Greek and Roman ideas. Muslim and Jewish scholars had copied, translated, and added to Greek and Roman ideas for hundreds of years. Now European thinkers began to build on these ideas as well.

Humanist writers tried to re-create classical styles. Francesco Petrarch, the most famous Renaissance poet, lived in Italy. He is most famous for a group of 366 poems to his love, Laura.

Quick Check

Make Inferences **How did the growth of cities lead to the use of a money economy?**

The Ponte Vecchio bridge in Florence ▼

B RENAISSANCE ART AND SCIENCE

The great humanist artists and thinkers were interested in so many different ideas at once that the term "Renaissance man" was used to describe them. The term means someone who is curious about everything. Artist, scientist, and engineer Leonardo da Vinci is the best known Renaissance man. His most famous painting is the *Mona Lisa*, a woman with a mysterious half-smile. It is now in a museum in Paris.

Painter and sculptor Michelangelo Buonarroti was another important Renaissance man. Michelangelo is famous for the painting he created on the ceiling of the Sistine Chapel in the Vatican in Rome. The Vatican is the headquarters of the Catholic Church and home of the pope. Michelangelo painted the ceiling while lying on his back on a high platform. It took him four years to finish the ceiling.

◀ Leonardo da Vinci's "The Lady with the Ermine"

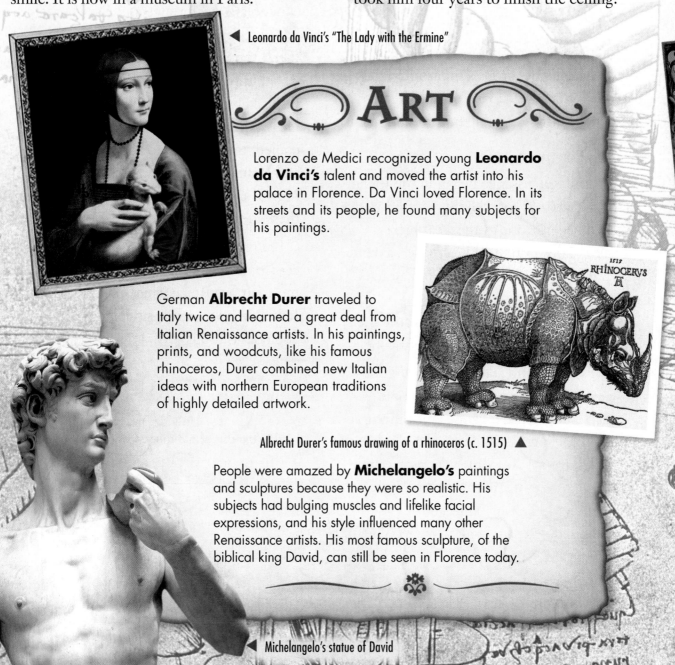

ART

Lorenzo de Medici recognized young **Leonardo da Vinci's** talent and moved the artist into his palace in Florence. Da Vinci loved Florence. In its streets and its people, he found many subjects for his paintings.

German **Albrecht Durer** traveled to Italy twice and learned a great deal from Italian Renaissance artists. In his paintings, prints, and woodcuts, like his famous rhinoceros, Durer combined new Italian ideas with northern European traditions of highly detailed artwork.

Albrecht Durer's famous drawing of a rhinoceros (c. 1515) ▲

People were amazed by **Michelangelo's** paintings and sculptures because they were so realistic. His subjects had bulging muscles and lifelike facial expressions, and his style influenced many other Renaissance artists. His most famous sculpture, of the biblical king David, can still be seen in Florence today.

◀ Michelangelo's statue of David

A Revolution in Science

For hundreds of years, religious leaders had taught Europeans that Earth was the center of the universe. Then, astronomer Nicolaus Copernicus realized that Earth could not be the center of the universe. He discovered that Earth, as well as the other planets in the solar system, had to revolve around the sun. Many Europeans refused to believe Copernicus, and no one would print his ideas. He died in 1543.

That same year his book, *On the Revolutions of the Heavenly Spheres*, was finally published. Copernicus's ideas—which were proven and expanded on by later scientists such as Johannes Kepler, Galileo Galilei, and Isaac Newton—would change humanity's knowledge about Earth and the universe.

Quick Check

Make Inferences **Why might religious and political leaders have rejected Copernicus's ideas?**

Science

Da Vinci filled hundreds of notebooks with scientific ideas and sketches of inventions. (See the background image on this page.) He drew plans for a machine gun, a submarine, and even a helicopter! Interestingly, he wrote all his notes backward.

◀ Copernicus appears at lower right in this map of the solar system from 1660.

Polish astronomer **Nicolaus Copernicus** studied Greek and Arab astronomy, then made careful observations of the night sky himself. He realized that Earth was not the center of the universe but actually rotated around the sun each year.

German mathematician **Johannes Kepler** built on Copernicus's work and discovered the law of planetary motion. He showed that the planets rotated around the sun in egg-shaped, not circular, orbits.

Spheres like this one show Kepler's ideas of planetary motion. ▶

C CHALLENGING THE CHURCH

While the Renaissance thrived in Italy, France and England fought a series of battles over who would rule France. In 1453 France finally defeated the English. The war lasted so long they called it the Hundred Years' War. The fighting helped to unite the people within both France and England. Both kingdoms became nations, or communities of people who share the same land as well as political, economic, and cultural goals.

The Inquisition

Muslim-Christain conflict began again in Spain in the late 1400s. Muslim groups had controlled parts of Spain since the 700s. As king and queen of Spain, Ferdinand and Isabella wanted to create a Christian country. They first drove out the Muslims, and then they drove out the Jews. Some Jews stayed, however, and tried to practice their religion secretly. To find these people, Ferdinand and Isabella used the **Inquisition**, a church-run court. People suspected of not being Christian were either driven out or killed.

Public executions were common during the Inquisition. ▼

The Reformation

During the Renaissance the idea of humanism led people to think about religion in a new way. Some people felt the Roman Catholic Church needed to change its interest in worldly things.

I do not accept the authority of popes and councils. . . .

—MARTIN LUTHER

In 1517 Martin Luther, a German religious leader, was angry that the church sold indulgences. An indulgence is a forgiveness of sins. Luther also did not like what political power some church leaders had. He wrote Ninety-five Theses, or arguments, about why the church needed to change. Luther nailed them to the door of his local church. By doing so, he started the **Reformation**, a movement to reform the church.

Luther's ideas spread quickly with the help of the printing press. A German named Johannes Gutenberg built the first European printing press that used metal moveable type. Now pages could be printed more quickly.

Shakespeare reciting a work before the court of Elizabeth I.

In 1520 the pope ordered Luther's books to be burned. Church leaders wanted to punish Luther, but German leaders protected him.

Luther's followers were called Protestants because they left the Catholic Church to protest its practices. Protestants prayed in their own languages instead of in Latin, and their churches did not accept the pope's leadership. The pope responded to the issues to which Protestants objected by forming the Council of Trent. This church council set up strict rules for how bishops and priests should behave.

After the Reformation the church in Rome became known as the Roman Catholic Church. By the mid-1500s, many different Protestant groups dominated northern Europe, while the Roman Catholic Church remained strong in Southern Europe.

Changes in England

England's King Henry VIII had no sons who could become king after him. In 1533 Henry asked the pope legally undo his marriage. He wanted to try to have a son with a new queen. The pope refused. At Henry's request, Parliament broke the Catholic Church in England from the pope in Rome. Henry declared himself head of the Church of England and divorced his wife.

King Henry did remarry, but he had a daughter, Elizabeth, not a son. During her reign as queen, William Shakespeare began producing his plays at the Globe Theater. Shakespeare based his plays on ancient Greek and Roman stories, as well as English history. His actors performed for Queen Elizabeth.

PLACES

Queen Elizabeth's interest in playwrights led to a golden age for English theater. The **Globe Theater**, in London, was a circular, unroofed structure. The Globe's admission charge of one or two pennies even let the lower classes attend.

Globe Theater

Quick Check

Make Inferences **Why was it difficult for the pope to stop the Reformation?**

D EXPLORATION

In the 1400s luxury goods from Asia were in great demand in Europe. Europeans were willing to pay high prices for Asia's products. It took luck—and several years—for merchants to travel across the Silk Road to reach Asian markets. Europeans began to search for another route to Asia.

Primary Sources

"They came swimming to the boats, bringing parrots, balls of cotton thread, javelins, and many other things which they exchanged for articles we gave them, such as glass beads, and hawk's bells; which trade was carried on with the utmost good will."

A selection from the Log of Christopher Columbus, 1492

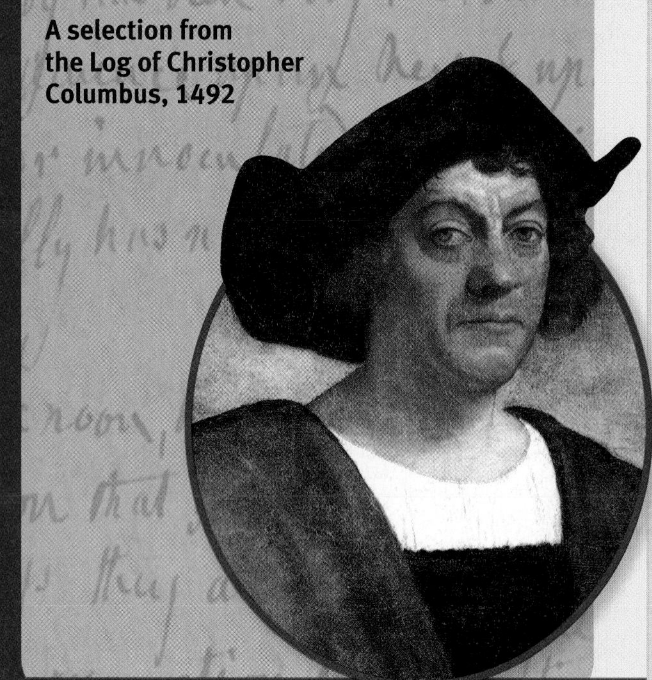

Write About It It is 1492, and you have just arrived in the Americas. Write a letter home describing the new foods you are tasting for the first time.

Portugal Leads the Way

Henry the Navigator, a Portuguese prince, believed Asia could be reached by sea. He established a school to train shipbuilders and sailors. With this help Portuguese shipbuilders designed a new ship, called a **caravel**. Caravels combined the wide body of a European ship with the three-sided sail of Arab boats. The caravel was a sturdy ship that maneuvered easily in all winds. The Portuguese also improved the compass and the astrolabe, an instrument used to pinpoint location.

In 1488 a Portuguese ship was the first to round Africa's southern tip. Vasco da Gama became the first European to sail around Africa to India. Prince Henry's dream had come true.

Across the Atlantic

When Christopher Columbus, an Italian-born explorer, set sail in 1492, he decided to find a different route to Asia. Instead of sailing south around the coast of Africa, he set sail west, across the unknown Atlantic Ocean.

Columbus's voyage took him to the Americas, continents unknown in Europe at the time. Columbus sailed to the Americas four times for Spain, looking for wealth. He brought strange animals and new foods back to Europe, but he never found gold. Columbus died in 1506, never knowing he had reached the Americas.

Around the World

By 1519 Europeans realized that the Americas blocked a straight voyage to Asia. In that year Ferdinand Magellan set out from Spain to sail around South America to Asia.

In the middle of their trip, food and water ran out. They faced a choice. Should they sail east or west home? In the end one ship sailed in each direction. The ship sailing east was lost. The other ship, the *Victoria*, reached Spain in 1522. It was the first ship to **circumnavigate**, or sail around, Earth.

The successes of these explorers made other European countries, such as England and France, eager to send out their own voyages. Conquests followed these voyages. Europeans began founding colonies, or overseas settlements, in the Americas, Asia, and Africa. Trade with these new colonies brought Europe great wealth and power.

QUICK CHECK

Make Inferences **Why did European countries want to reach Asia?**

Check Understanding

1. **VOCABULARY** Write a sentence for each of the following words.

   Renaissance **Inquisition**
   Reformation

2. **READING SKILL** Make Inferences
   Use your chart from page 198 to explain how art and writing can change a civilization.

Text Clues	What You Know	Inference

3. **Write About It** Write about how the Renaissance and Reformation changed Europe.

Replica of a caraval from Christopher Columbus's voyage

Lesson 6

Enlightenment and Revolution

VOCABULARY

heliocentric p. 207
Enlightenment p. 207
divine right p. 208
union p. 211
imperialism p. 212
nationalism p. 212

READING SKILL

Make Inferences

Copy the chart below. Use it to write details about this lesson.

Text Clues	What You Know	Inference

STANDARDS FOCUS

SOCIAL STUDIES Culture

GEOGRAPHY Human Systems

Scientific instruments belonging to Italian scientist Galileo in Florence, Italy

Visual Preview

How did new ways of thinking change how people lived and worked?

A Europeans used reason to study science and improve society.

B New ideas led to revolutions in England and France.

C The Industrial Revolution brought jobs and growth to towns and cities.

D European nations looked for colonies in Asia and Africa.

Ⓐ NEW IDEAS

From the 1600s to the 1800s and beyond, new ideas and discoveries helped Europe become a global power.

After 1400 Europeans turned to science as a way to explain the world. Europeans developed a process called the scientific method. In this method scientists use experiments to see if they can prove their ideas. An idea that is unproven is called a theory. Theories are proven by study of additional facts.

An Italian scientist named Galileo Galilei thought that new knowledge could come from observing and measuring the natural world. According to one legend, Galileo decided to test the theory of Greek philosopher Aristotle that heavy objects would fall faster than lighter objects. He dropped two objects of different weights from the Tower of Pisa in Italy. Both objects hit the ground at the same moment. Galileo proved Aristotle's theory wrong.

Scientists began to question other ancient theories as well. Nicolaus Copernicus, a Polish mathematician, concluded that the sun, not Earth, is the center of the universe. This sun-centered system is called **heliocentric**.

The Enlightenment

These and other ideas sparked a revolution, or sweeping change, in the way people thought. During this Scientific Revolution, many Europeans used reason, instead of faith or tradition, to guide them.

As a result the 1700s became known as the Age of **Enlightenment**. During this era thinkers were excited about the new discoveries in science. They wanted to use reason just like the scientists had, but their goal was to improve society. They asked whether their governments and traditions were rational. Their questions paved the way for major revolutions in America and France.

QUICK CHECK

Make Inferences **How might scientists have influenced each other in this period?**

◀ The bell tower of the cathedral of Pisa, where Galileo supposedly tested his theory about gravity

Ⓑ REVOLUTIONS

In the 1600s Europe's kings claimed to rule by **divine right**. They believed that God had chosen them to be kings and had given them the right to rule in any way they liked.

The Glorious Revolution

In the 1600s King Charles I insisted that he did not need to uphold the Magna Carta. Parliament disagreed and sent him the Petition of Rights in 1628, reminding the king that he could not rule by divine right. When Charles did not listen, Parliament defeated him in a civil war in 1649. After several years without a king, Charles II was invited to rule in 1660, but he had to agree to Parliament's demands.

When Charles II died in 1685, his brother, James II, tried to rule by divine right but was forced to flee to France. Parliament offered the throne to James's daughter, Mary II, and her husband, William. In order to rule, they agreed to sign the English Bill of Rights in 1689. This document said that Parliament had the final say in any disagreement.

During this time John Locke, an important Enlightenment thinker from England, wrote that all people have natural rights, including the rights to life, liberty, and property. Locke also said that when a government did not protect these rights, citizens had the right to overthrow it. These ideas became important during the American Revolution.

The French Revolution

The French government had borrowed money to help the American colonists gain independence. By 1789 there was no money left to pay back the loans. King Louis XVI called a meeting of the Estates-General, France's parliament, in order to raise taxes.

At the time the French people were divided into three "estates," or classes.

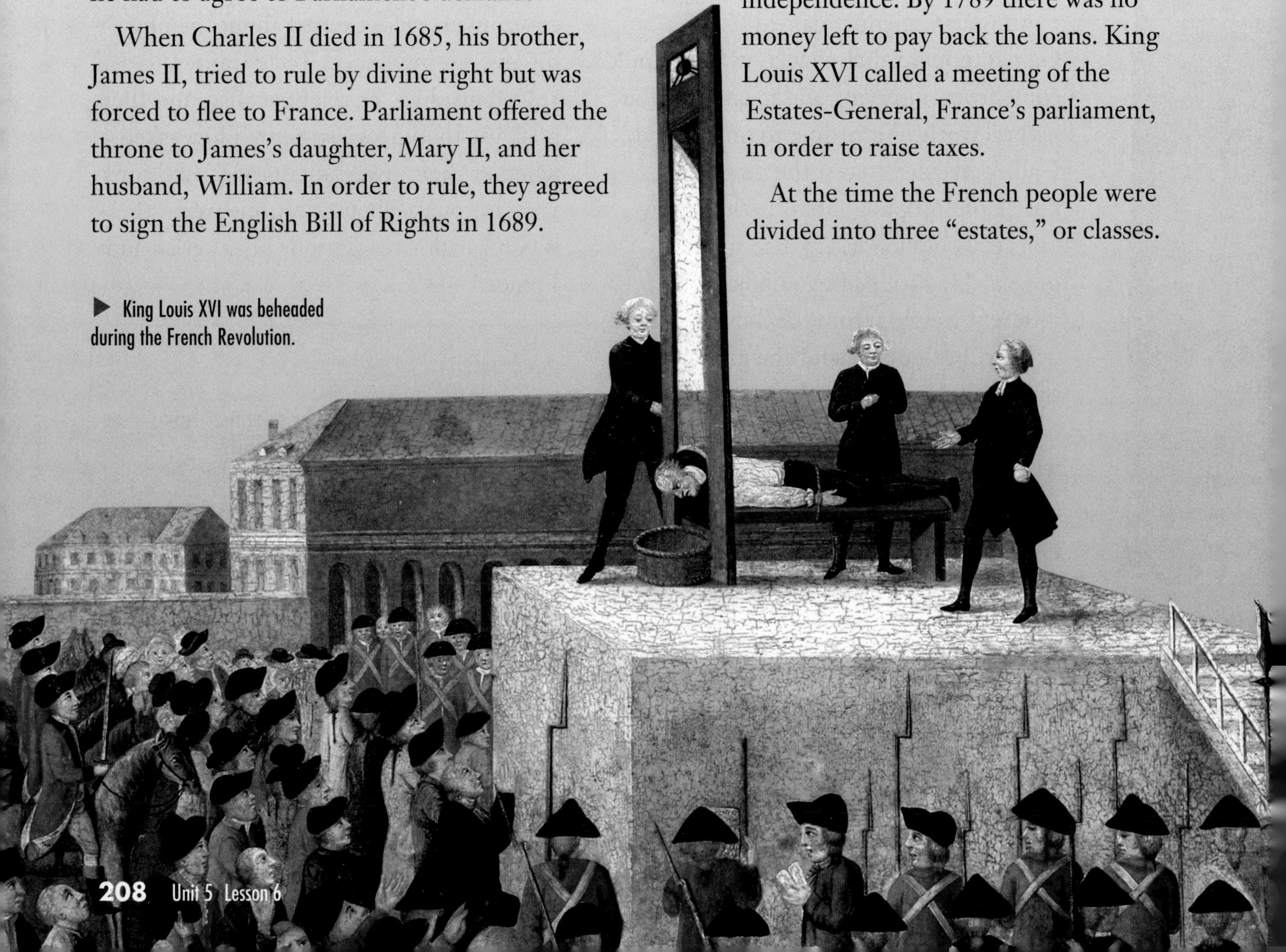

▶ King Louis XVI was beheaded during the French Revolution.

The First Estate was made up of the clergy of the Catholic Church. The Second Estate was the nobles of France. These two wealthy estates ran France, but they paid few taxes. The Third Estate included nearly 98 percent of the population. It was made up mostly of poor peasants who paid taxes but had no voice in government.

The leaders of the third Estate formed a National Assembly and demanded rights and a constitution. The poor seized the Bastille, a royal prison in Paris. There, they found weapons to defend their rights. The National Assembly wrote a document called the Declaration of the Rights of Man and the Citizen. It stated that all men were "born and remain free and equal."

In 1792 France's governing body, the National Convention, ended the monarchy and established a republic. The government then set up courts to place people opposed to their authority on trial. As a result, the king, the queen, and 40,000 others were executed during the "Reign of Terror."

Napoleon Bonaparte

In 1799 a brilliant general named Napoleon Bonaparte seized power in France. After he defeated several more European rulers, Napoleon made himself emperor in 1802.

Napoleon established public education and created the Napoleonic Code. This set of laws guaranteed religious freedom and gave men the right to vote.

Napoleon fought many wars. In 1815 he was defeated and forced to leave France. The ideas of equality and liberty continued to inspire revolutions throughout the 1800s.

Quick Check

Make Inferences **How might the American Revolution have influenced the French Revolution?**

▲ Napoleon Bonaparte

Ⓒ INDUSTRIAL REVOLUTION

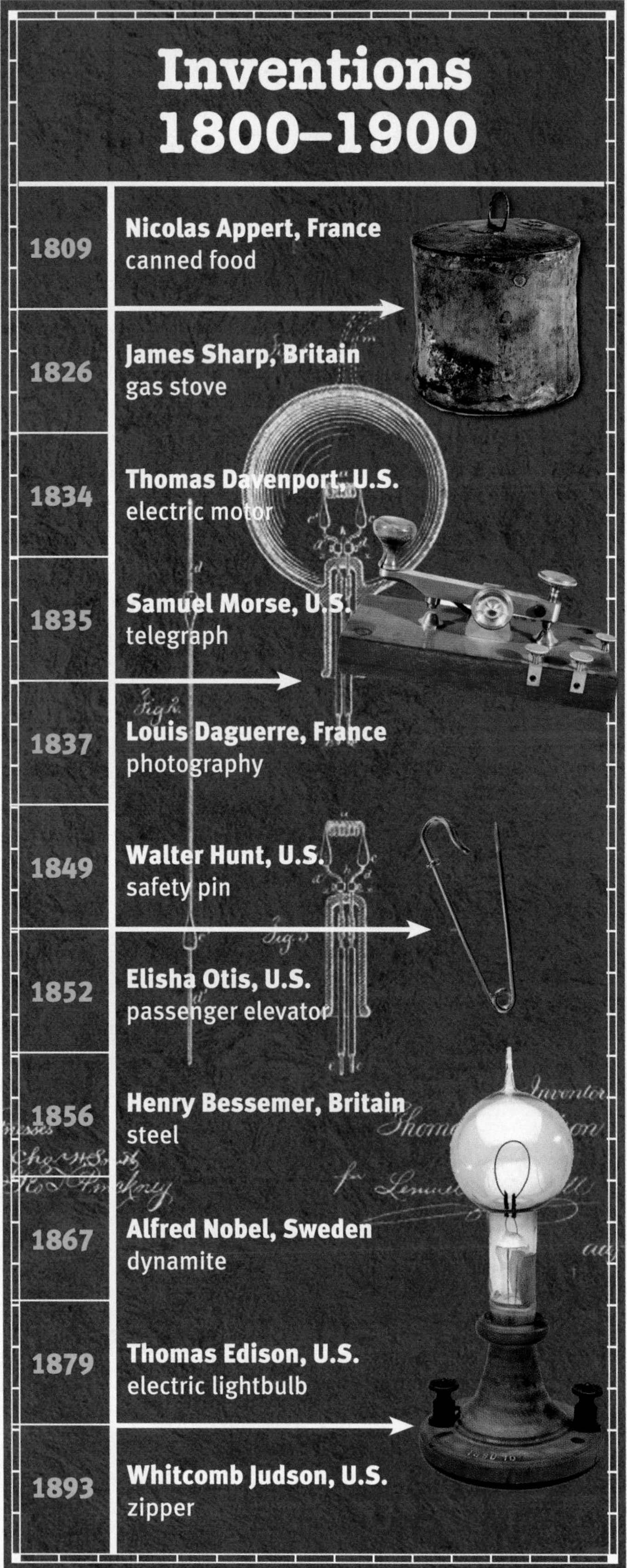

Inventions 1800–1900
1809 Nicolas Appert, France canned food
1826 James Sharp, Britain gas stove
1834 Thomas Davenport, U.S. electric motor
1835 Samuel Morse, U.S. telegraph
1837 Louis Daguerre, France photography
1849 Walter Hunt, U.S. safety pin
1852 Elisha Otis, U.S. passenger elevator
1856 Henry Bessemer, Britain steel
1867 Alfred Nobel, Sweden dynamite
1879 Thomas Edison, U.S. electric lightbulb
1893 Whitcomb Judson, U.S. zipper

Between 1750 and 1830, there was a change in how goods were produced in Europe. Instead of being made by hand, many goods were now manufactured, or made, with machines. This change radically affected the economy and also changed how and where people lived. We refer to this time period as the Industrial Revolution.

Factories Change the Landscape

The Industrial Revolution began in Britain. People began using machines and building factories, or large buildings where workers gathered to manufacture products. Machines could produce goods faster and at lower cost. People could afford more things, such as more comfortable clothing.

Many people left farms to find work near the factories. Soon small towns and cities grew. They continued to grow as more people came to work in the new factories.

New Inventions

Early factories relied on waterpower. Then, in 1769, James Watt invented the steam engine. It burned coal, which heated water and produced steam. By 1800 this technology spread across Europe and the United States. In 1807 the steam engine was used to power steamboats. By 1825 steam engines were used to move trains on iron rails. Soon railroads crossed Europe and the United States.

Farmers also developed new inventions and techniques. They learned to use fertilizers to make their fields more fertile. In 1831 Cyrus McCormick invented a mechanical reaper to harvest wheat.

The Development of Classes

The Industrial Revolution increased the power of two new social classes, the middle class and the working class. The middle class had included bankers, lawyers, doctors, and merchants. Now it also included the new factory owners and inventors. One of the greatest changes of this time period was the growth in the power of the middle class.

The working class—factory workers in towns and cities—did not gain power right away. They worked 12 or 15 hours a day for low wages. They lived in crowded houses and apartments in the cities. The factories spewed out pollution, and disease spread rapidly. Entire families had to work. Factory owners liked to hire children and women because they could pay them less than men.

Gradually, workers began to form unions. A **union** is a group of workers who unite to demand better working conditions. Unions threatened to go on strike if laws were not passed to improve their working conditions. While on strike they refused to work until their demands were met.

The Industrial Revolution changed the way people lived and worked. The industrial advances helped European countries grow more powerful. In many ways the Industrial Revolution began the path to the modern world we live in today.

Quick Check

Make Inferences **How did the Industrial Revolution help to create the world you live in?**

This factory in Berlin, Germany, made machines for other factories.

D IMPERIALISM

European nations needed markets for the products of the Industrial Revolution. They built empires to obtain raw materials and to provide markets for manufactured goods.

Empires Spread

Imperialism is the control of the economy and government of one country by another. The years between 1880 and 1914 are called the "Age of Imperialism" because European nations competed fiercely to establish colonies during this time.

Nationalism contributed to the fierce competition for colonies. Nationalism is intense feelings of devotion to one's own nation. This idea often led people to feel their nation was superior to other nations.

India and Southeast Asia

Asia was an attractive place for Europe's rulers and merchants. Asian spices, crops, and metals were very valuable in Europe.

During the late 1700s, Great Britain gradually expanded its control over India. Great Britain ruled through the British East India Company.

Europeans also established colonies in Southeast Asia. The Dutch claimed a chain of islands which are today the nation of Indonesia. This colony, called the Dutch East Indies, produced crops such as coffee, pepper, cinnamon, sugar, indigo, and tea. In the 1860s the French established colonies in what is now Laos, Cambodia, and Vietnam. The Europeans also were able to divide China into spheres of influence, or areas that they controlled.

Africa

In the late 1800s, European colonizers competed for control of Africa. Some European nations, including the Dutch, had trading posts in Africa. In 1869 the French got involved with Egypt when a French company got permission to build the Suez Canal. The canal connected the Mediterranean Sea to the Red Sea, making it a key trade route.

In the late 1880s, Belgium began claiming land along the Congo River. Other European nations worried that they were losing out on profits in Africa. They began claiming land there too. By 1900 only Liberia and Ethiopia were still independent countries in Africa.

▼ Europeans travel to Delhi for a meeting with India's mogul ruler, Akbar II, in 1815.

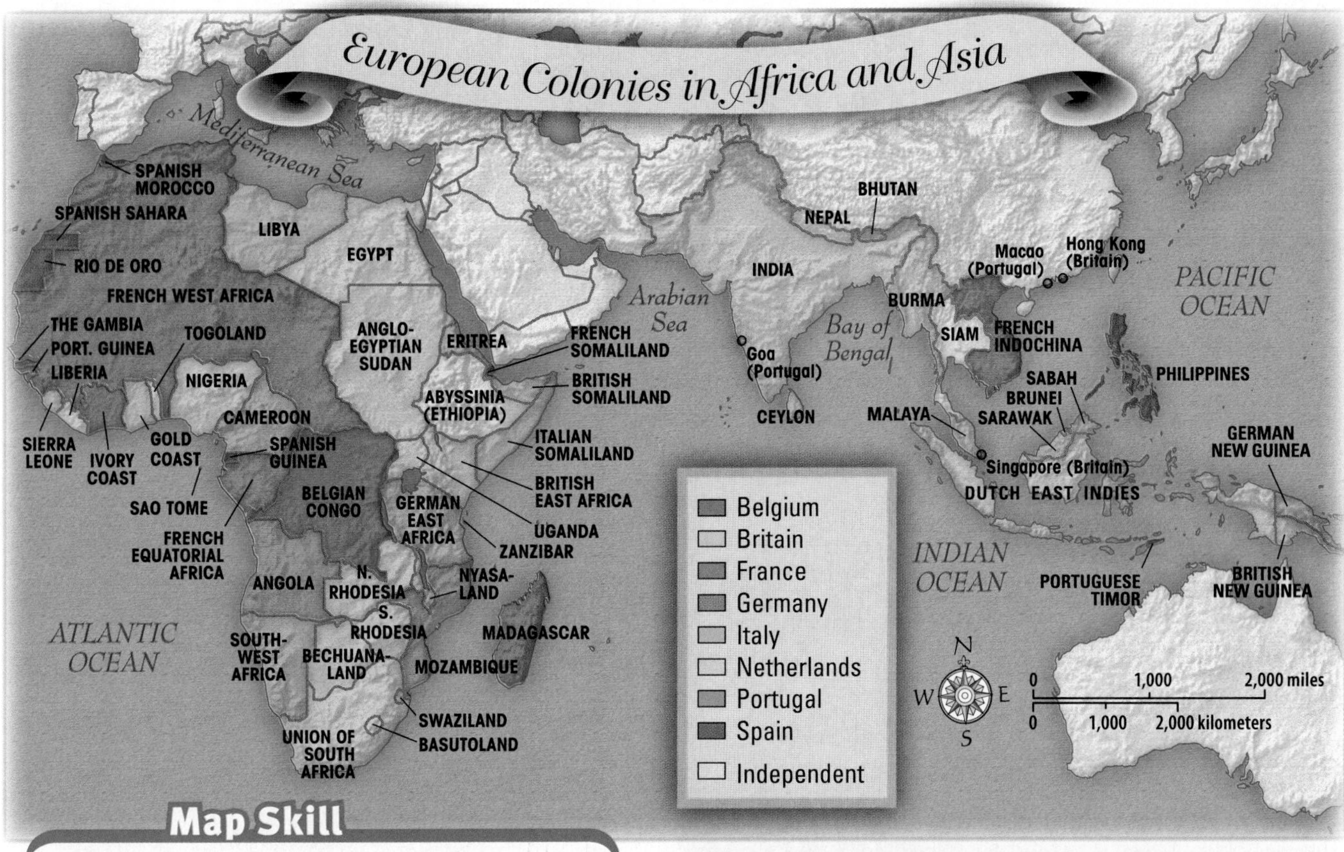

Map Skill

LOCATION List the areas that France controlled.

The End of Imperialism

Imperialism created a number of problems. Competition for colonies led to many arguments among European nations. People who lived in European colonies resented the rule of foreigners. The practice of making Indian crafts was destroyed. Colonial borders ignored Africa's history and local cultures.

The year1914 marked the end of the Age of Imperialism. European nations became wealthy from their colonies. Imperialism also caused friction among the nations, though. This friction increased nationalism, which contributed to the start of World War I.

Quick Check

Make Inferences How did the formation of European colonies affect Africans?

Check Understanding

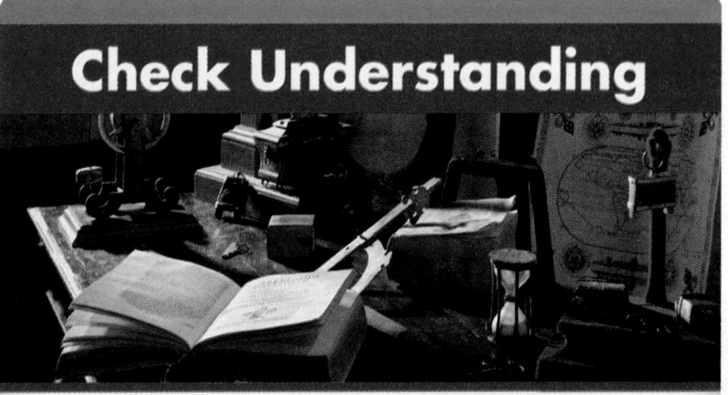

1. **VOCABULARY** Use each vocabulary word below in a sentence that shows you understand its meaning in this lesson.

Enlightenment **imperialism**
nationalism

2. **READING SKILL Make Inferences** Use your chart from page 206 to explain how the Industrial Revolution changed life in Europe.

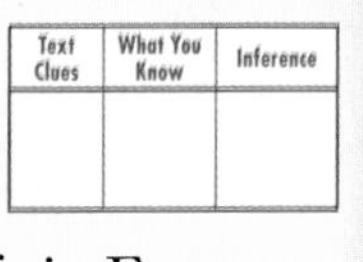

3. **Write About It** Explain why Europeans thought imperialism was a good idea.

Lesson 7

VOCABULARY

alliance p. 215
propaganda p. 218
genocide p. 219
Warsaw Pact p. 220

READING SKILL

Make Inferences
Copy the chart below. Use it to write details about modern Europe.

Text Clues	What You Know	Inference

STANDARDS FOCUS

SOCIAL STUDIES Culture

GEOGRAPHY Human Systems

MODERN EUROPE

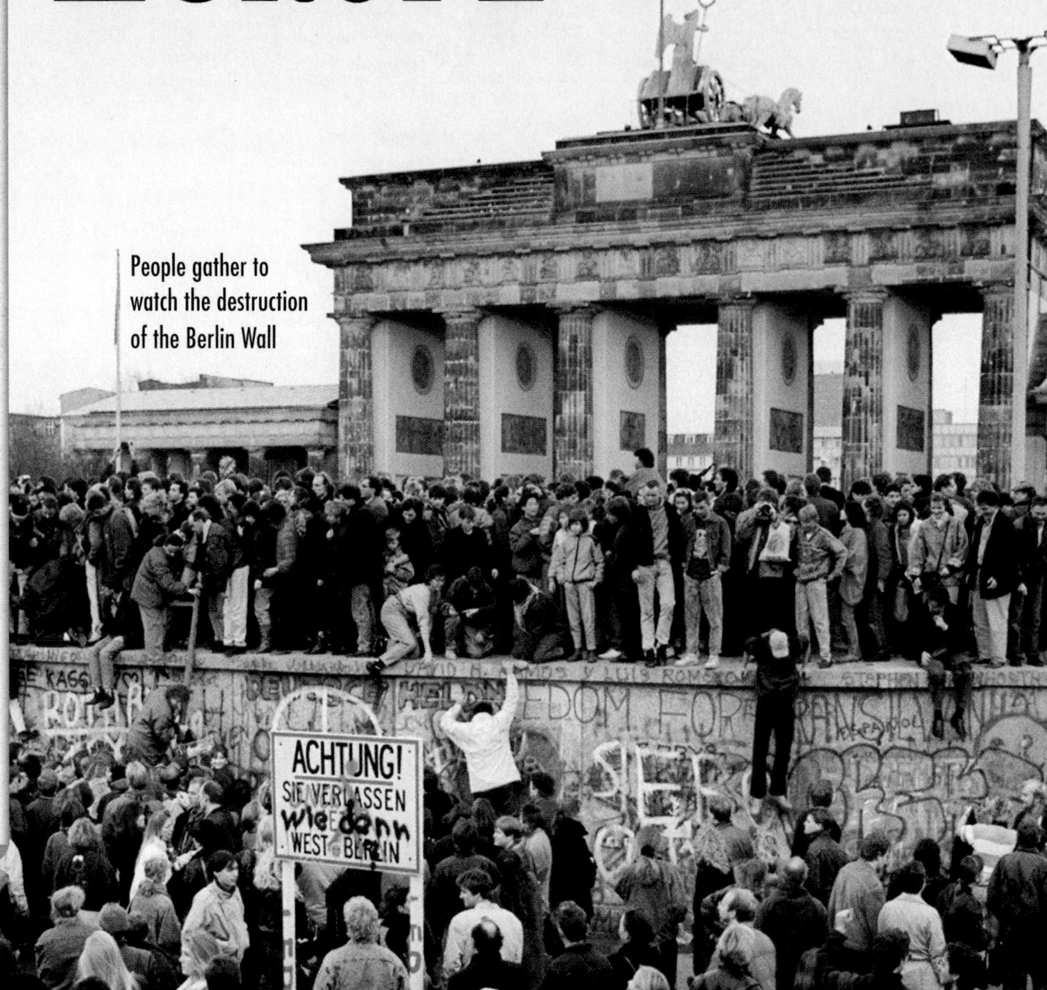

People gather to watch the destruction of the Berlin Wall

Visual Preview How did political and economic changes lead to conflict in Europe?

A European rivalries grew tense, and a murder drove the continent into war.

B Under communist leaders, Russia's economy grew, but many people suffered.

C In the 1930s new governments in Italy and Germany began a new world war.

D After World War II, the United States and the Soviet Union became bitter rivals.

Ⓐ WORLD WAR I

By 1910 many European nations were wealthy and powerful. Countries built up their armies to become more powerful than their neighbors. This made nations develop strong feelings of nationalism.

Governments began to make alliances with each other for protection. An **alliance** is a formal agreement to work together. In these alliances countries promised to defend each other in case of attack.

A Murder Leads to War

The spark that set off World War I occurred on June 28, 1914. The Archduke Franz Ferdinand of Austria-Hungary and his wife were killed by a Serbian gunman. Austria-Hungary's leaders in turn declared war on Serbia. Because of the alliances, almost every European country and many of their allies became involved. By August most of Europe was at war.

The war did not end quickly. Both sides dug long ditches, or trenches. In the trenches soldiers crouched in mud, waiting to attack and gaining little ground during battles. In all, more than 8.5 million people died during World War I. Millions more were wounded.

The United States at first announced that it was neutral. But on May 7, 1915, a German submarine sank the British passenger ship *Lusitania*, killing the more than 100 Americans that were on board. This convinced Congress to declare war on Germany in April 1917. With this support the Allies won the war.

In June 1919 Germany was forced to sign a peace agreement known as the Treaty of Versailles. The harsh treaty angered Germans. It blamed their country for the war and demanded that it pay huge sums of money to repair the damages.

The treaty also called for countries to join a League of Nations, a group that would work to prevent wars by resolving disputes between nations. Although American President Woodrow Wilson liked the idea, the U.S. Congress refused to join. An uneasy peace settled over Europe.

Quick Check

Make Inferences **Why might Germans believe that the Treaty of Versailles was not fair?**

New technology changed warfare during World War I. Weapons like the machine gun and poison gas could kill hundreds of soldiers in trenches in a single attack. ▶

Vladimir Lenin speaking in Moscow in 1919

B COMMUNISM

Life in Russia in 1900 was not very different than it had been in the Middle Ages. The ideas of the Enlightenment had not made it there. Russia was led by an absolute ruler called a tsar, the Russian word for emperor. Most Russians were serfs, or poor peasant farmers.

Revolution

The tsar lived in St. Petersburg, Russia's capital and a city of beautiful palaces. The city also had terrible slums. Peasants lived in shabby, crowded neighborhoods and worked long hours. In 1905 workers started refusing to work in these terrible conditions. They went on strike. On January 22, hundreds of peaceful strikers marched to the tsar's palace. The current tsar, Nicholas II, was not in the city. His generals panicked and ordered soldiers to fire. More than 100 marchers were killed on "Bloody Sunday."

Russia was still dealing with this crisis when it was forced into World War I. Russia was not ready for war. Soldiers went into battle without guns or bullets, and more than one million of them were killed.

In March 1917 thousands of workers met to strike in the streets of St. Petersburg. The strike became a revolution. Tsar Nicholas II was forced to give up his crown. In July 1918 he and his family were killed. After 300 years, the rule of the tsars was over.

A New Kind of Government

Many Russians found hope in the Bolshevik political party. It followed the ideas of the German thinker Karl Marx. He called his ideas socialism, or communism. Marx believed that workers should create new societies. He said all businesses should be owned and managed by a government controlled by the workers.

The leader of Russia's Communist Party was Vladimir Lenin. During the war he said he would seize private property and give it to the poor, so many poor Russian workers, peasants, and soldiers supported him. The temporary government turned over power without a fight. Once in power, Lenin began peace talks with Germany to get Russia out of the war.

Communist Russia

Lenin made many enemies. He took land and factories away from their owners. He demanded that ethnic groups across the country give up their traditional ways of life.

By 1918 Lenin's enemies and supporters were fighting a civil war. Millions died from battles, starvation, and disease. Finally, in 1920, Lenin's forces won, and Russia became the world's first communist nation. In 1922 it took a new name—the Union of Soviet Socialist Republics, or the Soviet Union. *Soviet* is a Russian term for a council of workers and soldiers.

Lenin died unexpectedly in 1924. Josef Stalin, another Communist leader, gained control of the Soviet government. Stalin forced all small family farms into huge collective farms, or large farms where everyone worked together. These collective farms produced grain and other crops for export rather than for the Russian people. Under Stalin the Soviet Union rapidly industrialized. Soviet factories produced more tractors than any other country.

Stalin's nation was a totalitarian state. The government controlled almost all public and private activity. It could also be a cruel state. Stalin ruled through terror. Those who complained were punished as "enemies of the state." The number of these enemies reached into the millions. More than 15 million Soviet citizens were killed or forced to work in labor camps in the remote region of Siberia.

Quick Check

Make Inferences **How did communism change Russia?**

Women cleaning grain on a collective farm in the Soviet Union

C WORLD WAR II

In the 1930s nations around the world, including Germany, suffered an economic depression, or a time when many people were out of work and few people had money to buy goods.

Germany and Italy

Adolf Hitler used **propaganda** to convince Germans that his Nazi party would lead them out of the depression. Propaganda is the spreading of persuasive, but sometimes false, ideas to influence people. Hitler blamed Germany's problems on the Treaty of Versailles, communists, and Jews. Hitler took power in 1933.

In 1922 Benito Mussolini had set up a fascist government in Italy. Fascist governments are totalitarian. They encourage nationalism, a strong military, a command economy and, often, racism. Hitler's government was also fascist. In 1936 Germany and Italy formed an alliance with Japan, called the Axis. Each began to seize new territory.

War in Europe

When Hitler's armies invaded Poland on September 1, 1939, France and Great Britain, called the Allies, declared war on Germany. The German forces defeated the Polish. In 1940 Hitler sent troops into Belgium, Denmark, the Netherlands, and France. Germany conquered all of these countries using its *blitzkrieg*, or "lightning war" strategy.

By the end of 1940, Great Britain was the last major European country fighting Germany. During the Battle of Britain, German forces bombed London for almost a year. The British refused to surrender. Finally, Hitler stopped the attacks. He decided to invade the Soviet Union.

Germany attacked the Soviet Union in 1941. For two-and-a-half years, German troops fought there. In 1942 Nazi troops attacked the city of Stalingrad. The Soviet troops stopped the German forces. After the deadliest battle in history, with more than 2 million deaths, the Nazis surrendered. This was a major turning point of World War II.

▼ German soldiers covered in snow and ice during the Battle of Stalingrad

▲ Allied troops landing on the beaches of Normandy, France

War in the Pacific

At the same time Germany was attacking the Soviet Union, Japan was trying to become a world power. On December 7, 1941, Japan attacked the American naval base at Pearl Harbor in Hawaii. The attack destroyed 19 ships, ruined 188 planes on the ground, and killed more than 2,200 people. The next day, President Franklin Roosevelt asked Congress to declare war on Japan. U.S. troops joined the Allies fighting in Europe and the Pacific.

D-Day

After three long years, Allied armies had not been able to push Nazi armies totally out of North Africa and the Soviet Union. They planned a surprise invasion of France to open up a third front, or battleground.

On June 6, 1944, or "D-Day," 2,700 ships carried 200,000 Allied soldiers toward the beaches of Normandy, in northern France. Thousands of Allied soldiers died as they fought through German gunfire. The surprise attack worked, though, and the Allied soldiers pushed back the Germans. Less than a year later, the Allies reached Germany. On April 30, 1945, Hitler killed himself, and a week later Germany surrendered.

The Holocaust

When the Allied troops defeated Germany, they found concentration camps where millions had been imprisoned or killed in Hitler's "Final Solution." This was **genocide**, or the planned destruction of a racial, political, or cultural group. About 6 million Jews were killed in what has become known as the Holocaust. Millions of Roma (often called Gypsies), the disabled, and political opponents also worked as slaves or were shot, starved, or gassed to death.

After the War

The victorious Allies agreed that each one of them would control one region of Germany and help rebuild the country after the war. The goal was for Germany to one day be reunited. The Allies also led a movement to create the United Nations to help countries avoid conflicts in the future.

Quick Check

Make Inferences **Why do you think many Germans supported Hitler?**

▲ Children trapped behind barbed wire at a Nazi concentration camp

▼Smoke rising over London, England, after a German air raid in 1940

D THE COLD WAR

Before the end of World War II in 1945, the three major Allied leaders met in the Soviet city of Yalta to discuss how to divide Europe. Things did not go as planned.

The Iron Curtain

Although Stalin had agreed to remove his troops from Eastern Europe, he never did. This created what Winston Churchill of Great Britain called an "Iron Curtain" that divided Europe between democratic nations and Soviet-controlled states.

In 1949, the United States and several Western European nations formed the North Atlantic Treaty Organization (NATO) to prepare for the possibility of war with the Soviet Union. In 1955 the Soviet Union created a similar alliance, the **Warsaw Pact**. The communist states in the pact agreed to defend each other if they were attacked.

After World War II, the United States and the Soviet Union were the world's two "superpowers," or the nations with the most military strength. For almost 50 years, they struggled for power, never fighting each other directly, during what was called the Cold War.

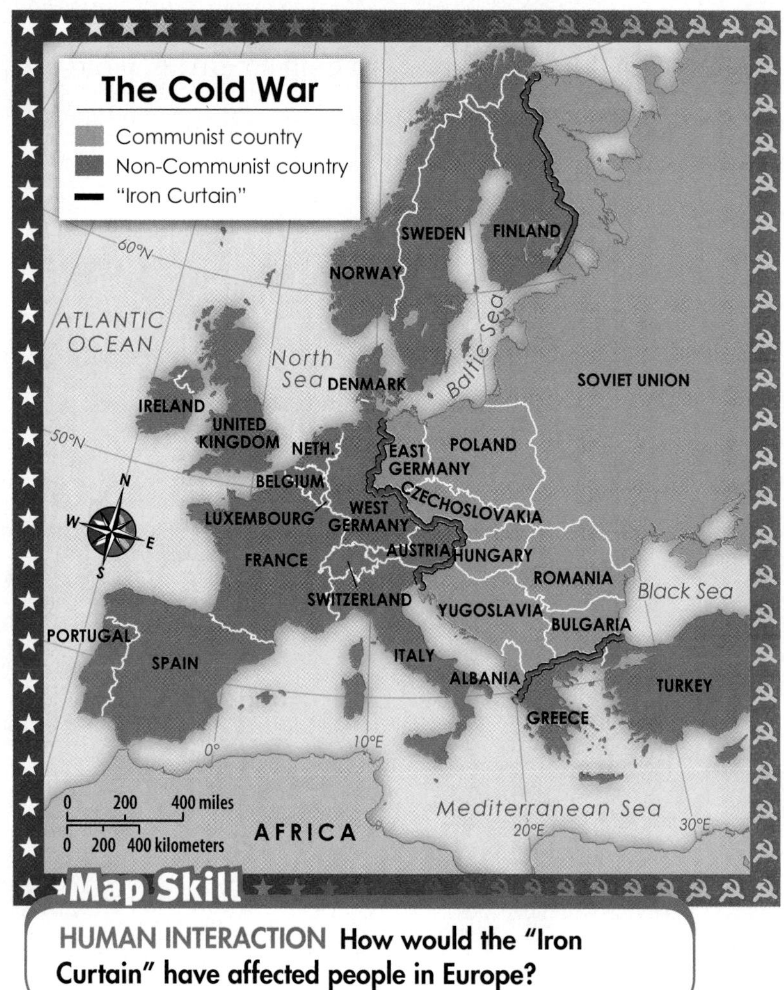

Map Skill

HUMAN INTERACTION **How would the "Iron Curtain" have affected people in Europe?**

Berlin Divided

The Soviet Union set up a communist government in East Germany. The Allied-controlled regions of Germany united as a democracy in West Germany. The capital of both countries, Berlin, was deep inside East Germany. The city was divided into East Berlin and West Berlin as well.

In 1948 the Soviets tried to gain control of West Berlin by cutting off all land routes to it. The United States, Britain, and France began flying supplies into the city. This "Berlin Airlift" kept the city from starving. Finally, the Soviets opened the roads and railroads again.

Many East Germans tried to escape to freedom by crossing into West Berlin. To stop them East German police built the Berlin Wall in 1961. The wall split the city in two. Barbed wire, minefields, and floodlights guarded the wall.

Cold War Races

The Soviets saw the power of the atomic bomb in World War II. By 1949 they had built one for themselves. The superpowers continued to develop more powerful nuclear weapons throughout the Cold War. The arms race, or competition to create nuclear weapons, made people fear the possibility of a nuclear war.

The superpowers also competed in a "space race." In 1957 the Soviets won an early victory by launching *Sputnik*, the first satellite into Earth's orbit.

The Cold War Ends

The Berlin Wall stood until 1989, when East Germany's communist leaders allowed it to be torn down. Germany reunified, as a democracy, in 1990.

Two years later the Soviet Union broke apart. All 15 Soviet republics declared their independence from the Soviet Union. The new president outlawed the communist party in Russia. Most of the Soviet republics then joined in a federation called the Commonwealth of Independent States.

In 1993, several democracies in Western Europe formed the European Union (EU). The goal of the organization, which now includes eastern European countries, is a united Europe. The EU allows goods, services, and workers to move freely among member countries.

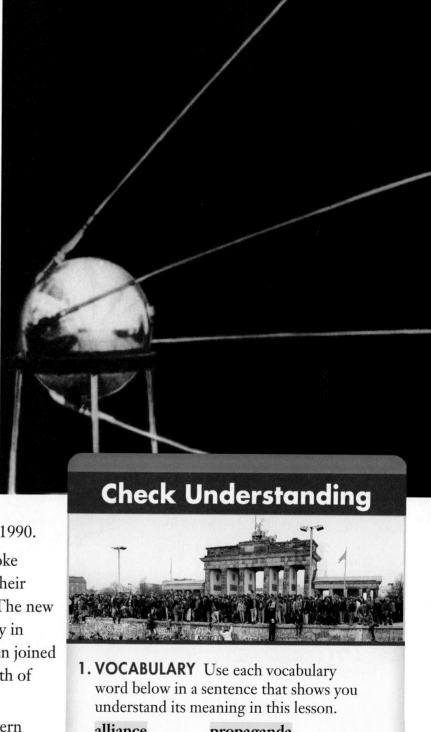

Quick Check

Make Inferences **What did Winston Churchill mean by the phrase "Iron Curtain?"**

Check Understanding

1. **VOCABULARY** Use each vocabulary word below in a sentence that shows you understand its meaning in this lesson.

   alliance **propaganda**
   Warsaw Pact

2. **READING SKILL** Make Inferences Use your chart from page 214 to explain the effects of World War I and World War II.

Text Clues	What You Know	Inference

3. **Write About It** How were science and technology important parts of the Cold War?

Review and Assess

Vocabulary

Write the word from the list that matches the definition.

caravel **city-state**
nation-state **navigable**

1. a river that is wide and deep enough for boats to use
2. a city and its nearby land and villages
3. a country consisting of people who share a common history or culture
4. a cargo ship designed for ocean travel in the 1400s

Comprehension and Critical Thinking

5. How did the location of Greece help its economy?
6. What are some of the characteristics of feudalism?
7. **Reading Skill** Explain why European countries explored.
8. **Critical Thinking** Why do you think many Russians supported Communism?

Skill

Use a Time Zone Map

Write a complete sentence to answer each question.

9. How many time zones are in Europe?
10. If it is 3:00 p.m. in London, what time is it in Paris?

Time Zones of Europe

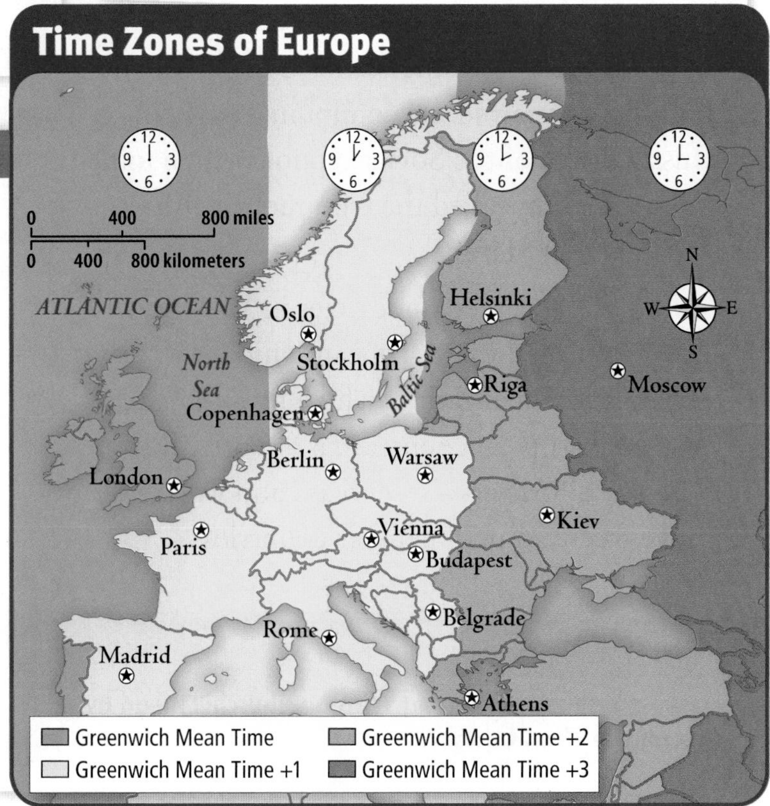

Test Preparation

Read the passage. Then answer the questions.

Roman Emperor Diocletian's successor, Constantine, moved the center of the Roman Empire's power to a city in the east named Byzantium. He renamed the city Constantinople in honor of himself. Even though the Roman Empire in the west declined, Constantine's Byzantine Empire prospered and lasted about a thousand years after the fall of Rome. The center of the Byzantine Empire was Constantinople. It grew rich from trade and manufacturing.

In A.D. 527, Justinian became emperor of Rome's eastern empire. Under his leadership, the Byzantine Empire reached its glory. He expanded its borders and even tried to reconquer the lands of the Western Roman Empire. Justinian reorganized the laws of the Roman Empire which became the basis for Byzantine law. His code of laws covered property, marriage, women, slaves, and criminals.

1. What is one reason the Byzantine Empire was so prosperous?

A. Constantine renamed the city.

B. Constantinople was rich from trade.

C. Constantinople's walls withstood attacks.

D. The western empire helped.

2. Which statement best summarizes the Byzantine Empire's success?

A. It grew rich from trade and manufacturing.

B. The Western Roman Empire declined.

C. Leadership changed.

D. Byzantium was changed to Constantinople.

3. What did Justinian's code of laws cover?

A. property, taxes, women, and marriage

B. slaves, criminals, women, and borders

C. property, trade, criminals, and marriage

D. marriage, women, criminals, and property

4. How did Justinian help the success of the eastern Roman Empire?

5. Describe the Byzantine Empire.

The Big Idea Activities

Why do civilizations change?

Write About the Big Idea

FOLDABLES™ Study Organizer

Narrative Essay
Use the Unit 5 foldable to help you write an essay about the Big Idea question, *Why do civilizations change?* Begin with an introduction in which you clearly explain why you think civilizations change. Write one paragraph for each set of notes under a tab on your foldable. End with a concluding paragraph.

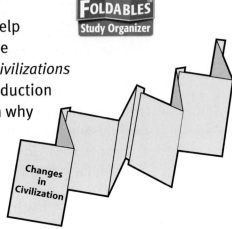

Changes in Civilization

Make a Poster

Work independently to prepare a poster. The subject will be "The Seven Wonders of the Ancient Greek and Roman Empires." Here's how to make your poster:

1. Research the accomplishments of ancient Greece and Rome.
2. Choose seven buildings or other large construction projects from the two ancient empires.
3. Draw a picture or find a photo to illustrate each of your choices.
4. Write a description of each of your choices.
5. Present your poster to your class. Be sure to explain why you chose each of your selections.

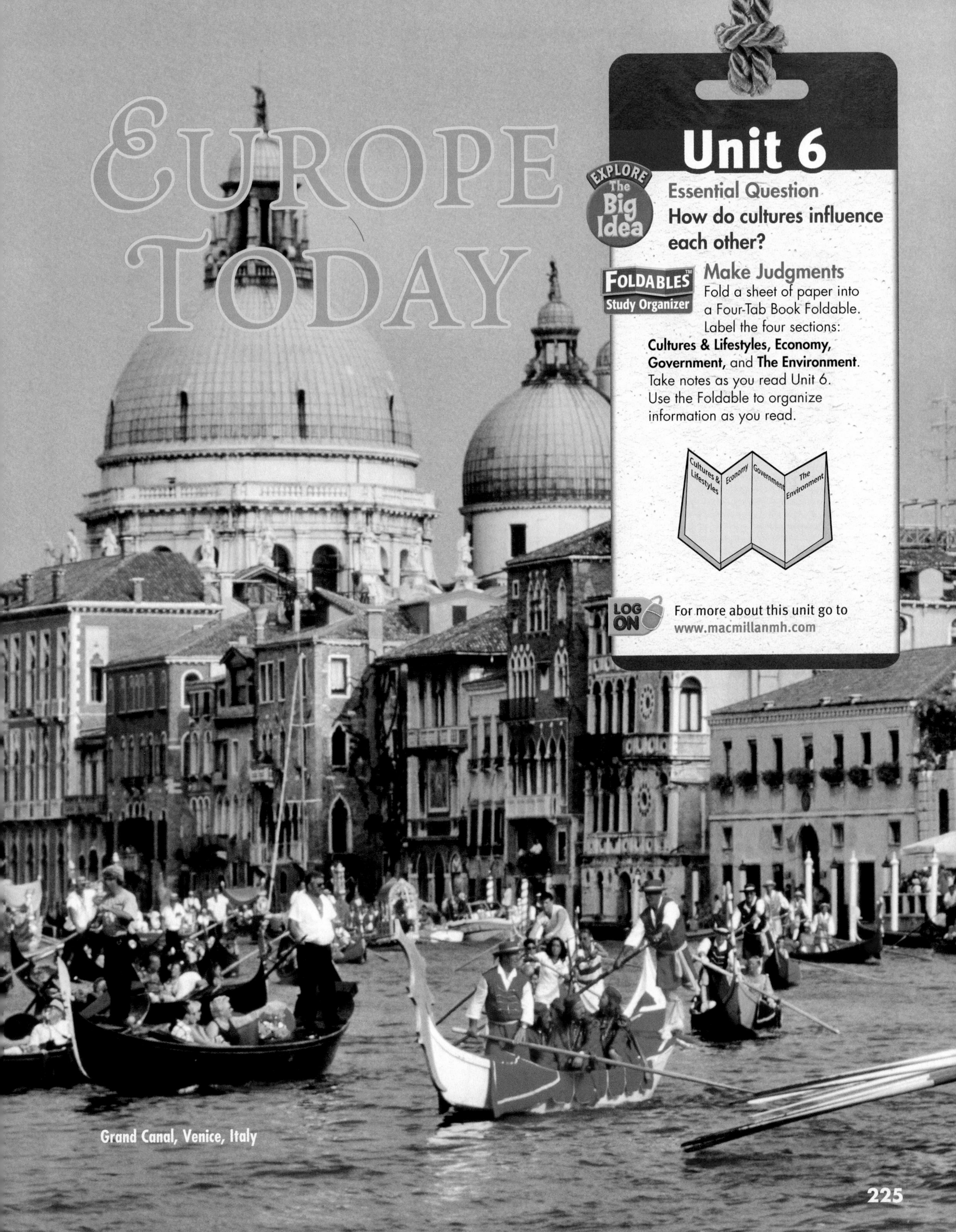

EUROPE TODAY
Unit 6
EXPLORE The Big Idea
Essential Question
How do cultures influence each other?
FOLDABLES Study Organizer
Make Judgments
Fold a sheet of paper into a Four-Tab Book Foldable. Label the four sections: Cultures & Lifestyles, Economy, Government, and The Environment. Take notes as you read Unit 6. Use the Foldable to organize information as you read.
Cultures & Lifestyles
Economy
Government
The Environment
LOG ON
For more about this unit go to www.macmillanmh.com

Grand Canal, Venice, Italy

PEOPLE, PLACES, AND EVENTS

Claude Monet

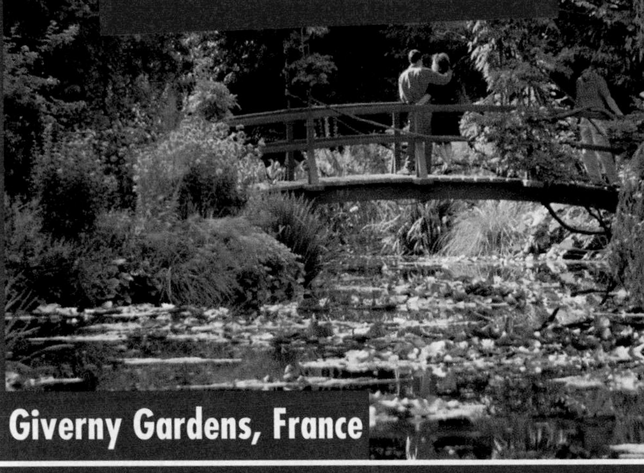

Giverny Gardens, France

1883 Monet started planting gardens at his home.

Queen Elizabeth II

Buckingham Palace, England

1953 Queen Elizabeth II lives and works in Buckingham Palace.

1875 1900 1925

Monet received artistic inspiration from the gardens at his house in **Giverny**, where artists from around the world visited him.

Today you can visit the gardens in the village of Giverny, France.

Queen Elizabeth II is one of the longest reigning monarchs.

Today areas of **Buckingham Palace** are open to visitors on a regular basis.

For more about People, Places, and Events, visit www.macmillanmh.com

Charles de Gaulle

Strasbourg, France

1959 Charles de Gaulle talks about a unified Europe in Strasbourg.

Adi Roche

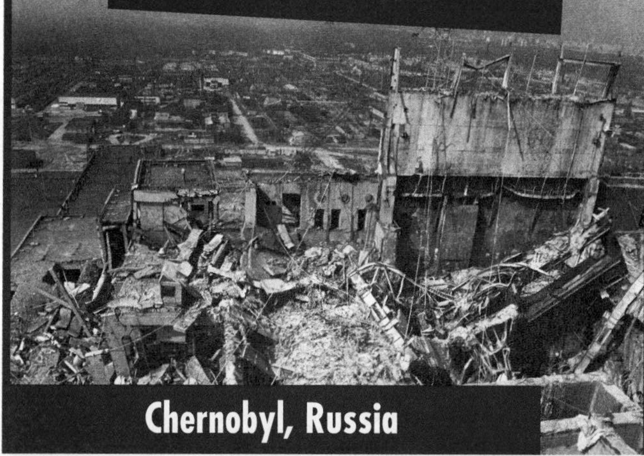

Chernobyl, Russia

1986 Adi Roche founded the Chernobyl Children's Project International.

1950 1975 2000

Parts of President **Charles de Gaulle's** speech have often been mentioned, especially the phrase, "Europe, from the Atlantic to the Urals."

Today Strasbourg is the location of the European Parliament of the European Union.

Adi Roche's Chernobyl Children's Project International offers medical aid for children in the areas most affected by the **Chernobyl** disaster.

Today plans are in place to replace the aging cover that protects Chernobyl's damaged reactor.

Lesson 1

VOCABULARY

- **fertility rate** p. 231
- **Romanticism** p. 234
- **Impressionism** p. 234

READING SKILL

Make Judgments

Complete the chart below with details about the cultures and lifestyles of Europeans. Use your notes to make a judgment about life in Europe today.

Action	→	Judgment
	→	
	→	
	→	

STANDARDS FOCUS

SOCIAL STUDIES — Culture

GEOGRAPHY — Places and Regions

CULTURES AND LIFESTYLES

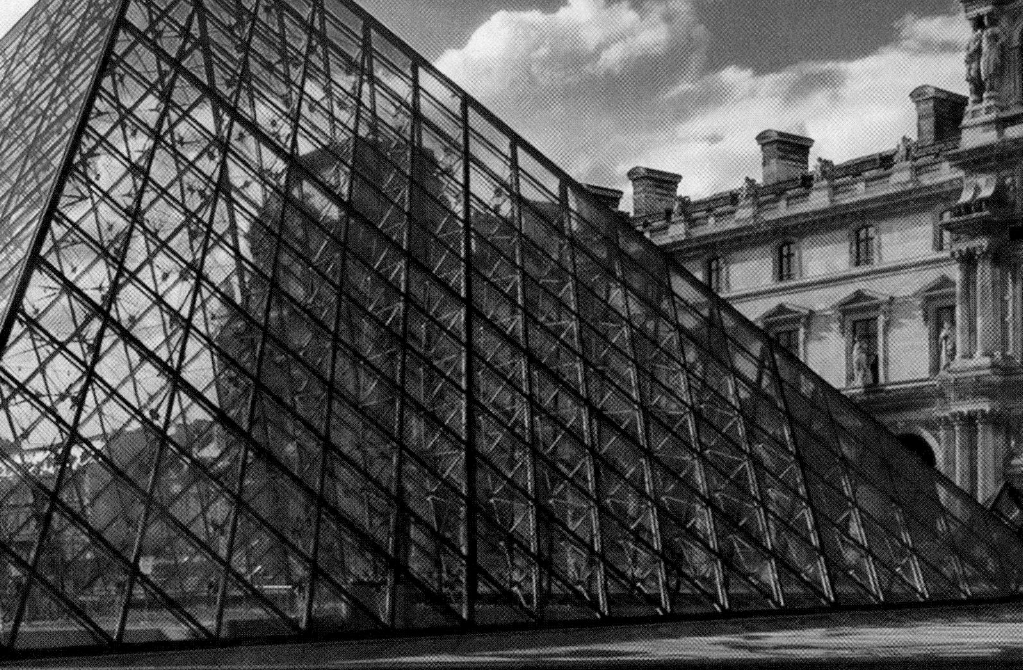

The Louvre Museum in Paris, France, houses some of the world's most famous paintings and sculptures.

Visual Preview

How do people affect the cultures and lifestyles in Europe?

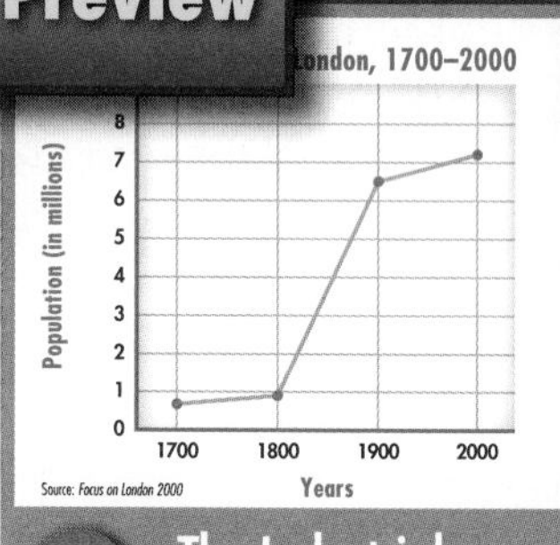

A The Industrial Revolution changed Europe into an urban, industrial society.

B Today, Europe is home to more than 160 different ethnic groups.

C Europeans enjoy sports and celebrate historical events.

D The arts have been an important part of European culture for centuries.

Ⓐ URBANIZATION

In recent years differences in lifestyles among Europeans have lessened as a result of industrial, economic, and urban growth.

In the late 1700s, the industrial revolution changed Europe from a rural, farming society to an urban, industrial society. Cities grew rapidly as rural villagers moved in large numbers to the developing urban areas. The growth was most remarkable in London, England, during the early 1800s.

Today, three out of every four Europeans live in cities. Paris and London are among the largest urban areas in the world. The next biggest cities are Milan, Italy, and Madrid, Spain.

Most European cities are a blend of old and new. It is common for ancient landmarks to stand near modern highways and skyscrapers. Europe's cities are crisscrossed by public transportation systems that bring people to jobs and urban attractions. In recent years, however, more Europeans have bought cars and moved to the suburbs outside of the cities.

Quick Check

Make Judgments **Why do you think more Europeans have moved to the cities in recent years?**

DataGraphic

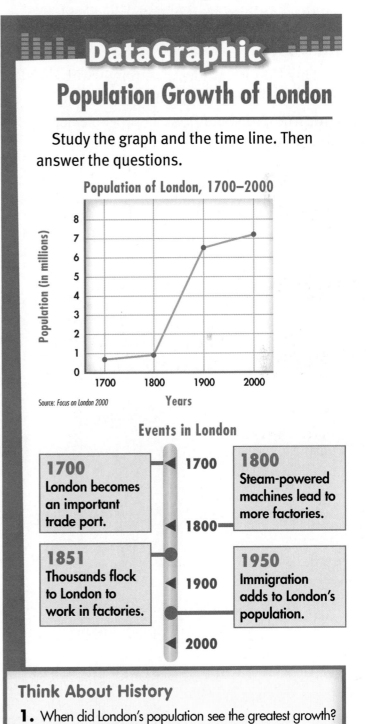

Population Growth of London

Study the graph and the time line. Then answer the questions.

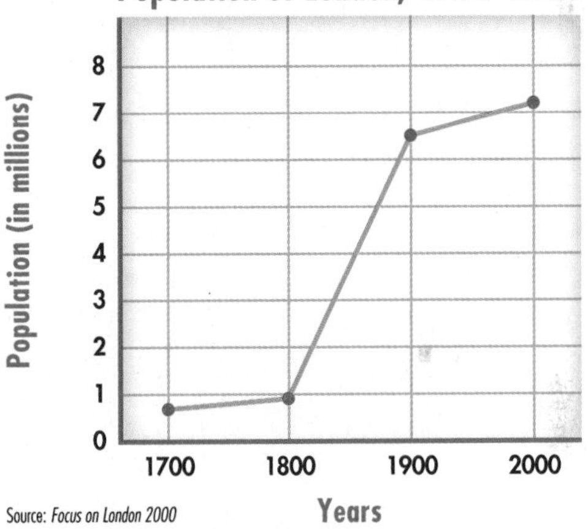

Population of London, 1700–2000

Source: *Focus on London 2000*

Events in London

1700 London becomes an important trade port.

1800 Steam-powered machines lead to more factories.

1851 Thousands flock to London to work in factories.

1950 Immigration adds to London's population.

Think About History

1. When did London's population see the greatest growth?
2. Use the timeline to find reasons for the growth.

B DIVERSE POPULATIONS

Europeans are crowded into a fairly small space. The population is not evenly distributed, and it continues to undergo change. There are areas of dense populations, but there are also areas of untouched land.

The People

Many Europeans identify strongly with their country as well as with their ethnic group. In some European countries, most people belong to the same ethnic group. For example, more than 90 percent of the people in Sweden are Swedes, descendants of people that settled the Scandinavian peninsula centuries ago. They share a common heritage, the Swedish language, and the Lutheran religion.

In other countries the population consists of a few different ethnic groups. Belgium, for example, has two leading ethnic groups—the Flemings and the Walloons. Flemings and Walloons share a common religion, Roman Catholicism, but they speak different languages.

Today, Europe is home to more than 160 separate ethnic groups. Europe's vast ethnic mix is a result of migrations, wars, and the changing of country boundaries.

National and ethnic loyalties, however, have also led to conflict. In the 1990s disputes among ethnic groups split Yugoslavia into six separate countries. Some of these new countries have seen some of the worst fighting since World War II.

These schoolgirls in London show Europe's growing immigrant population and ethnic diversity. .

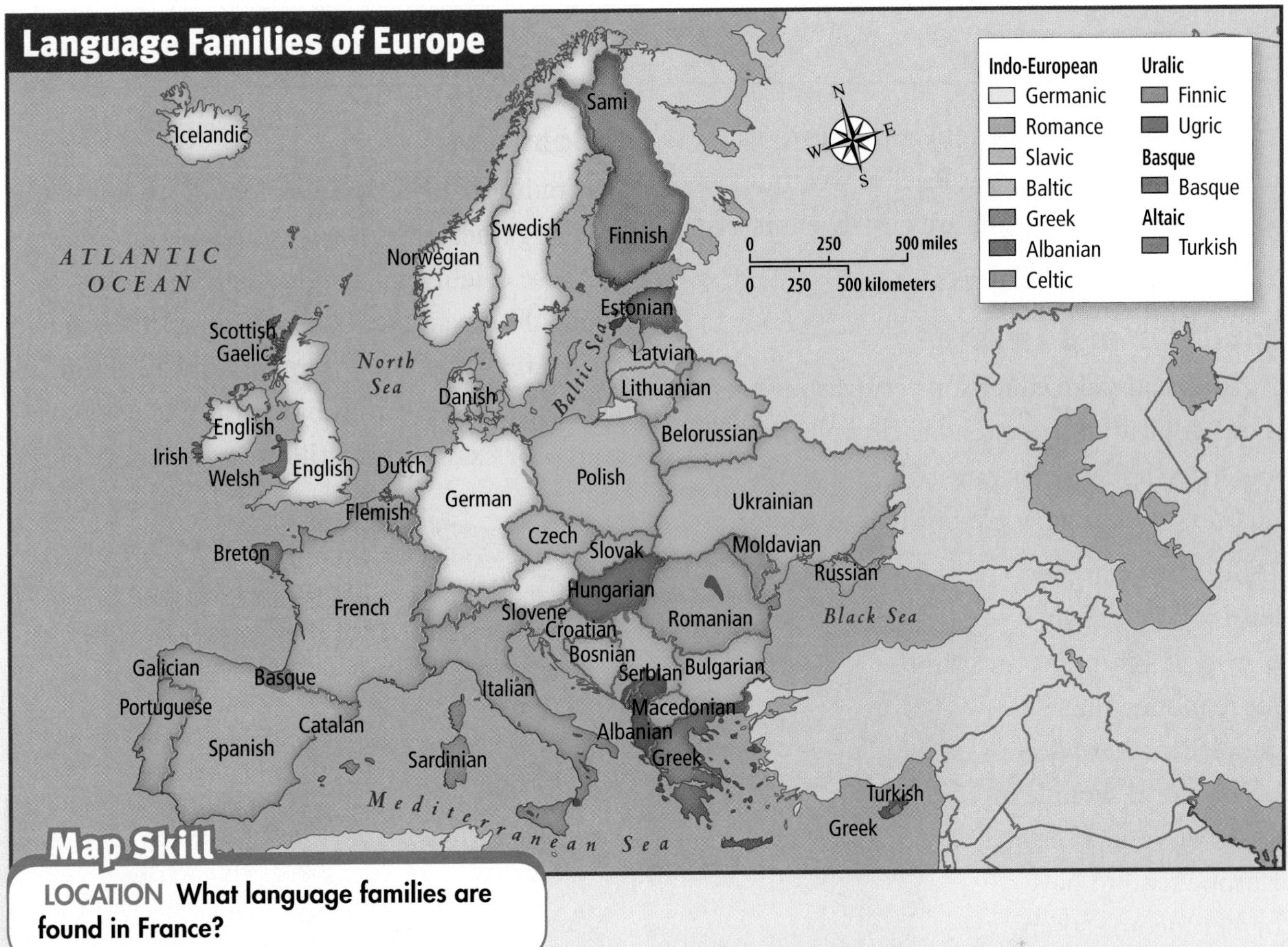

Map Skill

LOCATION **What language families are found in France?**

In spite of divisions, Europeans have a growing sense of unity today. They realize that their countries are linked by geography and that cooperation can help bring peace and prosperity to their region.

Population Changes

Since World War II, many people from Asia, Africa, and Latin America have settled in Europe. Some came from former European colonies. Others moved from different parts of the world. Many North Africans from the former French colonies have migrated to France. Germany and other Central European countries have admitted large numbers of people from Turkey and Greece, as well as the former Yugoslavia.

Although the number of immigrants to Europe is increasing, the continent's overall population is decreasing in number. Europe's **fertility rate**, the average number of children born to each woman, has dropped tremendously over the last few decades. Due to the low fertility rate, Europe is expected to have 10 percent fewer people by the year 2050.

This creates a problem for the countries because there will be fewer workers to keep Europe's economy growing. At the same time, Europeans are living longer because of better health care. Young workers will face higher taxes to support the older, retired workers.

Quick Check

Make Judgments **What other problems might Europe's low fertility rate cause?**

C DAILY LIFE

Lifestyles in Europe reflect the region's urban society and higher level of wealth. Today, most Europeans are city dwellers with comfortable incomes.

Education and Leisure

Europeans take education very seriously. The people of Europe tend to be well educated and have high literacy rates. More than three-quarters of young people finish high school.

Because of higher levels of education, Europeans earn more money than people in other parts of the world. People in Northern and Western Europe tend to have higher incomes than those in Southern and Eastern Europe, though.

Soccer is a popular sport in Europe

Their fairly high incomes allow many Europeans to enjoy leisure time. In most countries workers receive four weeks of vacation each year. Many people use this time to travel to places such as Italy and France.

Europeans take full advantage of their natural environment. Skiing is a popular winter sport. Swimming and rowing are favorite summer activities. People are passionate about playing and watching rugby and soccer, which Europeans call football. In fact soccer is the national sport in most European countries.

Celebrations

Traditional European celebrations include family gatherings for special occasions. Most of these celebrations include eating special foods. For example, Greeks celebrate Easter with a feast of lamb. Many European countries celebrate festivals to honor historical events as well. For example, Bastille Day, celebrated in France on July 14, honors the storming of Bastille prison in 1789 and the start of the French Revolution.

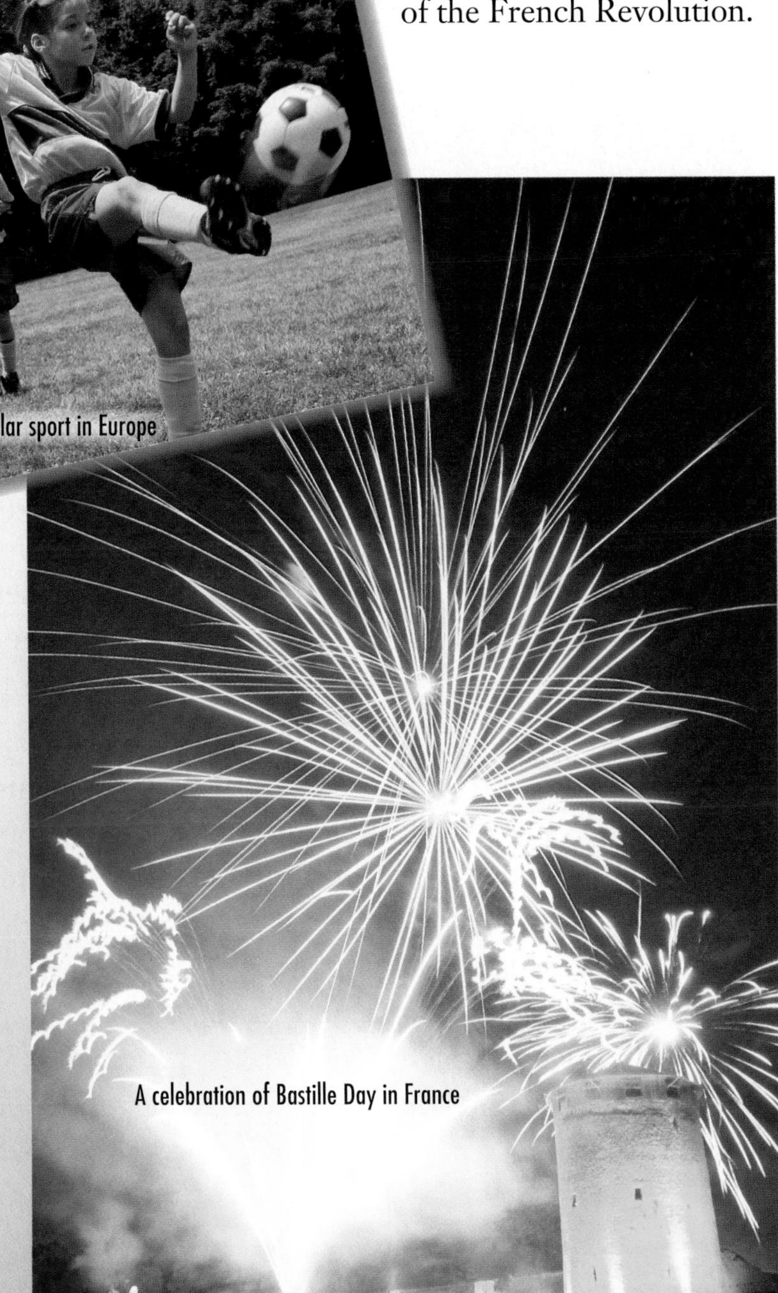

A celebration of Bastille Day in France

Religion

Christianity has been a major influence in European life for centuries. However, since the 1700s Europeans have become more secular, or nonreligious. Many Europeans do not belong to one particular religious group. However, Christian moral teachings remain important throughout much of the continent.

Most of Europe's Christians are Roman Catholic and live in the southern areas of Western Europe and in some Eastern European countries. Protestants are dominant in northern Europe. Eastern orthodoxy is strongest in the southern part of Eastern Europe.

Judaism and Islam have also influenced European culture. Despite times of discrimination, Jews have made many contributions to European life. Jewish communities thrive in all of the major European cities. Meanwhile, Muslim immigrants are moving to the region of Europe by the thousands.

Europe's Religions

- Roman Catholicism
- Eastern Orthodox
- Protestantism
- Islam
- Judaism

1. SLOVENIA
2. CROATIA
3. BOSNIA & HERZEGOVINA
4. MONTENEGRO
5. MACEDONIA
6. ALBANIA

Map Skill

PLACE Which religions are found in Germany?

For the most part, Europeans of different faiths live together peacefully. In some cases, however, Europe's religious differences have led to violence. For years, hostility between Catholics and Protestants created conflict in Northern Ireland. Currently, both sides share political power, but tensions remain.

Roman Catholic, Eastern Orthodox, and Muslim groups have had clashes in the Balkan Peninsula during the 1990s. Today, these groups are living together more peacefully, but experts believe that European nations will have to become more tolerant of religious differences.

PLACES

The Cologne Cathedral is the seat of the Roman Catholic Archbishop of Cologne. It is known as a monument of Christianity and of Gothic architecture. Today, the cathedral is a World Heritage Site and is one of the world's largest churches.

Cologne Cathedral

QUICK CHECK

Make Judgments Why do you think the French celebrate Bastille Day?

D THE ARTS

The arts have been an important part of European culture for centuries. Europe's churches and temples show the development of architecture and major religions. In ancient times the Greeks and Romans constructed temples with columns. During the Middle Ages, a new style of architecture, known as Gothic, arose. People built churches, called cathedrals, with pointed arches and stained-glass windows.

▲ Claude Monet's painting, *Water Lilies,* is an example of Impressionism.

During the Renaissance European artists began to use everyday subjects. The writings of England's William Shakespeare and Spain's Miguel de Cervantes told tales of characters with timeless problems.

In the 1800s musicians, writers, and European artists developed a style known as **Romanticism**, which aimed to stir emotions. This style drew ideas from nature and historical events.

In the late 1800s, artists began a style called **Impressionism**. This style showed the natural appearance of objects and light using bold colors and brushstrokes. European artists moved away from portraying the world as it appeared in the 1900s. Sculptures, buildings, and paintings became more abstract.

Quick Check

Make Judgments **How does Romanticism differ from Impressionism?**

Check Understanding

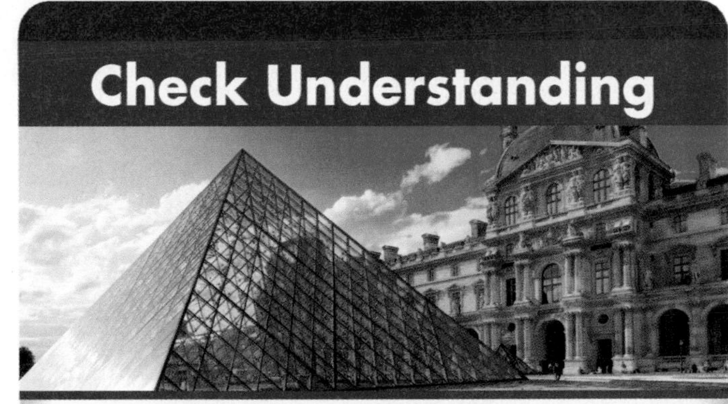

1. **VOCABULARY** Use each vocabulary word below in a sentence that shows you understand its meaning in this lesson

   fertility rate **Romanticism**
   Impressionism

2. **READING SKILL**
   Make Judgments Use your chart from page 228 to explain the diversity in Europe.

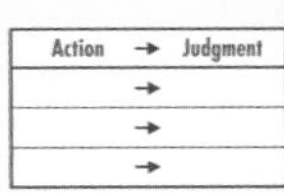

3. **Write About It** Write about a celebration or art showing that you have participated in your community.

Chart and Graph Skills

Use a Double Bar Graph

VOCABULARY

double bar graph

A **double bar graph** compares information. It shows information as two bars on the same graph. Look at the double bar graph on this page as you follow the steps.

Population Distribution Urban and Rural Areas

Percentage of Population

100
90
80
70
60
50
40
30
20
10
0

France
Greece
United Kingdom

Urban Areas
Rural Areas

Source: United Nations Statistics Division

Learn It

- A double bar graph uses bars side by side to compare information.
- The title shows the topic of the double bar graph.
- The bars use different colors to show each set of information clearly.
- The labels on each side of the graph tell you how to understand the information.

Try It

- Where do most French people choose to live?
- Which country has the biggest difference between urban and rural settlements?

Apply It

- Make a double bar graph showing the number of boys and the number of girls in each sixth-grade class in your school.

The Economy of Europe

Lesson 2

VOCABULARY

global economy p. 238

heavy industry p. 240

light industry p. 240

organic p. 241

READING SKILL

Make Judgments

Complete the chart below with details about the economy of Europe. Then use your notes to make a judgment about Europe's economy.

Action	→	Judgment
	→	
	→	
	→	

STANDARDS FOCUS

SOCIAL STUDIES — Production, Distribution, & Consumption

GEOGRAPHY — Human Systems

The German autobahn

Visual Preview

How does technology influence the economy?

A Europe is supported by high-tech transportation and communications.

B Europe buys and sells goods across the globe.

C Both industry and agriculture are important to Europe's economy.

Ⓐ TECHNOLOGY

Europe's system of highways, railroads, waterways, and airline routes is among the best in the world. Modern communications systems also link most parts of Europe to one another and to the rest of the world.

Many European countries have transportation systems that take people to and from jobs, city centers, and across the country. Each country is different, but most of Europe has an advanced transportation network.

Transportation

High-speed trains connect cities and towns across the continent. Highways also allow high-speed, long-distance travel. Cars can zip along Germany's autobahn at more than 80 miles per hour. Trucks use the roadways to carry goods.

Canals and rivers are also used to connect people and to transport goods. The Main-Danube Canal in Germany links hundreds of ports between the North Sea and the Black Sea. Europe's long coastline has many other important ports, such as Rotterdam in the Netherlands and Lisbon in Portugal.

Communications

Telephone and print media vary across Europe. Western Europeans benefit from high-quality satellite, Internet, and cell phone technology. These technologies are not as common in Eastern Europe yet, but they are starting to catch on.

Quick Check

Make Judgments **Why do you think cell phones are more common in Western Europe?**

The metro lines in Toulouse, France, help to connect metropolitan areas.

B GLOBAL ECONOMY

Europe's economy is influenced heavily by trade with nations around the globe. Europe has benefited from the rapid growth of the **global economy**, or the ability of companies to sell products all over the world.

Global Trade

In 1992 representatives from various European governments met in Maastricht, Netherlands, to form the European Union. The EU was developed first as an economic union. It unites most countries in Europe into one trading community.

The EU imports the second largest number of goods in the world. Some major imports are plastics and oil. The EU exports the largest number of goods in the world. Some major exports are dairy products and automobiles. EU members do not pay tariffs, or taxes added to the cost of foreign trade goods.

The Euro

One of the EU's first goals was to make Europe's economies more competitive. It removed limitations on the movement of goods and people across its members' borders.

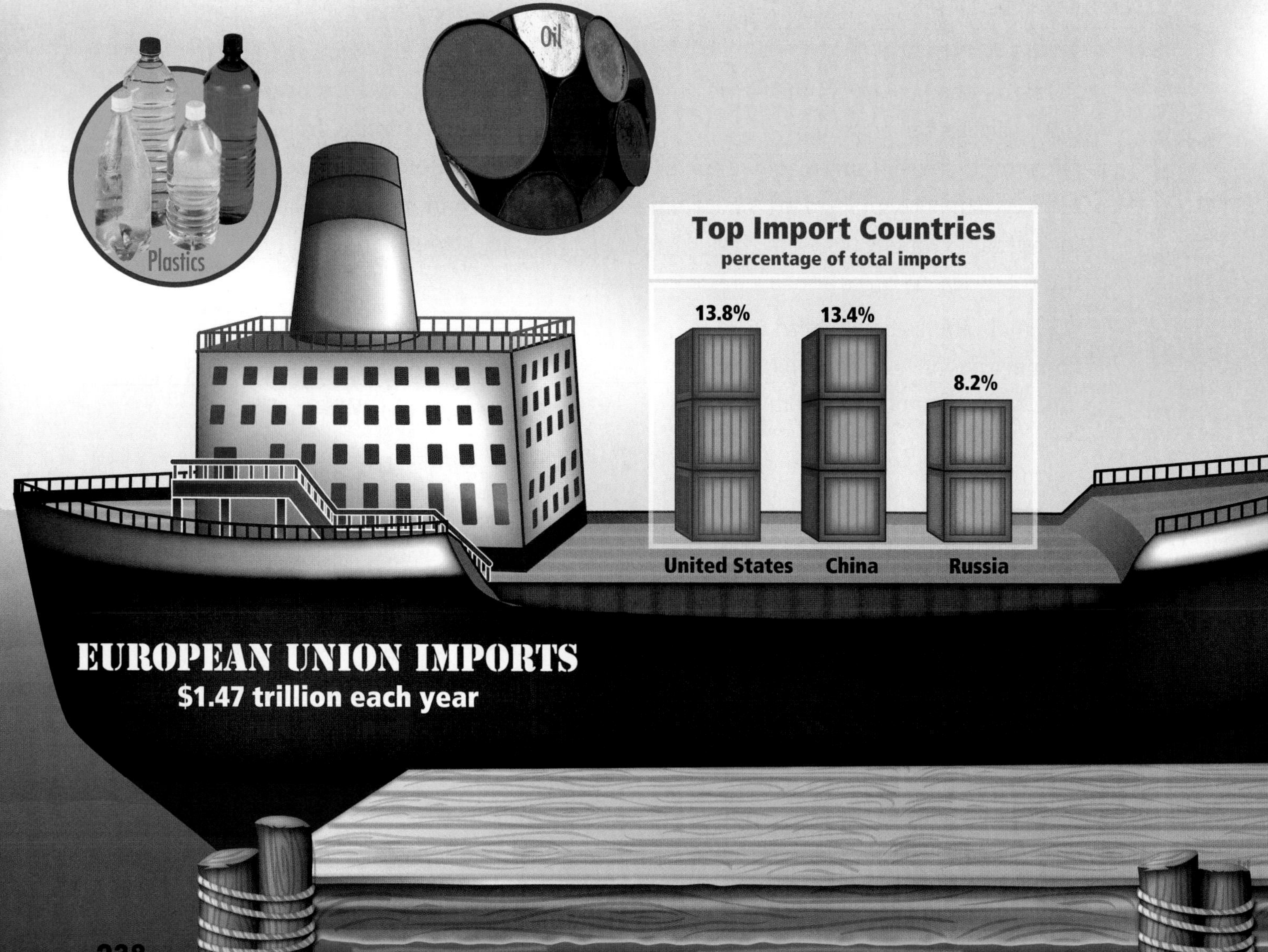

This paved the way for a single European currency, the euro. The EU also created a central bank and one foreign policy.

Fifteen members of the EU have adopted the euro. Together, the territories of these countries are called the eurozone. The currency is also used by a number of countries outside the EU. The euro is controlled by the European Central Bank.

Eastern Europe

Many former communist nations of Eastern Europe hope to join the EU for trade benefits. To be eligible to join, nations must meet strict standards, such as keeping their budgets close to balance or in surplus. Meeting these standards has been a long struggle for these nations.

After the fall of communism, the economy of Eastern Europe saw many changes. Previously, the state controlled the economy. With communist rule over, Eastern Europe had to change to compete in the global marketplace. Outdated equipment was replaced, and workers were retrained to find jobs in industries that use updated technologies. As a result, Eastern Europe's economy is growing.

QUICK CHECK

Make Judgments **Why should European nations have to meet standards to join the EU?**

C INDUSTRY AND AGRICULTURE

You learned about the Industrial Revolution in Unit 5. That era made Europe the birthplace of modern industry. Today, Europe manufactures items as varied as computer chips, automobiles, and clothing.

Manufacturing

During the 1800s Europe's industries relied on its large deposits of coal and iron. This resulted in the growth of **heavy industry**. Heavy industry is the production of machinery and industrial equipment. Today, automobiles and transportation equipment are also considered heavy industry. Countries that do not have these raw materials are involved in **light industry**. Light industry includes the production of high-end electronics and specialty tools.

Today, Europe's leading industrial centers include the Midlands region in the United Kingdom, the Ruhr and Middle Rhine districts in Germany, and the Upper Silesia-Moravia districts in Poland and the Czech Republic.

Service and Technology

Service industries are industries which provide a direct service to people or businesses. These include many diverse activities from pest control to entertainment. Service industries employ nearly 60 percent of Europe's population. Tourism is one of the largest service industries in Europe. Spain, Italy, and Greece, for instance, are visited by millions of vacationers each year.

Industries in Europe are diverse. They include heavy industries such as this car factory in Germany (left) and light industries like a computer parts laboratory in Ireland (top).

Agriculture

Even though most Europeans are employed in industries, Europe has fertile farmland and a long agricultural tradition. In some parts of Eastern Europe, nearly 50 percent of the population is involved in agriculture.

Crops vary between regions. In Southern Europe, farmers grow olives, dates, citrus fruit, and grapes. In Western and Eastern Europe, wheat, rye, and other grains are major products. Denmark and the Netherlands are major producers of dairy products such as cheese. The Dutch also export about two million tulip bulbs each year.

Current Issues

A developing technology in Europe is genetically modified food products. These are foods with genes that have been altered to make them bigger or more resistant to disease. These products are strictly regulated throughout Euope. Still, Europeans avoid these products as they do not believe they are safe. Some people also avoid foods grown in fields treated with chemicals. As a result, they only eat products which have been grown on **organic** farms, where no chemicals are used.

In 2001 the livestock industry of several European nations suffered from an outbreak of a disease called foot-and-mouth disease. In the United Kingdom, this resulted in the destruction of thousands of animals and damage to the economy. Today, countries have strict control on agriculture to prevent such outbreaks from occuring.

Quick Check

Make Judgments **Would you buy genetically modified food?**

Primary Sources

"When foot-and-mouth is fully eradicated, some will move on. But we know for farmers and the countryside in general this will remain a time of great change and great anxiety. We will do all we can to help people throughthose changes. Our work will not stop when foot-and-mouth is gone."

British Prime Minister Tony Blair's statement on the foot-and-mouth disease outbreak on May 3, 2001

Write About It Write an essay about how you would react to this speech if you were one of the farmers who was affected.

Check Understanding

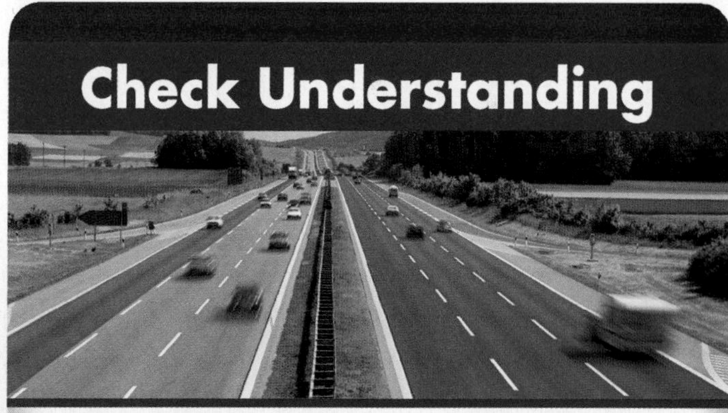

1. **VOCABULARY** Use these vocabulary words in a paragraph about Europe's economy.

   global economy **heavy industry**
   light industry **organic**

2. **READING SKILL Make Judgments** Use your chart from page 236 to write about how the EU brings Europeans together.

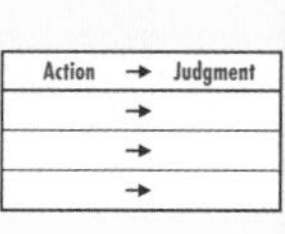

3. **Write About It** How does the global economy impact trade in Europe?

Lesson 3

VOCABULARY

parliamentary democracy p. 243

constitutional monarchy p. 244

figurehead p. 244

neutrality p. 245

READING SKILL

Make Judgments

Complete the chart below with judgments about democracy in Europe today.

Action	→	Judgment
	→	
	→	
	→	

STANDARDS FOCUS

SOCIAL STUDIES — Civics Ideals and Practices

GEOGRAPHY — World in Spatial terms

GOVERNMENT AND CITIZENSHIP

The British Parliament meets in the Palace of Westminster.

Visual Preview

How do governments influence each other?

A All European countries are democracies.

B Differences exist between European governments.

C Former communist countries are learning how democracy works.

A DEMOCRATIC GOVERNMENTS

Some European countries have a long history of being democratic. Other countries are still working on creating true and stable democratic governments.

All European citizens control and influence their governments through voting. Many countries are republics because people elect officials to represent them. Several countries also have a federal system of government, where power is shared between the national government and regional or local governments.

Branches of Government

Like the United States, most European countries have a legislative, executive, and judicial branch. The legislative branch is usually strong and powerful. In different countries the lawmaking body can be called different names, such as congress, council, or parliament.

Many countries have both a president and a prime minister. The prime minister is the head of the political party that has the most seats in the legislature. The role of judges varies between different countries.

Great Britain

The **parliamentary democracy** of Great Britain is the oldest in the world. In this type of government, citizens of a country elect officials to a legislature called parliament. Great Britain's system has served as a model for many other countries, including Belgium, Portugal, and Latvia.

The British Parliament has two houses, with the House of Commons having the real power. When needed, Parliament can remove the prime minister from office and call for new elections.

You may already know that Great Britain has a monarchy, or a king or queen. In a true monarchy, a king or queen has complete power for governing a country. Today, Great Britain's Queen Elizabeth II has only limited power.

Quick Check

Make Judgments **Why do you think other countries have modeled their governments after Great Britain?**

PEOPLE

Germany has a chancellor instead of a prime minister. **Angela Merkel** became the first female chancellor of Germany in 2005. The country also has a president, but he or she does not have much power in the government.

Angela Merkel

B VARIETIES OF GOVERNMENT

Many European countries have quite a few similarities among their governments, though interesting differences do exist. As you have already read, Great Britain has a monarchy.

Constitutional Monarchies

Great Britan can be described as a **constitutional monarchy**. The king or queen is the official head of state in this form of government, but he or she does not have much power or control. In countries with a constitutional monarchy, the king or queen is a **figurehead**, or a leader in name only. Elected officials activiely run the government.

The Netherlands, Denmark, Norway, Sweden and Spain are a few other countries in Europe that have constitutional monarchies. Queen Beatrix has been the monarch of the Netherlands since 1980. She has more power than most other monarchs.

Political Parties

Unlike the United States, many European countries have more than two main political parties. Italy, for example, has numerous political parties. The country does not require that a party receive a minimum amount of votes in order to hold a seat in parliament.

Usually, no single party is able to gain a majority in Italy. Party officials have to form coalition governments in order to pass legislation. A coalition government happens when members of different political parties work together to run the government.

▼ Queen Beatrix performing one of her many duties as the monarch of the Netherlands

Neutrality

Switzerland, in the middle of Europe, has a unique distinction. For over 700 years, the country has had a policy of **neutrality**. Neutrality is not supporting any side during a conflict. For example, Switzerland was not part of either side during World War II. Sweden also has a history of being a neutral country.

As a result, the Swiss have had a stable democratic government for more than 700 years, even as fighting has waged around them. Many international organizations are located in Switzerland. For example, the headquarters of the World Health Organization is located in Geneva, Switzerland. This group promotes public health worldwide.

QUICK CHECK

Make Judgments How has the role of a European monarch changed over time?

▼ The World Health Organization in Geneva, Switzerland

Citizenship

Express Your Disagreement

In a democracy citizens participate in and shape their government through voting. Free and fair elections are essential to any democracy. If citizens disagree with something in government, they have the opportunity to seek answers from the government.

In November 2005 the presidential election in the former communist country of Ukraine upset many people. Citizens discovered that the election was not run fairly. People successfully protested for a new election in Independence Square in the capital Kiev. This movement became known as the Orange Revolution. These citizens showed that, in a democracy, change can be accomplished peacefully.

Write About It How can you work to change something that you don't agree with?

C FORMER COMMUNIST STATES

After World War II, the Soviet Union set up communist governments in several Eastern European countries. During the early 1990s, former communist states declared independence and began to reform their societies, including their governments. Today, several Eastern European countries, such as Poland and Bulgaria, are young democracies.

Germany

Germany had been divided into east and west following World War II. East Germany had a communist government. West Germany was democratic, with a federal republic like the United States. In 1989 people in East Germany began to protest against their harsh government. The following year Germany was reunified into one democratic country. Today, Germany is a federal republic.

Balkan States

Following World War II, a dictator named Josip Tito to ruled all of Yugoslavia. He ruled it as a communist country.

Beginning in 1990 different ethnic groups began to seek independence. In some areas fighting broke out and thousands of people were killed. Today, six countries now exist in the area that used to be just one country.

Czech Republic and Slovakia

In the middle of Europe, two ethnic groups found a way to resolve their differences peacefully. Communists controlled the country of Czechoslovakia following World War II. This country gained its independence after the fall of communism, but problems remained. In 1993 the country split into the Czech Republic and Slovakia.

The image to the right shows a market square in communist-ruled Warsaw, Poland. The image below shows the same market square in Warsaw after the fall of communism. Notice how alive it looks today.

Former Communist Countries

Western Europe
Eastern Europe

Former boundaries of:
- Czechoslovakia
- East Germany
- Yugoslavia

1. SLOVENIA
2. CROATIA
3. BOSNIA & HERZEGOVINA
4. MONTENEGRO
5. MACEDONIA
6. ALBANIA

Map Skill

REGION **Which nations make up the former Yugoslavia?**

Russia

After the fall of communism, the Soviet Union was renamed Russia. It wrote a new constitution and held democratic elections. Russia had some success building a democracy and a market economy. However, it still struggles to be truly democratic. Government controls have increased. The president has strong powers and can issue laws that do not need approval by the legislature. The government puts limits on free expression. Also, the courts do not always treat everyone fairly.

Quick Check

Make Judgments **Why do you think Russia has trouble being truly democratic?**

Check Understanding

1. **VOCABULARY** Use these vocabulary words in a paragraph about European governments.
   parliamentary democracy **figurehead**
   constitutional monarchy

2. **READING SKILL** Make Judgments Use your chart from page 242 to write about democracy in Europe today.

Action →	Judgment
→	
→	
→	

3. **Write About It** How did the fall of the Soviet Union affect Eastern Europe?

ISSUES TODAY

Lesson 4

VOCABULARY

ethnic cleansing p. 251

separatist movement p. 251

READING SKILL

Make Judgments

Complete the chart below with details about the issues in Europe today. Use your notes to make a judgment about an issue affecting Europe today.

Action	→	Judgment
	→	
	→	
	→	

STANDARDS FOCUS

SOCIAL STUDIES Global Connections

GEOGRAPHY World in Spatial Terms

European Union committees meet at the Berlaymont building in Brussels, Belgium.

Visual Preview

How do issues in Europe today affect its people?

A The European Union has brought the countries of Europe together.

B Europeans are trying to solve some regional conflicts.

Years	Estimated Number of Immigrants in Europe	Percent of European Population
1965	16,662,207	3.8
1975	20,170,448	4.3
1985	23,471,785	4.8
1995	55,286,554	7.6
2005	64,115,850	8.8

C Immigrants from all over the world have changed Europe's make up.

D Some European countries have become targets of terrorists.

Ⓐ THE EUROPEAN UNION

Shortly after the end of World War II, several countries in Europe met to discuss ways to work together. This group established the foundation for the European Union.

Twelve original member countries officially established the European Union in 1993. The EU has three governing bodies. The Council of the European Union represents member governments, the European Parliament represents the people, and the European Commission represents the common interest of the EU. The EU has its own anthem, flag, holiday, and motto. It also has laws that must be obeyed by member countries. By 2020 the EU plans to have 30 member countries.

Other Functions

The EU is more than an economic organization, though. For instance, the EU has brought greater political unification among its member countries. For example, people today can get EU passports instead of passports from their countries.

The EU is also working to protect the environment. By 2010 the EU hopes that its member countries will have reduced their pollution levels by 15 percent from the levels of 1990. The group also monitors equality and human rights issues, and it has its own military force.

Quick Check

Make Judgments **How has the EU improved people's lives in Europe?**

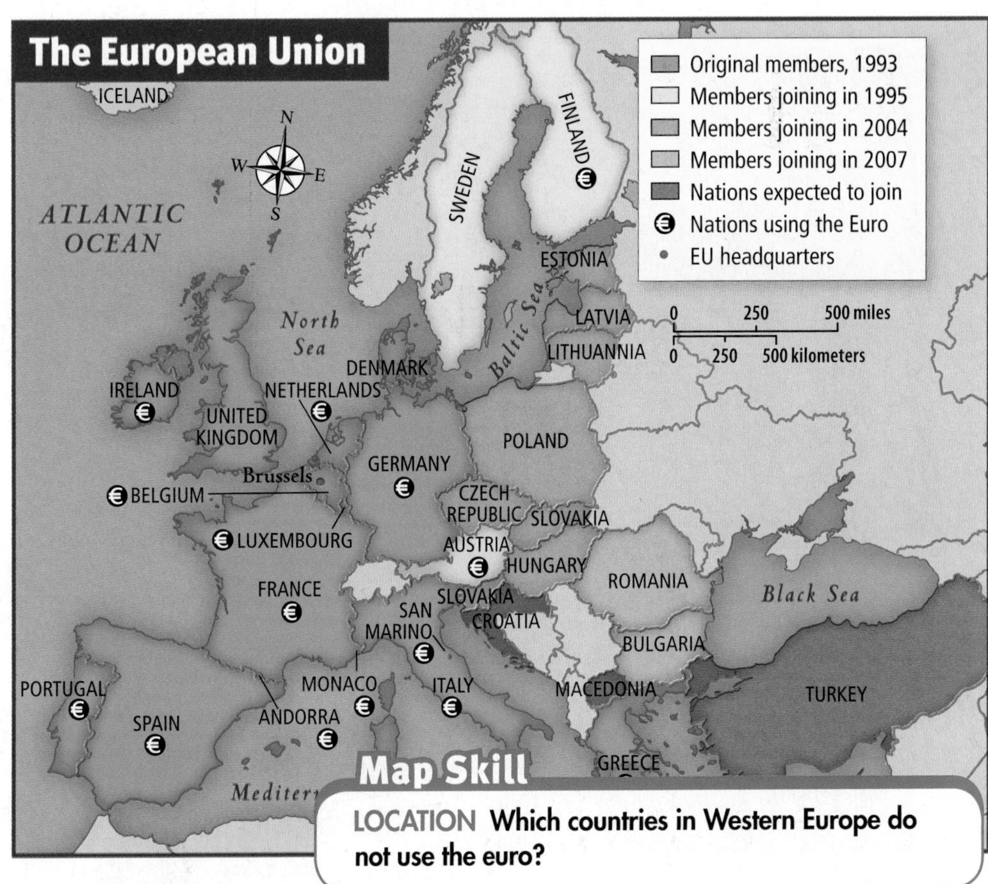

Map Skill

LOCATION **Which countries in Western Europe do not use the euro?**

B REGIONAL CONFLICTS

European countries are coming together to join the European Union, but national and ethnic loyalties have also led to conflict. These conflicts have been going on for many years and are based on long histories of tension.

The Struggle for Northern Ireland

The country of Ireland had won its independence from the United Kingdom in 1922. The British, meanwhile, kept control of Northern Ireland, where most people are Protestants.

Northern Ireland has been the site of violence between Catholics and Protestants for many years. The Catholics of Northern Ireland would like to unite with their Catholic neighbors in Ireland. Most Protestants in Northern Ireland wish to remain a part of the United Kingdom.

The dispute over Northern Ireland has led to conflict, especially from the 1960s to the 1990s. In 1998 leaders of the United Kingdom and the Republic of Ireland met with leaders of both sides in Northern Ireland. They signed the Good Friday Agreement to end the violence, but disputes have continued. The future of Northern Ireland remains uncertain.

Yugoslavia

When communism collapsed in Eastern Europe, many different ethnic groups saw their chance for independence. Some took action.

In the early 1990s, four parts of Yugoslavia, including Bosnia and Herzegovina, declared their independence. Meanwhile, another strong part, Serbia, wanted to keep Yugoslavia together under Serbian rule.

Students in a youth group in Ireland learn to work together despite their differences (above). Fighting in Northern Ireland escalated on January 30, 1972. On this day, known as "Bloody Sunday," British troops fired on a crowd of civil rights protestors and killed 13 people (right).

Villages burned during the heavy fighting in Bosnia (below). A growing tourism industry, due to Bosnia's beautiful beaches, is helping to rebuild the country (left).

Serbia's leaders used force to gain power. The heaviest fighting took place in Bosnia and Herzegovina. Here the Serbs carried out **ethnic cleansing**—the removing or killing of an entire ethnic group—against the Bosnian population. Thousands of people were forced to leave their homes and became refugees. Many more people died. The conflicts have left the region badly scarred.

Today, Serbia has given up hope of reclaiming Yugoslavia. Where Yugoslavia once was, there are now six separate nations. Since the Dayton Peace Agreements ended the war in the former Yugoslavia in 1995, the country of Bosnia and Herzegovina has made tremendous progress in rebuilding. Today, it is working toward joining the European Union.

Chechnya

Russia has controlled Chechnya for many years. When the Russian government was weakened, Chechen rebels launched a **separatist movement**, or a campaign to break away from the national government.

In the early 1990s, Russia's President Boris Yeltsin gave Chechnya more self-rule. However, many Chechens wanted complete independence from Russia. Yeltsin feared that other regions would also demand independence. In 1994 he sent the Russian army into Chechnya to crush Chechen forces. Both sides suffered heavy losses.

The Chechen separatists continued to carry out attacks against the Russian government. Agreements between the two sides have failed. The situation remains unstable today.

Quick Check

Make Judgments **Why do you think the fall of communism caused different ethnic groups to fight for independence?**

Russian occupation and destruction are a part of everyday life in Chechnya (above). Today, humanitarian aid, such as shipments of bread, help the Chechen people (right).

C PEOPLE ON THE MOVE

In recent years the population of Europe has become more diverse. Immigration to Europe has changed the make up of the continent. European governments, as well as the European Union, are working to develop balanced immigration policies. Immigration issues will be important for many years to come.

People migrate, or move from one country to another, for a variety of reasons. Economics motivates many people to come to Europe. Europe provides not only more jobs but also higher-paying ones than are often not available in immigrants' home countries.

Freedoms, including speech, assembly, and religion, attract other people, especially those who face discrimination in their native countries. For many people Europe provides more opportunities for a better life.

The Need for Labor

Immigration might also help solve the problem of labor shortage in several nations. These countries need skilled workers to fill positions across the economy, especially in high-tech fields.

◀ Immigration to Europe from all over the world has made it a more diverse continent.

Manual laborers, such as those who pick crops, are also needed. Immigrants can help fill these positions. In Europe an estimated 50 to 75 million immigrants will be needed during the next 50 years to fill jobs.

Also, the population of Europe is getting older and families are having fewer children. As a result, there are fewer people in the workforce to support the welfare and retirement systems. Immigrant workers can help support these European institutions.

Impact of Immigration

While solving some problems, immigration has also created problems in Europe. More people put pressure on a country's resources. Overcrowding may occur, and welfare systems, such as healthcare, may get overwhelmed.

European Immigration

Years	Estimated Number of Immigrants in Europe	Percent of European Population
1965	16,662,207	3.8
1975	20,170,448	4.3
1985	23,471,785	4.8
1995	55,286,554	7.6
2005	64,115,850	8.8

Source: World Migrant Stock, United Nations

Chart Skill

What percentage of the European population were immigrants in 2005?

Muslims stage a rally to protest the printing of cartoons of the prophet Muhammad.

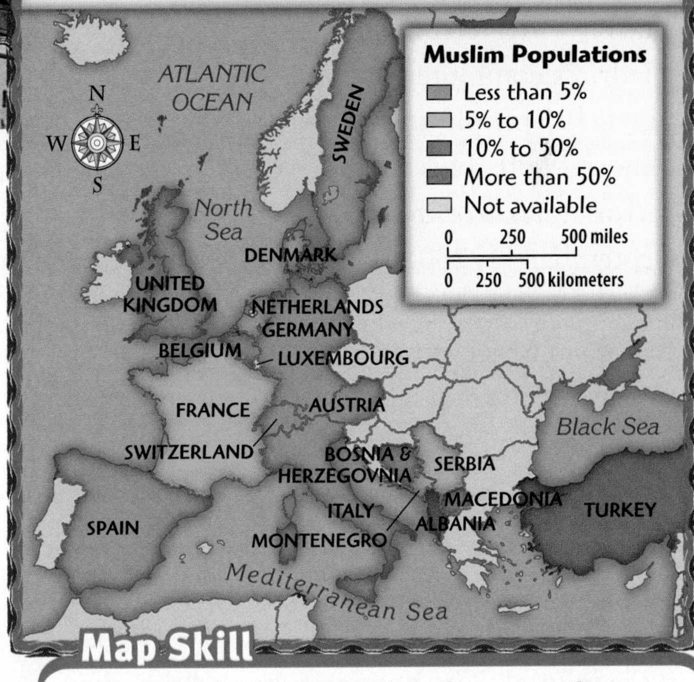

Map Skill

PLACE **Which countries have the largest Muslim populations?**

Immigration has increased fear in some people. Some native Europeans worry about the loss of national and cultural identities as more immigrants come into European countries. They are concerned that traditional ways will disappear when new people and cultures enter their society. These concerns can sometimes cause conflict.

Religious Issues

Many groups of different faiths, other than Christianity, have moved to Europe. Millions of immigrants, many of them Muslims from North Africa, Turkey, and Southwest Asia, have left their homelands to start new lives in European nations. Sometimes, not understanding different religious backgrounds and different religious beliefs can cause bad feelings and conflict among people.

One instance of religious conflict happened in 2006. A newspaper published cartoons that presented the prophet Muhammad negatively. Muhammad is an important figure in Islam. Muslims in Europe and around the world were angered by the paper. They believed that it was disrespectful to their religion. They participated in protests to voice their concern.

Quick Check

Make Judgments **Do you think immigration is positive or negative? Why?**

D TERRORISM

You have learned about the impact of terrorism on life in the United States. Several European countries have joined the United States in international efforts to stop terrorism. Some of these countries have become targets themselves.

A memorial for those killed in the Madrid bombings calls for "Peace" (above). Flowers cover a memorial for those killed in the London terrorist attacks (right).

Spain and England

On March 11, 2004, Spain was shaken when terrorist attacks on Madrid's commuter train system killed 191 people and injured almost 2,000. This was the worst terror attack worldwide, since the September 11, 2001, strikes on the United States. The Madrid attacks led Spain to reevaluate its involvment in the war in Iraq. It decided to start pulling its troops out in 2004, ahead of schedule.

On July 7, 2005 London, England, was hit with a series of terrorist bombings on its public transportation system during the morning rush hour. Fifty-two people were killed and 700 were injured. The bombings moved the issue of terrorism to the forefront in England.

Terrorism continues to be an ongoing issue throughout Europe today. The European Union developed a counter-terrorism "action plan" that was passed in December 2005. It is based on the following four pillars: prevention, protection, pursuit, and response.

Quick Check

Make Judgments **How has terrorism affected the lives of people today?**

Check Understanding

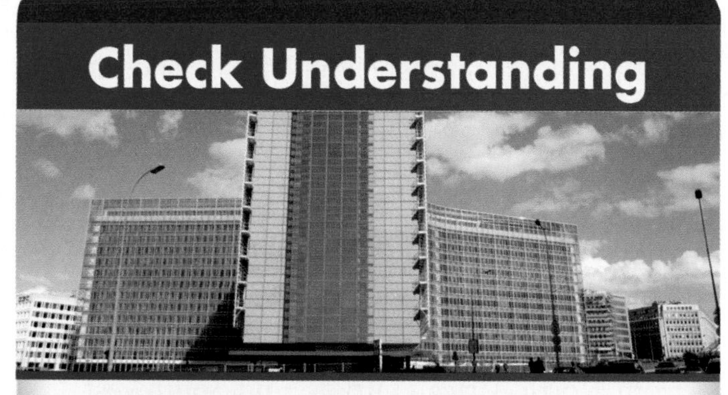

1. **VOCABULARY** Use each vocabulary word below in a sentence that shows you understand its meaning in this lesson.

   ethnic cleansing **separatist movement**

2. **READING SKILL Make Judgments** Use your chart from page 248 to explain immigration in Europe.

Action	→	Judgment
	→	
	→	
	→	

3. **Write About It** Write about how regional conflicts affect Europe today.

Map and Globe Skills

Use Map Projections

VOCABULARY

projection

All flat maps have one big problem: since Earth is curved, the maps can never be completely accurate. Mapmakers have invented ways of drawing Earth on flat surfaces. These drawings are called **projections**. Each type has advantages and disadvantages. Follow the steps below to learn more about two popular kinds of map projections.

Learn It

- The first map is a Mercator projection. The lines of latitude and longitude are straight, but land areas on either side of the equator are stretched. They look bigger than they really are.
- The second map is a Winkel Tripel projection. The lines of latitude and longitude are curved, so the size of land areas is not distorted. Since the lines are not straight, however, this projection is not good for showing directions.

Mercator Projection: Europe

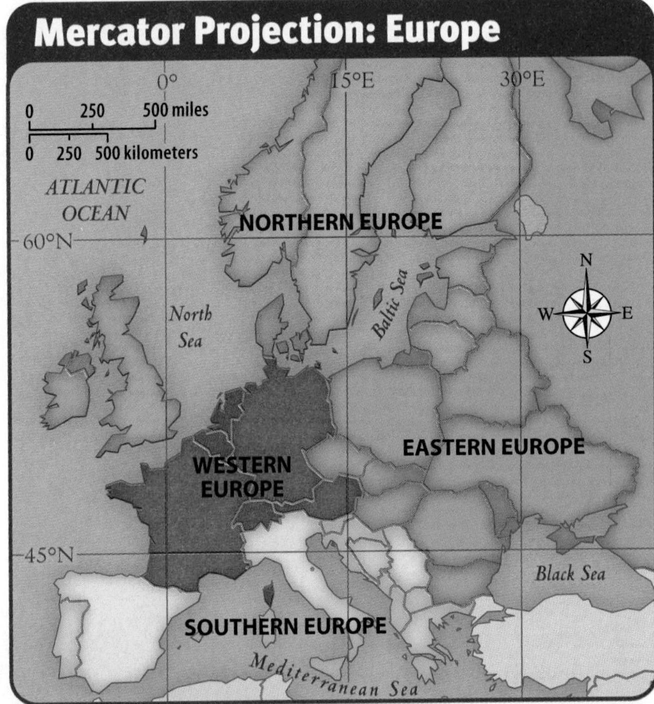

Try It

Use the maps to answer the questions.

- Which projection most accurately shows the size of landmasses?
- Which projection would you use for finding direction?

Winkel Tripel Projection: World

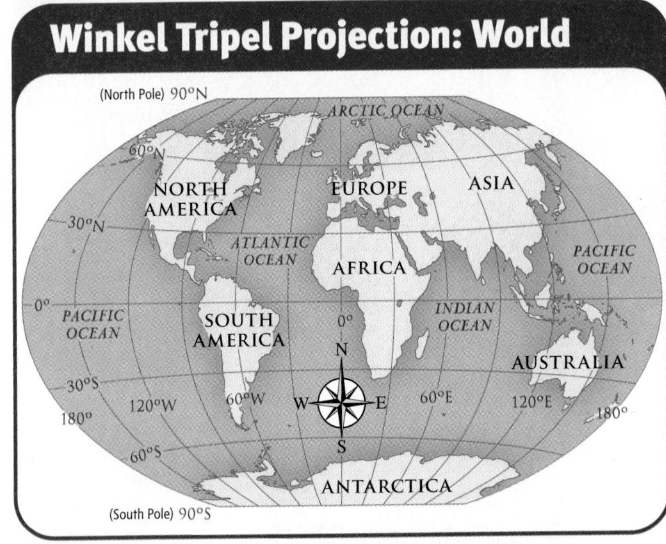

Apply It

- Which projection would be better for a map of your town? Why?

Lesson 5

VOCABULARY

- **reforestation** p. 257
- **erosion** p. 257
- **runoff** p. 258
- **nuclear waste** p. 259
- **greenhouse effect** p. 259

READING SKILL

Make Judgments

Complete the chart below with judgments about the solutions to environmental problems in Europe today.

Action	→	Judgment
	→	
	→	
	→	

STANDARDS FOCUS

SOCIAL STUDIES — People, Places, & Environment

GEOGRAPHY — Environment and Society

The Environment

Air polution from industrial plants can destroy forests, such as this one in Poland.

Visual Preview

How do environmental issues affect people in Europe today?

A Europeans are planting trees to reduce the effects of erosion.

B Europeans are concerned about air and water pollution.

C Today, European countries are uniting to find ways to protect the environment.

Ⓐ MANAGING RESOURCES

Europe's abundant natural resources have helped its economy, but environmental problems are a growing concern.

Mistreatment of the land has caused environmental problems in Europe. Today, Europeans must manage their natural resources wisely in order to repair the damages done.

Deforestation

It is believed that long ago four-fifths of Europe was covered by forest. Today, however, two-thirds of these forests have been removed. People removed trees for firewood and to build cities and farms. The largest amount of tree removal has occurred in the Mediterranean region and industrial Western Europe. Today, the healthiest, most untouched forests are found in Northern Europe.

To stop the effects of forest loss, many countries have started to practice **reforestation**, or the replanting of trees. Many other countries have taken steps to manage the cutting down of trees more responsibly. Sweden, for example, has had a strict system of cutting and replanting trees since the 1800s.

Soil Erosion

Soil **erosion**, or wearing away, has increased in Europe due to human activity. Rapid erosion can be caused by many human practices. These practices include over-farming, poor farming practices, the clearing of vegetation, and overgrazing by livestock.

Soil erosion is a serious problem on the Mediterranean coast. Since the 1980s scientists have done studies to learn how widespread the problem is and to develop solutions in order to reduce erosion. Forest destruction in the Mediterranean is one reason for the area's severe problems with erosion. As a result, Europeans have begun reforestation in this area.

Quick Check

Make Judgments **Why is it important for Europeans to practice reforestation?**

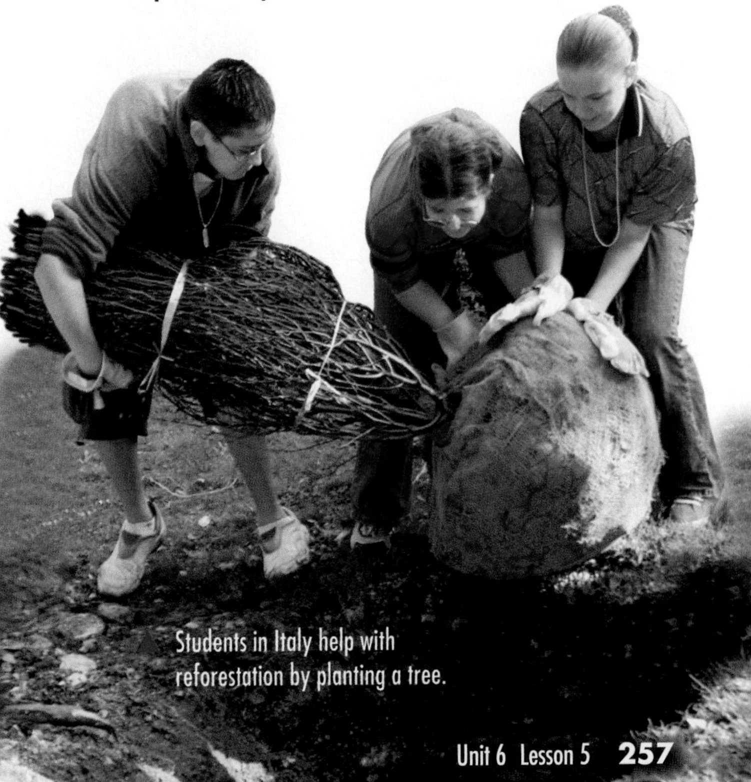

Students in Italy help with reforestation by planting a tree.

B THE HUMAN IMPACT

Population growth and industrialization have affected Europe's environment in some harmful ways. Europeans must deal with pollution, nuclear waste, and global warming.

Air Pollution and Acid Rain

The industrial growth of Europe has created air pollution and health risks. Car exhaust, industrial plants, and smoke from burning oil and coal have caused breathing problems, eye irritations, and lung disease.

Air pollution also produces acid rain. This can make trees vulnerable to attack from insects and disease. Acid rain also poses a problem for Europe's historic buildings. The Tower of London, Germany's Cologne Cathedral, and ancient Greek and Roman buildings all show damage from acid deposits.

Water Pollution

Water pollution is another challenge for Europe. Sewage, garbage, and waste from industry have all been dumped into the region's waterways. As populations and tourism have increased, the problem has become worse.

Runoff from farms has also caused pollution. Runoff is precipitation that flows over the ground, often picking up pesticides and fertilizers along the way. The runoff spilling into the Danube River, for example, has killed much of its marine life.

▼ Exhaust from industrial plants, such as this one in Wales, can cause damage to ancient Greek buildings, such as the Acropolis in Athens (inset).

Nuclear Waste

Nuclear waste has caused environmental problems, particularly in parts of Russia. Nuclear wastes are the by-products of producing nuclear power and weapons. Some nuclear wastes can remain radioactive for thousands of years, posing dangers to people and the environment. Under Soviet rule, Russians placed most of their nuclear wastes in storage facilities, but some radioactive materials were dumped into the Barents Sea, the Baltic Sea, and the Bering Sea.

Global Warming

Many of the world's scientists think that Earth's climate is getting warmer. Average temperatures have been rising for decades. Measurements and photos show that glaciers are gradually melting. In 2003 Western Europe suffered its worst heat wave since the Middle Ages.

EVENT

On April 26, 1986, the world's worst nuclear disaster occurred at the **Chernobyl** nuclear power plant in Ukraine. A reactor at the plant exploded and sent dangerous radioactive material into the sky. Ukraine, Belarus, and other parts of Europe still feel the effects today.

Chernobyl

There is a debate about whether this global warming is part of nature's cycle or is related to human activities instead. Most scientists believe that burning coal and oil contributes to the **greenhouse effect**, or gas buildup in the atmosphere that traps large amounts of warm air near Earth's surface.

Many European leaders are worried about global warming. They fear the melting glaciers will create higher ocean levels which will flood low-lying areas such as the Netherlands. Most European governments have signed the Kyoto Protocol, an international treaty, or agreement, to limit the output of greenhouse gases.

Quick Check

Make Judgments **How has pollution impacted the environment in Europe?**

C THE FUTURE

Few areas in Europe remain unchanged by human impact. Today, European countries are uniting to develop ways of protecting and restoring the region's environment.

Solutions

Europeans want to preserve what little wilderness areas are left. One of the largest still in its natural state is the Bialowieza Forest in Belarus and Poland. This forest was put on the World Heritage List in 1992 and became internationally known as a Biosphere Reserve in 1993. It is home to animals such as the wolf, lynx, wild boar, elk, and European bison, all of which are rare in other parts of Europe.

Norway and Sweden are adding lime to their lakes. This stops the damage caused by acid rain and allows fish to multiply again. Europeans are also making their rivers and lakes cleaner by treating waste and sewage. In addition some countries encourage farmers to use less fertilizer to reduce runoff. Farmers are trying to find natural ways to care for their crops. Cities in Western Europe now protect buildings and statues with acid-resistant coatings.

The Bialowieza Forest is one of the few places where European bison roam free (inset).

Recycling

Recycling is another way Europeans help protect the environment. Europe now recycles more paper, plastics, and glass than ever before. This saves energy that would otherwise be needed to produce these goods and cuts down on waste. Recycling paper also helps to stop trees from being cut down and helps to preserve Europe's forests.

Recycling is popular in Europe.

European Union Protection

The first European Union environmental policy was started in 1972. Since then the European Union has continued to develop ways to protect the environment. For instance, EU member countries face legal action if they do not respect environmental protection laws. To be admitted into the EU, countries are expected to meet all EU environmental standards.

By 2010 all EU members must lower their emissions to 15 percent below their 1990 levels in order to reduce greenhouse gases. More cars and trucks in member countries will be required to run on cleaner fuels. Sweden, for example, introduced the first biogas-powered passenger train in 2005. Biogas is made from decomposing organic material and is much less damaging to the atmosphere than fossil fuels that are currently used.

Quick Check

Make Judgments What more do you think the EU can do to protect the environment in Europe?

Check Understanding

1. **VOCABULARY** Use these vocabulary words in a paragraph about Europe's environment.

   erosion **reforestation**
   runoff **greenhouse effect**

2. **READING SKILL**
   Make Judgments Use your chart from page 256 to write about the effects of pollution in Europe today.

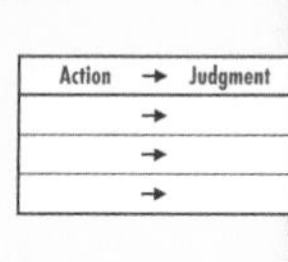

3. **Write About It** How do humans impact the environment in Europe?

Unit 6 Review and Assess

Vocabulary

Write the word from the list that matches the definition.

impressionism **organic**
neutrality **reforestation**

1. no chemicals were used
2. the replanting of trees
3. a painting style that uses bold colors and brushstrokes
4. not supporting any side during a conflict

Comprehension and Critical Thinking

5. Why is Europe's population still changing?
6. What are the benefits of being a member of the European Union?
7. Reading Skill Why did ethnic groups in Yugoslavia seek independence?
8. Critical Thinking If you were in a debate about global warming, what would your argument be? Why?

Skill

Use a Double Bar Graph

Write a complete sentence to answer each question.

9. What countries had an increase in carbon dioxide emissions from 1990 to 2003?
10. Why do you think Russia has seen a drop in carbon dioxide emissions?

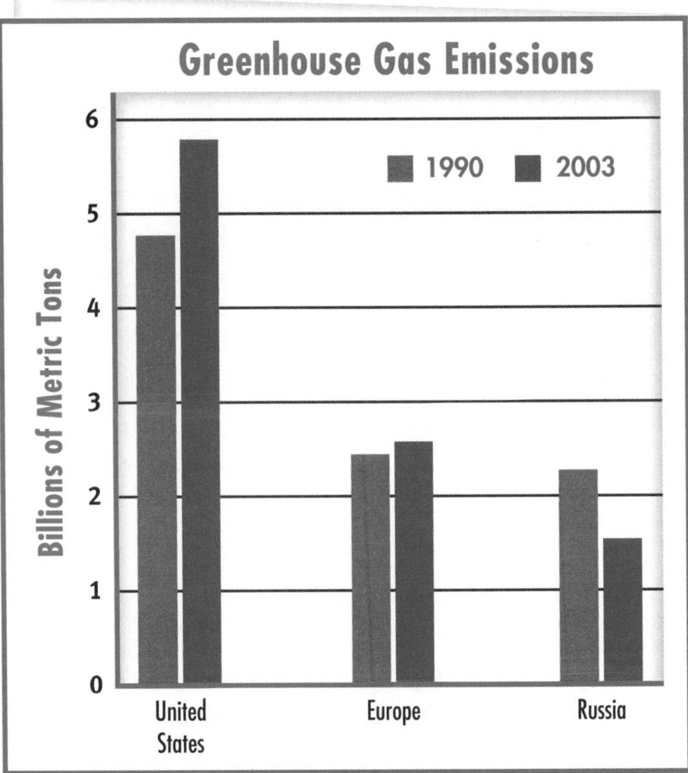

Test Preparation

Read the passage. Then answer the questions.

> "Under the Kyoto Protocol, industrialized countries are to reduce their combined emissions of six major greenhouse gases during the five-year period 2008–2012 to below 1990 levels. The European Union, for example, is to cut its combined emissions by eight percent, while Japan should reduce emissions by six percent. For many countries, achieving the Kyoto targets will be a major challenge that will require new policies and new approaches. . . .
>
> Developing countries, including Brazil, China, India and Indonesia, are also Parties to the Protocol but do not have emission reduction targets. Many developing countries have already demonstrated success in addressing climate change."
>
> —UNEP, "Kyoto Protocol to Enter into Force 16 February 2005"

1. What countries have targets set by the Kyoto Protocol?

A. developing nations
B. northern nations
C. industrialized nations
D. immigration nations

2. By what percent does the European Union have to cut its emissions?

A. 2 percent
B. 4 percent
C. 6 percent
D. 8 percent

3. How many years do the industrialized nations have to reach their targets?

A. 8 years
B. 5 years
C. 6 years
D. 10 years

4. According to this press release, what is the purpose of the Kyoto Protocol?

5. Why will it be a challenge for countries to achieve the Kyoto targets?

The Big Idea Activities

Write About the Big Idea

Narrative Essay
Use the Unit 6 foldable to help you write an essay about the Big Idea question, *How do cultures influence each other?* Begin with an introduction in which you clearly explain why you think cultures influence each other. In the body of the essay, be sure to summarize how the cultures of Europe influence each other. Write one paragraph for each set of notes under a tab on your foldable. End with a concluding paragraph.

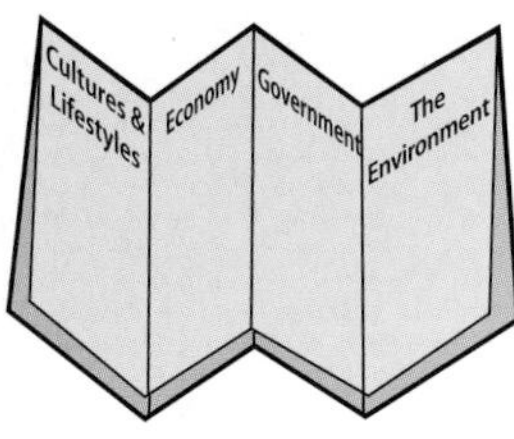

Create a Web

Work with a partner to prepare a web on poster paper.

1. Choose a European country and write its name in the center of your web.
2. Write the title of your web—"How Cultures Influence Each Other" at the top of your poster paper.
3. Draw four spokes extending from the center and label them with these categories: Culture and Lifestyle, Economy, Government, and The Environment.
4. Research on the Internet or in books to find examples of how the country you chose has influenced other countries. Write or draw one or two examples for each category.
5. Share your findings with your class.

Reference Section

The Reference Section is a collection of tools that can be used to help you understand the information you read in this textbook.

Unit 1 • Reading Skills

Cause and Effect

A cause is a person or event that makes something else happen. An effect is the result of the cause. When one event causes another event to happen, the two events have a cause-and-effect relationship. Connecting causes with effects will help you understand more about reading social studies.

Learn It

- After you finish reading a section, ask yourself, "What happened?" The answer to that question will help you identify an effect.
- Then ask yourself "Why did that happen?" The answer to this question helps you identify a cause.
- Look for the clue words *because, so,* and *as a result*. These words point to cause-and-effect relationships.
- Now read the passage below. Use the steps above to pick out cause-and-effect relationships.

Cause
This is a cause. It tells why.

Effect
This is an effect. It tells what happened.

Cause and Effect
This has a cause and an effect.

The American Revolution

The people in Great Britain's 13 colonies soon grew angry over British taxes and trade policies. In 1776 the colonists declared their independence from Great Britain. However, Great Britain would not give up its colonies without a fight.

The Americans fought back and won several battles. The Revolutionary War lasted eight long years. Finally, in 1783 the United States won the war, and Britain recognized American independence. A new nation called the United States was born.

Try It

Copy and complete the cause-and-effect chart below. Then fill in the chart with another cause and effect from the paragraph.

Cause	→	Effect
	→	
	→	
	→	

How did you figure out the causes and effects?

Apply It

- Review the steps for understanding cause and effect in Learn It.
- Read the passage below. Then use a chart to list the causes and effects from the passage.

After the American Revolution, the British population increased in Canada. About 50,000 Loyalists, American colonists who had remained loyal to Britain, fled to Canada. They set up farms along the Atlantic coast and in what is now Ontario. French-speaking Canadians lived mostly in present-day Quebec. The Loyalists wanted their own government, so in 1791 the British divided Quebec into two colonies, Lower Canada and Upper Canada. Each had its own elected assembly, or group of people who make laws.

Unit 2 • Reading Skills

Fact and Opinion

When people write about events, they often include both facts and opinions. Facts are statements that can be proven true. Opinions state feelings and beliefs. Opinions cannot be proven true or false. Being able to distinguish facts from opinions will help you understand what you read in social studies.

Learn It

- Facts can be checked and proven true.
- Opinions are personal views. They cannot be proven true or false.
- Clue words such as *think, felt, believe,* and *it seems* often state opinions.
- Now read the passage below. Look for facts and opinions.

The Constitutional Convention

Fact
On Many 25, 1787, a total of 55 delegates were sent to a convention in Philadelphia.

Opinion
Many delegates felt that the Articles of Confederation did not meet the needs of the nation.

On May 25, 1787, a total of 55 delegates, or representatives from each state, were sent to a convention in Philadelphia. The purpose of this convention was to fix the problems of the government. Many delegates felt that the Articles of Confederation did not meet the needs of the nation. Creating this new plan of government was not easy.

Try It

Copy and complete the chart below. Fill in the chart with two facts and two opinions from the paragraph about the Constitutional Convention on page R4.

Fact	Opinion

How did you figure out which phrases were facts and which were opinions?

Apply It

- Review the steps for understanding fact and opinion from Learn It.
- Read the paragraph below. Then make a chart that lists two facts and opinions from the paragraph.

Canada has welcomed many immigrant families to its shores over the years. These families believed that it was important to keep many of the customs of their homelands. These customs appear in the form of some of the best foods from around the world found in different parts of Canada. You may find Italian and Eastern European food in Toronto and French cuisine in Quebec.

Canadians are also big sports fans. Hockey is the national sport in Canada. Lacrosse is another popular sport that is fun to play. Many Canadians enjoy outdoor activities, such as skiing, boating, hunting, and fishing.

Unit 3 • Reading Skills

Draw Conclusions

Reading for understanding is more than noticing the details in a passage. Readers need to think about what the details tell them. Often the details in a passage will help you draw a conclusion. Drawing a conclusion is reaching an opinion based on the details you read.

Learn It

- Identify the subject of the passage.
- Gather details and other evidence in a reading passage.
- Look for connections between the pieces of information. Ask yourself what the evidence says about the subject.
- Draw a conclusion based on what you have read.
- Now read this passage and think about what conclusions you can draw from it.

Text clue
600 Spanish soldiers marched to the city.

Text clue
The city might have gold.

Text clue
The Spanish kidnapped Moctezuma.

Text clue
Native Americans joined the Spanish to defeat the Aztec.

Cortés and the Aztec

In 1519 a Spanish army led by Hernán Cortés landed on Mexico's Gulf Coast. He and about 600 soldiers marched to Tenochtitlán. They heard Tenochtitlán was filled with gold.

Scouts of the Aztec emperor, Moctezuma, reported Cortés's movements. Moctezuma was dazzled by the Spanish, with their horses and guns, which he had never seen before. He welcomed them into the city.

His welcome became the beginning of the downfall of his empire. The Spanish kidnapped Moctezuma. He was later killed in a riot. Native Americans who opposed the harsh rule of the Aztec signed treaties with the Spanish and joined them. The Aztec's simple weapons were no match for the guns, cannons, and horses of the Spanish. Cortés defeated the Aztec within two years.

Try It

Copy and complete the conclusions chart below. Fill in lines on the left with the text clues. Fill in the box on the right with a conclusion based on the evidence you gathered.

Text Clues	Conclusion

What conclusion did you draw about Cortés and the Aztec?

Apply It

- Review the steps for drawing a conclusion in Learn It.
- Read the passage below. Then use the chart to draw a conclusion about the fall of the Inca empire.

A Spanish explorer named Francisco Pizarro wanted the gold and silver of the Inca. In 1532 Pizarro took a small group of Spanish soldiers to South America. The Inca emperor, Atahualpa, had heard about the arrival of Pizarro and had planned on meeting him. Instead, the Spanish attacked the Inca, killing mainly government officials.

Pizarro captured Atahualpa and held him prisoner for months. While Pizarro was waiting for more soldiers from Spain, Atahualpa offered to fill his room with gold in exchange for his freedom. On the same day Atahualpa finished filling the room with gold, Pizarro ordered him killed.

The death of their leaders and European diseases weakened the Inca. Pizarro then quickly conquered the empire.

Unit 4 • Reading Skills

Make Generalizations

When you read, sometimes it helps to make a generalization. A generalization is a broad statement that shows how different facts, people, or events have something in common. Being able to make generalizations will help you uncover similarities that you might otherwise not notice. Generalizations can also help you make sense of new information you will learn later.

Learn It

- Identify text clues with similarities or relationships.
- Apply what you already know about the topic.
- Make a generalization that is true about all of your text clues and what you know.
- Read the passage below. Think about a generalization you could make.

Text Clue
These activities involve clearing trees.

Text Clue
Rain forest soil is easily damaged.

Text Clue
Once the land is worked, it is ruined.

Deforestation

In the 1980s Brazil's government encouraged mining, logging, farming, and cattle ranching in the rain forest. Unfortunately, the soil in the rain forest is very fragile. Once the land has been cleared, it becomes almost useless. Farmers must move on, hoping to find better soil elsewhere. These activities lead to soil erosion.

Try It

Copy and complete the generalization chart below. Then make a generalization about the rain forest.

Text Clues	What You Know	Generalization

How did you figure out how to make a generalization?

Apply It

- Review the steps to make generalizations in Learn It.
- Read the next paragraph. Then make a generalization about the rain forest using a generalizations chart.

Rain forests are home to a huge variety of plants and animals. Three-quarters of Earth's living things are found in rain forests. In addition, tropical forests give off huge amounts of oxygen and play a role in maintaining Earth's climate patterns. Most of the Amazon rain forest belongs to the country of Brazil. However, the destruction of the rain forest is an issue that concerns many people across the globe.

Unit 5 • Reading Skills

Make Inferences

Writers want their readers to think about what they have read and to make inferences, or guesses, about what happened. To do this, you think about what you know from other reading or from your own experience. You use both kinds of information to make an inference about something.

Learn It

As you read, identify the details and clues in the text.

- Combine the clues and details with what you already know.
- Make an inference by "reading between the lines."
- Read the passage below. Think about an inference you could make.

Clue
Leonardo was left by his mother at a young age.

Detail
Leonardo became a very good painter.

Leonardo da Vinci was born in Vinci, Italy, to a peasant woman named Caterina. Shortly after Leonardo's birth, she left him in the care of his father. By the time Leonardo was 15 years old, his father knew his had artistic talent. He arranged for Leonardo to become an apprentice to the famous painter Andrea del Verrocchio.

By 1472 Leonardo had become a master in the painters' guild of Florence. In 1481 Leonardo moved to the city of Milan. There he had a large workshop with many apprentices. During this time, Leonardo began keeping a sketch pad tucked in his belt at all times. Later he organized the drawings by theme and assembled the pages into notebooks.

Try It

Copy the chart below. Then fill in the chart in order to make inferences about Leonardo da Vinci.

Text Clues	What You Know	Inference

What inferences can you make about Leonardo da Vinci when he moved to Milan?

Apply It

Read the paragraphs below. Then use the information to make a new inference chart like the one above.

In 1498 Leonardo returned to Florence, where he was welcomed with great honor. During this time, Leonardo painted some of his masterpieces, such as the *Mona Lisa*. He also made scientific studies, including dissections, observations of the flight of birds, and research on the movements of water currents.

In 1516 Leonardo accepted an invitation to live in France. The French king admired Leonardo and gave him freedom to pursue his interests. During the last three years of his life, Leonardo lived in a small house near the king's summer palace. He spent most of his time sketching and working on scientific studies.

Unit 6 • Reading Skills

Make Judgments

People make judgments as they read. Making a judgment means forming an opinion about an event, issue, or the actions of a person. As you read, look for clues that either support or change your judgment.

Learn It

- Think about an issue you are studying. What choices are involved in it?
- Make a judgment. Do you think the choices are good ones? Would you have made the same choices?
- Read the passage below. Make a judgment about actions taken by many Germans as described in the passage.

Action
Germans recycle their trash with a complicated process.

Germans like to think of themselves as the world champions of the environment. When it comes to separating their household trash, the process can get very complicated. According to surveys, about 90 percent of Germans sort their trash.

Germans have at least five types of trash bins. The bins are color-coded, to avoid any confusion. Yellow bins are for packaging. Blue bins are for paper. There are specially designed bins for glass that are separated into clear, green, and brown. "Bio" bins are designed to hold left-over food and plant waste. Finally, there is a black bin for the rest of the trash.

Judgment
What do you think about many Germans' decision to separate and recycle their trash?

Try It

Copy the chart below. Complete it with actions and your judgments about the paragraph on the previous page.

Action	→	Judgment
	→	
	→	
	→	

What judgment would you make about recycling in Germany?

Apply It

Review the steps for making judgments. Complete a new chart for the paragraph below. Make a judgment about Switzerland's recycling efforts.

Switzerland is very proud of its recycling efforts. There are not many things the Swiss simply just throw away. Glass-bottle banks are located at every supermarket. Every town has a free paper collection once a month. Most people recycle everything made of cardboard or paper. Garden trimmings are put out on the street for free pick up every two weeks. Aluminum and tin are taken to local depots and batteries are handed over at the supermarket. Almost 80 percent of all plastic bottles are recycled in Switzerland, a far higher percentage than any other European country.

Geography Handbook

Geography and You

Many people think geography means learning about the location of cities, states, and countries, but geography is much more than that. Geography is the study of our Earth and all its people. Geography includes learning about bodies of water such as oceans, lakes, and rivers. Geography helps us learn about landforms such as plains and mountains. Geography also helps us learn about using land and water wisely.

People are an important part of the study of geography. Geography includes the study of how people adapt to live in new places. How people move, how they transport goods, and how ideas travel from place to place are also parts of geography.

In fact, geography has so many parts that geographers have divided the information into smaller groups to help people understand its ideas. These groups are called the six elements of geography.

Six Elements of Geography

The World in Spatial Terms: Where is a place located, and what land or water features does that place have?

Places and Regions: What is special about a place, and what makes it different from other places?

Physical Systems: What has shaped the land and climate of a place, and how does this affect the plants, animals, and people there?

Human Systems: How do people, ideas, and goods move from place to place?

Environment and Society: How have people changed the land and water of a place, and how have land and water affected the people who live in a place?

Uses of Geography: How has geography influenced events in the past, and how will it influence events now and in the future?

Five Themes of Geography

You have read about the six elements of geography. The five themes of geography are another way of dividing the ideas of geography. The themes, or topics, are **location, place, region, movement**, and **human interaction**. Using these five themes is another way to understand events you read about in this book.

1. Location

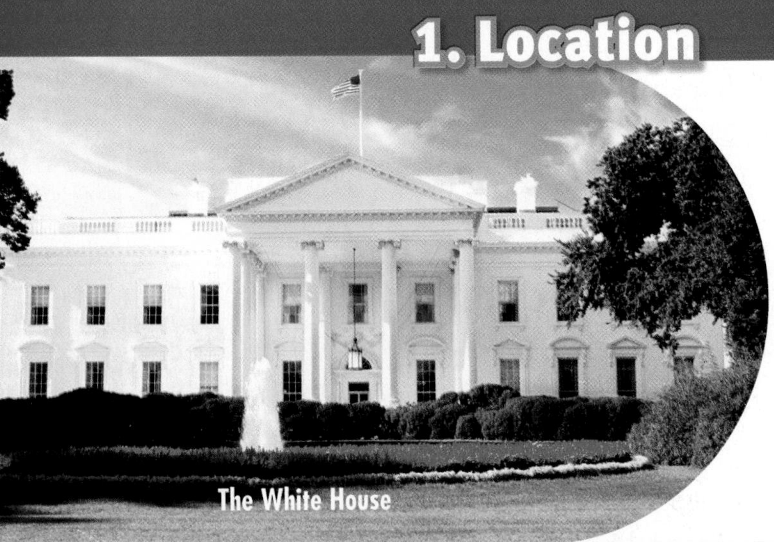
The White House

In geography *location* means an exact spot on the planet. A location is usually a street name and number. You write a location when you address a letter.

2. Place

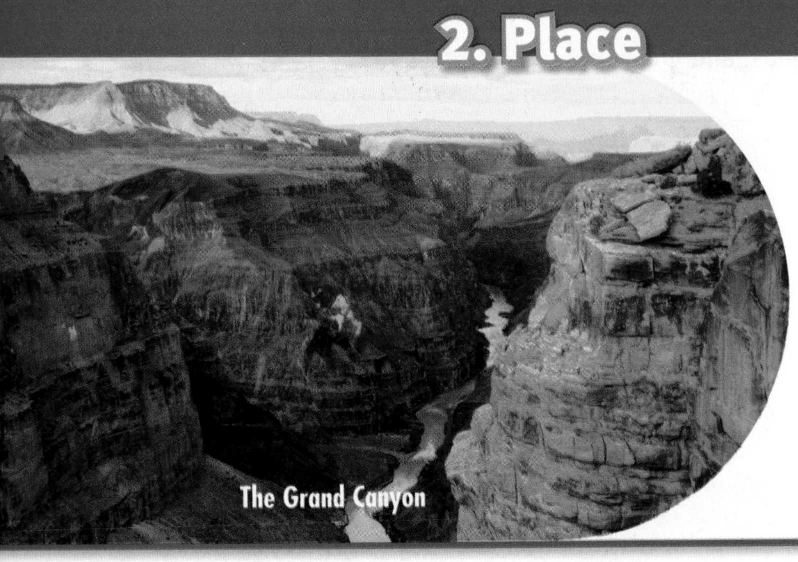
The Grand Canyon

A *place* is described by its physical features, such as rivers, mountains, or valleys. Human features, such as cities, language, and traditions can also describe a place.

3. Region

Wheat field in the Midwest

A *region* is larger than a place or location. The people in a region are affected by landforms. Their region has typical jobs and customs. For example, the fertile soil of the Mississippi lowlands helps farmers in the region grow crops.

4. Movement

Passenger train

Throughout history, people have moved to find better land or a better life. Geographers study why these *movements* occurred. They also study how people's movements have changed a region.

5. Human Interaction

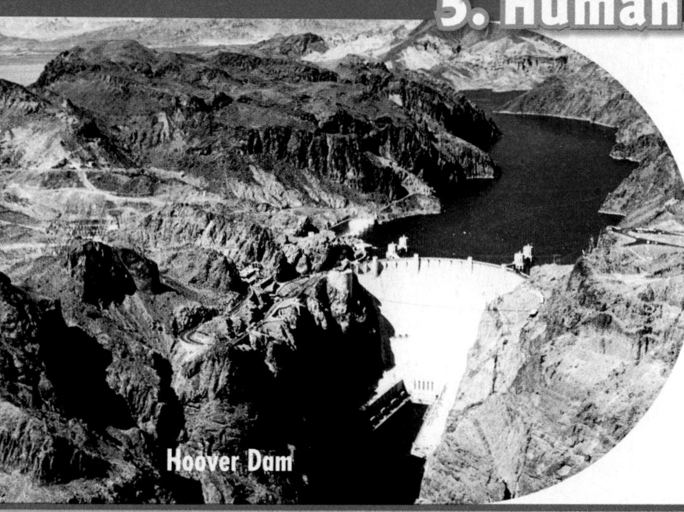
Hoover Dam

Geographers study the ways that people adapt to their environment. Geographers also study how people change their environment. The *interaction* between people and their environment explains how land is used.

Dictionary of Geographic Terms

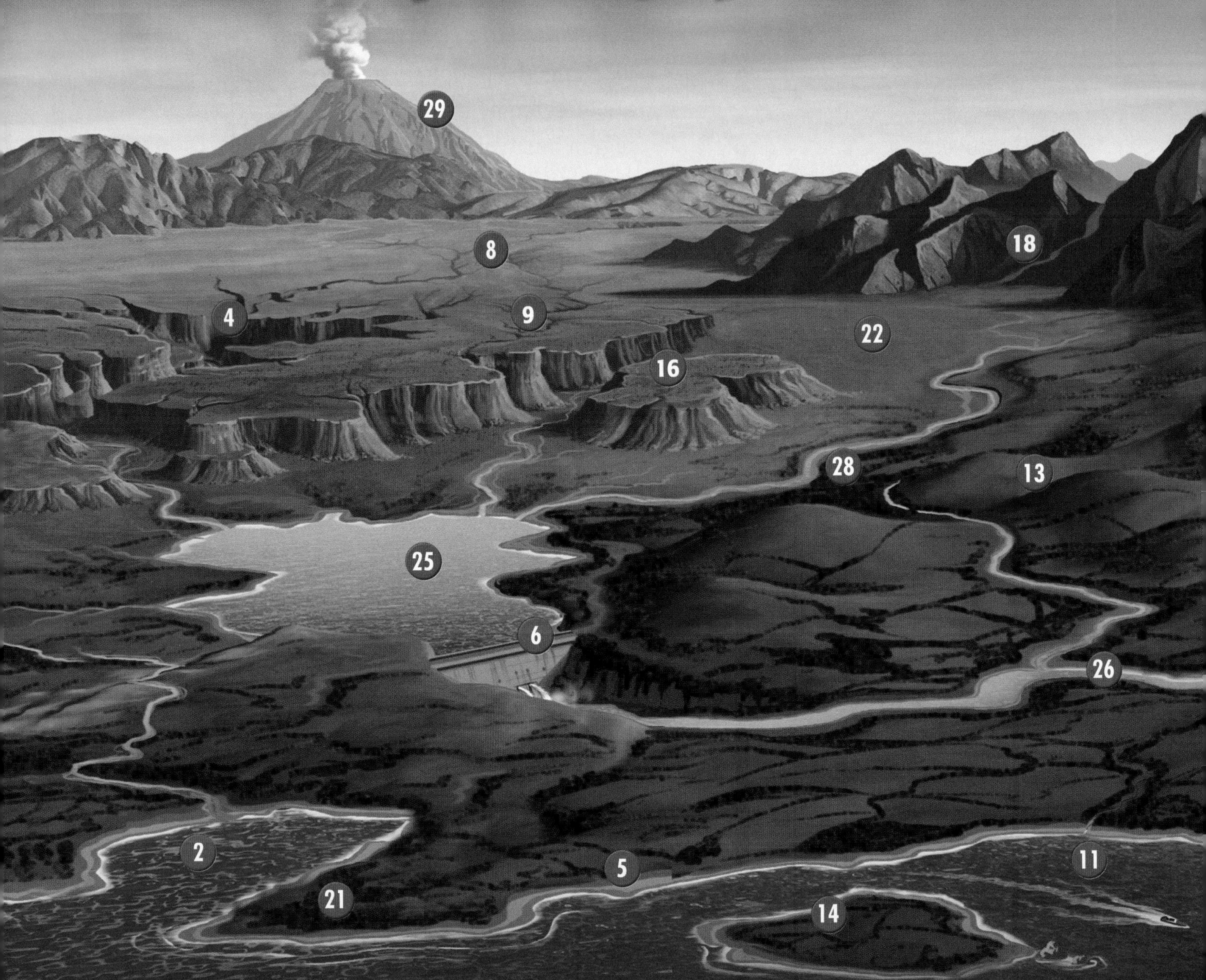

29
8
18
4
9
22
16
28
13
25
6
26
2
5
11
21
14

1 **BASIN** A bowl-shaped landform surrounded by higher land

2 **BAY** Part of an ocean or lake that extends deeply into the land

3 **CANAL** A channel built to carry water for irrigation or transportation

4 **CANYON** A deep, narrow valley with steep sides

5 **COAST** The land along an ocean

6 **DAM** A wall built across a river, creating a lake that stores water

7 **DELTA** Land made of soil left behind as a river drains into a larger body of water

8 **DESERT** A dry environment with few plants and animals

9 **FAULT** The border between two of the plates that make up Earth's crust

10 **GLACIER** A huge sheet of ice that moves slowly across the land

11 **GULF** Part of an ocean that extends into the land; larger than a bay

12 **HARBOR** A sheltered place along a coast where boats dock safely

13 **HILL** A rounded, raised landform; not as high as a mountain

14 **ISLAND** A body of land completely surrounded by water

15 **LAKE** A body of water completely surrounded by land

16 **MESA** A hill with a flat top; smaller than a plateau

17 MOUNTAIN A high landform with steep sides; higher than a hill

18 MOUNTAIN PASS A narrow gap through a mountain range

19 MOUTH The place where a river empties into a larger body of water

20 OCEAN A large body of salt water; oceans cover much of Earth's surface

21 PENINSULA A body of land nearly surrounded by water

22 PLAIN A large area of nearly flat land

23 PLATEAU A high, flat area that rises steeply above the surrounding land

24 PORT A place where ships load and unload their goods

25 RESERVOIR A natural or artificial lake used to store water

26 RIVER A large stream of water that empties into another body of water

27 SOURCE The starting point of a river

28 VALLEY An area of low land between hills or mountains

29 VOLCANO An opening in Earth's surface through which hot rock and ash are forced out

30 WATERFALL A flow of water falling vertically

Reviewing Geography Skills

Read a Map

Maps are drawings of places on Earth. Most maps have standard features to help you read the map. They also use color and symbols to show information. Physical maps show and label landforms, such as mountains and deserts, and water features. Map makers use shading and color to show different physical features, such as blue to show water or dark shading to show mountains.

Map Title Maps in this book have titles. The map title names the area shown on the map. A map title can include additional identification, such as population, political boundaries, or a particular period in history.

Inset Map An inset map is a small map set onto a larger map. It may show an area that is too small or too far away to be included on the main map. The inset maps on this page include maps of Alaska and Hawaii.

Map Key The key or legend on a map helps you understand the colors or special symbols on a map.

Map Scale A map scale helps you to determine the relationship between real distances on Earth and the same distances represented on the map.

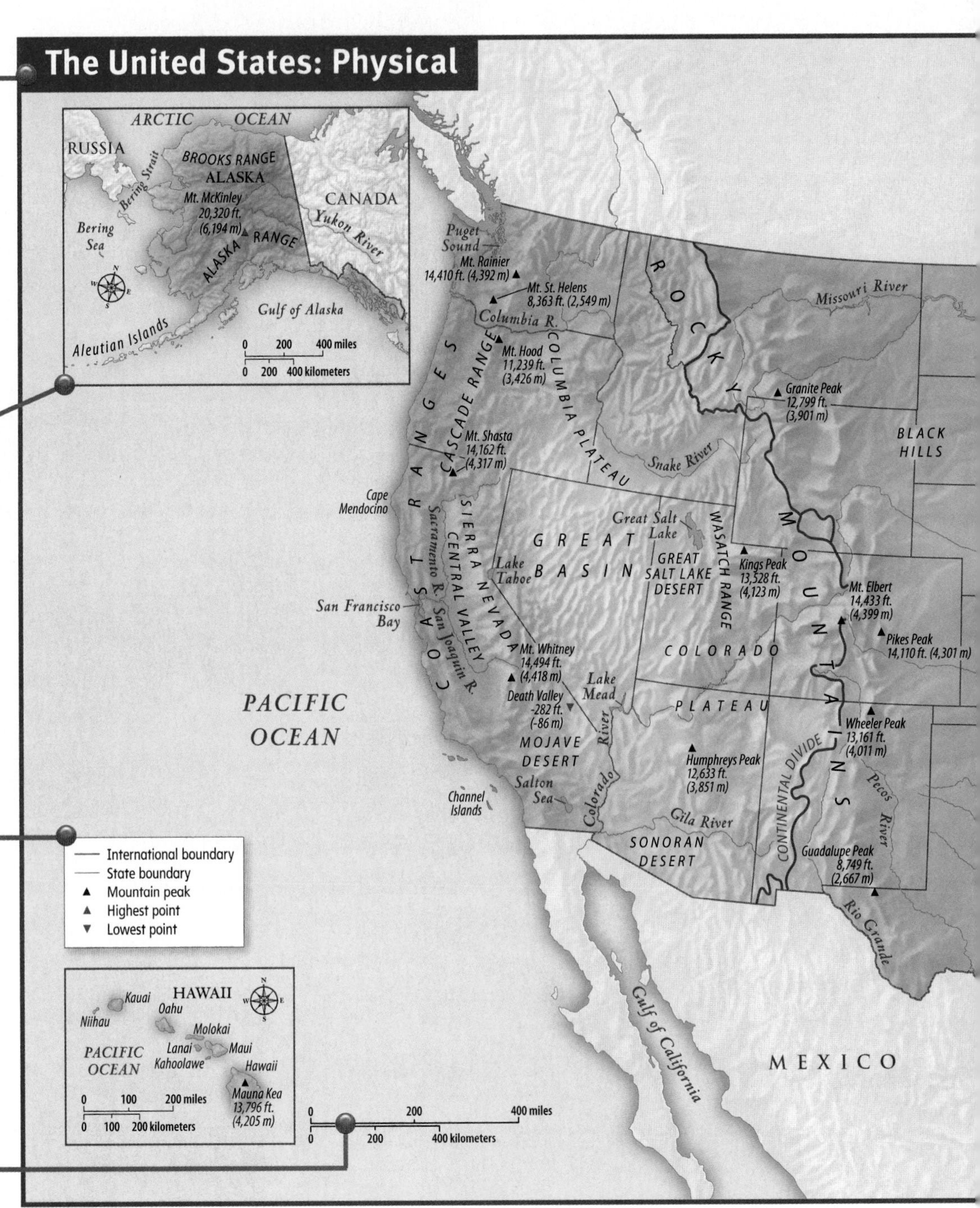

Some important information you get from a map is direction. The main directions are north, south, east, and west. These are called cardinal directions. Usually, these directions on a map are indicated by a compass rose. The areas between the cardinal directions are called intermediate directions. These are northeast, southeast, southwest, and northwest. You use these directions to describe one place in relation to another.

Think About It What mountain range is east of San Francisco Bay?

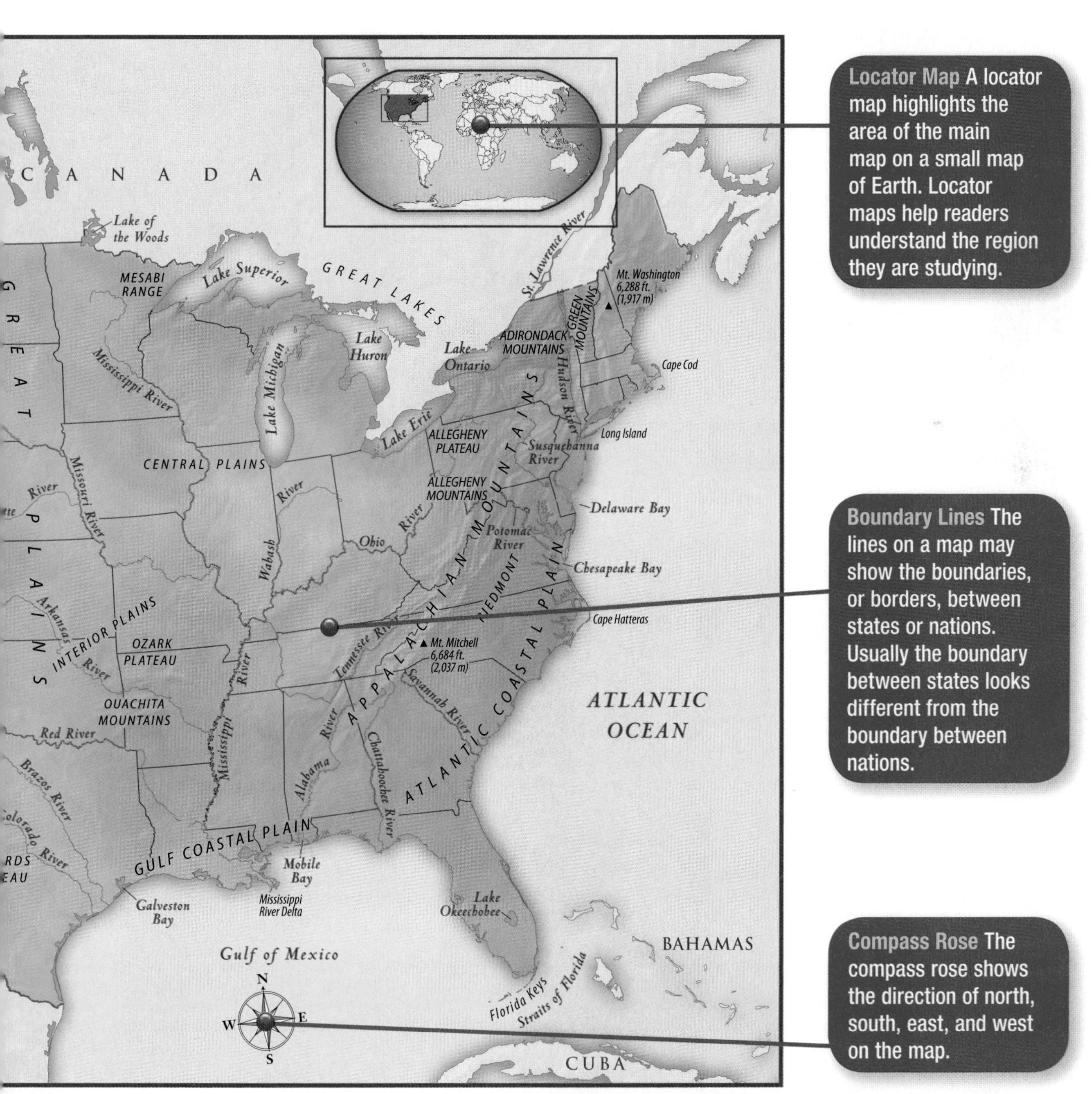

Special Purpose Maps

Some maps show specific information about a place or a period in history. These specific maps are called special purpose maps. One type of special purpose map may show how many people live in an area. Another may show the roads of a region. Still another might show the movement of an army during a historic battle.

Read Historical Maps

Some special purpose maps capture a period in time. These are called historical maps. They show information about past events and the places where they occurred. Read the title of the map on this page and study the key to understand its information. The map shows information about the routes of the First Crusade between the years 1095 to 1099. Pope Urban II called on the European Christians to march to Jerusalem to take the city. The Crusaders were victorious in capturing the city.

Think About It Why did the Crusaders travel through Christian lands to get to Jerusalem?

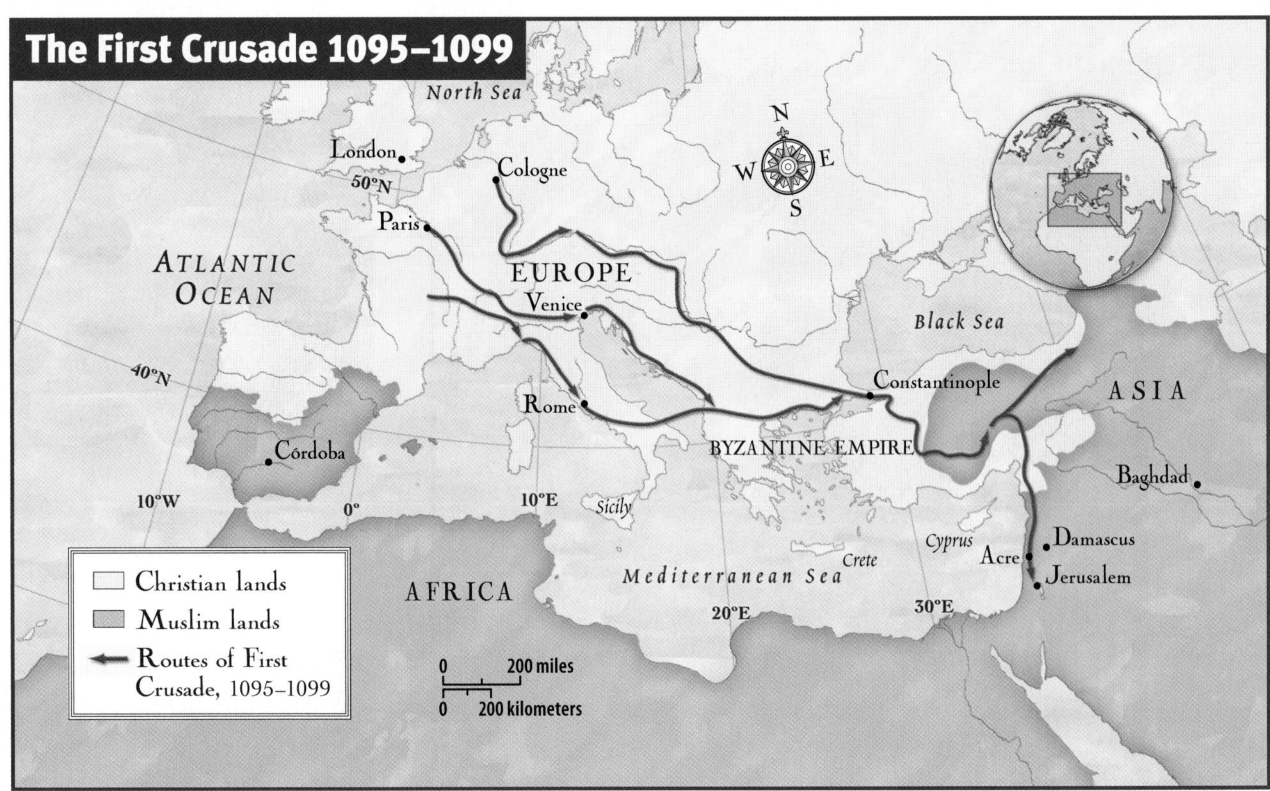

Use Elevation Maps

An elevation map is a physical map that uses colors to show the elevation, or height of land above or below sea level. The height is usually measured in feet or meters. Sea level is measured as 0 feet or meters around the world. Read the key to understand what each color means. The map on this page uses purple to show land below sea level.

Think About It Identify the area of your town or city on the map. How high above sea level is your area?

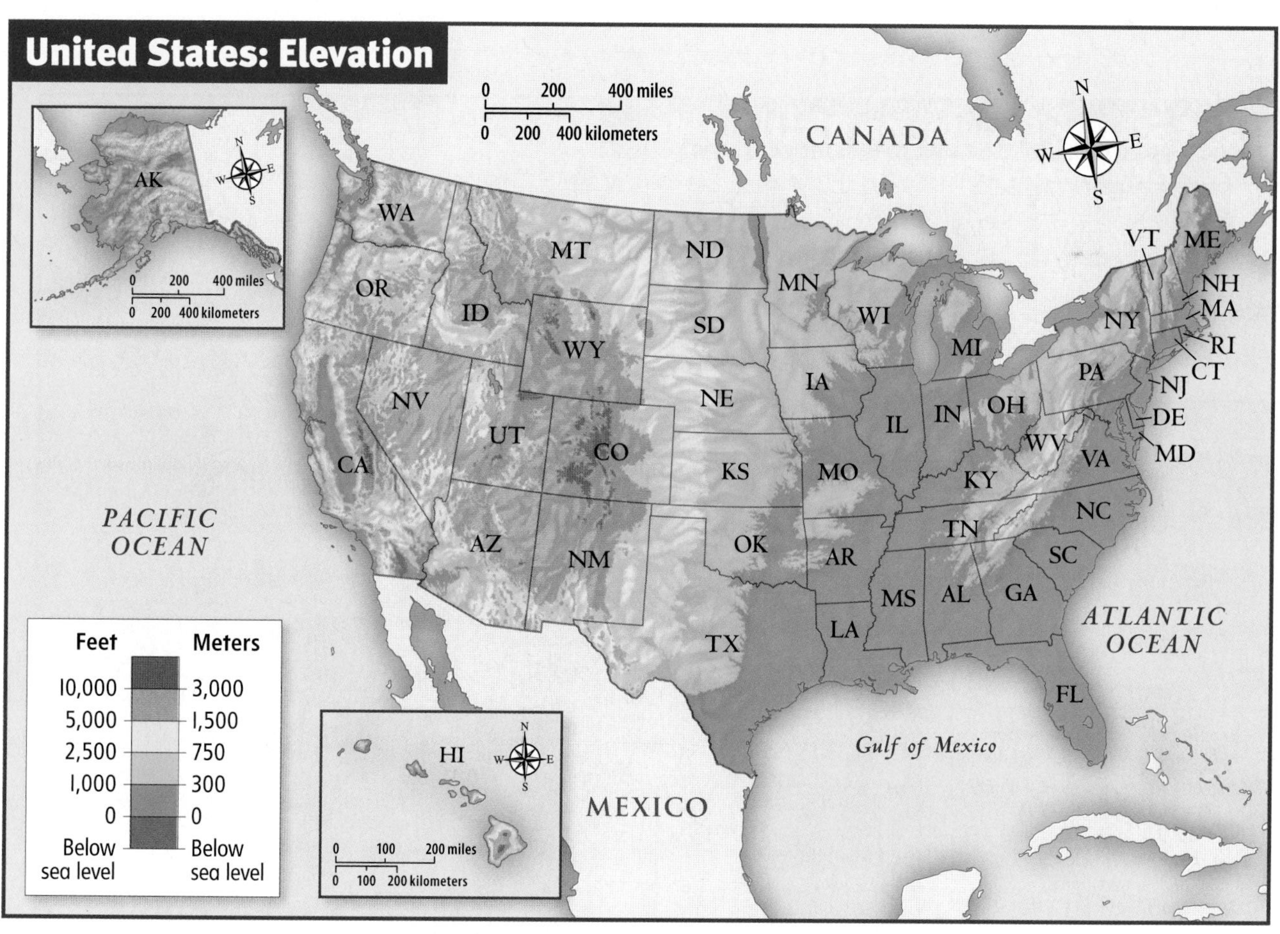

Use Population Maps

When you need to know the number of people who live in a place, or where people live, you can look at a population map. Most population maps show population density—how many people live in a certain area. Another kind of population map shows population distribution—where people live in an area.

Look at the population distribution map of the United States below. Population distribution maps often use different colors to stand for numbers of people per square mile or kilometer. The map key shows the number each color stands for. For example, between 5 and 24 people per square mile live in areas that are shaded yellow.

Think About It Which color is used to show the areas with the most people?

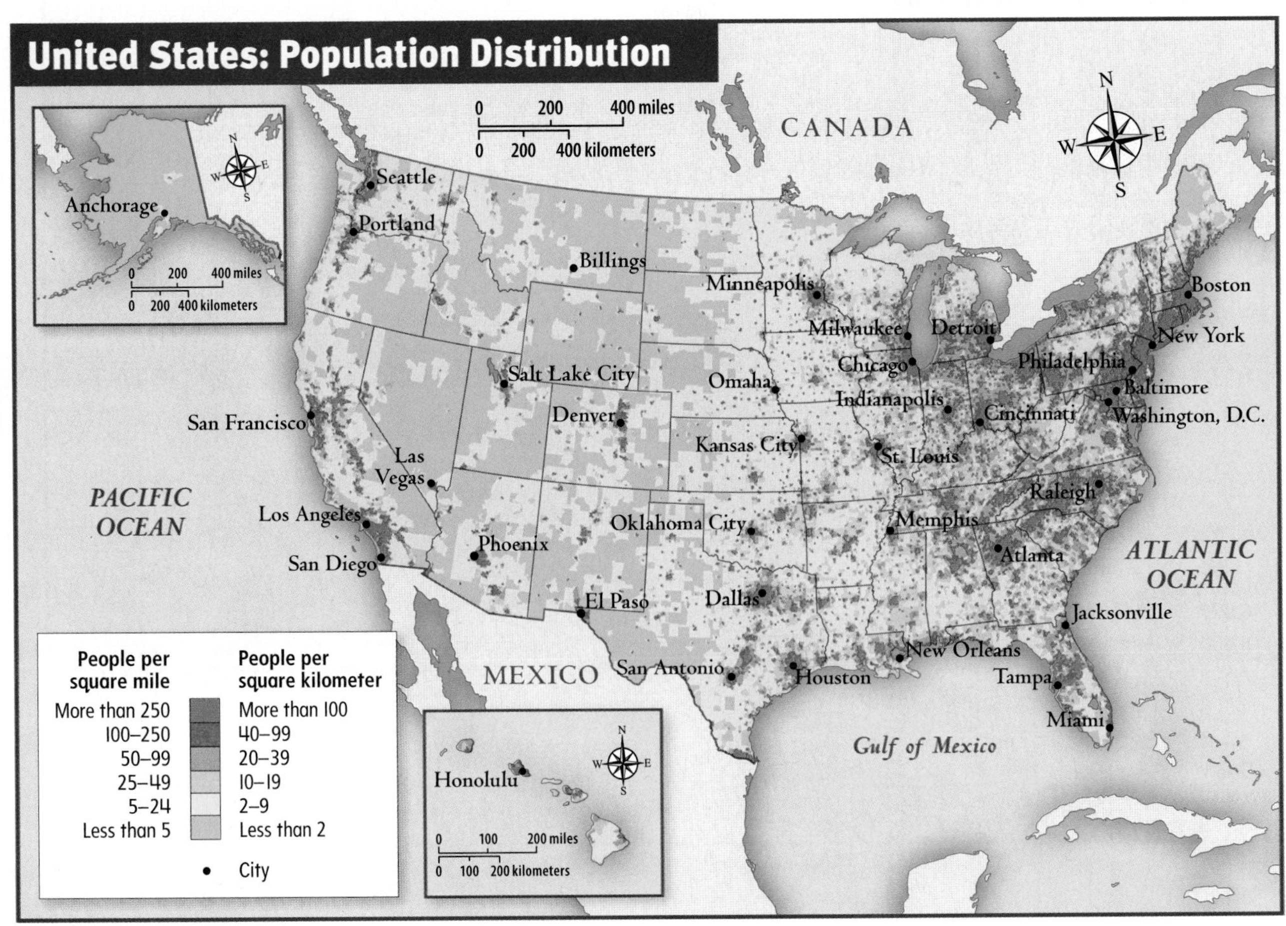

Use Road Maps

Suppose you want to go somewhere you have never been before. How do you know what road to take? You could use a road map. Road maps show where the roads in a certain area go. By reading a road map, you can figure out how to get from one place to another.

Look at the road map of Indiana. The map key tells you which kinds of roads are shown on the map. Interstate highways run through two or more states and have two or more lanes in each direction. U.S. highways are usually two-lane highways that also connect states. State highways stop at a state's borders. The name of each highway is a number. Notice the different symbols for each of the three kinds of highways.

Think About It Which roads would you use to get from South Bend to Terre Haute?

Use a Cartogram

A cartogram is a special kind of map that helps you to compare information about countries on the map. A cartogram does not show the physical sizes of countries. It compares information about countries, such as populations or economies. A country that is geographically quite large, such as Canada, may appear small on a cartogram comparing the size of the national economies of North America.

It is important to understand that a cartogram compares information among nations. You need to read the title of a cartogram to understand what is being compared. It may be population, or economies, or how much is spent on health and welfare by each nation in the cartogram.

You will also need to bring some of your own knowledge to read a cartogram. You have to know that Canada is one of the largest countries in the world to understand that its economy is not as large as its land size.

Think About It Why might the sizes of countries get larger or smaller on different cartograms?

Use a Time Zone Map

You may already know that people who live in different states set their clocks at different times. This happens because Earth spins. While the sun is shining in one area, it may be dark in another. If it were the same time all over Earth, the sun would be shining in the middle of the night at some point on our planet.

This is why Earth is divided into 24 time zones. Each time zone is set to a different hour of the day. To help you figure out what time it is someplace else in the world, you would use a time zone map. This kind of map shows the number of hours that any place is ahead or behind the time at the Prime Meridian.

For example, find North America on the map. How many different time zones do you see? As you travel west, you gain an hour. As you travel east, you lose an hour.

Think About It What is the time difference between the east coast of the United States and England?

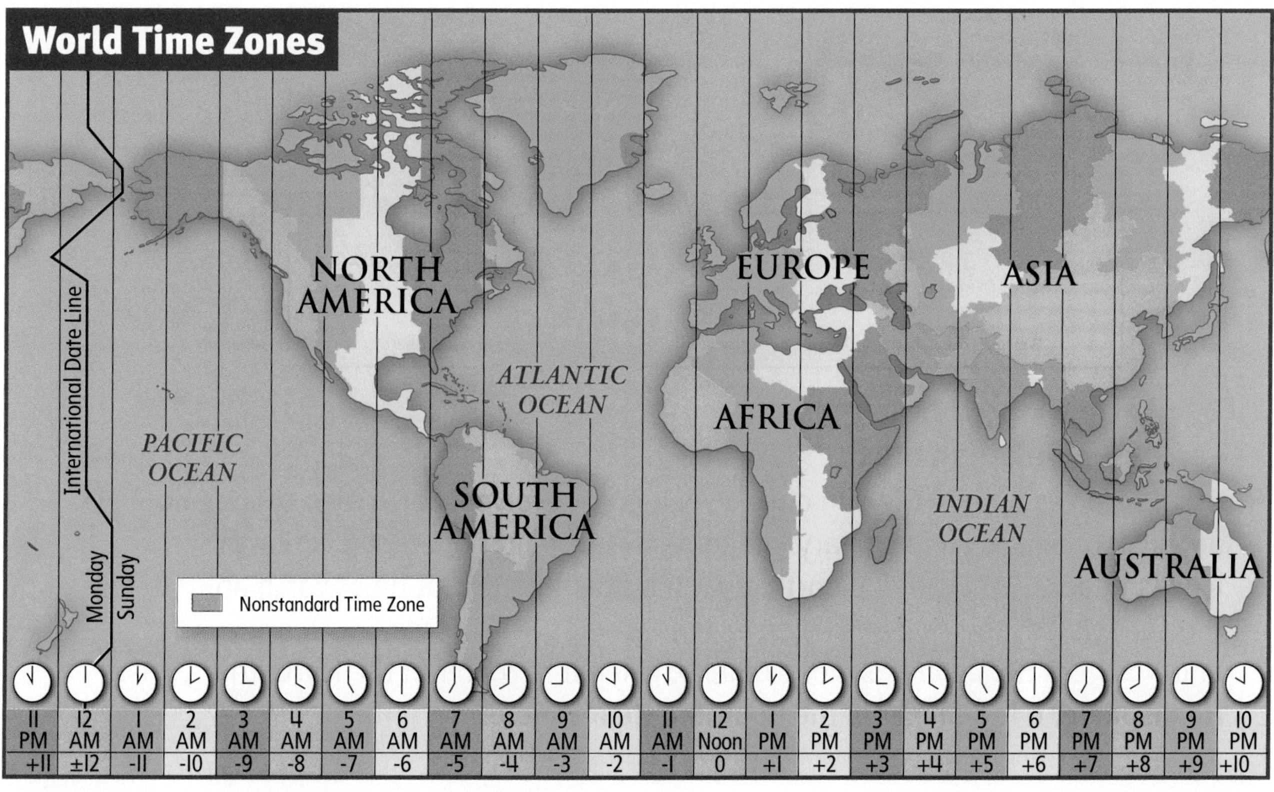

Understand Earth

Hemispheres

The equator is an imaginary line on Earth. It divides the sphere of Earth in half. A word for half a sphere is *hemisphere*. The prefix "hemi" means half. Geographers divide Earth into four hemispheres.

All land and ocean north of the equator are in the Northern Hemisphere. All the land and ocean south of the equator are in the Southern Hemisphere.

Another imaginary line on Earth runs from the North Pole to the South Pole. It is called the prime meridian. It divides Earth into the Eastern Hemisphere and the Western Hemisphere.

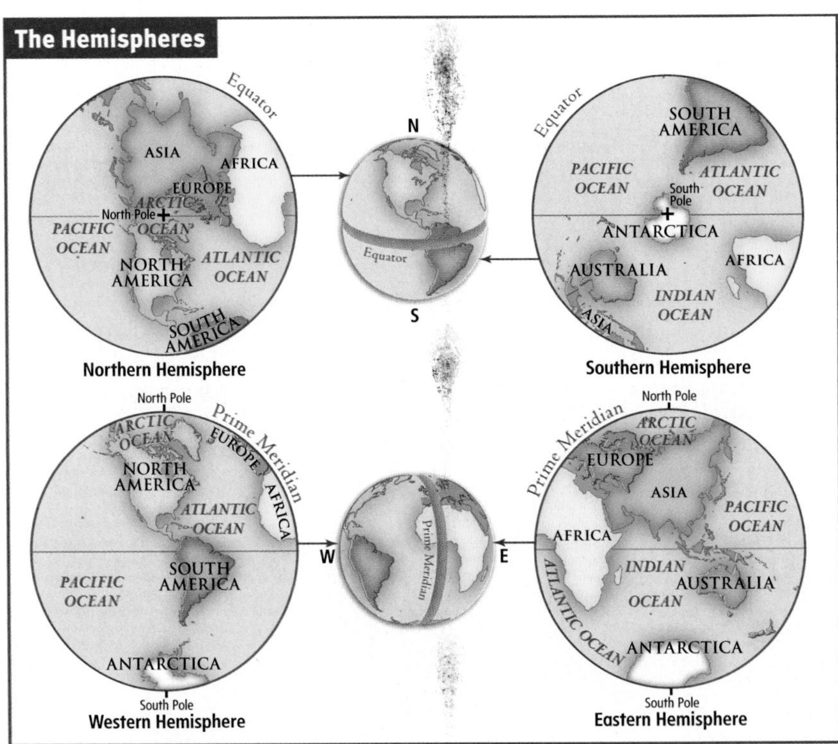

Earth-Sun Relationships

Earth revolves around the sun once a year. As it revolves, Earth also rotates on an axis. An axis is an imaginary line through the center of an object. Earth's axis is tilted 23.5° from due north. That tilt, plus the revolution of Earth around the sun, causes the seasons. The seasons are opposite in the Southern and Northern Hemispheres. For example, when it is winter in the Northern Hemisphere, it is summer in the Southern Hemisphere.

Latitude and Longitude

Geographers have created an imaginary system of lines on Earth. These lines form a grid to help locate places on any part of the globe. Lines of latitude go from east to west. Lines of longitude go from north to south.

The Prime Meridian runs north-south through Greenwich, England. Everything east of the Prime Meridian for 180 degrees is the Eastern Hemisphere. Everything west of the Prime Meridian for 180 degrees is the Western Hemisphere.

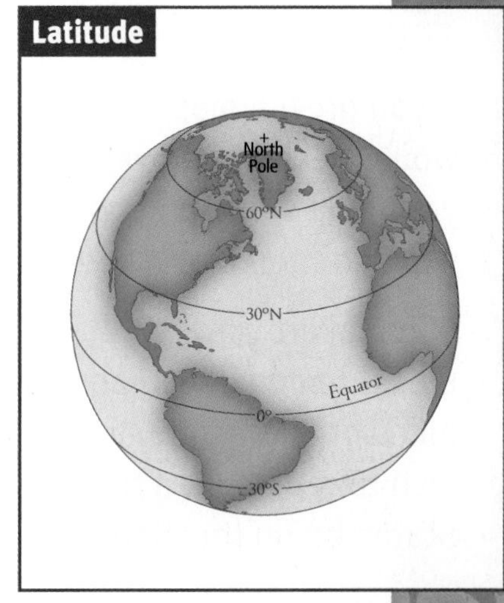

Latitude

Lines of latitude are called parallels because they are always at an equal distance from one another. Lines of latitude are numbered from 0 at the equator to 90 degrees north at the North Pole and 90 degrees south at the South Pole. Maps with latitude lines have N or S to indicate the Northern or Southern Hemisphere.

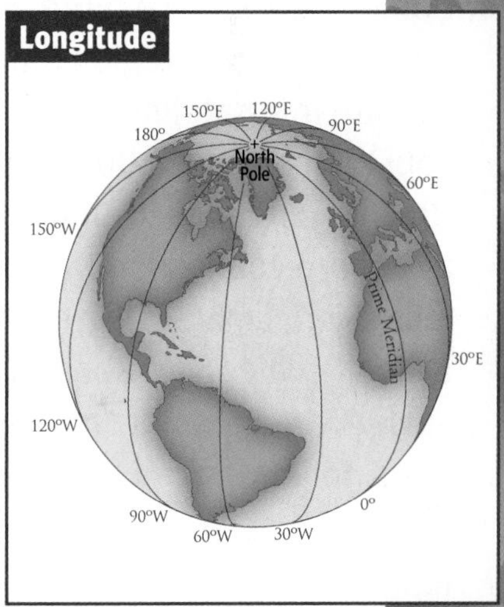

Longitude

Lines of longitude, or meridians, circle Earth from pole to pole. These lines measure the distance from the Prime Meridian, 0 degrees longitude. Lines of longitude are not parallel. They grow closer together near the North and South Poles. At the equator, they are far apart. Maps have an E or a W next to the number to indicate the Eastern or Western Hemisphere.

Absolute and Relative Location

You can locate any place on Earth using lines of latitude and longitude. Each line is identified by degrees (°). The spaces between the degree lines are measured in minutes ('). Each location has a unique number where one line of latitude intersects, or crosses, a line of longitude. This is absolute location. Each spot on Earth has an absolute location identified by a single set of degrees and minutes.

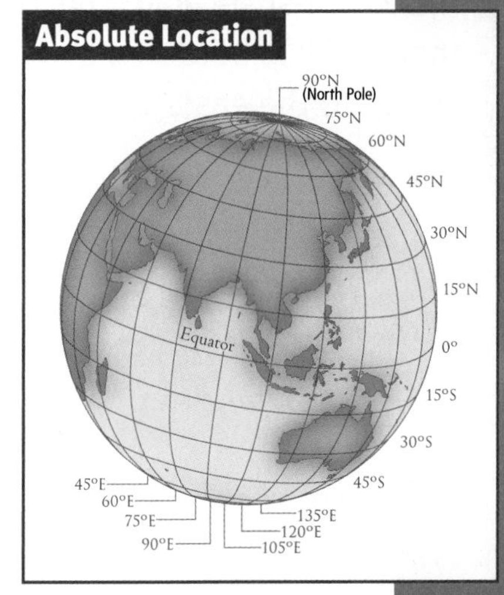

Relative location is the location of a place in relation to other landmarks. For example, St. Louis, Missouri, is located in eastern Missouri, along the Mississippi River.

Think About It What is your absolute location? Use the map of the United States on pages GH22–GH23 to find the lines of latitude and longitude that are closest to your home.

Maps at Different Scales

If you drew a map of the United States at its real size, your map would have to be over 3,000 miles wide. The Mississippi River on your map would be more than 2,000 miles long. A map this size would be too big to use!

Mapmakers draw maps to scale. A map scale uses some unit of measurement, such as an inch, to represent a certain number of miles or kilometers on Earth. If a map of the United States used one inch to represent a thousand miles—how wide would the United States be on the map?

Small-Scale Maps

Some maps show a large area, such as a continent, or a region. Imagine that you are in a satellite orbiting Earth. Your spaceship is 100 miles above Brazil. From this altitude you can see the entire country of Brazil. Everything looks very small—like the locations on a small-scale map. Because it covers such a large area, a small-scale map does not show many details.

From your satellite you might see the lights of Rio de Janeiro. You can also find the location of Rio de Janeiro on this small-scale map. This map shows that Brazil is bordered by the Atlantic Ocean to the east.

Large-Scale Maps

Now imagine that your satellite is flying only a few miles above Earth. You can see the city of Rio de Janeiro. You can see buildings, beaches, and landmarks. You can also see roads and highways. This is like looking at a large-scale map. The large-scale map shows a small area, but it has more detail than a small-scale map.

The large-scale map on this page shows the streets of the city of Rio de Janeiro in Brazil. If you wanted to find Copacabana, a famous beach in Rio de Janeiro, you would use the large-scale map that shows only the city and some of its landmarks.

Compare the scales on the two maps. What is the scale on page GH16? Is it larger or smaller than the scale on page GH17? Why do you think this is so? People choose the map that contains the information they need.

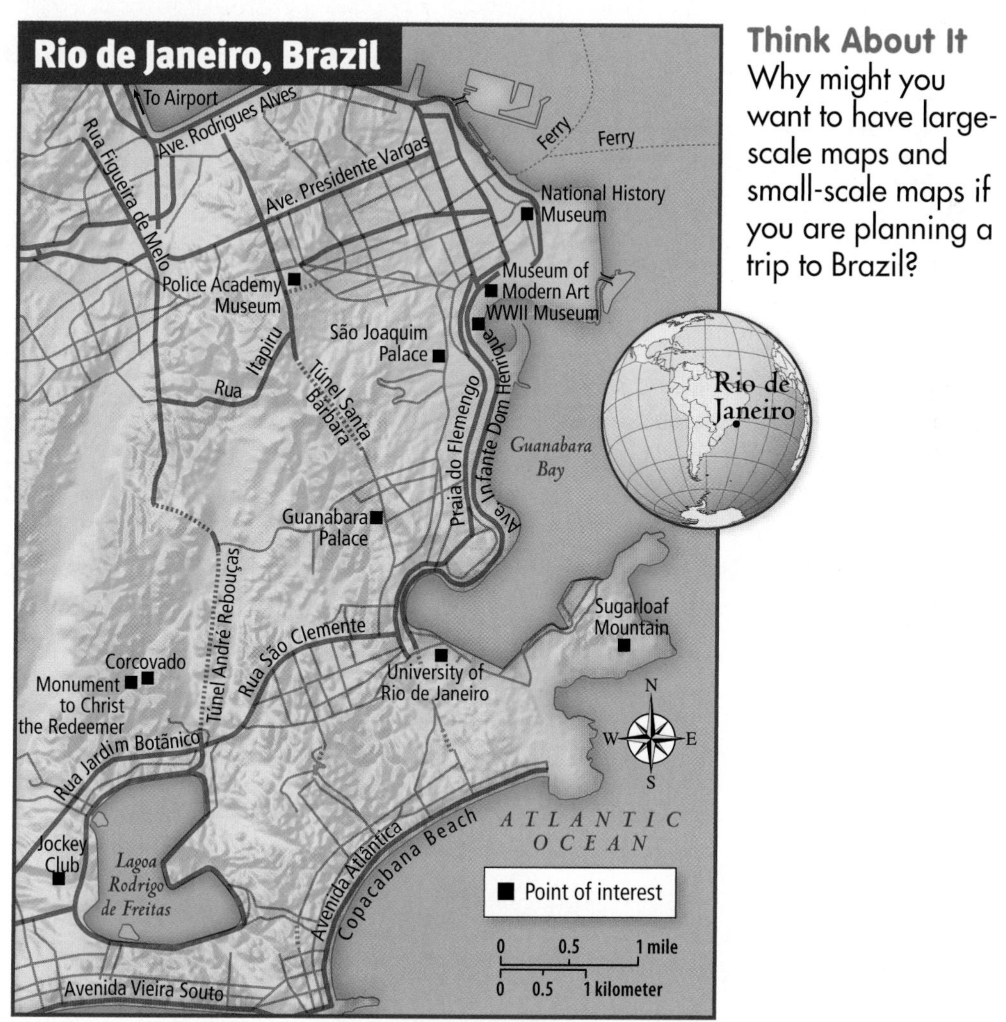

Think About It
Why might you want to have large-scale maps and small-scale maps if you are planning a trip to Brazil?

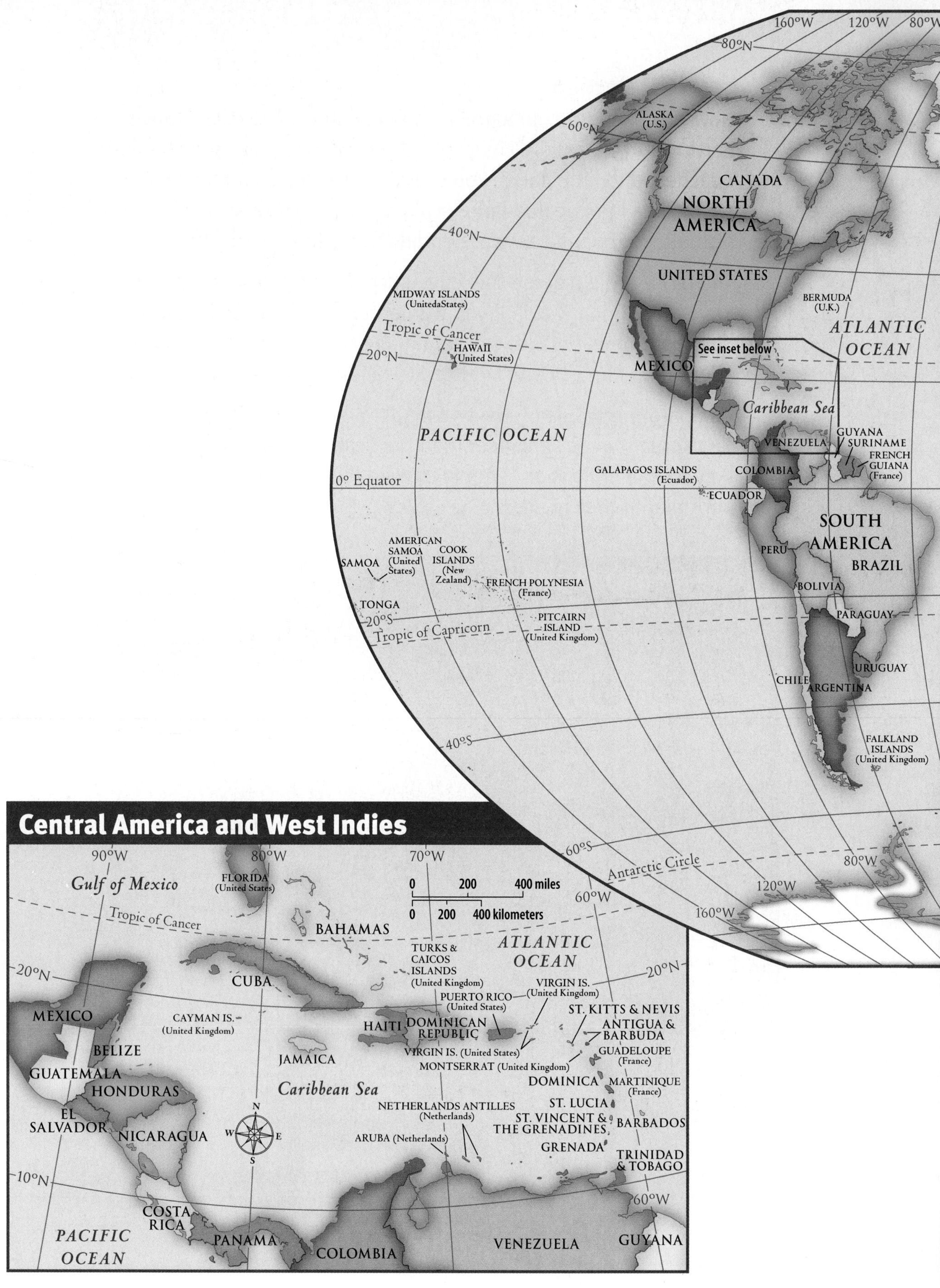

160°W
120°W
80°W
80°N
60°N
40°N
20°N
0° Equator
20°S
40°S
60°S
ALASKA (U.S.)
CANADA
NORTH AMERICA
UNITED STATES
MIDWAY ISLANDS (UnitedaStates)
BERMUDA (U.K.)
ATLANTIC OCEAN
Tropic of Cancer
HAWAII (United States)
See inset below
MEXICO
Caribbean Sea
PACIFIC OCEAN
GUYANA
SURINAME
FRENCH GUIANA (France)
VENEZUELA
GALAPAGOS ISLANDS (Ecuador)
COLOMBIA
ECUADOR
SOUTH AMERICA
BRAZIL
PERU
BOLIVIA
AMERICAN SAMOA (United States)
COOK ISLANDS (New Zealand)
SAMOA
FRENCH POLYNESIA (France)
TONGA
PARAGUAY
PITCAIRN ISLAND (United Kingdom)
Tropic of Capricorn
URUGUAY
CHILE
ARGENTINA
FALKLAND ISLANDS (United Kingdom)
Antarctic Circle
Central America and West Indies
90°W
80°W
70°W
60°W
Gulf of Mexico
FLORIDA (United States)
0 200 400 miles
0 200 400 kilometers
BAHAMAS
TURKS & CAICOS ISLANDS (United Kingdom)
ATLANTIC OCEAN
CUBA
VIRGIN IS. (United Kingdom)
PUERTO RICO (United States)
MEXICO
CAYMAN IS. (United Kingdom)
HAITI
DOMINICAN REPUBLIC
ST. KITTS & NEVIS
ANTIGUA & BARBUDA
BELIZE
VIRGIN IS. (United States)
GUADELOUPE (France)
JAMAICA
GUATEMALA
MONTSERRAT (United Kingdom)
DOMINICA
MARTINIQUE (France)
HONDURAS
Caribbean Sea
NETHERLANDS ANTILLES (Netherlands)
ST. LUCIA
EL SALVADOR
NICARAGUA
ST. VINCENT & THE GRENADINES
BARBADOS
ARUBA (Netherlands)
GRENADA
TRINIDAD & TOBAGO
10°N
N
S
E
W
COSTA RICA
PACIFIC OCEAN
PANAMA
COLOMBIA
VENEZUELA
GUYANA

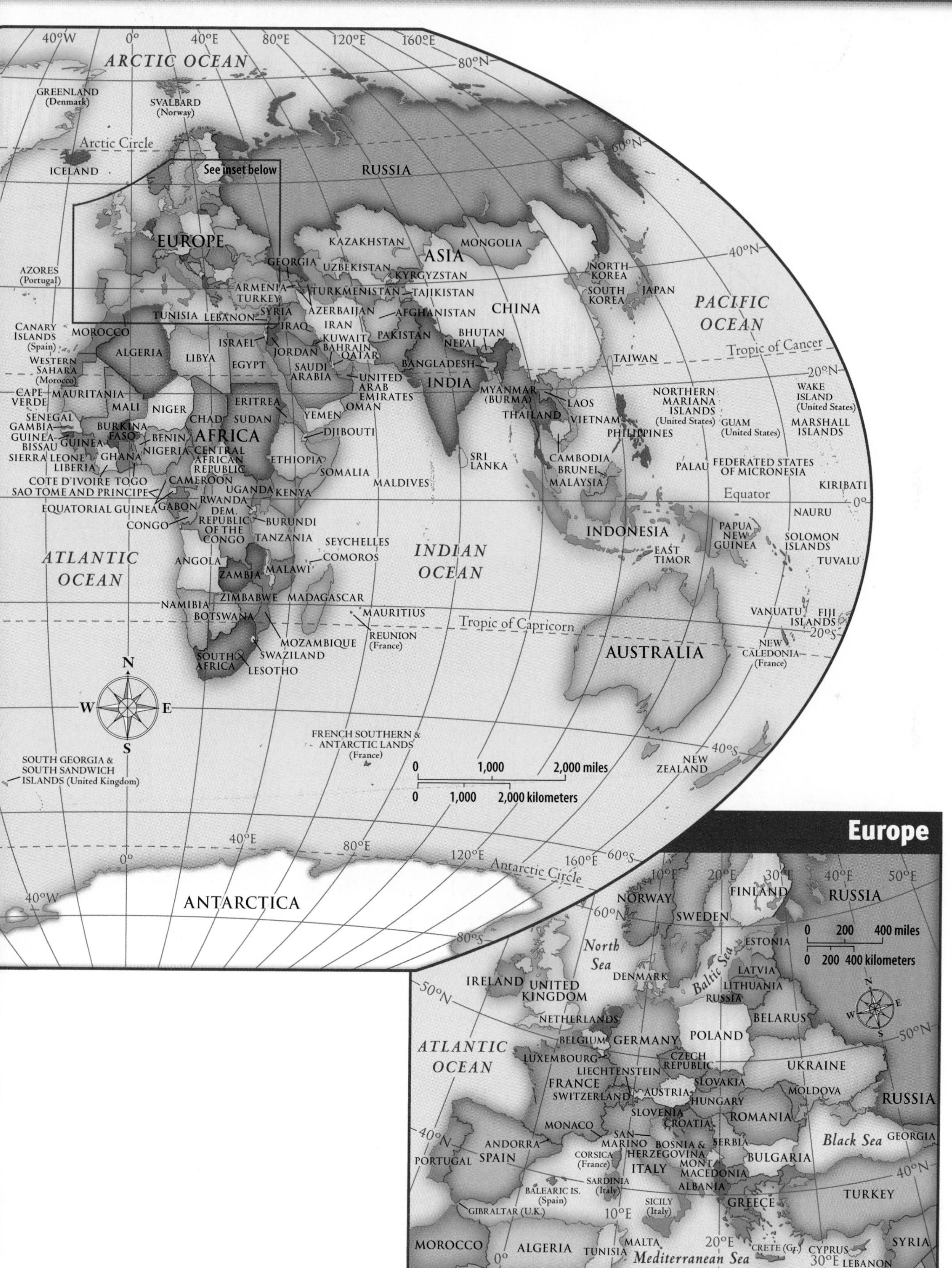
ARCTIC OCEAN
GREENLAND (Denmark)
SVALBARD (Norway)
Arctic Circle
ICELAND
See inset below
RUSSIA
EUROPE
AZORES (Portugal)
KAZAKHSTAN
ASIA
MONGOLIA
GEORGIA
UZBEKISTAN
KYRGYZSTAN
ARMENIA
TURKEY
TURKMENISTAN
TAJIKISTAN
NORTH KOREA
SOUTH KOREA
JAPAN
SYRIA
AZERBAIJAN
AFGHANISTAN
CHINA
PACIFIC OCEAN
TUNISIA
LEBANON
IRAQ
IRAN
CANARY ISLANDS (Spain)
MOROCCO
ISRAEL
KUWAIT
BAHRAIN
QATAR
PAKISTAN
NEPAL
BHUTAN
Tropic of Cancer
ALGERIA
LIBYA
EGYPT
JORDAN
SAUDI ARABIA
BANGLADESH
TAIWAN
WESTERN SAHARA (Morocco)
UNITED ARAB EMIRATES
INDIA
CAPE VERDE
MAURITANIA
MALI
NIGER
ERITREA
OMAN
MYANMAR (BURMA)
LAOS
NORTHERN MARIANA ISLANDS (United States)
WAKE ISLAND (United States)
SENEGAL
GAMBIA
GUINEA-BISSAU
GUINEA
SIERRA LEONE
LIBERIA
BURKINA FASO
GHANA
BENIN
NIGERIA
CHAD
SUDAN
AFRICA
YEMEN
DJIBOUTI
THAILAND
VIETNAM
PHILIPPINES
GUAM (United States)
MARSHALL ISLANDS
CENTRAL AFRICAN REPUBLIC
ETHIOPIA
SRI LANKA
CAMBODIA
BRUNEI
MALAYSIA
PALAU
FEDERATED STATES OF MICRONESIA
COTE D'IVOIRE
TOGO
CAMEROON
SOMALIA
MALDIVES
KIRIBATI
SAO TOME AND PRINCIPE
UGANDA
KENYA
Equator
EQUATORIAL GUINEA
GABON
RWANDA
DEM. REPUBLIC OF THE CONGO
BURUNDI
NAURU
CONGO
TANZANIA
SEYCHELLES
INDONESIA
PAPUA NEW GUINEA
SOLOMON ISLANDS
ATLANTIC OCEAN
ANGOLA
COMOROS
INDIAN OCEAN
EAST TIMOR
TUVALU
ZAMBIA
MALAWI
NAMIBIA
ZIMBABWE
MADAGASCAR
MAURITIUS
BOTSWANA
Tropic of Capricorn
VANUATU
FIJI ISLANDS
MOZAMBIQUE
REUNION (France)
NEW CALEDONIA (France)
SOUTH AFRICA
SWAZILAND
LESOTHO
AUSTRALIA
N
W
E
S
FRENCH SOUTHERN & ANTARCTIC LANDS (France)
SOUTH GEORGIA & SOUTH SANDWICH ISLANDS (United Kingdom)
0 1,000 2,000 miles
0 1,000 2,000 kilometers
NEW ZEALAND
Antarctic Circle
ANTARCTICA
40°W 0° 40°E 80°E 120°E 160°E
80°N 60°N 40°N 20°N 0° 20°S 40°S 60°S 80°S
Europe
NORWAY
SWEDEN
FINLAND
RUSSIA
ESTONIA
North Sea
0 200 400 miles
0 200 400 kilometers
DENMARK
Baltic Sea
LATVIA
LITHUANIA
IRELAND
UNITED KINGDOM
RUSSIA
BELARUS
NETHERLANDS
POLAND
GERMANY
BELGIUM
ATLANTIC OCEAN
LUXEMBOURG
CZECH REPUBLIC
UKRAINE
LIECHTENSTEIN
SLOVAKIA
FRANCE
AUSTRIA
MOLDOVA
SWITZERLAND
HUNGARY
RUSSIA
SLOVENIA
ROMANIA
CROATIA
MONACO
SAN MARINO
BOSNIA & HERZEGOVINA
SERBIA
Black Sea
GEORGIA
ANDORRA
PORTUGAL
SPAIN
CORSICA (France)
ITALY
MONT.
BULGARIA
MACEDONIA
ALBANIA
SARDINIA (Italy)
TURKEY
BALEARIC IS. (Spain)
GREECE
GIBRALTAR (U.K.)
SICILY (Italy)
MOROCCO
ALGERIA
TUNISIA
MALTA
Mediterranean Sea
CRETE (Gr.)
CYPRUS
SYRIA
LEBANON
10°E 20°E 30°E 40°E 50°E 0°
60°N 50°N 40°N

160°W
120°W
80°W
40°W
80°N
ARCTIC OCEAN
GREENLAND
Arctic Circle
Mackenzie River
60°N
ALASKA RANGE
Mt. McKinley
20,320 ft.
(6,194 m)
ROCKY MOUNTAINS
NORTH AMERICA
CANADIAN SHIELD
40°N
Mississippi River
APPALACHIAN MTS.
PACIFIC OCEAN
Rio Grande
ATLANTIC OCEAN
Gulf of Mexico
Tropic of Cancer
20°N
Caribbean Sea
0° Equator
Amazon River
SOUTH AMERICA
ANDES MOUNTAINS
20°S
Tropic of Capricorn
Mt. Aconcagua
22,834 ft.
(6,960 m)
ATLANTIC OCEAN
40°S
PACIFIC OCEAN
Cape Horn
60°S
Antarctic Circle
80°W
Weddell Sea
120°W
40°W
160°W
Vinson Massif
16,067 ft.
(4,897 m)

ARCTIC OCEAN
40°E
80°E
120°E
160°E
80°N
60°N
40°N
20°N
0°
20°S
40°S
60°S
80°S
Lena River
Yenisey River
Ob River
URAL MTS.
Volga River
Sea of Okhotsk
EUROPE
ALPS
Mont Blanc 15,711 ft. (4,807 m)
Black Sea
Mt. Elbrus 18,510 ft. (5,642 m)
Caspian Sea
ASIA
GOBI
HINDU KUSH
Mediterranean Sea
SYRIAN DESERT
HIMALAYA
Yangtze River
Tropic of Cancer
SAHARA
Nile River
Red Sea
Ganges River
Mt. Everest 29,035 ft. (8,850 m)
DECCAN PLATEAU
Arabian Sea
South China Sea
Philippine Sea
PACIFIC OCEAN
AFRICA
Congo River
Mt. Kilimanjaro 19,340 ft. (5,895 m)
Equator
INDIAN OCEAN
Coral Sea
GREAT SANDY DESERT
NAMIB DESERT
KALAHARI DESERT
Tropic of Capricorn
AUSTRALIA
Darling River
Mt. Kosciuszko 7,310 ft. (2,228 m)
Cape of Good Hope
N
W
E
S
0 1,000 2,000 miles
0 1,000 2,000 kilometers
Antarctic Circle
ANTARCTICA

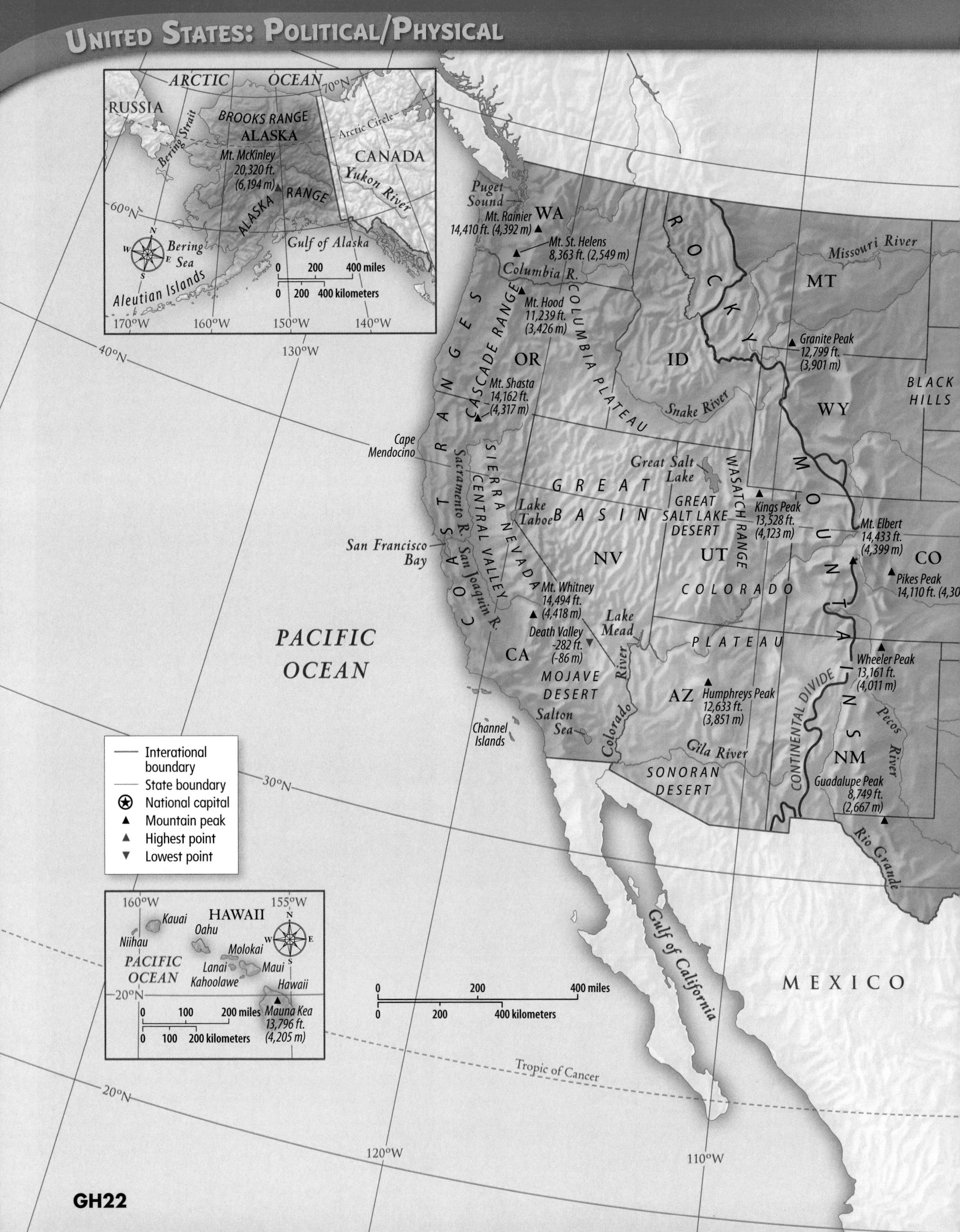
ARCTIC OCEAN
70°N
RUSSIA
BROOKS RANGE
ALASKA
Arctic Circle
Bering Strait
Mt. McKinley 20,320 ft. (6,194 m)
CANADA
Yukon River
ALASKA RANGE
60°N
Bering Sea
Gulf of Alaska
0 200 400 miles
0 200 400 kilometers
Aleutian Islands
170°W
160°W
150°W
140°W
40°N
130°W
Puget Sound
WA
Mt. Rainier 14,410 ft. (4,392 m)
Mt. St. Helens 8,363 ft. (2,549 m)
Columbia R.
ROCKY MOUNTAINS
Missouri River
MT
Mt. Hood 11,239 ft. (3,426 m)
COLUMBIA PLATEAU
CASCADE RANGE
COAST RANGES
Granite Peak 12,799 ft. (3,901 m)
OR
ID
BLACK HILLS
Mt. Shasta 14,162 ft. (4,317 m)
Snake River
WY
Cape Mendocino
SIERRA NEVADA
Sacramento R.
CENTRAL VALLEY
Great Salt Lake
WASATCH RANGE
GREAT BASIN
Kings Peak 13,528 ft. (4,123 m)
Lake Tahoe
GREAT SALT LAKE DESERT
Mt. Elbert 14,433 ft. (4,399 m)
San Francisco Bay
San Joaquin R.
NV
UT
CO
Pikes Peak 14,110 ft.
Mt. Whitney 14,494 ft. (4,418 m)
COLORADO PLATEAU
Lake Mead
Death Valley -282 ft. (-86 m)
PACIFIC OCEAN
CA
Wheeler Peak 13,161 ft. (4,011 m)
MOJAVE DESERT
Colorado River
AZ
Humphreys Peak 12,633 ft. (3,851 m)
CONTINENTAL DIVIDE
Pecos River
Salton Sea
Channel Islands
Gila River
NM
Interational boundary
State boundary
National capital
Mountain peak
Highest point
Lowest point
30°N
SONORAN DESERT
Guadalupe Peak 8,749 ft. (2,667 m)
Rio Grande
Gulf of California
MEXICO
160°W
155°W
HAWAII
Kauai
Oahu
Niihau
Molokai
PACIFIC OCEAN
Lanai
Maui
Kahoolawe
Hawaii
20°N
0 100 200 miles
0 100 200 kilometers
Mauna Kea 13,796 ft. (4,205 m)
0 200 400 miles
0 200 400 kilometers
Tropic of Cancer
20°N
120°W
110°W

CANADA
Lake of the Woods
Lake Superior
GREAT LAKES
Lake Michigan
Lake Huron
Lake Ontario
Lake Erie
St. Lawrence River
MESABI RANGE
GREAT PLAINS
CENTRAL PLAINS
INTERIOR PLAINS
OZARK PLATEAU
OUACHITA MOUNTAINS
ADIRONDACK MOUNTAINS
GREEN MOUNTAINS
ALLEGHENY PLATEAU
ALLEGHENY MOUNTAINS
APPALACHIAN MOUNTAINS
PIEDMONT
ATLANTIC COASTAL PLAIN
GULF COASTAL PLAIN
EDWARDS PLATEAU
Mt. Washington 6,288 ft. (1,917 m)
Mt. Mitchell 6,684 ft. (2,037 m)
ND
SD
NE
KS
OK
TX
MN
IA
MO
AR
LA
WI
IL
MI
IN
OH
KY
TN
MS
AL
GA
FL
SC
NC
VA
WV
MD
DE
PA
NJ
NY
CT
RI
MA
VT
NH
ME
Washington, D.C.
Mississippi River
Missouri River
Platte River
Arkansas River
Red River
Brazos River
Colorado River
Wabash River
Ohio River
Tennessee River
Alabama River
Chattahoochee River
Savannah River
Potomac River
Susquehanna River
Hudson River
Cape Cod
Long Island
Delaware Bay
Chesapeake Bay
Cape Hatteras
Mobile Bay
Galveston Bay
Mississippi River Delta
Lake Okeechobee
Gulf of Mexico
Florida Keys
Straits of Florida
ATLANTIC OCEAN
BAHAMAS
CUBA
N
S
E
W
50°N
40°N
30°N
20°N
100°W
90°W
80°W
1 m)

NORTH AMERICA: POLITICAL/PHYSICAL
ASIA
EUROPE
ARCTIC OCEAN
Oodaaq Island
Lincoln Sea
Greenland Sea
Gunnbjorn 12,139 ft. (3,700 m)
ICELAND
Queen Elizabeth Islands
Ellesmere Island
HAYES PENINSULA
Greenland
Chukchi Sea
Point Barrow
Bering Sea
Bering Strait
SEWARD PENINSULA
NORTH SLOPE
BROOKS RANGE
Beaufort Sea
Banks Island
Melville Island
Devon Island
Baffin Bay
Somerset I.
Prince of Wales I.
Victoria Island
BOOTHIA PENINSULA
Baffin Island
MELVILLE PEN.
Davis Strait
Cape Farewell
Foxe Basin
Mt. McKinley 20,320 ft. (6,194 m)
Yukon R.
ALASKA
ALASKA RANGE
KENAI PENINSULA
YUKON PLATEAU
MACKENZIE MTS.
Mackenzie R.
Great Bear Lake
Great Slave Lake
Southampton Island
Hudson Strait
Ungava Bay
Labrador Sea
Kodiak Island
Gulf of Alaska
Mt. Logan 19,551 ft. (5,959 m)
ALEXANDER ARCHIPELAGO
COAST MOUNTAINS
CANADA
Hudson Bay
Peace R.
Slave R.
Lake Athabasca
Athabasca R.
Churchill R.
CANADIAN SHIELD
Belcher Islands
James Bay
Island of Newfoundland
AVALON PENINSULA
Queen Charlotte Islands
ROCKY MOUNTAINS
FRASER PLATEAU
COLUMBIA MTS.
Saskatchewan R.
Lake Winnipeg
LAURENTIAN MTS.
Gulf of St. Lawrence
GASPÉ PEN.
Cape Breton Island
Prince Edward Island
Vancouver Island
OLYMPIC PENINSULA
CASCADE RANGE
St. Lawrence R.
Nova Scotia
Ottawa
Lake Superior
Lake Ontario
Bay of Fundy
Gulf of Maine
Snake R.
COLUMBIA PLATEAU
GREAT PLAINS
Missouri River
Lake Michigan
Lake Huron
APPALACHIAN MOUNTAINS
Great Salt Lake
Platte R.
Lake Erie
Cape Cod
Long Island
ATLANTIC OCEAN
Cape Mendocino
COAST RANGES
SIERRA NEVADA
GREAT BASIN
COLORADO PLATEAU
HIGH PLAINS
CENTRAL LOWLAND
Washington, D.C.
UNITED STATES
Chesapeake Bay
Cape Hatteras
Bermuda (U.K.)
Mt. Whitney 14,494 ft. (4,418 m)
Colorado R.
Death Valley -282 ft. (-86 m)
Grand Canyon
OZARK PLATEAU
Arkansas River
Mississippi R.
Ohio R.
Red River
Channel Islands
SONORAN DESERT
COASTAL PLAIN
PACIFIC OCEAN
BAJA CALIFORNIA
Gulf of California
SIERRA MADRE OCCIDENTAL
SIERRA MADRE ORIENTAL
Rio Grande
MEXICO
Gulf of Mexico
Florida Keys
BAHAMAS
Nassau
Tropic of Cancer
DOMINICAN REPUBLIC
WEST INDIES
Havana
CUBA
Hispaniola
HAITI
Virgin Islands
Guadeloupe
Martinique
Orizaba 18,855 ft. (5,747 m)
YUCATÁN PENINSULA
Cozumel Island
Cayman Islands (U.K.)
Port-au-Prince
Santo Domingo
Puerto Rico (U.S.)
Kingston
JAMAICA
México City
GUATEMALA
BELIZE
Belmopan
Isthmus of Tehuantepec
TRINIDAD & TOBAGO
Port-of-Spain
Caribbean Sea
HONDURAS
Guatemala City
Tegucigalpa
San Salvador
NICARAGUA
EL SALVADOR
Lake Nicaragua
Managua
COSTA RICA
San José
Isthmus of Panama
Panamá
PANAMA
CENTRAL AMERICA
SOUTH AMERICA
Equator
Arctic Circle
International boundary
National capital
Mountain peak
N
S
E
W
0 300 600 miles
0 300 600 kilometers
140°E
150°E
160°E
170°E
180°
170°W
160°W
150°W
140°W
130°W
120°W
110°W
100°W
90°W
80°W
70°W
60°W
50°W
40°W
30°W
20°W
10°W
0°
10°E
20°E
80°N
70°N
60°N
50°N
40°N
30°N
20°N
10°N
0°

SOUTH AMERICA: POLITICAL/PHYSICAL
Caribbean Sea
NORTH AMERICA
ISTHMUS OF PANAMA
Maracaibo
Caracas
Orinoco R.
VENEZUELA
GUIANA HIGHLANDS
Georgetown
GUYANA
Paramaribo
SURINAME
Cayenne
FRENCH GUIANA (France)
ATLANTIC OCEAN
Bogotá
Cali
COLOMBIA
Negro River
Quito
Equator
ECUADOR
Guayaquil
Galápagos Islands (Ecuador)
Amazon River
AMAZON BASIN
River
Tapajos River
Xingú River
Madeira River
Tocantins River
São Francisco River
BRAZIL
PERU
ANDES MOUNTAINS
Lima
Lake Titicaca
La Paz
Arequipa
BOLIVIA
Santa Cruz
Sucre
Paraguay R.
BRAZILIAN HIGHLANDS
Brasília
River
Paraná
ATACAMA DESERT
PARAGUAY
Rio de Janeiro
São Paulo
Asunción
Mt. Ojos del Salado 22,572 ft. (6,880 m)
Tropic of Capricorn
River
Paraná
CHILE
Mt. Aconcagua 22,834 ft. (6,960 m)
Rosario
Salto
URUGUAY
Valparaíso
Santiago
ARGENTINA
Montevideo
Buenos Aires
Rio de la Plata
PACIFIC OCEAN
PAMPAS
Concepción
ATLANTIC OCEAN
PATAGONIA
Falkland Islands (Islas Malvinas) (U.K.)
Strait of Magellan
TIERRA DEL FUEGO
Cape Horn
South Georgia (U.K.)
N
S
E
W
15°N
0°
15°S
30°S
45°S
105°W
90°W
75°W
60°W
45°W
30°W
0 250 500 miles
0 250 500 kilometers
International boundary
National capital
Other city
Mountain peak

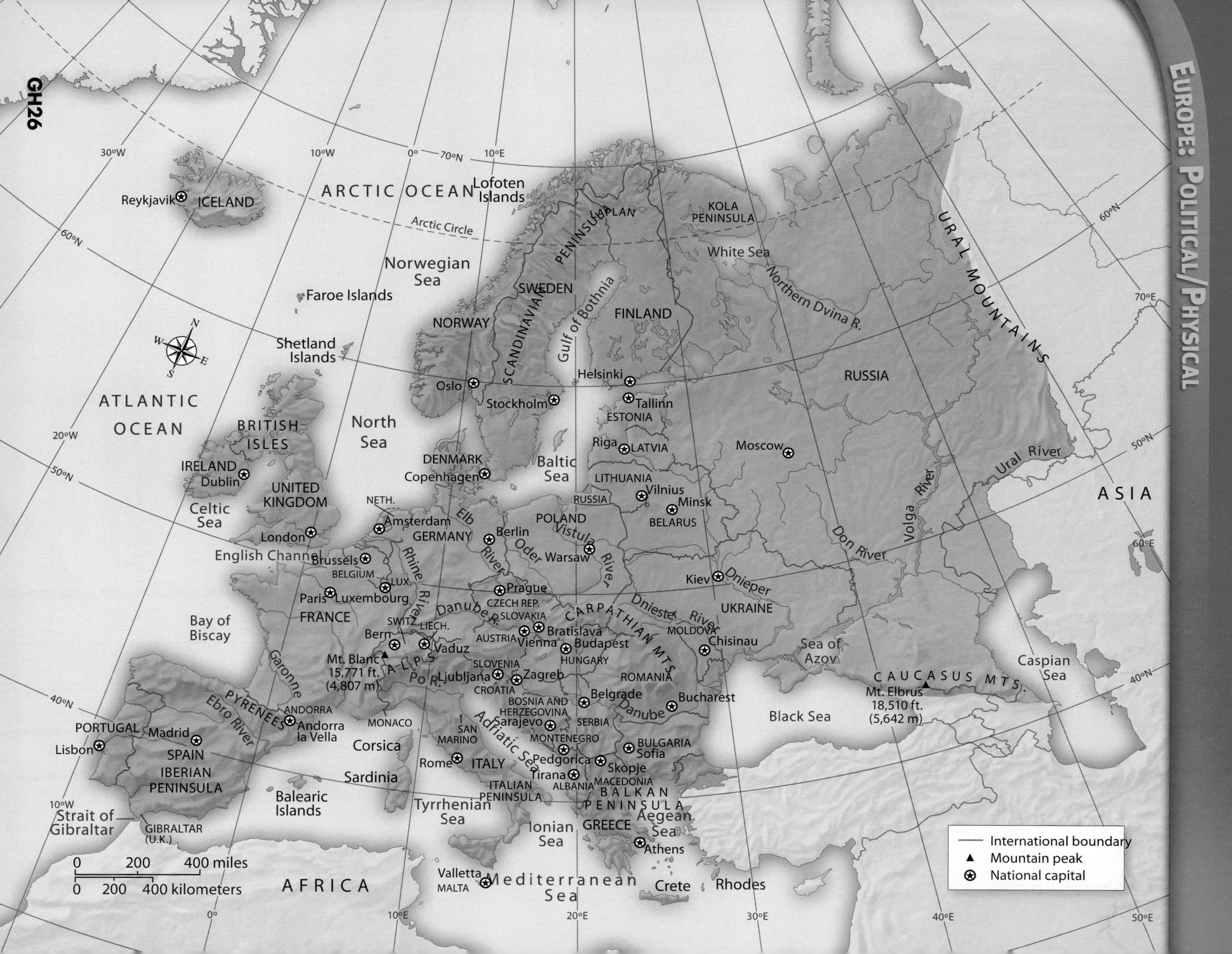

ARCTIC OCEAN
Lofoten Islands
Reykjavik
ICELAND
Arctic Circle
LAPLAND
KOLA PENINSULA
White Sea
URAL MOUNTAINS
Norwegian Sea
Faroe Islands
SCANDINAVIAN PENINSULA
SWEDEN
Gulf of Bothnia
FINLAND
Northern Dvina R.
NORWAY
Shetland Islands
Oslo
Helsinki
Stockholm
Tallinn
ESTONIA
RUSSIA
ATLANTIC OCEAN
BRITISH ISLES
North Sea
Riga
LATVIA
Moscow
DENMARK
Copenhagen
Baltic Sea
IRELAND
Dublin
UNITED KINGDOM
LITHUANIA
Vilnius
Minsk
BELARUS
RUSSIA
Ural River
Volga River
ASIA
Celtic Sea
NETH.
Amsterdam
Elb
GERMANY
Berlin
POLAND
Vistula River
Oder River
Warsaw
London
English Channel
Brussels
BELGIUM
LUX.
Luxembourg
Paris
Don River
Kiev
Dnieper
Rhine River
Prague
CZECH REP.
SLOVAKIA
Danube R.
Dniester River
UKRAINE
Bay of Biscay
FRANCE
SWITZ.
LIECH.
Bern
Vaduz
AUSTRIA
Vienna
Bratislava
Budapest
CARPATHIAN MTS.
MOLDOVA
Chisinau
Sea of Azov
Caspian Sea
Mt. Blanc 15,771 ft. (4,807 m)
ALPS
Po R.
SLOVENIA
Ljubljana
Zagreb
CROATIA
HUNGARY
ROMANIA
CAUCASUS MTS.
Mt. Elbrus 18,510 ft. (5,642 m)
Garonne
PYRENEES
Ebro River
ANDORRA
Andorra la Vella
MONACO
BOSNIA AND HERZEGOVINA
Sarajevo
Belgrade
SERBIA
Danube
Bucharest
Black Sea
PORTUGAL
Lisbon
Madrid
SPAIN
IBERIAN PENINSULA
Corsica
SAN MARINO
Adriatic Sea
MONTENEGRO
Podgorica
BULGARIA
Sofia
Rome
ITALY
Sardinia
Tirana
ALBANIA
Skopje
MACEDONIA
BALKAN PENINSULA
ITALIAN PENINSULA
Balearic Islands
Tyrrhenian Sea
Strait of Gibraltar
GIBRALTAR (U.K.)
Ionian Sea
GREECE
Aegean Sea
Athens
0 200 400 miles
0 200 400 kilometers
AFRICA
Valletta
MALTA
Mediterranean Sea
Crete
Rhodes
International boundary
Mountain peak
National capital
N
E
S
W
30°W
10°W
0°
70°N
10°E
60°N
70°E
20°W
50°N
60°E
40°N
10°E
20°E
30°E
40°E
50°E

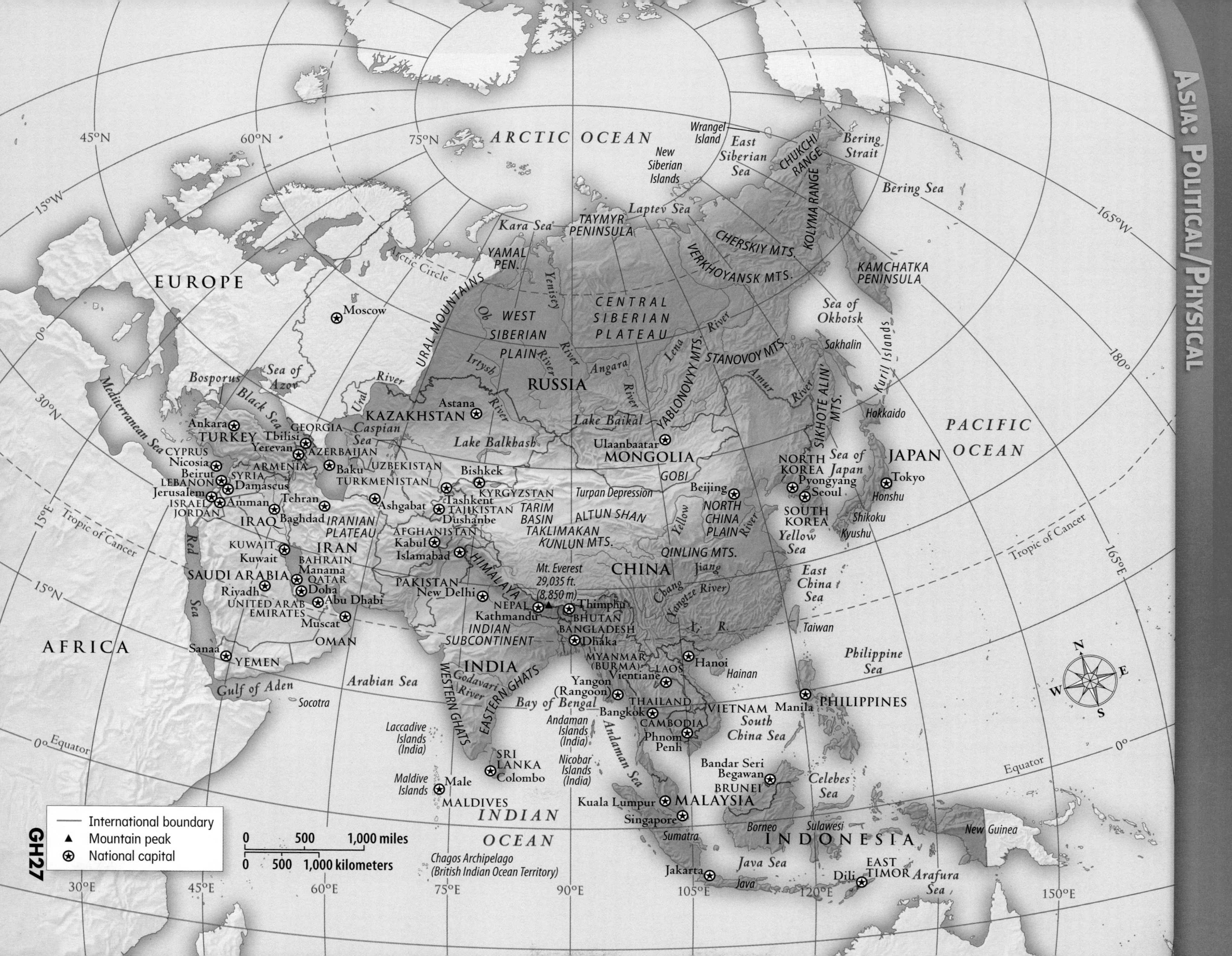

ASIA: POLITICAL/PHYSICAL
ARCTIC OCEAN
PACIFIC OCEAN
INDIAN OCEAN
EUROPE
AFRICA
RUSSIA
CHINA
MONGOLIA
KAZAKHSTAN
INDIA
JAPAN
INDONESIA
PHILIPPINES
IRAN
SAUDI ARABIA
TURKEY
PAKISTAN
AFGHANISTAN
IRAQ
SYRIA
JORDAN
ISRAEL
LEBANON
CYPRUS
GEORGIA
ARMENIA
AZERBAIJAN
TURKMENISTAN
UZBEKISTAN
KYRGYZSTAN
TAJIKISTAN
KUWAIT
BAHRAIN
QATAR
UNITED ARAB EMIRATES
OMAN
YEMEN
NEPAL
BHUTAN
BANGLADESH
MYANMAR (BURMA)
THAILAND
LAOS
CAMBODIA
VIETNAM
MALAYSIA
BRUNEI
SRI LANKA
MALDIVES
NORTH KOREA
SOUTH KOREA
EAST TIMOR
Moscow
Ankara
Nicosia
Beirut
Damascus
Jerusalem
Amman
Baghdad
Tbilisi
Yerevan
Baku
Tehran
Kuwait
Manama
Doha
Abu Dhabi
Muscat
Riyadh
Sanaa
Ashgabat
Tashkent
Dushanbe
Bishkek
Astana
Kabul
Islamabad
New Delhi
Kathmandu
Thimphu
Dhaka
Colombo
Male
Yangon (Rangoon)
Bangkok
Vientiane
Phnom Penh
Hanoi
Kuala Lumpur
Singapore
Jakarta
Bandar Seri Begawan
Manila
Dili
Beijing
Ulaanbaatar
Pyongyang
Seoul
Tokyo
URAL MOUNTAINS
WEST SIBERIAN PLAIN
CENTRAL SIBERIAN PLATEAU
YAMAL PEN.
TAYMYR PENINSULA
KAMCHATKA PENINSULA
CHUKCHI RANGE
KOLYMA RANGE
CHERSKIY MTS.
VERKHOYANSK MTS.
STANOVOY MTS.
YABLONOVYY MTS.
SIKHOTE ALIN' MTS.
GOBI
Turpan Depression
ALTUN SHAN
TARIM BASIN
TAKLIMAKAN
KUNLUN MTS.
QINLING MTS.
NORTH CHINA PLAIN
HIMALAYA
Mt. Everest 29,035 ft. (8,850 m)
INDIAN SUBCONTINENT
EASTERN GHATS
WESTERN GHATS
IRANIAN PLATEAU
Kara Sea
Laptev Sea
East Siberian Sea
Bering Sea
Bering Strait
Sea of Okhotsk
Sea of Japan
Yellow Sea
East China Sea
South China Sea
Philippine Sea
Celebes Sea
Java Sea
Arafura Sea
Andaman Sea
Bay of Bengal
Arabian Sea
Gulf of Aden
Red Sea
Mediterranean Sea
Black Sea
Sea of Azov
Caspian Sea
Bosporus
Lake Balkhash
Lake Baikal
Ob
Irtysh
Yenisey River
Angara River
Lena River
Amur River
Ural River
Yellow River
Chang Jiang (Yangtze River)
Xi R.
Godavari River
Wrangel Island
New Siberian Islands
Sakhalin
Kuril Islands
Hokkaido
Honshu
Shikoku
Kyushu
Taiwan
Hainan
Borneo
Sumatra
Java
Sulawesi
New Guinea
Andaman Islands (India)
Nicobar Islands (India)
Laccadive Islands (India)
Maldive Islands
Chagos Archipelago (British Indian Ocean Territory)
Socotra
Arctic Circle
Tropic of Cancer
Equator
75°N
60°N
45°N
30°N
15°N
0°
15°W
165°W
180°
165°E
150°E
120°E
105°E
90°E
75°E
60°E
45°E
30°E
15°E
N
E
S
W
0 500 1,000 miles
0 500 1,000 kilometers
International boundary
Mountain peak
National capital

AFRICA: POLITICAL/PHYSICAL

EUROPE
ASIA
ATLANTIC OCEAN
Madeira Islands (Portugal)
Strait of Gibraltar
Rabat
MOROCCO
Canary Islands (Spain)
ATLAS MOUNTAINS
Algiers
Tunis
Mediterranean Sea
Gulf of Gabes
TUNISIA
Tripoli
Gulf of Sidra
NILE DELTA
Suez Canal
SINAI PENINSULA
Cairo
WESTERN SAHARA (Morocco)
ALGERIA
LIBYA
EGYPT
Nile R.
Red Sea
S A H A R A
Cape Blanc
Tropic of Cancer
AHAGGAR MOUNTAINS
LIBYAN DESERT
Lake Nasser
NUBIAN DESERT
MAURITANIA
Nouakchott
AIR RANGE
TIBESTI MOUNTAINS
MALI
Senegal R.
Niger
Dakar
SENEGAL
Banjul
GAMBIA
NIGER
CHAD
Khartoum
Atbara R.
ERITREA
Asmara
DJIBOUTI
Djibouti
Gulf of Aden
Bamako
BURKINA FASO
Niger River
Niamey
Lake Chad
SUDAN
White Nile R.
Blue Nile R.
GUINEA-BISSAU
Bissau
GUINEA
Ouagadougou
N'Djamena
ETHIOPIAN HIGHLANDS
SOMALI PENINSULA
Conakry
SIERRA LEONE
Freetown
COTE D'IVOIRE
GHANA
BENIN
NIGERIA
Abuja
Addis Ababa
TOGO
Lake Volta
Porto-Novo
Monrovia
LIBERIA
Yamoussoukro
Accra
Lome
Benue River
CENTRAL AFRICAN REPUBLIC
ETHIOPIA
GREAT RIFT VALLEY
SOMALIA
Cape Palmas
Gulf of Guinea
Malabo
EQUATORIAL GUINEA
CAMEROON
Yaounde
Bangui
SUDD
Lake Turkana
Lake Albert
UGANDA
Mogadishu
SAO TOME AND PRINCIPE
Sao Tome
Equator
Libreville
Ubangi R.
Congo R.
Kampala
KENYA
Cape Lopez
GABON
CONGO
CONGO BASIN
Lomami R.
Kigali
Lake Victoria
Nairobi
INDIAN OCEAN
Mt. Kilimanjaro 19,340 ft. (5,895 m)
Brazzaville
Kasai R.
Kinshasa
RWANDA
Bujumbura
BURUNDI
Pemba Island
Dodoma
Zanzibar Island
Dar es Salaam
CABINDA (Angola)
Kwango R.
DEMOCRATIC REPUBLIC OF THE CONGO
Lake Tanganyika
TANZANIA
Cape Delgado
SEYCHELLES
Luanda
BIE PLATEAU
MALAWI
Moroni
COMOROS
Lake Malawi
Mayotte (France)
Lilongwe
ANGOLA
ZAMBIA
Cuando R.
Cubango R.
Lake Kariba
Lusaka
Zambezi R.
Mozambique Channel
MADAGASCAR
Harare
NAMIBIA
OKAVANGO BASIN
Victoria Falls
ZIMBABWE
Antananarivo
NAMIB DESERT
Windhoek
BOTSWANA
Limpopo R.
MOZAMBIQUE
Tropic of Capricorn
KALAHARI DESERT
Gaborone
Pretoria
Maputo
SWAZILAND
Mbabane
Vaal R.
Maseru
Bloemfontein
LESOTHO
Orange River
DRAKENSBERG
SOUTH AFRICA
Cape Town
Cape of Good Hope
Cape Agulhas
N
E
S
W
40°N
30°N
20°N
10°N
0°
10°S
20°S
30°S
40°S
20°W
10°W
0°
10°E
20°E
30°E
40°E
50°E
National capital
International boundary
Disputed boundary
Mountain peak
Waterfall
0
500
1,000 miles
0
500
1,000 kilometers

Glossary

This glossary will help you to pronounce and understand the meanings of the vocabulary terms in this book. The page number at the end of the definition tells you where the word first appears.

A

absolute location (ab′ sə lüt lō kā shən) the exact location of a place expressed by longitude and latitude or street address (p. 37)

acid rain (a′sid rān) precipitation containing harmful chemical pollution that can poison water and destroy trees and wildlife; see **precipitation** (p. 77)

alliance (ə lī′əns) an agreement to work together (p. 215)

altitude (al′ti tüd) height of something above the ground or above sea level (p. 94)

amendment (ə mend′mənt) an addition to the Constitution (p. 64)

amnesty (am nə stē) a pardon (p. 67)

annex (an′ eks) to make a country or territory part of another country (p. 26)

aqueduct (ak′ wə dukt) a bridge-like structure that carries water to cities (p. 187)

archipelago (är kə pel′a gō) a cluster of many islands (p. 85)

arid (ar′id) dry (p. 16)

arms race (ärmz rās) the competition to design and build the most powerful weapons (p. 35)

B

battle map (bat′əl map) a map that shows the events of a conflict between two groups of armed forces (p. 119)

bilingual (bī ling′wəl) having two languages (p. 47)

C

campesino (käm pə sē′ nō) a poor farmer in Latin America (p. 144)

caravel (kar′a vel) a cargo ship designed for ocean travel in the 1400s (p. 204)

carnival (kär′nä väl) a festival held on the last day before the Christian holy period of Lent (p. 137)

Pronunciation Key

a	at	ē	me	ō	old	ū	use	ng	song
ā	ape	i	it	ô	fork	ü	rule	th	thin
ä	far	ī	ice	oi	oil	u̇	pull	th	this
âr	care	î	pierce	ou	out	ûr	turn	zh	measure
e	end	o	hot	u	up	hw	white	ə	about, taken, pencil, lemon, circus

cartogram (kär'tə gram) a map that shows information by changing the sizes of places (p. 147)

cash crop (kash krop) a crop that is grown to be sold for profit (p. 111)

caudillo (kou dē'yō) military dictator in nineteenth-century Latin America (p. 121)

circumnavigate (sûr kum nav'ə gāt) to sail completely around Earth (p. 205)

citizenship (si tə zən ship) the position of being a member of a country with all the rights, duties, and privileges (p. 64)

city-state (si' tē stāt) a city with its nearby land and villages that governs itself (p. 184)

climograph (klī'mō graf) graph that shows information about the temperature and precipitation of a place over time (p. 89)

coalition government (kō əli shən guv'ərn mənt) is members of different political parties working together to run the nation (p. 151)

Columbian Exchange (kə lum'bē ən eks chānj') the movement of people, plants, animals, and germs in either direction across the Atlantic Ocean following the voyages of Columbus (p. 108)

command economy (kə mand' ē kon'ə mē) an economy completely controlled by the government (p. 124)

commonwealth (kom' ən welth) a partially self-governing territory; as a United States commonwealth, Puerto Rico has control over its local affairs (p. 152)

communism (kom'ūn izm) the political system in which the government owns all property and distributes resources to its citizens (p. 124)

coniferous (kō'ni fə rəs) cone-bearing (p. 180)

conservation (kon sər vā'shən) protection and careful use of natural resources (p. 77)

constitutional monarchy (kon'sti tū'shə nəl mon'ər kē) a type of government where the king or queen is the official head of state, but has little power or control (p. 244)

consul (kon' səl) elected leader of ancient Rome (p. 186)

current (kûr'ənt) a portion of water or air that flows continuously in approximately the same path (p. 14)

D

deciduous (di sig'ə wəs) dropping leaves every year (p. 180)

decree (di krē') a royal command (p. 117)

demand (di mand') the desire for a product or service; see **supply** (p. 51)

dictator (dik'tā tər) ruler or leader with absolute power (p. 121)

divine right (di vīn' rīt) the belief that monarchs receive the right to rule from God and that they need answer only to God (p. 208)

double bar graph (dub'əl bär graf) a graph that compares information with parallel rectangles (p. 235)

drought (drout) long period of little or no rainfall (p. 15)

E

ecosystem (ē'kō sis təm) all the living and nonliving things in a certain area (p. 162)

El Niño (el nē'nyō) weather event marked by very heavy rains in western South America, often causing flooding; reduced rainfall in Southern Asia, Australia, and Africa; and severe storms in North America; opposite of La Niña (p. 95)

emigrate (e mi grāt) to leave one's own country to live in another (p. 158)

empire (em'pīr) several territories and nations ruled by one authority (p. 102)

encomienda (en kō mē en'də) a Spanish grant of land that included all the Native Americans living on the land (p. 111)

Enlightenment (en līt' ən ment) movement in Europe during the 1600s and 1700s that sought to use scientific discoveries and reason to improve society (p. 207)

erosion (i rō'zhən) the wearing away of land (p. 257)

ethnic cleansing (eth nik klenz ing) the removal or killing of an entire ethnic group (p. 251)

F

federalism (fed'ər əl izm) a system of government in which power in the nation is shared between the central government and the state governments (p. 61)

fertility rate (fər 'ti lə tē 'rāt) the average number of children born to each woman (p. 231)

feudalism (fū'dəl izm) a political and economic system based on loyalty to a lord (p. 192)

figurehead (fig'yər hed) a leader in name only (p. 244)

free enterprise (frē en'tər prīz) economic system in which people can own property and businesses and are free to decide what to make, how much to produce, and what price to charge (p. 51)

G

genocide (jen ō sīd) the planned destruction of an ethnic, political, or cultural group (p. 219)

geographer (jē og'rə fer) one who studies geography (p. 71)

global economy (glō'bəl I kon'ə mē) the flow of goods, services, and currency among nations (p. 238)

global grid (glō'bəl grid) a set of squares formed by crisscrossing lines that can help you determine the absolute location of a place on a globe (p. 37)

Global Positioning System (GPS) (glō'bəl pə zish'əning) a group of satellites that use radio signals to determine the exact location of places on Earth (p. 71)

Pronunciation Key

a	at	**ē**	me	**ō**	old	**ū**	use	**ng**	song
ā	ape	**i**	it	**ô**	fork	**ü**	rule	**th**	thin
ä	far	**ī**	ice	**oi**	oil	**u̇**	pull	**th**	this
âr	care	**î**	pierce	**ou**	out	**ûr**	turn	**zh**	measure
e	end	**o**	hot	**u**	up	**hw**	white	**ə**	about, taken, pencil, lemon, circus

global warming (glō'bəl wär'ming) the gradual increase of Earth's temperature (p. 73)

glyph (glif) a picture symbol (p. 98)

GMT (abbreviation) abbreviation for Greenwich Mean Time, the line of longitude where each day begins; see Greenwich Mean Time (p. 177)

greenhouse effect (grēn'hous i fekt') gas buildup in the atmosphere that traps large amounts of warm air near Earth's surface (p. 259)

Greenwich Mean Time (GMT) (gren' ich mēn tīm) the starting point for counting hours across the world's time zones, located in Greenwich, England (p. 177)

gross domestic product (grōs' də məs'tik prod' əkt) the value of all the goods and services in one nation produced in one year (p. 57)

guild (gild) an organized group of artisans in the same industry or trade during the Middle Ages in Europe (p. 193)

H

heavy industry (hev'ē in'dəs trē) production of machinery and industrial equipment (p. 240)

heliocentric (hē lē ō sen' trik) a sun-centered description of the universe (p. 207)

humanism (hū' mən izm) a philosophy based on human values and achievement (p. 199)

I

immigrant (im'i grənt) a person who comes to live in a country in which he or she was not born (p. 46)

imperialism (im pîr'ē əl izm) claiming colonies to increase a nation's wealth and power (p. 212)

Impressionism (im'pre shə ni zəm) a painting style that uses bold colors and brushstrokes to create "impressions" of the real world (p. 234)

indigenous (in di'jə nəs) people descended from an area's first inhabitants (p. 19)

Inquisition (in kwə zi'shun) a church-run court (p. 202)

interdependence (in'tər di pen'dəns) dependence on each other to meet needs and wants (p. 56)

Internet (in'tər net) a network of computers that connects people around the world (p. 68)

L

La Niña (lä nē'nyə) weather event marked by unusually cool waters and low amounts of rainfall in the eastern Pacific and heavier rains with a better chance of hurricanes in the western Pacific; opposite of El Niño (p. 95)

landlocked (land' läkt) enclosed by land without access to an ocean or sea (p. 173)

latitude (lat'i tüd) an imaginary line, or parallel, measuring distance north or south of the equator; see **parallel** (p. 37)

Line of Demarcation (līn əv di mär kā'shən) an agreed-upon imaginary line dividing the Americas into Spanish and Portuguese territories in 1494 (p. 105)

light industry (līt in'dəs trē) production of high-end electronics and specialty tools (p. 240)

literacy rate (li'tə rə sē rāt) percentage of people who can read and write (p. 153)

Llanos ('lä'nōs) tropical grasslands that stretch through eastern Columbia and Venezuela (p. 87)

longitude (lon'ji tüd) an imaginary line, or meridian, measuring distance east or west of the prime meridian; see **meridian** and **prime meridian** (p. 37)

Glossary

M

manor (man′ər) an area of land controlled by a lord during the Middle Ages in Europe (p. 192)

maquiladora (mə′ke lə dor ə) foreign-owned factory in Mexico where workers assemble parts made in other countries (p. 142)

meridian (mə rid′ē ən) a meridian is any line of longitude east or west of Earth's prime meridian (p. 37)

mestizo (mās tē′zō) a person of mixed Spanish and Native American heritage (p. 114)

migrate (mī′grāt) to move from one place to another (p. 158)

mineral (min′ər el) a natural resource found in nature that is not an animal or plant (p. 10)

mistral (mi′ sträl) a strong, cold, dry, northerly wind of southern France (p. 180)

mural (myur′əl) a large painting drawn on a wall (p. 138)

N

national debt (na′shən nəl det) the amount of money a country owes to other countries (p. 143)

nationalism (nash′ ə nə liz əm) loyalty to one's country (p. 212)

nation-state (nā′ shən stāt) country made up of people who share a common culture or history (p. 195)

natural resource (na′ chə rəl rē′sôrs) material found in nature that people use (p. 10)

navigable (na′vi gə bəl) waterway that is deep enough and wide enough for ships to steer through (p. 173)

neutrality (nü′trəl it ē) not supporting any side during a conflict (p. 245)

Northwest Passage (nôrth′west pas′ij) a water route believed to flow through North America to Asia that European explorers searched for from the 1500s to the 1700s (p. 20)

nuclear waste (nü′klē ər wāst) the by-product of producing nuclear power and weapons (p. 259)

O

organic (ôr gan′ik) using or grown by farming or gardening methods in which manufactured chemicals are not used (p. 241)

Pronunciation Key

a	at	ē	me	ō	old	ū	use	ng	song
ā	ape	i	it	ô	fork	ü	rule	th	thin
ä	far	ī	ice	oi	oil	u̇	pull	th	this
âr	care	î	pierce	ou	out	ûr	turn	zh	measure
e	end	o	hot	u	up	hw	white	ə	about, taken, pencil, lemon, circus

P

Pampas (pam′ pəz) treeless grassland of Argentina and Uruguay (p. 87)

parallel (par′ ə lel) a line of latitude; see **latitude** (p. 37)

parallel time line (par′ ə lel tīm līn) a diagram of events arranged in time order for two different regions or people's lives (p. 29)

parliament (pä′lə mənt) an assembly of people who pass laws and govern a nation (p. 62)

parliamentary democracy (pär′lə mənt ərē də mok′rə sē) a type of government where citizens elect officials to a legislature called parliament (p. 243)

pass (pas) a low area between mountains (p. 175)

peninsula (pə nin′sə lə) a body of land almost entirely surrounded by water, projecting out from a large land mass (p. 174)

pidgin language (pij′ən lang′gwij) language formed by combining several different languages (p. 135)

philosopher (fə los′ə fər) someone who seeks truth and the right way to live (p. 184)

plantation (plan tā′shən) a large farm that often grows one cash crop (p. 111)

plateau (pla′ tō) a flat area of raised land (p. 7)

polytheism (pol ē thē′iz əm) belief in many gods (p. 185)

popular sovereignty (pop′yə lar′ sä və rən tē) the idea that the power of the government belongs to all of the people in a nation (p. 60)

prairie (prâr′ē) flat or rolling land covered with grass (p. 6)

precipitation (pri sip i tā′shən) moisture that falls to the ground in the form of rain, sleet, hail, or snow (p. 14)

prime meridian (prīm mə rid′ē ən) the line of longitude labeled 0° longitude. Any place east of the prime meridian is labeled E. Any place west of it is labeled W; see **longitude** (p. 37)

projection (prə jek′shən) the method of transferring information from a globe onto a flat surface (p. 255)

propaganda (prop ə gand′ə) spreading ideas to influence opinion (p. 218)

province (prov′ins) a political division of a country (p. 28)

R

reforestation (rē for′ist ā shən) the replanting of trees to stop the effects of forest loss (p. 257)

Reformation (re′fər mā′shən) a movement that established the Christian Protestant churches in Europe (p. 202)

relative location (rel′ə tiv lō kā ′shən) the location of a place in relation to another place (p. 37)

Renaissance (ren′ə säns) a period of cultural growth in Europe in the 1500s (p. 199)

Romanticism (ro man′ tə si zəm) artistic style developed by European musicians, writers, and artists in the 1800s (p. 234)

runoff (rən ôf) precipitation that flows over the ground, often picking up pesticides and fertilizers along the way (p. 258)

Glossary

S

satellite (sa tə līt) an object that circles another object (p. 35)

scarcity (skâr'si tē) shortage of available goods and services (p. 11)

selva (sel'və) Brazilian name for the Amazonian rain forest (p. 162)

separation of powers (sep'ə rā'shən uv pou' ərz) each branch has its own powers and can limit the power of the other branches (p. 60)

separatist movement (sep'ə rə tist müv mənt) a campaign to break away from the national government (p. 251)

serf (sûrf) a servant in Europe in the Middle Ages who farmed the land (p. 192)

sirocco (shə rä kō) a hot, dusty wind from Africa that blows on the northern Mediterranean coast, chiefly in Italy, Malta, and Sicily (p. 181)

slavery (slā'və rē) the practice of treating people as property and forcing them to work (p. 26)

smog (smog) thick haze of smoke and chemicals (p. 164)

socialism (sō'shə liz'əm) economic system under which all land, banks, factories, and large businesses are owned and controlled by the government, not by individuals (p. 125)

subregion (sub rē'jen) smaller area of a region (p. 85)

supply (sə' plī) quantity of something needed or ready for use; see **demand** (p. 51)

T

technology (tek nol'ə jē) tools and methods used to help humans perform tasks (p. 25)

temperate climate (tem'pər it klī'mit) mild weather that is neither too hot nor too cold, with changing seasons (p. 13)

territory (ter'i tôr ē) an area of land controlled by a nation that lacks the full rights of a province (p. 28)

terrorism (ter'ər izm) the use of fear and violence by non-government groups against civilians to achieve political goals (p. 36)

time line (tīm' līn) a diagram showing the order in which events took place (p. 29)

time zone (tīm zōn) one of the 24 areas into which Earth is divided for measuring time (p. 177)

tributary (trib'yə ter ē) a river or stream that flows into a larger river (p. 8)

Pronunciation Key

a	at	ē	me	ō	old	ū	use	ng	song
ā	ape	i	it	ô	fork	ü	rule	th	thin
ä	far	ī	ice	oi	oil	ú	pull	th	this
âr	care	î	pierce	ou	out	ûr	turn	zh	measure
e	end	o	hot	u	up	hw	white	ə	about, taken, pencil, lemon, circus

U

union (ūn'yən) a group of workers who unite to improve working conditions (p. 211)

urbanization (ûr bə nə zā'shən) population movement from rural areas to cities (p. 47)

V

vassal (vas'əl) one who swore loyalty to a lord (p. 192)

voyageur (vwä yä zhûr) trader who transported furs by canoe in New France (p. 21)

W

Warsaw Pact (wôr sô pakt) an alliance between the Soviet Union and Eastern European communist countries organized to oppose NATO (p. 220)

westerlies (wes tər lēz) winds from the west (p. 179)

Index

This index lists many topics that appear in the book, along with the pages on which they are found. Page numbers after a *c* refer you to a chart or diagram, after a *g*, to a graph, after an *m*, to a map, and after a *p*, to a photograph or picture.

A

B

H

I

J

Index

Q

R

S

Credits

Illustration Credits: 12-13: Paul Mirocha. 19: (tl) Gary Overacre. 26-27: Inklink. 30-31: Richard Hook. 32: Gary Overacre. 44: Inklink. 47: Gary Overacre. 49: Inklink. 50-51: Richard Hook. 54-55: Richard Hook. 131: (tl) Steve Chorney. 226: (tr) Steve Chorney. 236: Roger Stewart. 252: Marc Sott. 291: John Kurtz.

Photo Credits: All Photographs are by Macmillan/McGraw-Hill (MMH) except as noted below.

CVR (c) Blend Images/Superstock, (b) Bettmann/CORBIS, (l) Photodisc/ Superstock,(r) Brand X/SuperStock; **1** Frank Krahmer/Getty Images; **2** (tl) The Granger Collection, New York, (bl) Robert Estall photo agency / Alamy, (tr) Stock Montage/Stock Montage/Getty Images, (br) Associated Press; **3** (tl) The Corcoran Gallery of Art/CORBIS, (bl) David Muench/CORBIS, (tr) ullstein bild / The Granger Collection, New York, (br) Wm. Baker / GhostWorx Images / Alamy; **4** (bl) Bryan & Cherry Alexander Photography / Alamy, (bcl) Craig Tuttle/ CORBIS, (bcr) Cathlyn Melloan/Getty Images, (br) Roger Ressmeyer/CORBIS, (t) Royalty-Free/CORBIS; **5** Bryan & Cherry Alexander Photography / Alamy; **6** Craig Tuttle/CORBIS; **7** Lowell Georgia/CORBIS; **8** Cathlyn Melloan/Getty Images; **10** (t) Associated Press, (b) Roger Ressmeyer/CORBIS; **11** (b) Robert Glusic/CORBIS/PunchStock, (t) Ragnar Th. Sugurosson; **12** (t) Douglas Peebles/ CORBIS, (bl) Lowell Georgia/CORBIS, (bc) DEBORAH DAVIS/GETTY IMAGES, (br) Michael Dwyer / Alamy; **13** Lowell Georgia/CORBIS; **14** (r) Danita Delimont / Alamy, (l) DEBORAH DAVIS/GETTY IMAGES; **16** (t) Associated Press, (b) Michael Dwyer / Alamy; **17** (b) Douglas Peebles/CORBIS, (t) Steve Dunwell Photography Inc /Jupiter Images; **18** (bl) The Granger Collection, New York, (br) North Wind / North Wind Picture Archives, (t) Bettman/CORBIS; **20** The Granger Collection, New York; **21** (tr) Purchased with the assistance of the National Art, Art Gallery of New South Wales, Sydney, Australia / The Bridgeman Art Library International, (tl) North Wind / North Wind Picture Archives, (b) CP PHOTO/ Jacques Boissinot; **22** The Granger Collection, New York; **23** (t) North Wind / North Wind Picture Archives, (b) Bettman/CORBIS; **24** (bl) Lewis Hine/Museum of Photography at George Eastman House, (bc) Bettmann/CORBIS; **24** (t) CP PHOTO/The Ottawa Sun - Jeff Bassett, (br) The Granger Collection, New York; **25** Lewis Hine/Museum of Photography at George Eastman House; **26** Bettmann/ CORBIS; **27** (b) CORBIS, (tl) The Granger Collection, New York, (tr) The Granger Collection, New York; **28** (r) CP PHOTO/The Ottawa Sun - Jeff Bassett, (l) The Granger Collection, New York; **30** (bc) Larry Burrows/ Timepix, (t) Associated Press, (br) CP Photo/Murray Brewster, (bl) CORBIS; **32** (br) courtesy Ford Motor Company, (t) CORBIS, (b) CORBIS; **33** (b) Time Life Pictures/Getty Images, (c) St. Paul Daily News/Minnesota Historical Society, (t) Hulton Archive/Getty Images; **34** (r) Larry Burrows/ Timepix, (l) Hulton Archive/Getty Images; **34-35** (bkgd) Bettmann/CORBIS; **35** (c) Bettmann/CORBIS, (l) Paul Fusco/Magnum Photos; **36** (t) Associated Press, (b) CP Photo/Murray Brewster; **38** Associated Press; **40** (b) C Squared Studios/Getty Images, (c) Jules Frazer/Getty Images, (t) Photographer's Choice RF/PunchStock; **41** Miles Ertman/Masterfile; **42** (tl) Associated Press, (bl) MONSERRATE J. SCHWARTZ / Alamy, (tr) Alfred Eisenstaedt//Time Life Pictures/Getty Images, (br) Michael P. Gadomski; **43** (tr) Associated Press, (br) LUCAS JACKSON/Reuters/CORBIS, (tl) REBECCA COOK/ Reuters/CORBIS, (bl) Dan Lamont/CORBIS; **44** (bl) Scott B. Rosen, (bc) Bob Daemmrich / PhotoEdit, (t) Blend Images/Image Stock, (br) ADRIAN DENNIS/ AFP/Getty Images; **45** Scott B. Rosen; **46** (l) Bettmann/CORBIS, (r) Bob Daemmrich / PhotoEdit; **47** Scott Mills / Alamy; **48** (tr) The Granger Collection, New York, (tl) Jacket Cover from ANNE OF GREEN GABLES (JACKET COVER) by L.M. Montgomery. Used by permission of Random House Value Publishing, a division of Random House, Inc., (b) Gift of the J.S.McLean Collection by Canada Packers Inc 1990, Art Gallery of Ontario, Toronto, Canada / The Bridgeman Art Library International; **49** (tl) RICHARD CORKERY/Newscom, (b) Blend Images/Image Stock, (tr) ADRIAN DENNIS/AFP/Getty Images; **50** (t) Reuters/CORBIS, (br) DUNG VO TRUNG/CORBIS SYGMA, (bcr) Roger Ressmeyer/CORBIS, (bl) Jack Star/PhotoLink/Getty Images, (bcl) Car Culture/CORBIS; **51** Jack Star/ PhotoLink/Getty Images; **52** (t) AP Photo/M. Spencer Green, (b) Car Culture/ CORBIS; **54** (t) Roger Ressmeyer/CORBIS, (b) Associated Press; **55** George F. Herben/Getty Images; **56** (b) Nik Wheeler/CORBIS, (t) JIM YOUNG/Reuters/ CORBIS; **57** Reuters/CORBIS; **58** (bl) Joseph Sohm; Visions of America/CORBIS, (br) Bob Daemmrich / PhotoEdit, (t) Garry Black/Masterfile, (bcr) Associated Press, (bcl) Danilo Donadoni/Bruce Coleman Inc.; **59** Joseph Sohm; Visions of America/CORBIS; **60** (c) Danilo Donadoni/Bruce Coleman Inc., (l) SuperStock, (r) Wendell Metzen/Bruce Coleman Inc.; **61** (l) Reuters/CORBIS, (br) www.in.gov, (tr) AP Photo/Michael Conroy; **62** Associated Press; **63** (l) C Squared Studios/ Getty Images, (r) Jules Frazer/Getty Images; **64** (r) Bob Daemmrich / PhotoEdit, (l) PH2 CHANTEL M. CLAYTON, USN/Department of Defense; **65** (b) Mark Wilson/ Getty Images/Newscom, (t) Garry Black/Masterfile; **66** (t) CP PHOTO/Adrian Wyld; **67** Pablo San Juan/CORBIS; **68** (r) Ian Shaw/Alamy Images, (l) Dinodia Photo Library/Brand X/CORBIS; **69** (l) Parque/zefa/CORBIS, (c) Lawrence Manning/CORBIS, (r) IStockPhoto:Copyright: Manuela K; **70** (t) CP PHOTO/ Adrian Wyld, (b) Joseph Sohm/Visions of America/CORBIS; **71** iStockphoto Copyright: roberta casaliggi; **72** (bc) Benjamin Lowy/CORBIS, (bl) Associated Press, (t) David Leadbitter / Alamy, (br) Ted Streshinsky/CORBIS; **73** Associated Press; **74** (l) Bettmann/CORBIS, (r) Benjamin Lowy/CORBIS; **75** (b) Macduff Everton/CORBIS, (t) Associated Press; **76** (l) Associated Press; **76-77** (b) Ted Streshinsky/CORBIS; **77** (r) David Leadbitter / Alamy; **78** Car Culture/CORBIS; **80** (t) Photodisc/Getty Images, (b) Digital Vision/PunchStock; **81** Schalkwijk/Art Resource, NY; **82** (tl) The Art Archive/CORBIS, (bl) North Wind / North Wind Picture Archives, (tr) Erich Lessing / Art Resource, NY, (br) Reeve, James (Contemporary Artist) / Private Collection, / The Bridgeman Art Library International; **83** (tr) EVARISTO SA/AFP/Getty Images, (br) Digital Vision/ PunchStock, (tl) Visual Arts Library (London)/Alamy, (bl) Ken Welsh / Alamy; **84** Clive Tully / Alamy; **86** (t) Danny Lehman/CORBIS, (b) Bob Krist/CORBIS; **87** (c) Kit Houghton/CORBIS, (r) Brent Winebrenner/LPI, (l) Clive Tully / Alamy; **88** Schalkwijk/Art Resource, NY; **96** (t) The Art Archive/National Bank of Mexico/ Dagli Orti, (bcr) The Art Archive/Museo Ciudad Mexico/Dagli Orti, (others) Scott B. Rosen; **98-99** (bkgd) Scott B. Rosen; **99** (r) Erich Lessing / Art Resource, NY; **100** (l) The Art Archive/Museo Ciudad Mexico/Dagli Orti, (r) Scott B. Rosen; **101** (l) The Art Archive/Museo Ciudad Mexico/Dagli Orti, (r) Scott B. Rosen; **102** (bkgd) Scott B. Rosen, (r) Scott B. Rosen; **103** (b) The Art Archive/National Bank of Mexico/Dagli Orti, (t) Jane Sweeney/Robert Harding World Imagery/CORBIS; **104** (bc) Photographer's Choice/PunchStock, (t) Kean Collection/Getty Images, (bl) Time Life Pictures/Mansell/Time Life Pictures/Getty Images, (br) The Granger Collection, New York; **106** The Granger Collection, New York; **107** Time Life Pictures/Mansell/Time Life Pictures/Getty Images; **108** Photographer's Choice/PunchStock; **110** The Granger Collection, New York; **111** (b) Kean Collection/Getty Images, (tl) The British Library / HIP / The Image Works, (tr) The Art Archive/Biblioteca National do Rio de Janiero Brazil/Dagli Orti; **112** (br) Giraudon/Art Resource, NY, (t) Hisham Ibrahim / Photov.com / Alamy, (bl) 2005 Roger-Viollet / Topham / The Image Works, (bcr) Archivo Iconografico, S.A./ CORBIS, (bcl) Jose Maria Morelos (1765-1815) (gouache on paper), Embleton, Ron (1930-88) / Private Collection, Look and Learn / The Bridgeman Art Library; **113** 2005 Roger-Viollet / Topham / The Image Works; **114** (r) The Granger Collection, New York, (l) Jose Maria Morelos (1765-1815) (gouache on paper), Embleton, Ron (1930-88) / Private Collection, Look and Learn / The Bridgeman Art Library; **115** (t) The Granger Collection, New York, (b) Associated Press; **116** Salas, Tito (b.1887) / Private Collection, Index / The Bridgeman Art Library; **117** Archivo Iconografico, S.A./CORBIS; **118** (l) Giraudon/Art Resource, NY, (r) Hisham Ibrahim / Photov.com / Alamy; **120** (t) Mary Evans Picture Library, (br) Alejandro Ernesto/epa/CORBIS, (bl) Blaine Harrington III/CORBIS, (bc) REUTERS/Juan Carlos Ulate; **121** Blaine Harrington III/CORBIS; **122** REUTERS/ Juan Carlos Ulate; **123** (r) David J. & Janice L. Frent Collection/CORBIS, (bl) The Granger Collection, New York; **124** Alejandro Ernesto/epa/CORBIS; **125** (b) Mary Evans Picture Library, (t) REUTERS/Max Montecinos; **126** Scott B. Rosen; **128** (t) Dave Mager/Index Stock Imagery; **129** Organization of American States.; **130** (tr) AFP/Getty Images, (tl) Time Life Pictures/Time Magazine, Copyright Time Inc./Time Life Pictures/Getty Images, (bl) Stephanie Maze/CORBIS, (br) Brand X Pictures/PunchStock; **131** (tl) Reuters/CORBIS, (bl) Alfredo Maiquez, (tr) TIMOTHY A. CLARY/AFP/Getty Images; **132** (t) Caroline Webber/AGE Fotostock, (bl) Scott B. Rosen, (bc) Larry Dale Gordon/Getty Images; **134** (bl) Scott B. Rosen, (tl) Medioimages/PunchStock, (tr) Associated Press, (br) MAURICIO LIMA/AFP/Getty Images; **135** (tr) Patrick Robert/Sygma/CORBIS, (bl) Jean-Yves Rabeuf-Valette / The Image Works, (tl) Hans Neleman/Getty Images, (br) Kevin Schafer/CORBIS; **136** (b) Dennis Welsh/Getty Images; **137** (t) Associated Press, (t) Scott B. Rosen, (b) Larry Dale Gordon/Getty Images; **138** (br) LAURA BOUSHNAK/AFP/Getty Images, (tr) Albright-Knox Art Gallery/CORBIS, (tl) Diego Giudice/CORBIS, (bl) Rufus F. Folkks/CORBIS; **139** (cr) Scott B. Rosen, (b) Hulton Archive/Getty Images, (t) Archivo Iconografico, S.A./CORBIS, (cl) AP Images; **140** (bl) Keith Dannemiller/CORBIS, (bcl) ASSOCIATED PRESS, (bcr) Associated Press, (br) Photographer's Choice/PunchStock, (t) Greg Smith/CORBIS; **141** Keith Dannemiller/CORBIS; **142** (r) ASSOCIATED PRESS, (l) ASSOCIATED PRESS; **143** (l) Andre Vieira/Stringer/Getty Images, (r) Tim Brakemeier/Newscom; **144** (l) Associated Press, (r) JORDI CAMÍ/Alamy Images; **145** (b) Kit Houghton/ CORBIS, (t) Jeremy Horner/CORBIS; **146** (bkgd) Photographer's Choice/ PunchStock, (r) Greg Smith/CORBIS; **148** (bl) Central Press/Getty Images, (t) Stephanie Maze/CORBIS, (br) David R. Frazier / Danita Delimont Agency / drr. net, (bc) Fausto Albuquerque/Alamy; **149** Central Press/Getty Images; **150** (t) Julia Waterlow; Eye Ubiquitous/CORBIS, (br) Bjanka Kadic/Alamy, (bl) Fausto Albuquerque/Alamy; **151** Christie's Images/CORBIS; **152** G.RACINAN/WITNESS/ CORBIS SYGMA; **153** (b) Stephanie Maze/CORBIS, (t) David R. Frazier / Danita Delimont Agency / drr.net, (c) ImageState/Alamy Images; **154** (br) Jim Sugar/ CORBIS, (bl) YURI CORTEZ/AFP/Getty Images, (bc) Yoray Liberman/Getty Images, (t) Royalty-Free/CORBIS; **155** YURI CORTEZ/AFP/Getty Images; **156** (t) Eric Vernazobres/CORBIS, (b) Susanna Bennett/Alamy Images; **157** (t) Yoray Liberman/Getty Images, (b) Jeffrey L. Rotman/CORBIS; **158** (bkgd) Karl Kummels / SuperStock, (inset) David Young-Wolff / PhotoEdit; **159** (t) Jim Sugar/CORBIS, (b) Royalty-Free/CORBIS; **160** (bc) Jacques Jangoux/Photo Researchers, Inc., (t) Jochen Schlenker/Masterfile, (bl) Daniel Aguilar/Reuters/CORBIS, (br) Jeff Greenberg/Alamy Images; **161** Daniel Aguilar/Reuters/CORBIS; **162** Jacques Jangoux/Photo Researchers, Inc.; **163** (b) Photodisc/PunchStock, (t) Worldwide Picture Library / Alamy; **164** Stephanie Maze/CORBIS; **165** (br) Jochen

Schlenker/Masterfile, (t) AP Photo/John Moore, (bl) Jeff Greenberg/Alamy Images; **168** (b) Nicholas Prior/Getty Images, (t) Michael Newman / PhotoEdit; **169** SuperStock; **170** (tl) Araldo de Luca/CORBIS, (bl) Robert Harding Picture Library Ltd./Alamy Images, (tr) SuperStock, (br) Dagli Orti/The Art Archive; **171** (tl) Gianni Dagli Orti/CORBIS, (bl) Museo Civico Revoltella Trieste/Dagli Orti (A)/ The Art Archive, (tr) The Granger Collection, New York, (br) CORBIS; **172** (br) age fotostock/SuperStock, (bl) Atlantide Phototravel/CORBIS, (t) Adam Woolfitt/ CORBIS; **174-175** Atlantide Phototravel/CORBIS; **176** (l) age fotostock/ SuperStock, (r) Adam Woolfitt/CORBIS; **178** (t) SIME s.a.s/eStock Photo, (b) Robert Harding Picture Library Ltd/Alamy Images; **180-181** (bkgd) Robert Harding Picture Library Ltd/Alamy Images; **181** (r) SIME s.a.s/eStock Photo; **182** (bl) Travelshots.com/Alamy Images, (br) Blaine Harrington III/Alamy Images, (bl) Peter Connolly/akg-images, (t) Roy Rainford/Robert Harding World Imagery/ Getty Images; **183** Peter Connolly/akg-images; **184** (l) PoodlesRock/CORBIS; **184-185** (bkgd) Travelshots.com/Alamy Images; **187** David McNew/Hulton Archive/Getty Images; **188** Erich Lessing/Art Resource, Inc.; **189** (b) Blaine Harrington III/Alamy Images, (t) Roy Rainford/Robert Harding World Imagery/ Getty Images; **190** (bl) The Gallery Collection/CORBIS, (t) The Granger Collection, New York, (br) Saint Sebastian Chapel Lanslevillard Savoy/Dagli Orti/The Art Archive; **193** Stock Montage; **195** (b) The Gallery Collection/ CORBIS, (t) Archivo Iconografico, S.A./CORBIS; **197** (t) The Granger Collection, New York, (b) Saint Sebastian Chapel Lanslevillard Savoy/Dagli Orti/The Art Archive; **198** (br) Les Stone/Sygma/CORBIS, (t) Erich Lessing/Art Resource, Inc., (bl) Erich Lessing/Art Resource, Inc., (bcl) The Granger Collection, New York, (bcr) The Granger Collection, New York; **199** Joe Malone/ Jon Arnold Images/ Alamy Images; **200** (tl) Czartoryski Museum, Krakow, Poland/Bridgeman Art Library, (bl) Scala/Art Resource, Inc., (cr) Bettmann/CORBIS; **201** (l) The Granger Collection, New York, (r) Alinari/Art Resource, Inc.; **202** (b) The Granger Collection, New York, (t) akg-images; **203** (t) Archive Photos/Getty Images, (b) Jason Hawkes/CORBIS; **204** The Granger Collection, New York; **205** (b) Les Stone/Sygma/CORBIS, (t) Erich Lessing/Art Resource, Inc.; **206** (bcl) Erich Lessing/Art Resource, NY, (t) Erich Lessing/Art Resource, Inc., (bl) Ray Juno/ CORBIS, (bcr) akg-images, (br) HIP/Art Resource, Inc.; **207** Ray Juno/CORBIS; **208-209** Erich Lessing/Art Resource, Inc.; **209** Erich Lessing/Art Resource, NY; **210** (t) SSPL/The Image Works, Inc., (tc) SEF/Art Resource, Inc., (bc) Charles Nesbit/Photonica/Getty Images, (b) SSPL/The Image Works, Inc.; **211** akg-images; **212** HIP/Art Resource, Inc.; **213** Erich Lessing/Art Resource, Inc.; **214** (t) AFP/Getty Images, (br) KEYSTONE-FRANCE/Imagestate, (bl) Hulton Archive/ Getty Images, (bcl) Bettmann/CORBIS, (bcr) Hulton-Deutsch Collection/CORBIS; **215** Hulton Archive/Getty Images; **216** Keystone/Hulton Archive/Getty Images; **217** Bettmann/CORBIS; **218** (r) Hulton-Deutsch Collection/CORBIS, (l) Hulton Archive/Getty Images; **218-219** (bkgd) USIA/Landov; **219** (l) Keystone/Getty Images; **221** (b) AFP/Getty Images, (t) KEYSTONE-FRANCE/Imagestate; **222** Les Stone/Sygma/CORBIS; **224** (t) Amos Morgan/Getty Images, (c) Steve Vidler/ SuperStock, (b) Cosmo Condina/Alamy Images; **225** Roberto Gerometta/Lonely Planet Images; **226** (tl) Bettmann/CORBIS, (bl) Franz-Marc Frei/CORBIS, (tr) Tim Graham Picture Library, (br) Formcourt (Form Advertising)/Alamy Images; **227** (bl) PHOVOIR/FCM Graphic/Alamy Images, (tl) LIBRARY OF CONGRESS, (tr) AP Photo/John Coghill, (br) Igor Kostin/Sygma/CORBIS; **228** (bl) Gideon Mendel/ CORBIS, (t) scenicireland.com/Christopher Hill Photographic/Alamy Images, (bc) The McGraw-HillCompanies Inc./Ken Cavanagh Photographer, (br) Claude Monet; **230** Gideon Mendel/CORBIS; **232** (t) The McGraw-HillCompanies Inc./ Ken Cavanagh Photographer, (b) Trevor pearson/Alamy Images; **233** Glow Images/Alamy Images; **234** (b) scenicireland.com/Christopher Hill Photographic/Alamy Images, (t) Claude Monet; **235** Hemis/CORBIS; **236** (br) Gideon Mendel/CORBIS, (t) JUPITERIMAGES/Comstock Images/Alamy Images, (bl) JUPITERIMAGES/Comstock Images/Alamy Images; **237** Jean-pierre VERGEZ; **238** (l) Comstock Images, (r) Aspix/Alamy Images; **239** (b) John A.Rizzo/Getty Images, (t) Car Culture/CORBIS; **240** (r) Gideon Mendel/CORBIS, (l) Getty Images; **241** (b) JUPITERIMAGES/Comstock Images/Alamy Images, (t) AP Photo/ Yun Jai-hyoung; **242** (t) Manfred Gottschalk/Lonely Planet Images, (bl) Manfred Gottschalk/Lonely Planet Images, (bc) AP Photo/Serkan Senturk, (br) Rick England/Getty Images; **243** AP Photo/Jockel Finck; **244** (l) AP Photo/Serkan Senturk; **244-245** Steve Turner/Alamy Images; **245** (r) AP Photo/Efrem Lukatsky; **246** (bkgd) Rick England/Getty Images, (inset) Roger Viollet/Getty Images; **247** Manfred Gottschalk/Lonely Planet Images; **248** (t) Van Parys Media/CORBIS, (bl) CFPNI.org, (br) AP Photo/Stefan Rousseau, PA; **250** (c) CFPNI.org, (b) Bettmann/CORBIS, (t) CARDINALE STEPHANE/CORBIS SYGMA; **251** (bl) Yuri Kadobnov/epa/CORBIS, (br) AFP/Getty Images, (t) Andrija Ilic/ reportdigital.co.uk; **252** RyanMcVay/Getty Images; **254** (b) Van Parys Media/ CORBIS, (tl) Visual&Written SL/Alamy Images, (tr) AP Photo/Stefan Rousseau, PA; **256** (t) Andra Maslennikov/Peter Arnold, Inc., (bl) Getty Images, (bc) CORBIS, (br) Alamy Images; **257** Getty Images; **258** (l) Andra Maslennikov/Peter Arnold, Inc., (c) JUPITERIMAGES/Brand X/Alamy Images; **258-259** (bkgd) CORBIS; **259** (t) AP Photo/Efrem Lukatsky; **260** (bkgd) Alamy Images, (inset) A&P/Alamy Images; **261** (b) Andra Maslennikov/Peter Arnold, Inc., (t) istockphoto; **264** (t) Amos Morgan/Photodisc/Getty Images, (b) Issouf Sanogo/ AFP/Getty Images; **R01** (t) CORBIS, (c) The Granger Collection, New York, (b) Stockdisc/Getty Images; **R03** North Wind / North Wind Picture Archives; R05 Scott Mills / Alamy; **R07** Time Life Pictures/Mansell/Time Life Pictures/Getty Images; **R09** Luiz Claudio Marigo/naturepl.com; **R11** Jean-Pierre Muller/AFP/ Getty Images; **R13** istockphoto; **GH2** (b) Panoramic Images/Getty Images, (t) Peter Gridley/Photographer's Choice/Getty Images; **GH3** (t) Photolibrarycom/ Getty Images, (c) CORBIS/PunchStock, (b) Larry Dale Gordon/The Image Bank/ Getty Images.

ACKNOWLEDGMENTS

Grateful acknowledgment is given to the following authors and publishers. Every effort has been made to trace the ownership of all copyrighted material and to secure the necessary permissions to reprint these selections. In the case of some selections for which acknowledgment is not given, extensive research has failed to locate the copyright holders.